The Welfare State

A Reader

Edited by
**Christopher Pierson
and Francis G. Castles**

Polity Press

First published in 2000 by Polity Press
in association with Blackwell Publishers Ltd

Editorial office:
Polity Press
65 Bridge Street
Cambridge CB2 1UR, UK

Marketing and production:
Blackwell Publishers Ltd
108 Cowley Road
Oxford OX4 1JF, UK

Published in the USA by
Blackwell Publishers Inc.
Commerce Place
350 Main Street
Malden, MA 02148, USA

ISBN 0–7456–2252–6
ISBN 0–7456–2253–4 (pbk)

A catalogue record for this book is available from the British Library.

Library of Congress Cataloging–in–Publication Data

The welfare state : a reader / edited by Christopher Pierson and Francis G. Castles.
 p. cm.
 Includes bibliographical references and index.
 ISBN 0–7456–2252–6. — ISBN 0–7456–2253–4
 1. Welfare state. I. Pierson, Christopher. II. Castles, Francis Geoffrey.
JC479.W44 2002
330.12′6–dc21   99–36410
                                                        CIP

Typeset in 10 on 12 pt Stemple Garamond
by Kolam Information Services Pvt Ltd, Pondicherry, India
Printed in Great Britain by T. J. International Ltd, Padstow, Cornwall

This book is printed on acid-free paper.

Contents

Acknowledgements   viii

Editors' Note   xii

Editors' Introduction   1

I APPROACHES TO WELFARE

The First Welfare State?   *Thomas Paine*   11

'Classical'

The Welfare State in Historical Perspective   *Asa Briggs*   18

Citizenship and Social Class   *T. H. Marshall*   32

Universalism versus Selection   *Richard Titmuss*   42

Perspectives on the Left

What is Social Justice?   *Commission on Social Justice*   51

The Fiscal Crisis of the State   *James O'Connor*   63

Some Contradictions of the Modern Welfare State   *Claus Offe*   67

The Power Resources Model   *Walter Korpi*   77

Responses from the Right

The Meaning of the Welfare State   *Friedrich von Hayek*   90

The Two Wars against Poverty   *Charles Murray*   96

The New Politics of the New Poverty   *Lawrence M. Mead*   107

Feminism

Feminism and Social Policy   *Mary McIntosh*   119

The Patriarchal Welfare State   *Carole Pateman*   133

II DEBATES AND ISSUES

Welfare Regimes

Three Worlds of Welfare Capitalism   *Gøsta Esping-Andersen*   154

The Real Worlds of Welfare Capitalism   *Robert E. Goodin,
      Bruce Headey, Ruud Muffels and Henk-Jan Dirven*   170

A European Welfare State?

Towards a European Welfare State?   *Stephan Leibfried*   190

Is the European Social Model Fragmenting?   *John Grahl and
                                        Paul Teague*   207

Competitiveness and Globalization: Economic Challenges to the Welfare State

Social Welfare and Competitiveness   *Ian Gough*   234

Negative Integration: States and the Loss of Boundary Control
                                        Fritz Scharpf   254

Challenges to Welfare: External Constraints   *Martin Rhodes* 257

National Economic Governance   *Paul Hirst and Grahame
                                        Thompson*   263

Demographic and Social Change

Social Security around the World   *Estelle James*   271

On *Averting the Old Age Crisis*   *R. Beattie and W. McGillivray* 281

Intergenerational Conflict and the Welfare State: American and
                      British Perspectives   *Chris Phillipson* 293

Political Challenges to the Welfare State

The New Politics of the Welfare State   *Paul Pierson*   309

Welfare State Retrenchment Revisited   *Richard Clayton and
                                        Jonas Pontusson*   320

Contents

III   THE FUTURES OF WELFARE

High-Risk Strategy   *Will Hutton*   337

The Implications of Ecological Thought for Social Welfare
                                        Tony Fitzpatrick   343

Basic Income and the Two Dilemmas of the Welfare State
                                        Philippe van Parijs   355

The Welfare State and Postmodernity   *Kirk Mann*   360

Positive Welfare   *Anthony Giddens*   369

Subject Index   380

Name Index   400

Acknowledgements

The editors and publishers gratefully acknowledge permission to reprint from the following:

R. Beattie and W. McGillivray: from debate on 'Averting the Old Age Crisis' from *International Social Security Review*, 48, 3/4, 1995, by permission of International Social Security Association, c/o Blackwell Publishers.

Richard Clayton and **Jonas Pontusson**: 'Welfare State Retrenchment Revisited' from *World Politics*, 51, 1998, copyright © 1998 Center of International Studies, Princeton University, by permission of the Johns Hopkins University Press.

Gøsta Esping-Andersen: 'Three Worlds of Welfare Capitalism' from *The Three Worlds of Welfare Capitalism* (Polity Press / Princeton University Press, 1990), copyright © 1990 Princeton University Press, by permission of the publishers.

Tony Fitzpatrick: 'The Implications of Ecological Thought for Social Welfare' from *Critical Social Policy*, 18, 1, 1998, copyright © Journal of Critical Social Policy 1998, by permission of the author and the publisher, Sage Publications Ltd.

Anthony Giddens: 'Positive Welfare' from *The Third Way* (Polity Press, 1998), by permission of the publisher.

Robert E. Goodin, Bruce Headey, Ruud Muffels and **Henk-Jan Dirven**: 'The Real Worlds of Welfare Capitalism' summarized and adapted for this volume by the authors, from *The Real Worlds of Welfare Capitalism* (Cambridge University Press, 1999), by permission of the authors and Cambridge University Press.

Ian Gough: 'Social Welfare and Competitiveness' from *New Political Economy*, 1, 2, 1996, by permission of Carfax Publishing, Taylor & Francis Group.

John Grahl and **Paul Teague**: 'Is the European Social Model Fragmenting?' from *New Political Economy*, 2, 3, 1997, by permission of Carfax Publishing, Taylor & Francis Group.

Friedrich von Hayek: 'The Meaning of the Welfare State' from F. A. Hayek: *The Constitution of Liberty* (Routledge / University of Chicago Press, 1959), by permission of the Literary Executor of the Estate of F. A. Hayek and the publishers.

Paul Hirst and **Grahame Thompson**: 'National Economic Governance' from P. Hirst and G. Thompson: *Globalization in Question* (Polity Press, 1996), by permission of the publisher.

Will Hutton: 'High Risk Strategy' first published in the *Guardian*, 30 October 1995, copyright © the *Guardian* 1995, by permission of the *Guardian*.

Institute for Public Policy Research: 'What is Social Justice?' from *The Justice Gap*, Commission on Social Justice (IPPR, 1993), by permission of the IPPR.

Estelle James: 'Social Security Around the World' first published in P. A. Diamond *et al.* (eds): *Social Security: What Role for the Future?* (Brookings Institution, 1996), by permission of the Brookings Institution Press.

Walter Korpi: 'The Power Resources Model' from W. Korpi: *The Democratic Class Struggle* (Routledge & Kegan Paul, 1983), by permission of the publisher.

J. Lewis: 'Gender and the Development of Welfare Regimes' from *Journal of European Social Policy*, 2, 3, 1992, copyright © Sage Publications Ltd 1992, by permission of the publisher, Sage Publications Ltd.

Stephan Leibfried: 'Towards a European Welfare State?' from C. Jones (ed.): *New Perspectives on the Welfare State* (Routledge, 1993), by permission of the publisher.

Mary McIintosh: 'Feminism and Social Policy' from *Critical Social Policy*, 1, 1981, copyright © *Journal of Critical Social Policy* 1981, by permission of the author and the publisher, Sage Publications Ltd.

Kirk Mann: 'The Welfare State and Postmodernity' from *Critical Social Policy*, 18, 1, 1998, copyright © *Journal of Critical Social Policy* 1998, by permission of the author and the publisher, Sage Publications Ltd.

T. H. Marshall: 'Citizenship and Social Class' from *Citizenship and Social Class and Other Essays* (CUP, 1950), originally delivered in Cambridge as the Marshall Lecture in 1949, by permission of Mrs N. Marshall.

Lawrence M. Mead: 'The New Politics of Poverty' from *The Public Interest*, 103, Spring 1991, copyright © 1991 National Affairs, Inc., by permission of the author and the publishers.

Charles Murray: 'The Two Wars Against Poverty' from *The Public Interest*, 69, Winter 1982, copyright © 1982 National Affairs, Inc., by permission of the author and the publishers.

James O'Connor: 'Fiscal Crisis of State' from the Introduction to J. O'Connor: *The Fiscal Crisis of State* (St Martin's Press, 1973), by permission of the author.

Claus Offe: 'Some Contradiction of the Modern Welfare State' from *Critical Social Policy*, 2, 2, 1982, copyright © *Journal of Critical Social Policy* 1982, by permission of the author and the publisher, Sage Publications Ltd.

Philippe van Parijs: 'Basic Income and the Two Dilemmas of the Welfare State' from *Political Quarterly*, 67, 1, 1996, by permission of Political Quarterly Publishing Co., Blackwell Publishers.

Carole Pateman: 'The Patriarchal Welfare State' from *The Disorder of Women* (Princeton University Press, 1988), copyright © 1988 Princeton University Press, by permission of the publisher.

Chris Phillipson: 'Intergenerational Conflict and the Welfare State: American and British Perspectives' from A. Walker (ed.): *The New Generational Contract* (UCL Press, 1996), by permission of the publisher.

Paul Pierson: 'The New Politics of the Welfare State' from *World Politics*, 48, 1996, copyright © 1996 Center of International Studies, Princeton University, by permission of the Johns Hopkins University Press.

Martin Rhodes: 'Challenges to Welfare: External Constraints' from M. Rhodes *et al.* (eds): *Developments in West European Politics* (Macmillan, 1997), by permission of Macmillan Press Ltd and of St Martin's Press.

Fritz Scharpf: 'Negative Integration: The Loss of Boundary Control' from G. Marks *et al.* (eds): *Governance in the EU* (Sage, 1996), copyright © Sage Publications Ltd 1996, by permission of Sage Publications Ltd.

Richard Titmuss: 'Universalism Versus Selection' from R. Titmuss: *Commitment to Welfare* (Allen & Unwin, 1968), by permission of Ann Oakley.

Despite every effort to trace and contact copyright owners prior to publication we have been unable to do so in one case. If notified, the publisher will be pleased to rectify any errors or omissions at the earliest opportunity.

Editors' Note

An ellipsis within square brackets indicates an omission from the original publication, thus: [...]. Where more than a paragraph has been excluded, a line space appears above and below such ellipses. Apart from minor amendments (e.g. capitalization, British rather than American spellings and the presentation of reference material), the few editorial interventions necessitated by publishing these extracts in a single volume also appear in square brackets. The authors' opinions are, of course, those held at the time of writing; dates of original publication are reflected in the Notes to each reading.

Editors' Introduction

For many people, what to do about welfare is *the* key social, economic and political question of the new millennium. In bringing together this extensive selection from the very best and most influential writing on welfare of the past fifty years, our ambition is to show how, why and for whom the politics of welfare has attained this newly central status. We show where the main traditions of welfare state analysis have come from and what have been the changing objects of their study. We demonstrate both major continuities and substantive changes in the welfare debate. We chart the interplay of theoretical and empirical concerns and we anticipate the terrain over which the next battles for welfare will be fought. We cannot hope to represent every aspect of the contemporary welfare debate and important issues, such as disability, ethnicity and the problems of service delivery, lie beyond our scope. But a slightly narrower scope enables us to focus upon a series of welfare *debates*. There are (at least) two sides to almost every argument in the welfare field and anyone who has read the extraordinary range of contrasting opinions and judgements in this volume will have begun to grasp why this is such a crucial and *contested* field of contemporary debate.

I Approaches to Welfare

Thomas Paine is our sole representative of thinking about welfare *before* the rise of the modern welfare state. Paine was writing more than two hundred years ago, and many of his thoughts have a strikingly contemporary resonance. His views on the interaction of poverty, criminality, indolence and employment are often simply a more elegant and direct expression of the kinds of arguments that go on today. It is as well to remember that thinking about welfare did not begin in 1945!

It used to be said that we lacked any serious theoretical account of where welfare states came from and what they are for. The business of the welfare state was social administration: the mundane tasks of mopping up poverty and improving public services. This was always, in part, a caricature. There have always been sharp and insightful critics of this dreary-but-worthy view of the welfare state. But we now have a wealth of competing theoretical accounts of the welfare state to choose from and the principal aim of Part I of the Reader is to offer a representative survey of the best and the most influential of this literature. We begin with a series of writings from the years immediately following the end of the Second World War. These are not, for the most part, the years in which welfare states were founded. The origins of welfare states among most developed countries actually lie in the twenty-five years *preceding* the First World War. But this was a period of unprecedented and, at least to some extent, consensual growth in welfare states. It is also the time that gave us the most authoritative and enduring social democratic accounts of welfare and state. Here we have included three 'Classical' statements of the social democratic approach drawn from the work of Asa Briggs, T. H. Marshall and Richard Titmuss. The views of social democratic writers on the welfare state have always been vulnerable to misrepresentation, especially as they have so often been glossed as holding a rather simple-minded and wholly benign view of both the state and the human condition, a view which it is difficult to reconcile with a *careful* reading of what they actually said. But certainly these authors stand at the fount of a view of the welfare state which sees it as essentially a 'good thing', capable of forging a new and stable reconciliation between the seemingly competing claims of economic efficiency and social justice. Much of the rest of the literature on the welfare state is a more or less explicit engagement with these positions.

In the section headed 'Perspectives on the Left', we carry this approach forward towards our own time. Not all of the contributions here are social democratic. Indeed, James O'Connor and Claus Offe are quite explicitly critical of a form of political compromise which they see as unsustainable over the medium term. In slightly differing ways, they argue that capitalist welfare states are vulnerable to a series of deep-seated contradictions which make them politically quite unstable. By contrast, the selections from the Commission on Social Justice's *The Justice Gap* and Walter Korpi's *The Democratic Class Struggle* represent rather differing attempts to refashion social democratic impulses under the duress of changing (and more difficult) circumstances.

The views represented in 'Responses from the Right' have been extra-ordinarily influential upon welfare debates over the past twenty-five years. Friedrich von Hayek probably remains the most sophisticated representative of the view that welfare state institutions are essentially irreconcilable with a social order premised on the value of human freedom. In Hayek's wake have come a vast array of critics who have condemned the welfare state, variously, as uneconomic, unproductive, inefficient, ineffective, despotic and inconsistent with freedom. Two of the most influential spokespersons for a tradition which has always been at its strongest in the Anglo-Saxon world (above all, in North America) are Charles Murray and Lawrence M. Mead. Murray has become strongly identified with the idea that welfare state institutions tend to produce a social 'underclass' wedded to criminality, while Mead is similarly associated with the idea that welfare generates new forms of poverty and dependency in which the appeal to rights swamps any corresponding sense of social obligations. The views of both authors are given characteristically robust expression in the articles chosen here.

Among the most influential interventions in reshaping the entire debate about the politics of welfare over the past twenty-five years have been the contributions of feminist authors. Starting (at least in its contemporary form, since there are many precursors) with Elizabeth Wilson's book *Women and the Welfare State* (1977), the intervening period has seen the growth of a literature which has challenged the very terms upon which all previous discussions of state and welfare had proceeded. Though a diverse literature, feminist writers have consistently sought to show how the nature of welfare states and, within them, of the interplay of public and private institutions and of formal and informal labour markets, voluntary and family care and so on have generated welfare regimes which can be seen to be very clearly gendered in their structures and outcomes but in which, at the same time, this aspect of gender is effectively concealed. The two readings in the section, McIntosh's 'Feminism and Social Policy' and Pateman's 'The Patriarchal Welfare State', are outstanding examples of this approach.

II Debates and Issues

The second part of the Reader involves a change in focus. Whereas the primary concern of Part I is with normative and theoretical accounts of the welfare state, Part II adopts a more empirical and comparative approach. The selections here are chosen with three goals in mind. The first is to convey something of the range and variety of welfare state activity as demonstrated in the contemporary practice of advanced, industrial nations. The second is to use the experience of contemporary practice to identify the major challenges, problems and prospects of the advanced welfare state in the coming years of the new millennium. The third is to provide a guide to the major debates and policy issues which have preoccupied scholars from the many disciplines – including sociology, political science, economics and social administration – which see the welfare state and the public sector more broadly as among their central concerns. Since social provision in its many forms is now the predominant activity of the state in all modern societies, these are debates and issues which are clearly pivotal to understanding how such societies function and how they are changing.

Our preference for comparative studies has a double rationale. Partly, we want to avoid the parochialism that comes from identifying *our own* welfare state as the template for welfare states in general. More importantly, comparison is a key to better understanding. By the standards of the classic contributors to the welfare state literature discussed in Part I, virtually all modern states are welfare states, but that does not mean that they are all the same. Different welfare states achieve different degrees of poverty alleviation, income inequality and risk reduction. Their welfare systems have different implications for welfare dependency and they structure gender inequalities in different ways. Such differences are relevant to both policy goals and normative concerns, because they help us to establish the conditions under which desired social policy objectives may be achieved in practice.

A comparative approach also helps us to locate sources of weakness and strength in welfare state arrangements and institutions. A major theme of the contemporary literature is the extent and range of challenges to the viability of the welfare state in recent years. But again there are important differences between countries. Some appear to have coped better with economic and demographic problems than others. In some, support for the welfare state project seems to have remained rock solid, while in others there has been a strong political backlash against at least some forms of public intervention. Locating the reasons why such differences occur may tell us why some welfare states are more vulnerable to attack than others and may even provide us with the knowledge required to redesign welfare state institutions so that they are less vulnerable in future.

All the readings in Part II have been selected in order to present arguments central to major debates in the literature. Two of these debates are about the way we classify different types of welfare state. The initial section, 'Welfare Regimes', starts out from Gøsta Esping-Andersen's well-known distinction between what he describes as 'liberal', 'conservative' and 'social democratic' regime types. This typology has been widely welcomed for at least three reasons. It moves away from expenditure as the sole criterion of welfare effort, replacing it with the more sociological notion of the 'de-commodifying' impact of diverse systems of social rights. It suggests that the welfare state is about more than just services and transfers and argues that diverse patterns of social provision are premised on distinctive labour market formations. Finally, it provides plausible connections between the class origins of welfare regimes, their distinctive modes of provision and their consequences for social and economic inequality. The paper by Robert E. Goodin and his colleagues interrogates the empirical validity and relevance of Esping-Andersen's typology. Goodin's team investigates whether countries which are representative of each regime type actually achieve their stated social and economic objectives. The authors' conclusion – that the social democratic regime type is more effective than the others in alleviating poverty, reducing income inequality and spreading the fruits of economic growth – is worth remembering in light of later contributions which insist that there is an inherent trade-off between economic efficiency and the achievement of social goals.

A second debate with a classificatory focus raises a question: is it possible to identify 'A European Welfare State?' The issue is again one of similarities and differences among contemporary welfare states and how much they matter. The extract from Stephan Leibfried echoes the previous debate by pointing to the variety of regime types among countries constituting the European Union, noting that as well as 'liberal', 'conservative' and 'social democratic' types, there is also a 'Latin rim' type consisting of the newly democratized countries of Southern Europe. Leibfried discusses various scenarios by which greater similarity might emerge, but is not optimistic about such an outcome, given the primarily economic charter of EU development. John Grahl and Paul Teague see things differently. They argue that in the period of rapid post-war economic growth a common European social model did, indeed, emerge, defined both by its high levels of welfare provision and its institutionalized regulation of labour markets. However, in their view, changing economic realities challenge the continued viability of the model in some countries, making for a real possibility of greater diversity in the future. Both contributions see further progress towards European integration as the key to the emergence or consolidation of a European welfare state. Conceivably, their somewhat pessimistic conclusions might be revisited in an era when the EU's social agenda has been revivified by the presence of so many social democratic faces in the Council of Ministers and when 'harmonization' of tax and social policy is seen by many as the next stage in the process of European unification.

The notion that the modern welfare state is under serious threat and subject to challenge on many fronts is a dominant theme in the contemporary literature. Following on quite naturally from the debate on the viability of the European social model, the section on 'Competitiveness and Globalization: Economic Challenges to the Welfare State' examines arguments that welfare development on the scale of recent years is incompatible with the realities of an effectively functioning economy. One variant of the argument is that welfare state expansion has reduced economic efficiency and competitiveness and so has become a source of major economic problems, including declining productivity growth and high levels of unemployment. Another is the currently fashionable view that high levels of welfare state spending and highly regulated labour markets are incompatible with the new realities of a globalized economy, which impose heavy constraints on the policy autonomy of the modern state. If nations do not heed the demands of international markets, domestic economic actors will vote with their feet, leaving countries increasingly bereft of supplies of mobile capital and skilled labour. For both variants the bottom line is the same: countries which do not reduce high levels of social spending and taxation are, quite literally, likely to go out of business!

The authors in this section subject these views to critical scrutiny. Ian Gough's extensive survey of the evidence on 'competitiveness' reveals a much more complex picture than the advocates of 'compete and survive' have suggested. The shorter extracts from the work of Fritz Scharpf and Martin Rhodes reflect on the nature of the external constraints on domestic social policy making. Paul Hirst and Grahame Thompson, well known for their scepticism about the general phenomenon of 'globalization', offer a correspondingly robust defence of the scope still left for national governments to determine what goes on within their borders (while recommending further policy integration at the international level).

The supposedly inescapable trade-off between desired social and economic objectives is generally seen as the primary problem for the contemporary welfare state, just as it was for Marxist and conservative writers of an earlier generation. The literature has, however, concerned itself with other challenges to the existing character of welfare provision as well. In 'Demographic and Social Change', we look at several issues concerning the changing population structures of modern welfare states. One hugely influential strand of argument has been the view that population ageing combined with excessive state pensions have together seriously compromised the integrity of public finances and that what is required are reforms to reduce basic pension rights and to privatize provision for the middle class. Crucial to this international debate has been the impact of the World Bank's report *Averting the Old Age Crisis*, which was published in 1994 and has found its way onto the desk of virtually every senior civil servant concerned with pensions reform around the globe. Here we include a summary of the World Bank's case written by Estelle James, a World Bank insider, and a detailed critical response by R. Beattie and W. McGillivray. The question of pension reform has prompted a further and more general debate about the patterns of distribution of welfare goods *between* generations and the potential for conflict between young and old that further change may bring. This is the subject of Chris Phillipson's study of recent developments in Britain and America.

The final threat to the welfare state we consider here is that of politically driven cutbacks to existing levels of provision. In 'Political Challenges to the Welfare State', we examine how far the economic and demographic problems of advanced welfare states have been translated into pressures for public sector retrenchment and how far such retrenchment agendas have been successful. We present two opposing accounts. Paul Pierson's story is of the emergence of a 'new politics' of the welfare state, in which the natural wish of politicians to avoid blame for unpopular policies has combined with the development of strong constituencies of support for established welfare programmes to make retrenchment an issue of extreme political sensitivity. In Pierson's view, this is ultimately why both Thatcher and Reagan failed in their ideologically driven campaigns against public sector spending. But Richard Clayton and Jonas Pontusson tell a rather different story. Rather than focusing on public spending, they concentrate their attention on alternative measures of welfare state expansion and contraction. Looking at measures such as the level of public sector employment and the extent of direct, non-profit, service provision by the state, they find considerable evidence of welfare state decline and of a change in welfare state priorities. That change – away from services and towards income transfers directed to the old and the unemployed – may be indicative less of the emergence of a 'new politics' of the welfare state than of the re-emergence of an older politics, which views non-profit provision on the basis of need as a kind of covert state socialism that must be resisted at all costs.

III The Futures of Welfare

Part III is shorter and more speculative than the preceding parts, as we bring together a number of authors thinking about the 'coming' welfare state. We begin with a short piece by the influential economic journalist Will Hutton, who discusses the nature of the challenge that changing social and economic practices pose for our welfare institutions (especially those that relate to the governance of labour markets). He argues that in an increasingly uncertain world, competitiveness and real social security may require more (or at least more certain) welfare provision, not less. Next, Tony Fitzpatrick sets out to assess the strengths (and weaknesses) of the ecological critique of the practices of existing welfare states. The Green perspective on welfare has become increasingly prominent in recent years but, as Fitzpatrick shows, the move from criticism of the prevailing order to policy recommendations for its reform is far from easy. In a very short but incisive contribution, Philippe van Parijs sketches his ingenious plan to jettison most of the existing apparatus of the (income-transfer) welfare state by instituting a guaranteed basic income for every citizen. Even for those who doubt the political practicability of van Parijs' solution, it is a fascinating and challenging proposal which has provoked a wide-ranging and on-going debate. In the penultimate reading, Kirk Mann considers the impact that a rather elusive postmodernist approach has had upon welfare state thinking. If nothing else, this approach has heightened sensitivity to questions of diversity and difference in welfare state administration which have traditionally geared themselves to the needs of characteristically undifferentiated and 'standard' citizens. Our selection closes with a short extract from the work of Anthony Giddens, Director of the London School of Economics and thinker-in-residence to Britain's New Labour Administration. Drawing on his extraordinarily influential articulation of the 'third way', Giddens here discusses the ways in which welfare institutions might be remade in a radically changed social and economic environment to underpin a new form of 'positive welfare' built upon the shifting terrain of the new context set by 'reflexive modernity'.

This Reader reflects the extraordinary breadth and diversity of thinking about welfare being undertaken from almost every point of the political compass. It gives expression to the enormous challenges that we face but at the same time counsels against 'quick fixes' or ill-considered panic responses to problems which are undoubtedly real but may also be manageable. Having forced its way to the top of the political agenda over the past twenty years, welfare seems extremely unlikely to lose its salience in the years ahead.

Part I

Approaches to Welfare

The First Welfare State?

Thomas Paine

[...]

When, in countries that are called civilized, we see age going to the work-house and youth to the gallows, something must be wrong in the system of government. It would seem, by the exterior appearance of such countries, that all was happiness; but there lies hidden from the eye of common observation, a mass of wretchedness that has scarcely any other chance than to expire in poverty or infamy. Its entrance into life is marked with the presage of its fate; and until this is remedied, it is in vain to punish.

Civil government does not consist in executions; but in making that provision for the instruction of youth, and the support of age, as to exclude, as much as possible, profligacy from the one, and despair from the other. Instead of this, the resources of a country are lavished upon kings, upon courts, upon hirelings, impostors and prostitutes; and even the poor themselves, with all their wants upon them, are compelled to support the fraud that oppresses them.

Why is it, that scarcely any are executed but the poor? The fact is a proof, among other things, of a wretchedness in their condition. Bred up without morals, and cast upon the world without a prospect, they are the exposed sacrifice of vice and legal barbarity. The millions that are super-fluously wasted upon governments are more than sufficient to reform those evils, and to benefit the condition of every man in a nation, not included within the purlieus of a court.

[...]

In the present state of things, a labouring man, with a wife and two or three children, does not pay less than between seven and eight pounds a year in taxes. He is not sensible of this, because it is disguised to him in the articles which he buys, and he thinks only of their dearness; but as the taxes take from him, at least, a fourth part of his yearly earnings, he is consequently disabled from providing for a family, especially, if himself, or any of them, are afflicted with sickness.

The first step, therefore, of practical relief, would be to abolish the poor rates entirely, and in lieu thereof, to make a remission of taxes to the poor of double the amount of the present poor-rates, viz. 4 millions annually out of the surplus taxes. By this measure, the poor will be benefited 2 millions, and the housekeepers 2 millions.

[...]

I proceed to the mode of relief or distribution, which is,

To pay as a remission of taxes to every poor family, out of the surplus taxes, and in room of poor-rates, four pounds a year for every child under fourteen years of age; enjoining the parents of such children to send them to school, to learn reading, writing and common arithmetic; the ministers of every parish, of every denomination, to certify jointly to an office, for that purpose, that this duty is performed.

The amount of this expense will be,
For six hundred and thirty thousand children,
at four pounds *per ann.* each,   —   —   —   —   —   —   £2,520,000

By adopting this method, not only the poverty of the parents will be relieved, but ignorance will be banished from the rising generation, and the number of poor will hereafter become less, because their abilities, by the aid of education, will be greater. Many a youth, with good natural genius, who is apprenticed to a mechanical trade, such as a carpenter, joiner, millwright, shipwright, blacksmith, &c. is prevented getting forward the whole of his life, from the want of a little common education when a boy.

I now proceed to the case of the aged.

I divide age into two classes. First, the approach of age beginning at fifty. Secondly, old age commencing at sixty.

At fifty, though the mental faculties of man are in full vigour, and his judgement better than at any preceding date, the bodily powers for laborious life are on the decline. He cannot bear the same quantity of fatigue as at an earlier period. He begins to earn less, and is less capable of enduring wind and weather; and in those more retired employments where much sight is required, he fails apace, and sees himself, like an old horse, beginning to be turned adrift.

At sixty his labour ought to be over, at least from direct necessity. It is painful to see old age working itself to death, in what are called civilized countries, for daily bread.

[…]

[I propose] To pay to every such person of the age of fifty years, and until he shall arrive at the age of sixty, the sum of six pounds *per ann.* out of the surplus taxes; and ten pounds *per ann.* during life after the age of sixty. The expense of which will be,

> Seventy thousand persons at £6 *per ann.* 420,000
> Seventy thousand ditto at £10 *per ann.*   700,000
> £1,120,000

This support, as already remarked, is not of the nature of a charity, but of a right. Every person in England, male and female, pays on an average in taxes, two pounds eight shillings and sixpence *per ann.* from the day of his (or her) birth; and, if the expense of collection be added, he pays two pounds eleven shillings and sixpence; consequently, at the end of fifty years he has paid one hundred and twenty-eight pounds fifteen shillings; and at sixty, one hundred and fifty-four pounds ten shillings. Converting, therefore, his (or her) individual tax into a tontine, the money he shall receive after fifty years is but little more than the legal interest of the net money he has paid; the rest is made up from those whose circumstances do not require them to draw such support, and the capital in both cases defrays the expenses of government. It is on this ground that I have extended the probable claims to one third of the number of aged persons in the nation. Is it then better that the lives of one hundred and forty thousand aged persons be rendered comfortable, or that a million a year of public money be expended on any one individual, and him often of the most worthless or insignificant character?

[…]

After all the above cases are provided for, there will still be a number of families who, though not properly of the class of poor, yet find it difficult to give education to their children; and such children, under such a case, would be in a worse condition than if their parents were actually poor. A nation under a well-regulated government should permit none to remain uninstructed. It is monarchical and aristocratical government only that requires ignorance for its support.

Suppose then four hundred thousand children to be in this condition, which is a greater number than ought to be supposed, after the provisions already made, the method will be,

To allow for each of those children ten shillings a year for the expense of schooling, for six years each, which will give them six months schooling each year and half a crown a year for paper and spelling books.

The expense of this will be annually   £250,000

There will then remain one hundred and ten thousand pounds.

Notwithstanding the great modes of relief which the best instituted and best principled government may devise, there will be a number of smaller cases, which it is good policy as well as beneficence in a nation to consider.

Were twenty shilling to be given immediately on the birth of a child, to every woman who should make the demand, and none will make it whose circumstances do not require it, it might relieve a great deal of instant distress.

There are about two hundred thousand births yearly in England, and if claimed, by one fourth,

The amount would be   £50,000

And twenty shillings to every new-married couple who should claim in like manner. This would not exceed the sum of £20,000.

Also twenty thousand pounds to be appropriated to defray the funeral expenses of persons, who, travelling for work, may die at a distance from their friends. By relieving parishes from this charge, the sick stranger will be better treated.

I shall finish this part of the subject with a plan adapted to the particular condition of a metropolis, such as London.

[…]

First, To erect two or more buildings, or take some already erected, capable of containing at least six thousand persons, and to have in each of these places as many kinds of employment as can be contrived, so that every person who shall come may find something which he or she can do.

Secondly, To receive all who shall come, without enquiring who or what they are. The only condition to be, that for so much, or so many hours work, each person shall receive so many meals of wholesome food, and a warm lodging, at least as good as a barrack. That a certain portion of what each person's work shall be worth shall be reserved, and given to him, or her, on their going away; and that each person shall stay as long, or as short time, or come as often as he choose, on these conditions.

If each person stayed three months, it would assist by rotation twenty-four thousand persons annually, though the real number, at all times, would be but six thousand. By establishing an asylum of this kind, persons to whom temporary distresses occur would have an opportunity to recruit themselves and be enabled to look out for better employment.

Allowing that their labour paid but one half the expense of supporting them, after reserving a portion of their earnings for themselves, the sum of forty thousand pounds additional would defray all other charges for even a greater number than six thousand.

The fund very properly convertible to this purpose, in addition to the twenty thousand pounds, remaining of the former fund, will be the produce of the tax upon coals, so iniquitously and wantonly applied to the support of the Duke of Richmond. It is horrid that any man, more especially at the price coals now are, should live on the distresses of a community; and any government permitting such an abuse deserves to be dismissed. This fund is said to be about twenty thousand pounds *per annum*.

I shall now conclude this plan with enumerating the several particulars, and then proceed to other matters.

The enumeration is as follows:

First, Abolition of two million poor-rates.

Secondly, Provision for two hundred and fifty-two thousand poor families.

Thirdly, Education for one million and thirty thousand children.

Fourthly, Comfortable provision for one hundred and forty thousand aged persons.

Fifthly, Donation of twenty shillings each for fifty thousand births.

Sixthly, Donation of twenty shillings each for twenty thousand marriages.

Seventhly, Allowance of twenty thousand pounds for the funeral expenses of persons travelling for work, and dying at a distance from their friends.

Eighthly, Employment, at all times, for the casual poor in the cities of London and Westminster.

By the operation of this plan, the poor laws, those instruments of civil torture, will be superseded, and the wasteful expense of litigation prevented. The hearts of the humane will not be shocked by ragged and hungry children, and persons of seventy and eighty years of age begging for bread. The dying poor will not be dragged from place to place to breathe their last, as a reprisal of parish upon parish. Widows will have a maintenance for their children, and not be carted away, on the death of their husbands, like culprits and criminals; and children will no longer be considered as increasing the distresses of their parents. The haunts of the wretched will be known, because it will be to their advantage; and the number of petty crimes, the offspring of distress and poverty, will be lessened. The poor, as well as the rich, will then be interested in the support of government, and the cause and apprehension of riots and tumults will cease. – Ye who sit in ease, and solace yourselves in plenty, and such there are in Turkey and Russia, as well as in England, and who say to yourselves, 'Are we not well off', have ye thought of these things? When ye do, ye will cease to speak and feel for yourselves alone.

[…]

Note

Thomas Paine's *Rights of Man* was first published in London by J. S. Jordan in 1791–2. The same publisher produced several new editions in quick succession. The extract reproduced here is from the Penguin Classics reprint of 1985 (with introduction by Eric Foner and notes by Henry Collins), pp. 218, 240–48.

'Classical'

The Welfare State in Historical Perspective

Asa Briggs

[…]

A welfare state is a state in which organized power is deliberately used (through politics and administration) in an effort to modify the play of market forces in at least three directions – first, by guaranteeing individuals and families a minimum income irrespective of the market value of their work or their property; second, by narrowing the extent of insecurity by enabling individuals and families to meet certain 'social contingencies' (for example, sickness, old age and unemployment) which lead otherwise to individual and family crises; and third, by ensuring that all citizens without distinction of status or class are offered the best standards available in relation to a certain agreed range of social services.

The first and second of these objects may be accomplished, in part at least, by what used to be called a 'social service state', a state in which communal resources are employed to abate poverty and to assist those in distress. The third objective, however, goes beyond the aims of a 'social service state'. It brings in the idea of the 'optimum' rather than the older idea of the 'minimum'. It is concerned not merely with abatement of class differences or the needs of scheduled groups but with equality of treatment and the aspirations of citizens as voters with equal shares of electoral power.

Merely to define the phrase welfare state in this way points to a number of historical considerations, which are the theme of this article. First, the conception of 'market forces' sets the problems of the welfare state (and of welfare) within the context of the age of modern political economy. In societies without market economies, the problem of welfare raises quite different issues. Within the context of the age of modern political economy an attempt has been made, and is still being made, to create and maintain a self-regulating system of markets, including markets in the fictitious commodities, land, money and labour. The multiple motives lying behind the attempt to control these markets require careful and penetrating analysis.

Second, the conception of 'social contingencies' is strongly influenced by the experience of industrialism. Sickness, old age and death entail hardships in any kind of society. Ancient systems of law and morality include precepts designed to diminish these hardships, precepts based, for example, on the obligations of sons to support their parents or on the claims of charity, *obsequium religionis*. Unemployment, however, at least in the form in which it is thought of as a social contingency, is a product of industrial societies, and it is unemployment more than any other social contingency which has determined the shape and timing of modern welfare legislation. Before the advent of mass unemployment, 'unemployability', the inability of individuals to secure their livelihood by work, was a key subject in the protracted debates on poor law policy. The existence of 'chronic unemployment', structural or cyclical, has been a powerful spur from the nineteenth century onwards leading organized labour groups to pass from concentration on sectional interests to the consideration of 'social rights' of workers as a class; to philanthropic businessmen wishing to improve the 'efficiency' and strengthen the 'social justice' of the business system; and to politicians and governments anxious to avoid what seemed to be dangerous political consequences of unemployment. The memories of chronic unemployment in the inter-war years and the discovery of what it was believed were new techniques of controlling it reinforced welfare state policies in many countries after the Second World War.

Third, the idea of using organized power (through politics and administration) to determine the pattern of welfare services requires careful historical dating. Why not rely for welfare on the family, the church, 'charity', 'self help', 'mutual aid' (guild, trade union, friendly society) or 'fringe benefits' (business itself)? Whole philosophies of welfare have been founded on each of these ideas or institutions: often the philosophies and the interests sustaining them have been inimical to the suggestion that the state itself should intervene. The possibility of using governmental power has been related in each country to the balance of economic and social forces; estimates of the proper functions and, true or false, of the available resources of the state; effective techniques of influence and control, resting on knowledge (including expert knowledge); and, not least, the prevalence (or absence) of the conviction that societies can be shaped by conscious policies designed to eliminate 'abuses' which in earlier generations had been accepted as 'inevitable' features of the human condition.

Not only does the weighting of each of these factors vary from period to period, but it also varies from place to place. It was Bentham, scarcely distinguished for his historical sense, who in distinguishing between *agenda* (tasks of government) and *sponte acta* (unplanned decisions of individuals) wrote that 'in England abundance of useful things are done by individuals which in other countries are done either by government or not at all ... [while] in Russia, under Peter the Great, the list of *sponte acta* being a blank, that of *agenda* was proportionately abundant.'[1] This contrast was noted by many other writers later in the nineteenth century, just as an opposite contrast between Britain and the United States was often noted after 1945.

If the question of what constitutes welfare involves detailed examination of the nature and approach to 'social contingencies', the question of why the state rather than some other agency becomes the main instrument of welfare involves very detailed examination of a whole range of historical circumstances. The answer to the question is complicated, moreover, by differences of attitude in different countries, to the idea of 'the state' itself. Given these differences, a translation of basic terms into different languages raises difficulties which politicians and journalists may well have obscured. For example, is the term *Wohlfahrtsstaat* the right translation of welfare state? British and German approaches to 'the state' have been so different that they have absorbed the intellectual energy of generations of political scientists. In the nineteenth century there were somewhat similar difficulties (although on a smaller scale) surrounding the translation of the British term 'self help'. A French translator of Samuel Smiles's book of that title (1859) said that the term 'self help' was 'à peu près intraduisible'.

Fourth, the 'range of agreed social services' set out in the provisional definition of 'welfare state' is a shifting range. Policies, despite the finalism of much of the post-1945 criticism, are never fixed for all time. What at various times was considered to be a proper range shifts, as Dicey showed, and consequently must be examined historically. So too must changing areas of agreement and conflict. Public health was once a highly controversial issue in European societies: it still is in some other societies. The 'sanitary idea' was rightly regarded by the pioneers of public health as an idea which had large and far-reaching chains of consequences. It marked an assault on 'fate' which would be bound to lead to other assaults. Public health, in the administrative sphere of drains, sewers and basic 'environmental' services, has been taken outside the politics of conflict in Britain and other places, but personal health services remain controversial. There is controversy, very bitter indeed in the United States, not only about the range of services and who shall enjoy them but about the means of providing them. The choice of means influences all welfare state history. Welfare states can and do employ a remarkable variety of instruments, such as social insurance, direct provision in cash or in kind, subsidy, partnership with other agencies (including private business agencies) and action through local authorities. In health policy alone, although medical knowledge is the same in all countries of the West and the same illnesses are likely to be treated in much the same kind of way, there is a remarkable diversity of procedures and institutions even in countries which make extensive public provision for personal health services.

Fifth, there are important historical considerations to take into account in tracing the relationship between the three different directions of public intervention in the free (or partially free) market. The demand for 'minimum standards' can be related to a particular set of cumulative pressures. Long before the Webbs urged the need in 1909 for government action to secure 'an enforced minimum of civilized life', the case for particular minima had been powerfully advocated. Yet the idea of basing social policy as a whole on a public commitment to 'minimum' standards did not become practical politics in Britain until the so-called 'Beveridge revolution' of the Second World War. The third direction of 'welfare' policy, and the distinctive direction of the welfare state, can be understood only in terms of older logic and more recent history. The idea of separating welfare policy from 'subsistence' standards (the old minima, however measured) and relating it to 'acceptable' standards ('usual work income'), provides an indication of the extent to which 'primary poverty' has been reduced in 'affluent societies'. It may be related, however, to older ideas of equality, some of which would lead direct not to state intervention in the market but to the elimination of the market altogether, at least as a force influencing human relationships. A consideration of the contemporary debate is more rewarding if it is grounded in history. . . .

German experience in the nineteenth century was in certain important respects different from that of Britain. If before 1900 factory legislation was more advanced in Britain than in any other European country, Germany had established a 'lead' in social security legislation which the British Liberal governments of 1906 to 1914 tried to wipe out. Bismarck's reforms of the 1880s – laws of 1882, 1884 and 1889 introducing compulsory insurance against sickness, accidents, old age and invalidity – attracted immense interest in other European countries. Just as British factory legislation was copied overseas, so German social insurance stimulated foreign imitation. Denmark, for instance, copied all three German pension schemes between 1891 and 1898, and Belgium between 1894 and 1903. Switzerland by a constitutional amendment in 1890 empowered the federal government to organize a system of national insurance. In Britain itself a friendly observer noted in 1890 that Bismarck had 'discovered where the roots of social evil lie. He has declared in words that burn that it is the duty of the state to give heed, above all, to the welfare of its weaker members'.[2]

More recently Bismarck's social policy has been described by more than one writer as the creation of a welfare state.[3] The term is very misleading. Bismarck's legislation rested on a basic conservatism which Oastler himself would have appreciated and was sustained by a bureaucracy which had no counterpart in Britain except perhaps in Chadwick's imagination. The Prussian idea and history of the state and the British idea and history of the state diverged long before the 1880s, and it is not fanciful to attribute some of the divergences to the presence or absence a century before of 'cameralism', the idea of the systematic application to government of administrative routines.

Equally important, the history of political economy in the two countries diverged just as markedly. The development of a school of historical economics provided a powerful academic reinforcement in Germany for *Sozialpolitik*. The refusal of historical economists to 'isolate' economic phenomena, including 'economic man', their distrust of 'laws of political economy' covering all ages and all societies, their critique of the motives and institutions of contemporary capitalism and their underlying belief in a 'social order' distinguished them sharply from classical political economists in Britain. Their influence was considerable enough for Schmoller (1838–1917), the most important figure in the history of the school, to argue forcefully that no Smithian was fit to occupy an academic chair in Germany.[4]

Even among the 'precursors' of the historical school and among economists who stayed aloof from Schmoller and his circle, there was a powerful tradition linking social reform with conservative views of society.[5] J. K. Rodbertus (1805–75) was a conservative monarchist who combined dislike of the 'class struggle' and belief in state socialism. Adolf Wagner (1835–1917), who stayed aloof from Schmoller and admired Ricardo as the outstanding economic 'theorist', acknowledged his debt to Rodbertus when he gave a warm welcome to Bismarck's legislation.

According to Wagner Germany had entered a 'new social period', characterized by new economic ideas, new political views and new social programmes. National economy (*Volkswirtschaft*) had to be converted into state economy (*Staatswirtschaft*): the foundation of the new economy would have to be welfare. The idea of regarding 'labour power' as a commodity and wages as its price was 'inhuman' as well as 'unchristian'. Wagner proposed a number of practical measures, some of which went further than those introduced by Bismarck. Schmoller, too, advocated policies aiming at 'the re-establishment of a friendly relation between social classes, the removal or modification of injustice, a nearer approach to the principles of distributive justice, with the introduction of a social legislation which promotes progress and guarantees the moral and material elevation of the lower and middle classes.'[6]

Bismarck, for whom the idea of insurance had a particular fascination both in his domestic and foreign policies, did not envisage a social policy which would go anywhere near as far as some of the 'socialists of the chair' would have wished. He objected, for example, to the limitation by law of the hours of women and children in factories and he was at least as stubborn as any mill-owner of the Manchester School when 'theorists' talked of state officials interfering with private concerns in agriculture or industry. He also disliked extensions of direct taxation. He wanted the state, however, to be actively involved in the financing and administering of the insurance schemes which he proposed and he defended the introduction of these schemes – against both right-wing and left-wing opposition – in terms of 'the positive advancement of the welfare of the working classes'. 'The state', it was laid down in the preamble to the first and unsuccessful bill of 1881, 'is not merely a necessary but a beneficent institution.' Bismarck disagreed with Theodor Lohmann, who drafted his first social insurance legislation, about whether the state should contribute directly to the costs of insurance. Bismarck got his way that it should, but the political parties objected and his first attempts at legislation foundered. It was a measure of his recognition of political realities that the idea of state contributions was dropped in 1884 when his accident insurance bill was introduced. The law of 1889, providing for disability and old age pensions, did entail a flat-rate contribution from the imperial treasury of fifty marks for each person receiving a pension, but this was a small element in the total cost and fell far short of the amount Bismarck had originally envisaged.

Many of Bismarck's critics accused him, not without justification, of seeking through his legislation to make German workers 'depend' upon the state. The same charges have been made against the initiators of all welfare (and earlier, of poor law) policy often without justification, yet it was Bismarck himself who drew a revealing distinction between the degrees of obedience (or subservience) of private servants and servants at court. The latter would 'put up with much more' than the former because they had pensions to look forward to. Welfare soothed the spirit, or perhaps tamed it. Bismarck's deliberate invocation of 'subservience' is at the opposite end of the scale from the socialist invocation of 'equality' as the goal of the welfare state. It is brutally simple, too, when compared with sophisticated liberal attempts to define the conditions in which liberty and equality may be made to complement each other.[7] The invocation was, of course, bound up with conscious political calculation. Bismarck was anxious to make German social democracy less attractive to workingmen. He feared 'class war' and wanted to postpone it as long as possible. His talks with Lassalle in 1863 had ranged over questions of this kind,[8] and in 1884 he argued explicitly that if the state would only 'show a little more Christian solicitude for the workingman', then the social democrats would 'sound their siren song in vain'. 'The thronging to them will cease as soon as workingmen see that the government and legislative bodies are earnestly concerned for their welfare.'[9] It has been suggested that Bismarck was influenced by Napoleon III's successful handling of social policy as an instrument of politics. He certainly spent time seeking an 'alternative to socialism' and it was this aspect of his policy which gave what he did contemporary controversial significance throughout Europe.

His policy also provided a definite alternative to liberalism. During the last years of his life when he was prepared to contemplate insurance against unemployment and when he talked of the 'right to work' as enthusiastically as any Chartist, he was reflecting that sharp reaction against economic liberalism which could be discerned, in different forms, in almost every country in Europe. Disraeli's social policy in his ministry of 1874–80 had somewhat similar features. It also had the added interest of appearing to realize hopes first formulated by Disraeli in the age of Oastler and the Chartists. In 1874 also a royalist and clerical majority in the French National Assembly carried a factory act, limiting hours of work of children below the age of twelve, which went further than a law of 1848 on the same subject. A later and more comprehensive act of 1892 was the work of Conservative Republicans. The nineteenth century closed with a British Moneylenders Act which, Professor Clapham has argued, in effect revived the medieval law of usury, the last remnants of which had been swept away, it was thought for ever, in 1854.[10]

Medieval attitudes to welfare were echoed most strongly in Christian apologetics. Papal encyclicals, notably *Rerum Novarum* (1891), were not only manifestos in crusades against liberalism or socialism but were also important documents in the evolution of *Sozialpolitik*. De Mun, Von Ketteler and Von Vogelsang were writers who advocated particular or general welfare policies: so did Heinrich Pesch, who has been singled out for special treatment by Schumpeter. Among Protestants also there was renewed call for a 'social gospel'. It is not without interest that Lohmann, who had advised Bismarck and went on to advise William II in the formulation of the far-reaching Labour Code of 1891, was a deeply religious man, the son of a Westphalian Lutheran pastor. Canon W. L. Blackley (1830–1902), the pioneer of old-age pensions schemes not only in Britain but in other parts of the world and the founder of the National Providence League, was an honorary canon of Winchester Cathedral. On the Liberal side – and there was a close association in Britain between religious nonconformity and political liberalism – Seebohm Rowntree (1871–1954), one of the first systematic investigators of the facts of poverty, was a Quaker. The whole attack on the limitations of the poor law was guided, though not exclusively, by men of strong religious principles.

The complexity of the nineteenth-century background contrasts at first sight with the simplicity of the twentieth-century story. For a tangle of tendencies we have a 'trend', a trend culminating in greater 'order' and simplification. In fact, however, the twentieth-century story has its own complexities, which are now in the process of being unravelled. Professor Titmuss has shown, for instance, that Lloyd George's national health insurance legislation of 1911, a landmark in 'trend' legislation, was the culmination of a long and confused period in which doctors had been engaged in a 'Hobbesian struggle for independence from the power and authority exercised over their lives, their work and their professional values by voluntary associations and private enterprise.' He has maintained that the legislation of 1911 can only be understood if it is related, as so much else in the twentieth century must be related, to the history of hidden pressures from established interests and a sectional demand for an 'enlargement of professional freedom'.[11] Many of the complexities of twentieth-century history certainly lie buried in the records of the network of private concerns and of professional groups which came into existence in the nineteenth century. There can be no adequate historical explanation which concerns itself in large terms with the state alone. Just as the administration of welfare is complicated in practice and can be understood only in detail, so the outline of welfare state legislation only becomes fully intelligible when it ceases to be an outline, and when it looks beyond parliamentary legislation to such crucial twentieth-century relationships as those between governments and pressure groups and 'experts' and the 'public'.

Yet there are five factors in twentieth-century welfare history (other than warfare, one of the most powerful of factors) which are beyond dispute and dominant enough to need little detailed research. They are, first, the basic transformation in the attitude towards poverty, which made the nineteenth-century poor law no longer practicable in democratic societies; second, the detailed investigation of the 'social contingencies' which directed attention to the need for particular social policies; third, the close association between unemployment and welfare policy; fourth, the development within market capitalism itself of welfare philosophies and practices; and fifth, the influence of working-class pressures on the content and tone of welfare legislation.

The first and second of these five factors can scarcely be studied in isolation. The basis of the nineteenth-century British Poor Law of 1834 was economic logic. That logic was strained when empirical sociologists, like Charles Booth (1840–1916) and Rowntree, showed that a large number of poor people were poor through no fault of their own but because of tendencies within the market system. They pitted statistics against logic by attempting to count how many people were living in poverty and by surveying the various forms that the poverty assumed.[12] Prior to Booth's 'grand inquest', Beatrice Webb wrote, 'neither the individualist nor the socialist could state with any approach to accuracy what exactly was the condition of the people of England'.[13] Once the results of the 'inquest' had been published 'the net effect was to give an entirely fresh impetus to the general adoption of the policy of securing to every individual, as the very basis of his life and work, a prescribed natural minimum of the requisites for efficient parenthood and citizenship.'

Booth's thinking about economics was far less radical than his thinking about welfare, but Rowntree, who drew a neat distinction between 'primary' and 'secondary' poverty, the former being beyond the control of the wage-earner, went on to advocate specific welfare policies, ranging from old-age pensions to family allowances, public-provided housing to supervised welfare conditions in factories. The policies which he urged at various stages of his long life were, indeed, the main constituent policies of the welfare state.[14] Like the welfare state, however, Rowntree stopped short of socialism. He separated questions of welfare from questions of economic power, and remained throughout his life a 'new Liberal'. The main tenet of his liberalism was that the community could not afford the 'waste', individual and social, which was implied in an industrial society divided 'naturally' into 'rich' and 'very poor'. Poverty was as much of a social problem as 'pauperism'. The roots of poverty were to be found not in individual irresponsibility or incapacity but in social maladjustment. Poverty, in short, was not the fault of the poor: it was the fault of society. Quite apart from 'socialist pressure', society had to do something about poverty once it was given facts about its extent, its incidence (Rowntree drew attention to the cycle of poverty in families), its ramifications and its consequences. All facts were grist to the mill. They included facts not only about wages but about nutrition: subsistence levels could only be measured when nutritional criteria were taken into account.

Sharp turns of thought about poverty were by no means confined to people in Britain. There were signs of fundamental rethinking, allied [. . .] to 'feeling',[15] both in Europe and the United States at the end of the nineteenth and the beginning of the twentieth century.[16] The survey method, which Booth and Rowntree depended upon, was capable of general applicability.[17] The limitations of systematic 'charity' were noted at least as generally as the limitations of unsystematic charity had been at the beginning of the industrial age. It is no coincidence that in Britain and Sweden, two countries with distinct welfare histories, there was keen debate about the Poor Law at almost exactly the same time. In Sweden the Poor Relief Order of 1871, with its checks on poor relief, was criticized by the Swedish Poor Relief Association which was formed at the first General Swedish Poor Law Congress in 1906. A year later the government appointed a committee to draw up proposals for fresh legislation governing poor relief and the treatment of vagrants. In Britain the Royal Commission on the Poor Laws, which was appointed in 1905 and reported in 1909, covered almost all topics in social policy. The issues were clearly stated and both the social contingencies and the necessary policies of social control were carefully examined. Although new direct legislation was slow to come in both countries, there was much indirect legislation and in both countries there were demands for what Beatrice Webb called 'an enforced minimum of civilized life'.[18]

The main threat to that minimum in the later twentieth century came from 'mass involuntary unemployment'. This, of course, was a world phenomenon which strained poor law and social service systems in most countries and presented a threat – or a challenge – to politicians and administrators. In Britain, which was the first country to introduce compulsory unemployment insurance (1911; greatly extended in 1920), the system of relief broke down under the stresses of the 1930s. Insurance benefits, linked to contributions, were stringently restricted, and while tussles about the 'means test' were leading to extreme differences of outlook between socialists and their opponents, an Unemployment Assistance Board, founded in 1934, was providing a second-line income maintenance service, centrally administered. In Europe there was an extension of unemployment aid schemes, whether by insurance (the Swedes, for example, introduced state-subsidized unemployment insurance in 1934), 'doles' or in certain cases 'positive' state-run schemes of 'public works'. In the United States and Canada, where there had been entrenched resistance to government intervention in welfare provision, new legislation was passed,[19] while in New Zealand, which had long lost its reputation as a pioneer of welfare, there was a remarkable bout of state intervention after the return of a Labour government to power in 1935. The Social Security Act of 1938 contained a list of health services and pensions benefits which, while resting on previous legislation, were everywhere hailed as a bold and daring experiment. The Minister of Finance anticipated later welfare legislators in other countries by arguing unequivocally that 'to suggest the inevitability of slumps and booms, associated as they are with affluence for a limited number during a period, and followed by unemployment, destitution, hardship and privation for the masses, is to deny all conscious progressive purpose.'[20] According to the International Labor Office, the 1938 New Zealand Act 'has, more than any other law, determined the practical meaning of social security, and so has deeply influenced the course of legislation in other countries'.[21]

Twentieth-century social security legislation raises many interesting general issues – the relevance of the insurance principle, for example, the relationship between 'negative' social policy and 'positive' economic policy, and, underlying all else, the nature and extent of the responsibilities of the state. Insurance principles, actuarially unsound though they may be and inadequate though they have proved as instruments of finance at moments of crisis, have been historically significant. They removed the stigma of pauperism from a social service, reconciled 'voluntary' and 'compulsory' approaches to provision, and facilitated 'public approval' of state expenditures which otherwise would have been challenged. They thus served as a link between old ways of thinking ('self help' and 'mutual help') and new. 'Positive' economic policy was in the first instance, as in Roosevelt's America, the child of improvisation: its systematic justification had to await revolutions in political economy (Keynes and after) which accompanied shifts in social power. The difference in tone and content between two books by William Beveridge – his *Unemployment* (1909) and his *Full Employment in a Free Society* (1944) – is one of the best indications of the change in the world of ideas between the early and middle periods of the twentieth century. 'Beveridgism', an important British phenomenon during the Second World War, had sufficient popular appeal to show that the world of ideas and the world of practical politics were not very far apart. For the intellectuals and for the public the magnification of governmental power – and the enormous increase in government expenditure financed from taxation – were taken for granted.

The fourth and fifth factors are also related to each other. In all advanced industrial countries in the twentieth century there has been a movement towards welfare in industry – 'industrial betterment' it was originally called – which has been accompanied by the emergence of philosophies of 'human relations', 'welfare management' and industrial and labour psychology.[22] The movement has to be explained in terms of both economics and politics. A 'managerial revolution', limited though it may have been in its economic effects, has accelerated the tendencies making for 'welfare capitalism'. The need to find acceptable incentives for workers, to avoid labour disputes and to secure continuous production, to raise output in phases of technical change and (more recently) to hold labour 'permissively' in a period of full employment has often driven where 'human relations' philosophies have failed to inspire. Welfare, a word which was often resented by workers, when it was applied within the structure of the firm, was, indeed, used in a business context before it began to be applied to a new kind of state. Within state schemes of welfare employers have made, and are expected to make, sizeable contributions. In France and Italy, in particular, obligatory social charges as a percentage of assessable wages constituted the main source of welfare expenditure.[23] In the United States business rather than the state was, and is, expected directly to provide a network of welfare services. As in all such situations, the provision of welfare varies immensely from one firm (giant businesses are at one end of the scale) to another.

In contrast to these countries, such as Great Britain, which appear to regard government (for reasons which have been stated above) merely as the most effective of several possible institutions for the administration of income security programs or the provision of services, [...] a society like the United States that distrusts its government is likely to seek to organize its social security services in such a way as to keep government activity to a minimum.[24]

United States experience, in contrast to the experience described in other countries, shows that this likelihood has been converted into fact.

It is not accidental that the labour movement in the United States has showed little interest in socialism and that its leaders have chosen of their own volition to bargain for 'fringe benefits' at the level of the plant. In most European countries, particularly in Britain and in Scandinavia, there has been a tendency for working-class pressures to lead to greater state intervention. In Britain nineteenth-century patterns of 'mutual dependence' through 'voluntary action', which impressed so many observers from Tocqueville onwards, have become less dominant, except in the field of industrial relations where they have very tenaciously survived.[25]

As we have seen, the demand for state action has been related to the rights of citizenship, to equality as well as to security. During the critical period between the two World Wars, when economic and social conditions were very difficult, welfare measures were demanded and provided 'piecemeal' with varying conditions of regulation and administration, 'a frightening complexity of eligibility and benefit according to individual circumstances, local boundaries, degrees of need and so forth'.[26] The Second World War, which sharpened the sense of 'democracy', led to demands both for 'tidying up' and for 'comprehensiveness'. It encouraged the move from 'minima' to 'optima', at least in relation to certain specified services, and it made all residual paternalisms seem utterly inadequate and increasingly archaic. It was in the light of changes in working-class life within a more 'equal community' that post-war writers noted the extent to which the social services of the earlier part of the century had been shaped by assumptions about the nature of man, 'founded on outer rather than on inner observation', on the 'norms of behavior expected by one class from another'.[27] This period of criticism has already ended. The assumptions which shaped the welfare state have themselves been criticized,[28] and radical political slogans have concentrated more and more on differences of income between 'mature' and 'underdeveloped' countries rather than on differences within 'mature' countries themselves.

It may well be that in a world setting the five twentieth-century factors discussed in this article will be considered less important than other factors – the total size of the national income in different countries, for example, and the share of that income necessary for industrial (as, or when, distinct from social) investment, or even, on a different plane, the nature of family structure. Is not the making of the industrial welfare state in part at least the concomitant of the decline of the large, extended 'welfare family'? How far has the pressure of women (or just the presence of women voters) in industrial societies encouraged the formulation of welfare objectives? The historian does well to leave such large questions to be answered rather than to suggest that all or even the most important part of the truth is already known.

Notes

From C. Schottland, ed., *The Welfare State*, New York, Harper and Row, 1969, pp. 29–45.

1   J. Bentham, *Works*, ed. J. Bowring, 1843, vol. III, p. 35. Cf. J. M. Keynes's view of the 'agenda' of the state in *The End of Laissez Faire* (1926).
2   W. H. Dawson, *Bismarck and State Socialism* (1890), p. ix.
3   S. B. Fay, 'Bismarck's Welfare State', *Current History*, vol. XVIII (1950).
4   J. A. Schumpeter, *History of Economic Analysis* (1954), p. 765.
5   The pre-history of this approach leads back to Sismondi who has important links with Mill and the English utilitarians. He is a seminal figure in the critique of industrialism and the demand for welfare legislation.
6   A. Wagner, *Rede über die soziale Frage* (1872), pp. 8–9. G. von Schmoller, *Über einige Grundfragen des Rechts und der Volkswirtschaft* (1875), p. 92.
7   For the background of these attempts, see M. Ginsberg, 'The Growth of Social Responsibility', in M. Ginsberg, ed., *Law and Opinion in England in the Twentieth Century* (1959), pp. 3–26.
8   See G. Mayer, *Bismarck und Lassalle* (1927).
9   Dawson, op. cit., p. 35. This remark was made in 1884. Five years earlier the emperor, referring to the anti-socialist law of 1878, had said, 'a remedy cannot alone be sought in the repression of socialistic excesses; there must be simultaneously the positive advancement of the welfare of the working classes' (quoted ibid., p. 110).
10 J. H. Clapham, *An Economic History of Modern Britain*, vol. III (1938), p. 445.
11 R. M. Titmuss, 'Health', in Ginsberg, op. cit., p. 308. Cf. p. 313: 'The fundamental issue of 1911 was not [...] between individualism and collectivism, between contract and status; but between different forms of collectivism, different degrees of freedom; open or concealed power.'
12 C. Booth, *Life and Labour of the People in London*, 17 vols (1892–1903); B. S. Rowntree, *Poverty: A Study of Town Life* (1901).
13 B. Webb, *My Apprenticeship* (1926), p. 239.
14 For Booth, see T. S. and M. B. Simey, *Charles Booth, Social Scientist* (1960); for Rowntree, see A. Briggs, *Seebohm Rowntree* (1961). See also B. S. Rowntree and G. R. Lavers, *Poverty and the Welfare State* (1951).
15 'In intensity of feeling', Booth wrote, 'and not in statistics, lies the power to move the world. But by statistics must this power be guided if it would move the world aright.' *Life and Labour, Final Volume, Notes on Social Influences and Conclusion* (1903), p. 178.
16 See *inter alia* C. L. Mowat, *The Charity Organisation Society*; K. De Schweinitz, *England's Road to Social Security* (1943); C. W. Pitkin, *Social Politics and*

Modern Democracies, 2 vols (1931), vol. II being concerned with France; R. H. Bremner, *From the Depths: The Discovery of Poverty in the United States* (1956).

17 See M. Abrams, *Social Surveys and Social Action* (1951); P. V. Young, *Scientific Social Surveys and Research* (1950); D. C. Caradog Jones, *Social Surveys* (1955).

18 The British controversy is well described in U. Cormack, 'The Welfare State', *Loch Memorial Lecture* (1953). For Sweden, see The Royal Social Board, *Social Work and Legislation in Sweden* (1938).

19 J. C. Brown, *Public Relief, 1929–39* (1940); E. A. Williams, *Federal Aid for Relief* (1939); P. H. Douglas, *Social Security in the United States* (1939 edn).

20 Quoted in W. K. Hancock, *Survey of British Commonwealth Affairs*, vol. II (1940), p. 275.

21 International Labor Office, *Social Security in New Zealand* (1949), p. 111.

22 See A. Briggs, 'The Social Background', in H. Clegg and A. Flanders, eds, *Industrial Relations in Great Britain* (1955); L. Urwick and E. F. L. Brech, *The Human Factor in Management 1795–1943* (1944); E. D. Proud, *Welfare Work, Employers' Experiments for Improving Working Conditions in Factories* (1916); E. T. Kelly, ed., *Welfare Work in Industry* (1925); PEP, 'The Human Factor in Industry', *Planning* (March 1948).

23 PEP, 'Free Trade and Security', *Planning* (July 1957); 'A Comparative Analysis of the Cost of Social Security', in *International Labour Review* (1953).

24 E. M. Burns, *Social Security and Public Policy* (1956), p. 274.

25 For the nature of the nineteenth-century pattern, see J. M. Baernreither, *English Associations of Working Men* (1893). For industrial relations, see Clegg and Flanders, op. cit.

26 R. M. Titmuss, *Essays on the Welfare State* (1958), pp. 21–2.

27 Ibid., p. 19.

28 See A. Peacock, 'The Welfare Society', *Unservile State Papers* (1960); R. M. Titmuss, 'The Irresponsible Society', *Fabian Tracts* (1960); J. Saville, 'The Welfare State', *The New Reasoner*, no. 3 (1957).

Citizenship and Social Class
T. H. Marshall

[...]

I propose to divide citizenship into three parts. [...] I shall call these three parts, or elements, civil, political and social. The civil element is composed of the rights necessary for individual freedom – liberty of the person, freedom of speech, thought and faith, the right to own property and to conclude valid contracts, and the right to justice. The last is of a different order from the others, because it is the right to defend and assert all one's rights on terms of equality with others and by due process of law. This shows us that the institutions most directly associated with civil rights are the courts of justice. By the political element I mean the right to participate in the exercise of political power, as a member of a body invested with political authority or as an elector of the members of such a body. The corresponding institutions are parliament and councils of local government. By the social element I mean the whole range, from the right to a modicum of economic welfare and security to the right to share to the full in the social heritage and to live the life of a civilized being according to the standards prevailing in the society. The institutions most closely connected with it are the educational system and the social services. [...]

By 1832 when political rights made their first infantile attempt to walk, civil rights had come to man's estate and bore, in most essentials, the appearance that they have today.[1] 'The specific work of the earlier Hanoverian epoch', writes Trevelyan, 'was the establishment of the rule of law; and that law, with all its grave faults, was at least a law of freedom. On that solid foundation all our subsequent reforms were built.' This eighteenth-century achievement, interrupted by the French Revolution and completed after it, was in large measure the work of the courts, both in their daily practice and also in a series of famous cases in some of which they were fighting against parliament in defence of individual liberty. The most celebrated actor in this drama was, I suppose, John Wilkes, and, although we may deplore the absence in him of those noble and saintly qualities which we should like to find in our national heroes, we cannot complain if the cause of liberty is sometimes championed by a libertine.

In the economic field the basic civil right is the right to work, that is to say the right to follow the occupation of one's choice in the place of one's choice, subject only to legitimate demands for preliminary technical training. This right had been denied by both statute and custom; on the one hand by the Elizabethan Statute of Artificers, which confined certain occupations to certain social classes, and on the other by local regulations reserving employment in a town to its own members and by the use of apprenticeship as an instrument of exclusion rather than of recruitment. The recognition of the right involved the formal acceptance of a fundamental change of attitude. The old assumption that local and group monopolies were in the public interest, because 'trade and traffic cannot be maintained or increased without order and government', was replaced by the new assumption that such restrictions were an offence against the liberty of the subject and a menace to the prosperity of the nation. [...]

By the beginning of the nineteenth century this principle of individual economic freedom was accepted as axiomatic. You are probably familiar with the passage quoted by the Webbs from the report of the Select Committee of 1811, which states that:

> no interference of the legislature with the freedom of trade, or with the perfect liberty of every individual to dispose of his time and of his labour in the way and on the terms which he may judge most conducive to his own interest, can take place without violating general principles of the first importance to the prosperity and happiness of the community.[2] [...]

The story of civil rights in their formative period is one of the gradual addition of new rights to a status that already existed and was held to appertain to all adult members of the community – or perhaps one should say to all male members, since the status of women, or at least of married women, was in some important respects peculiar. This democratic, or universal, character of the status arose naturally from the fact that it was essentially the status of freedom, and in seventeenth-century England all men were free. Servile status, or villeinage by blood, had lingered on as a patent anachronism in the days of Elizabeth, but vanished soon afterwards. This change from servile to free labour has been described by Professor Tawney as 'a high landmark in the development both of economic and political society', and as 'the final triumph of the common law' in regions from which it had been excluded for four centuries. Henceforth the English peasant 'is a member of a society in which there is, nominally at least, one law for all men'.[3] The liberty which his predecessors had won by fleeing into the free towns had become his by right. In the towns the terms 'freedom' and 'citizenship' were interchangeable. When freedom became universal, citizenship grew from a local into a national institution.

The story of political rights is different both in time and in character. The formative period began, as I have said, in the early nineteenth century, when the civil rights attached to the status of freedom had already acquired sufficient substance to justify us in speaking of a general status of citizenship. And, when it began, it consisted, not in the creation of new rights to enrich a status already enjoyed by all, but in the granting of old rights to new sections of the population. [...]

It is clear that, if we maintain that in the nineteenth century citizenship in the form of civil rights was universal, the political franchise was not one of the rights of citizenship. It was the privilege of a limited economic class, whose limits were extended by each successive Reform Act. [...]

It was, as we shall see, appropriate that nineteenth-century capitalist society should treat political rights as a secondary product of civil rights. It was equally appropriate that the twentieth century should abandon this position and attach political rights directly and independently to citizenship as such. This vital change of principle was put into effect when the Act of 1918, by adopting manhood suffrage, shifted the basis of political rights from economic substance to personal status. I say 'manhood' deliberately in order to emphasize the great significance of this reform quite apart from the second, and no less important, reform introduced at the same time – namely the enfranchisement of women. [...]

The original source of social rights was membership of local communities and functional associations. This source was supplemented and progressively replaced by a Poor Law and a system of wage regulation which were nationally conceived and locally administered. [...]

As the pattern of the old order dissolved under the blows of a competitive economy, and the plan disintegrated, the Poor Law was left high and dry as an isolated survival from which the idea of social rights was gradually drained away. But at the very end of the eighteenth century there occurred a final struggle between the old and the new, between the planned (or patterned) society and the competitive economy. And in this battle citizenship was divided against itself; social rights sided with the old and civil with the new. [...]

In this brief episode of our history we see the Poor Law as the aggressive champion of the social rights of citizenship. In the succeeding phase we find the attacker driven back far behind his original position. By the Act of 1834 the Poor Law renounced all claim to trespass on the territory of the wages system, or to interfere with the forces of the free market. It offered relief only to those who, through age or sickness, were incapable of continuing the battle, and to those other weaklings who gave up the struggle, admitted defeat, and cried for mercy. The tentative move towards the concept of social security was reversed. But more than that, the minimal social rights that remained were detached from the status of citizenship. The Poor Law treated the claims of the poor, not as an integral part of the rights of the citizen, but as an alternative to them – as claims which could be met only if the claimants ceased to be citizens in any true sense of the word. For paupers forfeited in practice the civil right of personal liberty, by internment in the workhouse, and they forfeited by law any political rights they might possess. This disability of defranchisement remained in being until 1918, and the significance of its final removal has, perhaps, not been fully appreciated. The stigma which clung to poor relief expressed the deep feelings of a people who understood that those who accepted relief must cross the road that separated the community of citizens from the outcast company of the destitute.

The Poor Law is not an isolated example of this divorce of social rights from the status of citizenship. The early Factory Acts show the same tendency. Although in fact they led to an improvement of working conditions and a reduction of working hours to the benefit of all employed in the industries to which they applied, they meticulously refrained from giving this protection directly to the adult male – the citizen *par excellence*. And they did so out of respect for his status as a citizen, on the grounds that enforced protective measures curtailed the civil right to conclude a free contract of employment. Protection was confined to women and children, and champions of women's rights were quick to detect the implied insult. Women were protected because they were not citizens. If they wished to enjoy full and responsible citizenship, they must forgo protection. By the end of the nineteenth century such arguments had become obsolete, and the factory code had become one of the pillars in the edifice of social rights. [...]

By the end of the nineteenth century elementary education was not only free, it was compulsory. This signal departure from *laissez-faire* could, of course, be justified on the grounds that free choice is a right only for mature minds, that children are naturally subject to discipline, and that parents cannot be trusted to do what is in the best interests of their children. But the principle goes deeper than that. We have here a personal right combined with a public duty to exercise the right. Is the public duty imposed merely for the benefit of the individual – because children cannot fully appreciate their own interests and parents may be unfit to enlighten them? I hardly think that this can be an adequate explanation. It was increasingly recognized, as the nineteenth century wore on, that political democracy needed an educated electorate, and that scientific manufacture needed educated workers and technicians. The duty to improve and civilize oneself is therefore a social duty, and not merely a personal one, because the social health of a society depends upon the civilization of its members. And a community that enforces this duty has begun to realize that its culture is an organic unity and its civilization a national heritage. It follows that the growth of public elementary education during the nineteenth century was the first decisive step on the road to the re-establishment of the social rights of citizenship in the twentieth. [...]

Citizenship is a status bestowed on those who are full members of a community. All who possess the status are equal with respect to the rights and duties with which the status is endowed. There is no universal principle that determines what those rights and duties shall be, but societies in which citizenship is a developing institution create an image of an ideal citizenship against which achievement can be measured and towards which aspiration can be directed. The urge forward along the path thus plotted is an urge towards a fuller measure of equality, an enrichment of the stuff of which the status is made and an increase in the number of those on whom the status is bestowed. Social class, on the other hand, is a system of inequality. And it too, like citizenship, can be based on a set of ideals, beliefs and values. It is therefore reasonable to expect that the impact of citizenship on social class should take the form of a conflict between opposing principles. If I am right in my contention that citizenship has been a developing institution in England at least since the latter part of the seventeenth century, then it is clear that its growth coincides with the rise of capitalism, which is a system, not of equality, but of inequality. Here is something that needs explaining. How is it that these two opposing principles could grow and flourish side by side in the same soil? What made it possible for them to be reconciled with one another and to become, for a time at least, allies instead of antagonists? The question is a pertinent one, for it is clear that, in the twentieth century, citizenship and the capitalist class system have been at war. [...]

It is true that class still functions. Social inequality is regarded as necessary and purposeful. It provides the incentive to effort and designs the distribution of power. But there is no overall pattern of inequality, in which an appropriate value is attached, *a priori*, to each social level. Inequality therefore, though necessary, may become excessive. As Patrick Colquhoun said, in a much-quoted passage: 'Without a large proportion of poverty there could be no riches, since riches are the offspring of labour, while labour can result only from a state of poverty... Poverty therefore is a most necessary and indispensable ingredient in society, without which nations and communities could not exist in a state of civilization.[4] [...]

The more you look on wealth as conclusive proof of merit, the more you incline to regard poverty as evidence of failure – but the penalty for failure may seem to be greater than the offence warrants. In such circumstances it is natural that the more unpleasant features of inequality should be treated, rather irresponsibly, as a nuisance, like the black smoke that used to pour unchecked from our factory chimneys. And so in time, as the social conscience stirs to life, class-abatement, like smoke-abatement, becomes a desirable aim to be pursued as far as is compatible with the continued efficiency of the social machine.

But class-abatement in this form was not an attack on the class system. On the contrary it aimed, often quite consciously, at making the class system less vulnerable to attack by alleviating its less defensible consequences. It raised the floor-level in the basement of the social edifice, and perhaps made it rather more hygienic than it was before. But it remained a basement, and the upper storeys of the building were unaffected. [...]

There developed, in the latter part of the nineteenth century, a growing interest in equality as a principle of social justice and an appreciation of the fact that the formal recognition of an equal capacity for rights was not enough. In theory even the complete removal of all the barriers that separated civil rights from their remedies would not have interfered with the principles or the class structure of the capitalist system. It would, in fact, have created a situation which many supporters of the competitive market economy falsely assumed to be already in existence. But in practice the attitude of mind which inspired the efforts to remove these barriers grew out of a conception of equality which overstepped these narrow limits, the conception of equal social worth, not merely of equal natural rights. Thus although citizenship, even by the end of the nineteenth century, had done little to reduce social inequality, it had helped to guide progress into the path which led directly to the egalitarian policies of the twentieth century. [...]

This growing national consciousness, this awakening public opinion, and these first stirrings of a sense of community membership and common heritage did not have any material effect on class structure and social inequality for the simple and obvious reason that, even at the end of the nineteenth century, the mass of the working people did not wield effective political power. By that time the franchise was fairly wide, but those who had recently received the vote had not yet learned how to use it. The political rights of citizenship, unlike the civil rights, were full of potential danger to the capitalist system, although those who were cautiously extending them down the social scale probably did not realize quite how great the danger was. They could hardly be expected to foresee what vast changes could be brought about by the peaceful use of political power, without a violent and bloody revolution. The 'planned society' and the welfare state had not yet risen over the horizon or come within the view of the practical politician. The foundations of the market economy and the contractual system seemed strong enough to stand against any probable assault. In fact, there were some grounds for expecting that the working classes, as they became educated, would accept the basic principles of the system and be content to rely for their protection and progress on the civil rights of citizenship, which contained no obvious menace to competitive capitalism. Such a view was encouraged by the fact that one of the main achievements of political power in the later nineteenth century was the recognition of the right of collective bargaining. This meant that social progress was being sought by strengthening civil rights, not by creating social rights; through the use of contract in the open market, not through a minimum wage and social security.

But this interpretation underrates the significance of this extension of civil rights in the economic sphere. For civil rights were in origin intensely individual, and that is why they harmonized with the individualistic phase of capitalism. By the device of incorporation groups were enabled to act legally as individuals. This important development did not go unchallenged, and limited liability was widely denounced as an infringement of individual responsibility. But the position of trade unions was even more anomalous, because they did not seek or obtain incorporation. They can, therefore, exercise vital civil rights collectively on behalf of their members without formal collective responsibility, while the individual responsibility of the workers in relation to contract is largely unenforceable. These civil rights became, for the workers, an instrument for raising their social and economic status, that is to say, for establishing the claim that they, as citizens, were entitled to certain social rights. But the normal method of establishing social rights is by the exercise of political power, for social rights imply an absolute right to a certain standard of civilization which is conditional only on the discharge of the general duties of citizenship. Their content does not depend on the economic value of the individual claimant. There is therefore a significant difference between a genuine collective bargain through which economic forces in a free market seek to achieve equilibrium and the use of collective civil rights to assert basic claims to the elements of social justice. Thus the acceptance of collective bargaining was not simply a natural extension of civil rights; it represented the transfer of an important process from the political to the civil sphere of citizenship. But 'transfer' is, perhaps, a misleading term, for at the time when this happened the workers either did not possess, or had not yet learned to use, the political right of the franchise. Since then they have obtained and made full use of that right. Trade unionism has, therefore, created a secondary system of industrial citizenship parallel with and supplementary to the system of political citizenship. [...]

A new period opened at the end of the nineteenth century, conveniently marked by Booth's survey of *Life and Labour of the People in London* and the Royal Commission on the Aged Poor. It saw the first big advance in social rights, and this involved significant changes in the egalitarian principle as expressed in citizenship. But there were other forces at work as well. A rise of money incomes unevenly distributed over the social classes altered the economic distance which separated these classes from one another, diminishing the gap between skilled and unskilled labour and between skilled labour and non-manual workers, while the steady increase in small savings blurred the class distinction between the capitalist and the propertyless proletarian. Secondly, a system of direct taxation, ever more steeply graduated, compressed the whole scale of disposable incomes. Thirdly, mass production for the home market and a growing interest on the part of industry in the needs and tastes of the common people enabled the less well-to-do to enjoy a material civilization which differed less markedly in quality from that of the rich than it had ever done before. All this profoundly altered the setting in which the progress of citizenship took place. Social integration spread from the sphere of sentiment and patriotism into that of material enjoyment. The components of a civilized and cultured life, formerly the monopoly of the few, were brought progressively within reach of the many, who were encouraged thereby to stretch out their hands towards those that still eluded their grasp. The diminution of inequality strengthened the demand for its abolition, at least with regard to the essentials of social welfare.

These aspirations have in part been met by incorporating social rights in the status of citizenship and thus creating a universal right to real income which is not proportionate to the market value of the claimant. Class-abatement is still the aim of social rights, but it has acquired a new meaning. It is no longer merely an attempt to abate the obvious nuisance of destitution in the lowest ranks of society. It has assumed the guise of action modifying the whole pattern of social inequality. It is no longer content to raise the floor-level in the basement of the social edifice, leaving the superstructure as it was. It has begun to remodel the whole building, and it might even end by converting a skyscraper into a bungalow. It is therefore important to consider whether any such ultimate aim is implicit in the nature of this development, or whether, as I put it at the outset, there are natural limits to the contemporary drive towards greater social and economic equality. [...]

The degree of equalization achieved [by the modern system of welfare benefits] depends on four things: whether the benefit is offered to all or to a limited class; whether it takes the form of money payment or service rendered; whether the minimum is high or low; and how the money to pay for the benefit is raised. Cash benefits subject to income limit and means test had a simple and obvious equalizing effect. They achieved class-abatement in the early and limited sense of the term. The aim was to ensure that all citizens should attain at least to the prescribed minimum, either by their own resources or with assistance if they could not do it without. The benefit was given only to those who needed it, and thus inequalities at the bottom of the scale were ironed out. The system operated in its simplest and most unadulterated form in the case of the Poor Law and old age pensions. But economic equalization might be accompanied by psychological class discrimination. The stigma which attached to the Poor Law made 'pauper' a derogatory term defining a class. 'Old age pensioner' may have had a little of the same flavour, but without the taint of shame. [...]

The extension of the social services is not primarily a means of equalizing incomes. In some cases it may, in others it may not. The question is relatively unimportant; it belongs to a different department of social policy. What matters is that there is a general enrichment of the concrete substance of civilized life, a general reduction of risk and insecurity, an equalization between the more and the less fortunate at all levels – between the healthy and the sick, the employed and the unemployed, the old and the active, the bachelor and the father of a large family. Equalization is not so much between classes as between individuals within a population which is now treated for this purpose as though it were one class. Equality of status is more important than equality of income. [...]

I said earlier that in the twentieth century citizenship and the capitalist class system have been at war. Perhaps the phrase is rather too strong, but it is quite clear that the former has imposed modifications on the latter. But we should not be justified in assuming that, although status is a principle that conflicts with contract, the stratified status system which is creeping into citizenship is an alien element in the economic world outside. Social rights in their modern form imply an invasion of contract by status, the subordination of market price to social justice, the replacement of the free bargain by the declaration of rights. But are these principles quite foreign to the practice of the market today, or are they there already entrenched within the contract system itself? I think it is clear that they are. [...]

I have tried to show how citizenship, and other forces outside it, have been altering the pattern of social inequality. [...] We have to look, here, for the combined effects of three factors. First, the compression, at both ends, of the scale of income distribution. Second, the great extension of the area of common culture and common experience. And third, the enrichment of the universal status of citizenship, combined with the recognition and stabilization of certain status differences chiefly through the linked systems of education and occupation. [...]

I asked, at the beginning, whether there was any limit to the present drive towards social equality inherent in the principles governing the movement. My answer is that the preservation of economic inequalities has been made more difficult by the enrichment of the status of citizenship. There is less room for them, and there is more and more likelihood of their being challenged. But we are certainly proceeding at present on the assumption that the hypothesis is valid. And this assumption provides the answer to the second question. We are not aiming at absolute equality.

There are limits inherent in the egalitarian movement. But the movement is a double one. It operates partly through citizenship and partly through the economic system. In both cases the aim is to remove inequalities which cannot be regarded as legitimate, but the standard of legitimacy is different. In the former it is the standard of social justice, in the latter it is social justice combined with economic necessity. It is possible, therefore, that the inequalities permitted by the two halves of the movement will not coincide. Class distinctions may survive which have no appropriate economic function, and economic differences which do not correspond with accepted class distinctions. [...]

Notes

Originally delivered in Cambridge as the Marshall Lecture for 1949 and published in *Citizenship and Social Class and Other Essays*, ed. T. H. Marshall, Cambridge, Cambridge University Press, 1950. This version extracted from *States and Societies*, ed. D. Held, London, Open University/Martin Robertson, 1983, pp. 249–60.
1   G. M. Trevelyan, *English Social History* (1942), p. 351.
2   Sidney and Beatrice Webb, *History of Trade Unionism* (1920), p. 60.
3   R. H. Tawney, *The Agrarian Problem in the Sixteenth Century* (1916), pp. 43–4.
4   P. Colquhoun, *A Treatise in Indigence* (1806), pp. 7–8.

Universalism versus Selection

Richard Titmuss

[...]

Universalist and Selective Social Services

In any discussion today of the future of (what is called) 'The Welfare State'
much of the argument revolves around the principles and objectives of
universalist social services and selective social services.

[...]

Consider, first, the nature of the broad principles which helped to
shape substantial sections of British welfare legislation in the past,
and particularly the principle of universalism embodied in such post-
war enactments as the National Health Service Act, the Education
Act of 1944, the National Insurance Act and the Family Allowances
Act.

One fundamental historical reason for the adoption of this principle was
the aim of making services available and accessible to the whole population in such ways as would not involve users in any humiliating loss of
status, dignity or self-respect. There should be no sense of inferiority,
pauperism, shame or stigma in the use of a publicly provided service; no
attribution that one was being or becoming a 'public burden'. Hence the
emphasis on the social rights of all citizens to use or not to use as
responsible people the services made available by the community in
respect of certain needs which the private market and the family were
unable or unwilling to provide universally. If these services were not

provided for everybody by everybody they would either not be available at all, or only for those who could afford them, and for others on such terms as would involve the infliction of a sense of inferiority and stigma.

Avoidance of stigma was not, of course, the only reason for the development of the twin concepts of social rights and universalism. Many other forces, social, political and psychological, during a century and more of turmoil, revolution, war and change, contributed to the clarification and acceptance of these notions. The novel idea of prevention – novel, at least, to many in the nineteenth century – was, for example, another powerful engine, driven by the Webbs and many other advocates of change, which reinforced the concepts of social rights and universalism. The idea of prevention – the prevention and breaking of the vicious descending spiral of poverty, disease, neglect, illiteracy and destitution – spelt to the protagonists (and still does so) the critical importance of early and easy access to and use of preventive, remedial and rehabilitative services. Slowly and painfully the lesson was learnt that if such services were to be utilized in time and were to be effective in action in a highly differentiated, unequal and class-saturated society, they had to be delivered through socially approved channels; that is to say, without loss of self-respect by the users and their families.

Prevention was not simply a child of biological and psychological theorists; at least one of the grandparents was a powerful economist with a strongly developed streak of nationalism. As Professor Bentley Gilbert has shown in his [...] book *The Evolution of National Insurance: The Origins of the Welfare State*, national efficiency and welfare were seen as complementary.[1] The sin unforgivable was the waste of human resources; thus, welfare was summoned to prevent waste. Hence the beginnings of four of our present-day universalist social services: retirement pensions, the Health Service, unemployment insurance and the school meals service.

The insistent drumming of the national efficiency movement in those far-off days before the First World War is now largely forgotten. Let me then remind you that the whole welfare debate was a curious mixture of humanitarianism, egalitarianism, productivity (as we would call it today) and old-fashioned imperialism. The strident note of the latter is now, we may thank our stars, silenced. The Goddess of Growth has replaced the God of National Fitness. But can we say that the quest for the other objectives is no longer necessary?

Before discussing such a rhetorical question, we need to examine further the principal of universalism. The principle itself may sound simple but the practice – and by that I mean the present operational pattern of welfare in Britain [in the 1960s] – is immensely complex. We can see something of this complexity if we analyse welfare (defined here as all publicly provided and subsidized services, statutory, occupational and fiscal) from a number of different standpoints.

An Analytical Framework

Whatever the nature of the service, activity or function, and whether it be a service in kind, a collective amenity, or a transfer payment in cash or by accountancy, we need to consider (and here I itemize in question form for the sake of brevity) three central issues:

1   What is the nature of entitlement to use? Is it legal, contractual or contributory, financial, discretionary or professionally determined entitlement?
2   Who is entitled and on what conditions? Is account taken of individual characteristics, family characteristics, group characteristics, territorial characteristics or social-biological characteristics? What, in fact, are the rules of entitlement? Are they specific and contractual – like a right based on age – or are they variable, arbitrary or discretionary?
3   What methods, financial and administrative, are employed in the determination of access, utilization, allocation and payment?

Next we have to reflect on the nature of the service or benefit.

What functions do benefits, in cash, amenity or in kind, aim to fulfil? They may, for example, fulfil any of the following sets of functions, singly or in combination:

1   As partial compensation for identified disservices caused by society (for example, unemployment, some categories of industrial injuries benefits, war pensions, etc.). And, we may add, the disservices caused by international society as exemplified [...] by the oil pollution resulting from the Torrey Canyon disaster in 1967 costing at least £2 million.[2]
2   As partial compensation for unidentifiable disservices caused by society (for example, 'benefits' related to programmes of slum clearance, urban blight, smoke pollution control, hospital cross-infection and many other socially created disservices).
3   As partial compensation for unmerited handicap (for example, language classes for immigrant children, services for the deprived child, children handicapped from birth, etc.).
4   As a form of protection for society (for example, the probation service, some parts of the mental health services, services for the control of infectious diseases, etc.).

5 As an investment for a future personal or collective gain (education – professional, technical and industrial – is an obvious example here; so also are certain categories of tax deductibles for self-improvement and certain types of subsidized occupational benefits).

6 As an immediate and/or deferred increment to personal welfare or, in other words, benefits (utilities) which add to personal command-over-resources either immediately and/or in the future (for example, subsidies to owner-occupiers and council tenants, tax deductibles for interest charges, pensions, supplementary benefits, curative medical care, etc.).

7 As an element in an integrative objective which is an essential characteristic distinguishing social policy from economic policy. As Kenneth Boulding has said, '...social policy is that which is centred in those institutions that create integration and discourage alienation'.[3] It is thus profoundly concerned with questions of personal identity whereas economic policy centres round exchange or bilateral transfer.

This represents little more than an elementary and partial structural map which can assist in the understanding of the welfare complex [...]. Needless to say, a more sophisticated (inch to the mile) guide is essential for anything approaching a thorough analysis of the actual functioning of welfare benefit systems. I do not, however, propose to refine further this frame of study now, nor can I analyse by these classifications the several hundred distinctive and functionally separate services and benefits actually in operation in Britain [in the 1960s].

Further study would also have to take account of the pattern and operation of means-tested services. It has been estimated by Mr M. J. Reddin, my research assistant, that in England and Wales today local authorities are responsible for administering at least 3,000 means tests, of which about 1,500 are different from each other.[4] This estimate applies only to services falling within the responsibilities of education, child care, health, housing and welfare departments. It follows that in these fields alone there exist some 1,500 different definitions of poverty or financial hardship, ability to pay and rules for charges, which affect the individual and the family. There must be substantial numbers of poor families with multiple needs and multiple handicaps whose perception [...] of the realities of welfare is to see only a means-testing world. Who helps them, I wonder, to fill out all those forms?

I mention these social facts, by way of illustration, because they do form part of the operational complex of welfare in 1967. My main purpose, however, in presenting this analytical framework was twofold. First, to underline the difficulties of conceptualizing and categorizing needs, causes, entitlement or gatekeeper functions, utilization patterns, benefits and compensations. Second, to suggest that those students of welfare who are seeing the main problem today in terms of universalism versus selective services are presenting a naive and oversimplified picture of policy choices.

Some of the reasons for this simple and superficial view are, I think, due to the fact that the approach is dominated by the concept or model of welfare as a 'burden'; as a waste of resources in the provision of benefits for those who, it is said, do not need them. The general solution is thus deceptively simple and romantically appealing: abolish all this welfare complexity and concentrate help on those whose needs are greatest.

Quite apart from the theoretical and practical immaturity of this solution, which would restrict the public services to a minority in the population leaving the majority to buy their own education, social security, medical care and other services in a supposedly free market, certain other important questions need to be considered.

As all selective services for this minority would have to apply some test of need – eligibility, on what bases would tests be applied and, even more crucial, where would the lines be drawn for benefits which function as compensation for identified disservices, compensation for unidentifiable disservices, compensation for unmerited handicap, as a form of social protection, as an investment, or as an increment to personal welfare? Can rules of entitlement and access be drawn on purely 'ability to pay' criteria without distinction of cause? And if the causal agents of need cannot be identified or are so diffuse as to defy the wit of law – as they so often are [...] – then is not the answer 'no compensation and no redress'? In other words, the case for concentrated selective services resolves itself into an argument for allowing the social costs or diswelfares of the economic system to lie where they fall.

The emphasis [...] on 'welfare' and the 'benefits of welfare' often tends to obscure the fundamental fact that for many consumers the services used are not essentially benefits or increments to welfare at all; they represent partial compensations for disservices, for social costs and social insecurities which are the product of a rapidly changing industrial-urban society. They are part of the price we pay to some people for bearing part of the costs of other people's progress; the obsolescence of skills, redundancies, premature retirements, accidents, many categories of disease and handicap, urban blight and slum clearance, smoke pollution, and a hundred-and-one other socially generated disservices. They are the socially caused diswelfares; the losses involved in aggregate welfare gains.

What is also of major importance [...] is that modern society is finding it increasingly difficult to identify the causal agent or agencies, and thus to allocate the costs of disservices and charge those who are responsible. It is not just a question of benefit allocation – of whose 'Welfare State' – but also of loss allocation – whose 'Diswelfare State'.

If identification of the agents of diswelfare were possible – if we could legally name and blame the culprits – then, in theory at least, redress could be obtained through the courts by the method of monetary compensation for damages. But multiple causality and the diffusion of disservices – the modern choleras of change – make this solution impossible. We have, therefore, as societies to make other choices; either to provide social services, or to allow the social costs of the system to lie where they fall. The nineteenth century chose the latter – the *laissez-faire* solution – because it had neither a germ theory of disease nor a social theory of causality; an answer which can hardly be entertained today by a richer society equipped with more knowledge about the dynamics of change. But knowledge in this context must not, of course, be equated with wisdom.

If this argument can be sustained, we are thus compelled to return to our analytical framework of the functional concepts of benefit and, within this context, to consider the role of universalist and selective social services. Non-discriminating universalist services are in part the consequence of unidentifiable causality. If disservices are wasteful (to use the economists' concept of 'waste') so welfare has to be 'wasteful'.

The next question that presents itself is this: can we and should we, in providing benefits and compensation (which in practice can rarely be differentially provided), distinguish between 'faults' in the individual (moral, psychological or social) and the 'faults of society'? If all services are provided – irrespective of whether they represent benefits, amenity, social protection or compensation – on a discriminatory, means-test basis, do we not foster both the sense of personal failure and the stigma of a public burden? The fundamental objective of all such tests of eligibility is to keep people out; not to let them in. They must, therefore, be treated as applicants or supplicants; not beneficiaries or consumers.

It is a regrettable but human fact that money (and the lack of it) is linked to personal and family self-respect. This is one element in what has been called the 'stigma of the means test'. Another element is the historical evidence we have that separate discriminatory services for poor people have always tended to be poor quality services; read the history of the panel system under National Health Insurance; read Beveridge on workmen's compensation; Newsom on secondary modern schools; Plowden on standards of primary schools in slum areas; Townsend on Part III accommodations in *The Last Refuge*,[5] and so on.[6]

In the past, poor quality selective services for poor people were the product of a society which saw 'welfare' as a residual; as a public burden. The primary purpose of the system and the method of discrimination was, therefore, deterrence (it was also an effective rationing device). To this end, the most effective instrument was to induce among recipients (children as well as adults) a sense of personal fault, of personal failure, even if the benefit was wholly or partially a compensation for disservices inflicted by society.

The Real Challenge in Welfare

Today, with this heritage, we face the positive challenge of providing selective, high quality services for poor people over a large and complex range of welfare; of positively discriminating on a territorial, group or 'rights' basis in favour of the poor, the handicapped, the deprived, the coloured, the homeless, and the social casualties of our society. Universalism is not, by itself alone, enough: in medical care, in wage-related social security and in education. This much we have learnt in the past two decades from the facts about inequalities in the distribution of incomes and wealth, and in our failure to close many gaps in differential access to and effective utilization of particular branches of our social services.[7]

If I am right, I think that during the 1960s Britain was beginning to identify the dimensions of this challenge of positive, selective discrimination – in income maintenance, in education, in housing, in medical care and mental health, in child welfare, and in the tolerant integration of immigrants and citizens from overseas; of preventing especially the second generation from becoming (and of seeing themselves as) second-class citizens. We have continued to seek ways and means, values, methods and techniques, of positive discrimination without the infliction, actual or imagined, of a sense of personal failure and individual fault.

At this point, considering the nature of the search in all its ramifying complexities, I must now state my general conclusion. It is this. The challenge that faces us is not the choice between universalist and selective social services. The real challenge resides in the question: what particular infrastructure of universalist services is needed in order to provide a framework of values and opportunity bases within and around which can be developed socially acceptable selective services aiming to discriminate positively, with the minimum risk of stigma, in favour of those whose needs are greatest.

This, to me, is the fundamental challenge. In different ways and in particular areas it confronts the Supplementary Benefits Commission, the Seebohm Committee, the National Health Service, the Ministry of Housing and Local Government, the National Committee for Commonwealth Immigrants, the policy-making readers of the Newsom Report and the Plowden Report on educational priority areas, the Scottish Report, *Social Work and the Community*, and thousands of social workers and administrators all over the country wrestling with the problems of needs and priorities. In all the main spheres of need, some structure of universalism is an essential prerequisite to selective positive discrimination; it provides a general system of values and a sense of community; socially approved agencies for clients, patients and consumers, and also for the recruitment, training and deployment of staff at all levels; it sees welfare, not as a burden, but as complementary and as an instrument of change and, finally, it allows positive discriminatory services to be provided as rights for categories of people and for classes of need in terms of priority social areas and other impersonal classifications.

Without this infrastructure of welfare resources and framework of values we should not, I conclude, be able to identify and discuss the next steps in progress towards a 'Welfare Society'.

Notes

Lecture delivered at the British National Conference on Social Welfare, London, April 1967, and published in the *Proceedings of the Conference*. This extract from R. M. Titmuss, *Commitment to Welfare*, London, Allen and Unwin, 1968, pp. 128–37.

1 B. B. Gilbert, *The Evolution of National Insurance: The Origins of the Welfare State*, London, Michael Joseph, 1966.
2 *The Torrey Canyon*, Cmnd 3246, London, HMSO, 1967.
3 K. E. Boulding, 'The Boundaries of Social Policy', *Social Work*, vol. 12, no. 1, January 1967, p. 7.
4 This study is to be published by Mr M. J. Reddin as an *Occasional Paper on Social Administration*.
5 P. Townsend, *The Last Refuge*, London, Routledge, 1964.
6 See also R. M. Titmuss, *Problems of Social Policy*, London, HMSO, 1950.
7 See P. Townsend, *Poverty, Socialism and Labour in Power*, Fabian tract, 371, 1967, and R. J. Nicholson, 'The Distribution of Personal Income', *Lloyds Bank Review*, January 1967, p. 11.

Perspectives on the Left

What is Social Justice?

Commission on Social Justice

In deciding to develop a conceptual framework for thinking about social justice, the Commission made a big assumption, namely that there is such a thing as 'social justice'. Some people (particularly of the libertarian Right) deny that there is a worthwhile idea of *social* justice at all. They say that justice is an idea confined to the law, with regard to crime, punishment and the settling of disputes before the courts. They claim that it is nonsense to talk about resources in society being fairly or unfairly distributed. The free market theorist Friedrich von Hayek, for example, argued that the process of allocating wealth and property 'can be neither just nor unjust, because the results are not intended or foreseen, and depend on a multitude of circumstances not known in their totality to anybody'.

What libertarians really mean, however, is not that there is no such thing as social justice, but rather that there is only one criterion of a just outcome in society, namely that it should be the product of a free market. But this is not as simple as it may sound, because ideas of fairness (and not merely of efficiency) are themselves used in defining what counts as a free market. While it is often said that a given market competition is not fair because it is not being played 'on a level field', it is not clear what counts as levelling the field, as opposed to altering the result of the match. For example, anti-trust laws can be seen as an interference in a free market, or a device for making the field level.

In fact, people in modern societies *do* have strong ideas about social justice. We all know this from daily conversation, and opinion polls regularly confirm it. We are confident that at least in our belief that there is such a thing as 'social justice', we reflect the common sense of the vast majority of people. However, polls are not easy to interpret, and they make it clear that people's ideas about social justice are complex.

There is more than one notion associated with the term social justice. In some connections, for example, justice is thought to have something to do with *equality*. Sometimes it seems to relate to *need*: for example, it can seem notably unfair if bad fortune prevents someone from having something they really need, such as medical care, less unfair if it is something they just happen to want. Yet again, justice relates to such notions as *entitlement, merit* and *desert*. These are not the same as each other. For example, if someone wins the prize in the lottery, they are entitled to the money, and it would be unjust to take it away from them, but it has nothing to do with their merits, and they have done nothing to deserve it. Similarly, if talented people win prizes in an activity that requires no great practice or effort, they are entitled to the prize and get it on the strength of their merits (as opposed, for instance, to someone's getting it because he is the son of the promoter), but they may well have not done anything much to deserve it. People who are especially keen on the notion of desert may want there to be prizes only for effort; or, at least, think that prizes which command admiration (as the lottery prize does not) should be awarded only for effort. Humanity has shown so far a steady reluctance to go all the way with this view.

As well as being *complex* in this way, people's views about justice are also *indeterminate*. This means that it is often unclear what the just outcome should be – particularly when various considerations of social justice seem to pull in different directions, as they often do. Most people, for instance, think that inheritance is at least not intrinsically evil, and that parents are entitled to leave property to their children. But no one thinks that one can leave anything one likes to one's children – one's job, for instance – and almost everyone thinks that it can be just for the state to tax inheritances in order to deal with social injustice, or simply to help the common good.

The mere fact that people's ideas about justice are both complex and indeterminate has an important consequence for democratic politics. There is more than one step from general ideas to practical recommendations. There have to be *general* policies directed to social justice, and these are going to be at best an interpretation of people's ideas on such matters. General policies will hope to offer considerations which people can recognize as making sense in the light of their own experience and ideas (this need not exclude challenging some of those ideas). *Specific* policies, however, involve a further step, since they have to express general policies in a particular administrative form. A given scheme of taxation or social security is, in that sense, at two removes from the complex and indeterminate ideas that are its moral roots.

This is not to deny that some administrative practices may acquire a symbolic value of their own. In the 1940s, the death grant was a symbol of society's commitment to end paupers' funerals and ensure for every family the means to offer deceased relatives a proper burial. It is a matter of acute political judgement to decide whether one is dealing with an important example of such a value, as opposed to a fetish (in the more or less literal sense of an inert object that has been invested with value that does not belong to it in its own right). Not every arrangement that has been taken to be an essential embodiment of social justice is, in changing circumstances, really so.

Theories of Social Justice

There are important theories of social justice. The most ambitious give a general account of what social justice is, explain and harmonize the relations between the different considerations associated with it, do the same for the relations between justice and other goods, notably liberty, help to resolve apparent conflicts between different values, and in the light of all that, even give pointers to practical policies. The most famous such theory in modern discussion is that of John Rawls, which gives a very rich elaboration to a very simple idea: that the fair division of a cake would be one that could be agreed on by people who did not know which piece they were going to get.

Rawls invokes an 'Original Position', in which representatives of various parties to society are behind 'a veil of ignorance' and do not know what role each party will occupy in the society. They are asked to choose a general scheme for the ordering of society. The scheme that they would reasonably choose in these imagined circumstances constitutes, in Rawls's view, the scheme of a just society.

Rawls's theory, and others with similar aims, contains important insights, and anyone who is trying to think about these problems should pay attention to them. But there is an important question – one acknowledged by Rawls himself – of what relation such a theory can have to politics. Rawls thinks that his theory articulates a widely spread sense of fairness, but it is certain that the British public would not recognize in such a theory, or in any other with such ambitions, all its conflicting ideas and feelings about social justice. Even if the Commission, improbably, all agreed on Rawls's or some other such theory, we would not be justified in presenting our conclusions in terms of that theory. The Commission has a more practical purpose.

Our task is to find compelling ways of making our society more just. We shall be able to do so only if we think in ways that people can recognize and respect about such questions as how best to understand merit and need; how to see the effects of luck in different spheres of life; what is implied in saying, or denying, that health care is a morally special kind of good which makes a special kind of demand.

The Commission has to guard against all-or-nothing assumptions. It is not true that either we have a complete top-down theory, or we are left only with mere prejudice and subservience to polls. This particularly applies to conflict. Confronted, as will often be the case, with an apparent conflict within justice, or between justice and some other value, we may tend to assume that there are only two possibilities: the conflict is merely apparent, and we should understand liberty and equality (for instance) in such a way that they cannot conflict; or it is a real conflict, and then it can only be left to politics, majorities, subjective taste, or whatever. This will not do. Reflection may not eliminate all conflicts, but it can help us to understand them, and then arrive at policy choices.

The Equal Worth of Every Citizen

Social justice is often thought to have something specially to do with equality, but this idea, in itself, determines very little. A basic question is: equality of what? Furthermore, not all inequalities are unjust. For example, what people can do with money varies. Thus disabled people may well need more resources to reach a given quality of life than other people do, and if you are trying to be fair to people with regard to the quality of their life, unequal amounts of money is what fairness itself will demand. What this shows, as the philosopher and economist Amartya Sen has insisted, is that equality in one dimension goes with inequality in another. Since people have different capacities to turn resources into worthwhile activity (for instance because they are disabled), people will need different resources to be equally capable of worthwhile activity.

In fact, virtually everyone in the modern world believes in equality of *something*. All modern states are based on belief in some sort of equality and claim to treat their citizens equally. But what is involved in 'treating people equally'? Minimally, it implies political and civil liberties, equal rights before the law, equal protection against arbitrary arrest, and so forth. These things provide the basis of a 'civil society', a society of equal citizens.

However, these rights and freedoms cannot stand by themselves. More than this formal level of equality is needed if the minimal demands themselves are to be properly met. It is a familiar point that equality before the law does not come to much if one cannot afford a good lawyer. The 'equal freedom' of which modern democratic states boast should amount to more (as Anatole France observed) than the freedom to sleep on park benches and under bridges. Everyone needs the means to make use of their equal freedom, which otherwise would be hollow. Formal equalities have substantive consequences. Perhaps the most basic question about the nature of social justice in a modern society is what those substantive consequences are.

Meeting Basic Needs

People are likely to be restricted in what they can do with their freedom and their rights if they are poor, or ill, or lack the education which, to a greater extent today than ever before, is the basis of employment opportunities, personal fulfilment and people's capacities to influence what happens to them. These concerns define areas of *need*, and it is a natural application of the idea that everyone is of equal worth that they should have access to what they need, or at least to what they basically need.

Some basic needs are met by providing resources, or by helping people to save or acquire resources. This is the case with paid work; with financial security in old age; and with provisions for dealing with lack of resources, such as benefit in case of unemployment. In the case of health care and education, however, the most appropriate way of meeting needs seems to be not through money, but in kind; we think that someone who is ill has a right to access to treatment for their illness, but not that they have a right to funds which they can choose to spend on treatment or not. One way of expressing this commitment is that the state should itself provide the service. Another is that the state should provide means which command health care or education, but which cannot be converted into money. In the case of health, this may take the form of public insurance, though this can raise basic questions of fairness (with regard to individual risk) as well as of efficiency.

The case of health now raises a fundamental question which was not present fifty years ago. Health care has always seemed a very special good, in relation to social justice as in other respects. It involves our most basic interests, gives great power to certain professionals, and carries heavy symbolic value (brought out, for instance, in Richard Titmuss's famous discussion of blood donation *The Gift Relationship*). Treating health as one commodity, to be bought and sold like any other, is found offensive in most parts of the world (and Americans, though used to that attitude, seem to be turning against it). Our sentiments about health care merge with our sense of some very basic obligations: most people feel that resources should be used to save an identified person (as opposed to a merely statistical casualty) from death.

But today it is a fact that medicine's resources to extend life are expanding at an accelerating rate, and so is their cost. This raises hard questions not only about the distribution of resources devoted to health care (who gets the kidney machine?), but also about the amount of resources that should be devoted to health care at all. These hard questions are questions of justice, among other things. Confronted with the opportunity to save someone in the street from death, we will think that we should stop to save them even if the cost is not taking the children to school, but is it fair to save every saveable person from death at the cost of sending many children to quite inadequate schools?

To answer these questions, the Commission will need to consider what *sort* of goods we take health and health care to be. This was a less pressing question in the past, but it is now harder to avoid the issue of what we are distributing when we distribute medical care, and of what we most want it to do.

Education is also a good to which everyone has a right, because it is so closely tied to basic needs, to personal development, and to one's role in society. But it is also connected to equality in another way. Disadvantage is, notoriously, inherited, and an unfair situation in one generation tends to mean an unfair start for the next. Educational opportunity is still what it always has been, a crucial means for doing something about this unfairness.

This brings out a further point, that the ideal of 'equality of opportunity', which has often been thought by reformers to be a rather weak aspiration, is in fact very radical, if it is taken seriously. The changes required in order to give the most disadvantaged in our society the same life-chances as the more fortunate would be very wide-ranging indeed.

Opportunities and Life-chances

Self-respect and equal citizenship demand more than the meeting of basic needs for income, shelter and so on. They demand the opportunities and life-chances central to personal freedom and autonomy. In a commercial society (outside monasteries, kibbutzim, etc.), self-respect standardly requires a certain amount of personal property. As Adam Smith remarked, a working man in eighteenth-century Scotland needed to own a decent linen shirt as a condition of self-respect, even though that might not be true of every man everywhere.

This does not mean that Adam Smith's man should be issued with a shirt. In a commercial society, his need is rather for the resources to buy a shirt of his choice. This is connected with his needing it as a matter of self-respect, which suggests something else, namely that where resources are supplied directly, for instance to those who are retired or who are caring for members of their families, it must be in ways which affirm their self-respect. But most people, for most of their lives, want the opportunities to earn the resources for themselves. The obvious question is whether everyone therefore has a right to a job, or the right to the means to gain a job.

The trouble, clearly, is that it may not be in the power of government directly to bring this about. Having a job, at least as the world is now, is closely connected with self-respect and hence with the equality of citizens, and for this as well as other reasons it must be a high priority for any government to create the circumstances in which there are jobs for those who want them. To insist, however, on a right to work – a right, presumably, which each person holds against the government – may not be the best way of expressing this aim. The Commission will therefore consider not only ways in which employment may be increased, but also what provision social justice demands for those who are unable to do paid work, or who are engaged in valuable unpaid work, or when significant levels of unemployment persist, even for a temporary period. Tackling unemployment is, of course, central to the realization of social justice.

There are questions here of how resources and opportunities can be extended to the unemployed. But there is a wider question as well, that extends to the provision for other needs: how opportunities may be created for the expression of people's autonomy and the extension of their freedom to determine their own lives. There is no doubt that advocates of social justice have often been insensitive to this dimension. The designers of the welfare state wanted to put rights in the place of charity: the idea of *entitlement* to benefit was meant to undercut any notion that the better-off were doing the worse-off a good turn. But the entitlement was often still understood as an entitlement to be given or issued with certain goods and services, the nature of which it was, in many cases, the business of experts to determine. There is a much greater awareness today that what people need is the chance to provide for themselves: [...] 'there is a limit to what government can do for people, but there is no limit to what they can be enabled to achieve for themselves'.

Relatedly, there is a stronger sense today that the aims of social justice are served not only by redistribution, by bringing resources after the event to people who have done badly. Social justice requires as well that structures should be adapted and influenced in ways that can give more people a better chance in the first place. That is why opportunities, and breaking down barriers to them, are so important.

There are, without doubt, conflicts between these various considerations. You cannot both encourage people's freedom to live their own lives as they choose, and guarantee that they will not suffer if they do not live them well. You cannot both allow people to spend money, if they wish, on their children's education – a right that exists in every democratic country – and also bring it about that everyone gets exactly the same education whether they pay privately for it or not. Here there are questions, too, of how far publicly supported provision to meet need should aim only at a minimal level, available to those without other provision, and how far it should seek to provide a high level of service for everyone. The view of most people is probably that the first answer applies to some needs and the goods and services that meet them, while in the case of health care and education, at least, no one should be excluded by disadvantage from a very high level of provision. Exactly how those different aims should now be conceived, and the extent to which they can realistically be carried out, are central questions for the Commission.

Unjustified Inequalities

Proponents of equality sometimes seem to imply that *all* inequalities are unjust (although they usually hasten to add that they are not in fact arguing for 'arithmetical equality'). We do not accept this. It seems fair, for instance, that a medical student should receive a lower income than the fully qualified doctor; or that experience or outstanding talent should be rewarded, and so on. Different people may have different views about what the basis of differential rewards should be; but most people accept, as we do, that some inequalities are just. There is, however, a question about the justifiable *extent* of an inequality, even if we accept that the inequality *per se* is not unjust.

Similarly, most people believe that it is fair for people to bequeath their property as they see fit, even though this means that some will inherit more than others. Nonetheless, it is also accepted that society may claim a share of an inheritance through the taxation of wealth or gifts, particularly when the estate is large. It is, after all, offensive to most ideas of social justice that a growing number of people own two homes while others have nowhere to live at all. This does not imply that one person's property should be confiscated to house another; but it does suggest the need for a fundamental reform of housing policy, an issue the Commission will certainly be addressing.

But if some inequalities are just, it is obviously the case that not all are so. It would, for instance, be unjust to allow people to inherit jobs from their parents: employment should be open to all, on the basis of merit. Inheritance of a family title offends many people's views about a classless society, but could not be said to deny somebody else something which they deserved. But inheritance of a peerage, in the UK, carries with it automatic entitlement to a seat and vote in the Second Chamber of Parliament: and that is an inequality of power which seems manifestly unjust.

Entitlement and Desert

Parents can, however, pass on intelligence, talent, charm and other qualities, as well as property or titles. Rawls in his theory rests a lot on the fact that a person's talents, and his or her capacity to make productive use of those talents, are very much matters of luck and are also, in some part, the product of society. Nobody, he has rightly insisted, *deserves* his or her (natural) talents. From this he has inferred that nobody, at a level of basic principle, deserves the rewards of his or her talents. He argues that no one has a right to something simply because it is the product of his or her talents, and society has a right to redistribute that product in accordance with the demands of social justice.

This is a very strong and surprising claim. Some people might agree that no one deserves a reward that they get on the basis of some raw advantage, without any investment of effort. (Of course, given the existing rules, that does not mean that they are not entitled to it, or that it can merely be taken away from them. It means that it would not necessarily be an injustice to change the rules.) But those who agree to this are very likely to think that people who *do* invest effort deserve its rewards, at least up to a certain point. But Rawls's argument applies just as much to effort as to raw talent. First, it is practically impossible to separate the relative contributions of effort and talent to a particular product. Moreover, the capacity to make a given degree of effort is itself not equally distributed, and may plausibly be thought to be affected by upbringing, culture and other social factors. Virtually everything about a person that yields a product is itself undeserved. So no rewards, in Rawls's view, are, at the most basic level, a matter of desert.

Few people believe this. If someone has taken a lot of trouble in designing and tending a garden, for instance, they will be proud of it and appropriately think of its success as theirs. The same applies to many aspects of life. This does suggest that there is something wrong with the idea that basically people never earn anything by their talents or labours – that in the last analysis all that anyone's work represents is a site at which society has achieved something. Yet, certainly, one does not 'deserve' the talents of birth. It must be true, then, that one can deserve the rewards of one's talents without deserving one's talents. As the American philosopher Robert Nozick forcefully put it, why does desert 'have to go all the way down'?

What the various arguments about entitlement and desert suggest seems to be something close to what many people believe: that there is basic justice in people having some differential reward for their productive activities, but that they have no right to any *given* differential of their reward over others. It is not simply self-interest, or again scepticism about government spending programmes (though that is certainly a factor), that makes people resist the idea that everyone's income is in principle a resource for redistribution; that idea also goes against their sense of what is right. They rightly think that redistribution of income is not an aim in itself.

At the same time, they acknowledge that the needs of the less fortunate make a claim. Luck is everywhere, and one is entitled to some rewards of luck, but there are limits to this entitlement when one lives and works with other people. Even if one is entitled to some rewards from the product of one's efforts and talents, there is the further point that in a complex enterprise such as a company or family, there is rarely a product which is solely and definitely the product of a given person's efforts and talents.

This is no doubt one reason why people are sceptical about vast rewards to captains of industry. It is also a question of the relation of one person's activity to that of others. Few people mind that Pavarotti or Lenny Henry are paid large sums – there is only one of them, and they are undoubtedly the star of the show. But in some cases, one person's reward can be another person's loss. The Nobel Prize winning economist Professor James Meade argued in a submission to the Commission that 'Keynesian full-employment policy... collapsed simply and solely because a high level of money expenditures came to lead not to a high level of output and employment but to a high rate of money wages, costs and prices.... It is very possible that to absorb two million extra workers into employment would require a considerable reduction in real wage costs.'

This raises a crucial point, concerning the power to determine one's own rewards, and the relationship of that power to questions of justice and desert. In contrast to a simple focus on the distribution of rewards, this raises the question of the *generation* of rewards, the processes whereby inequalities are generated.

Unequal incomes are inherent in a market economy. Even if everyone started off with the same allocation of money, differences would soon emerge. Not all labour commands the same price; not all investments produce the same return; some people work longer hours, others prefer more leisure and so on. The resulting inequalities are not necessarily unjust – although the extent of them may be. In the real world, of course, people start off with very different personal and financial resources. The problem is that too many of these inequalities are exacerbated in the UK's system of market exchange.

But market economies are not all of a piece; different kinds of market produce different outcomes. For instance, Germany, Japan and Sweden all have more equal earnings distributions than the UK, where the gap between the highest and lowest paid is wider today than at any time since 1886. Social justice therefore has a part to play in deciding how a market is constructed, and not simply with the end result.

Fair Reward

Most people have some idea of a 'fair reward'. For example, it is clear to the vast majority of people that disadvantage and discrimination on grounds of sex or race or disability is unjust. However, once one gets beyond the general idea, there is less agreement on what fair rewards should be. Even if there were more agreement about this, it is very difficult, both practically and morally, to impose such notions on a modern economy. The very idea of a society that can be effectively managed from the top on the basis of detailed centralized decisions is now discredited. Moreover, our society does not stand by itself and happily does not have walls around it, and people can go elsewhere.

Ideas of social justice in this area are not, however, necessarily tied to the model of a command economy. It is often clear, at least, that given rewards in a market economy are not fair, because they are not being determined by such things as talent, effort and the person's contribution to the enterprise, but rather by established power relations. Real life does not conform to economic models: people are not paid for the 'marginal product' of their labour. They are paid, among other things, according to social norms. In one sense, such distortions are the product of the market: they are what we get if market processes, uncorrected, are allowed to reflect established structures and habits of power. Examples of this are the huge salaries and bonuses distributed to the directors of some large companies. [...] These salaries and bonuses are often quite unrelated to the performance of the company concerned, and are sometimes actually inversely correlated with company performance.

In another sense, unjust inequalities are themselves distortions of the market: it is not a fair market in talent and effort if it is not talent and effort that determine the outcome. This is most obviously demonstrated in the case of inequalities of pay between men and women. Although the 1970 Equal Pay Act eliminated overt pay inequities, it had a limited effect on the gap between men's and women's pay, which resulted in the main from job segregation and gender-biased views of what different jobs and different qualities were worth. Hence the concept of 'equal pay for work of equal value', which permits comparisons between two very different jobs performed for the same employer. Although designed to eradicate gender as a consideration in earnings, equal value claims may in practice require a complete transformation in an organization's pay-setting. Equal pay for work of equal value, after all, implies unequal pay for work of unequal value: thus, the basis for differentials has to be made explicit and justified.

Different organizations and people will have different views of what constitutes a fair basis for differentials: it should not be an aim of government to substitute its own view of fair wage settlements. It is, however, a legitimate aim of policy concerned with social justice to develop social institutions (of which equal value laws are one example) which will enable people to express their own ideas of a fair reward.

The Meaning of Social Justice: A Summary

In arriving at our principles of social justice, we reject the view, so fashionable in the 1980s, that human beings are simply selfish individuals, for whom there is 'no such thing as society'. People are essentially social creatures, dependent on one another for the fulfilment of their needs and potential, and willing to recognize their responsibilities to others as well as claiming their rights from them. We believe our four principles of social justice, based on a basic belief in the intrinsic worth of every human being, echo the deeply held views of many people in this country. They provide a compelling justification and basis for our work:

1 The foundation of a free society is the equal worth of all citizens.
2 Everyone is entitled, as a right of citizenship, to be able to meet their basic needs.
3 The right to self-respect and personal autonomy demands the widest possible spread of opportunities.
4 Not all inequalities are unjust, but unjust inequalities should be reduced and where possible eliminated.

[...]

Note

From Commission on Social Justice, *The Justice Gap*, London, Institute for Public Policy Research, 1993, pp. 4–16.

The Fiscal Crisis of the State

James O'Connor

[...]

Our first premise is that the capitalistic state must try to fulfil two basic and often mutually contradictory functions – *accumulation* and *legitimization*. [...] This means that the state must try to maintain or create the conditions in which profitable capital accumulation is possible. However, the state also must try to maintain or create the conditions for social harmony. A capitalist state that openly uses its coercive forces to help one class accumulate capital at the expense of other classes loses its legitimacy and hence undermines the basis of its loyalty and support. But a state that ignores the necessity of assisting the process of capital accumulation risks drying up the source of its own power, the economy's surplus production capacity and the taxes drawn from this surplus (and other forms of capital). This contradiction explains why President Nixon calls a legislated increase in profit rates a 'job development credit', why the government announces that new fiscal policies are aimed at 'stability and growth' when in fact their purpose is to keep profits high and growing, why the tax system is nominally progressive and theoretically based on 'ability to pay' when in fact the system is regressive. The state must involve itself in the accumulation process, but it must either mystify its policies by calling them something that they are not, or it must try to conceal them (e.g. by making them into administrative, not political, issues).

Our second premise is that the fiscal crisis can be understood only in terms of the basic Marxist economic categories (adapted to the problems taken up here). State expenditures have a twofold character corresponding to the capitalist state's two basic functions: social capital and social expenses. *Social capital* is expenditures required for profitable private accumulation; it is indirectly productive (in Marxist terms, social capital indirectly expands surplus value). There are two kinds of social capital: social investment and social consumption (in Marxist terms, social constant capital and social variable capital). [...] *Social investment* consists of projects and services that increase the productivity of a given amount of labour power and, other factors being equal, increase the rate of profit. A good example is state-financed industrial-development parks. *Social consumption* consists of projects and services that lower the reproduction costs of labour and, other factors being equal, increase the rate of profit. An example of this is social insurance, which expands the reproductive powers of the workforce while simultaneously lowering labour costs. The second category, *social expenses*, consists of projects and services which are required to maintain social harmony – to fulfil the state's 'legitimization' function. They are not even indirectly productive. [...] The best example is the welfare system, which is designed chiefly to keep social peace among unemployed workers. (The costs of politically repressed populations in revolt would also constitute a part of social expenses.)

Because of the dual and contradictory character of the capitalist state, nearly every state agency is involved in the accumulation and legitimization functions, and nearly every state expenditure has this twofold character. For example, some education spending constitutes social capital (e.g. teachers and equipment needed to reproduce and expand workforce technical and skill levels), whereas other outlays constitute social expenses (e.g. salaries of campus policemen). To take another example, the main purpose of some transfer payments (e.g. social insurance) is to reproduce the workforce, whereas the purpose of others (e.g. income subsidies to the poor) is to pacify and control the surplus population. The national income accounts lump the various categories of state spending together. (The state does not analyse its budget in class terms.) Clearly, the different categories cannot be separated if each budget item is not examined.

Furthermore, precisely because of the social character of social capital and social expenses, nearly every state expenditure serves these two (or more) purposes simultaneously, so that few state outlays can be classified unambiguously. For example, freeways move workers to and from work and are therefore items of social consumption, but they also transport commercial freight and are therefore a form of social investment. And, when used for either purpose, they may be considered forms of social capital. However, the Pentagon also needs freeways; therefore they in part constitute social expenses. Despite this complex social character of state outlays we can determine the political-economic forces served by any budgetary decision, and thus the main purpose (or purposes) of each budgetary item. [...]

The first basic thesis presented here is that the growth of the state sector and state spending is functioning increasingly as the basis for the growth of the monopoly sector and total production. Conversely, it is argued that the growth of state spending and state programmes is the result of the growth of the monopoly industries. In other words, the growth of the state is both a cause and effect of the expansion of monopoly capital. [...]

More specifically, the socialization of the costs of social investment and social consumption capital increases over time and increasingly is needed for profitable accumulation by monopoly capital. The general reason is that the increase in the social character of production (specialization, division of labour, interdependency, the growth of new social forms of capital such as education, etc.) either prohibits or renders unprofitable the private accumulation of constant and variable capital. The growth of the monopoly sector is irrational in the sense that it is accompanied by unemployment, poverty, economic stagnation and so on. To ensure mass loyalty and maintain its legitimacy, the state must meet various demands of those who suffer the 'costs' of economic growth. [...]

It might help to compare our approach with traditional economic theory. Bourgeois economists have shown that increases in private consumption beget increases in private investment via the accelerator effect. In turn, increases in private investment beget increases in private consumption via the multiplier effect. Similarly, we argue that greater social investment and social consumption spending generate greater private investment and private consumption spending, which in turn generate surplus capital (surplus productive capacity and a surplus population) and a larger volume of social expenses. Briefly, the supply of social capital creates the demand for social expenses. In effect, we work with a model of expanded reproduction (or a model of the economy as a whole) which is generalized to take into account the socialization of constant and variable capital costs and the costs of social expenses. The impact of the budget depends on the volume and indirect productivity of social capital and the volume of social expenses. On the one hand, social capital outlays indirectly increase productive capacity and simultaneously increase aggregate demand. On the other hand, social expense outlays do not increase productive capacity, although they do expand aggregate demand. Whether the growth of productive capacity runs ahead or behind the growth of demand thus depends on the composition of the state budget. In this way, we can see that the theory of economic growth depends on class and political analyses of the determinants of the budget.

This view contrasts sharply with modern conservative thought, which asserts that the state sector grows at the expense of private industry. We argue that the growth of the state sector is indispensable to the expansion of private industry, particularly monopoly industries. Our thesis also contrasts sharply with a basic tenet of modern liberal thought – that the expansion of monopoly industries inhibits the growth of the state sector. The fact of the matter is that the growth of monopoly capital generates increased expansion of social expenses. In sum, the greater the growth of social capital, the greater the growth of the monopoly sector. And the greater the growth of the monopoly sector, the greater the state's expenditures on social expenses of production.

The second basic thesis in this study is that the accumulation of social capital and social expenses is a contradictory process which creates tendencies toward economic, social and political crises. [...] Two separate but related lines of analysis are explored.

First, we argue that although the state has socialized more and more capital costs, the social surplus (including profits) continues to be appropriated privately. The socialization of costs and the private appropriation of profits creates a fiscal crisis, or 'structural gap', between state expenditures and state revenues. The result is a tendency for state expenditures to increase more rapidly than the means of financing them. While the accumulation of social capital indirectly increases total production and society's surplus and thus in principle appears to underwrite the expansion of social expenses, large monopoly-sector corporations and unions strongly resist the appropriation of this surplus for new social capital or social expense outlays. [...]

Second, we argue that the fiscal crisis is exacerbated by the private appropriation of state power for particularistic ends. A host of 'special interests' – corporations, industries, regional and other business interests – make claims on the budget for various kinds of social investment. [...] (These claims are politically processed in ways that must either be legitimated or obscured from public view.) Organized labour and workers generally make various claims for different kinds of social consumption, and the unemployed and poor (together with businessmen in financial trouble) stake their claims for expanded social expenses. Few if any claims are co-ordinated by the market. Most are processed by the political system and are won or lost as a result of political struggle. Precisely because the accumulation of social capital and social expenses occurs within a political framework, there is a great deal of waste, duplication and overlapping of state projects and services. Some claims conflict and cancel one another out. Others are mutually contradictory in a variety of ways. The accumulation of social capital and social expenses is a highly irrational process from the standpoint of administrative coherence, fiscal stability and potentially profitable private capital accumulation.

Notes

From J. O'Connor, *The Fiscal Crisis of the State*, New York, St Martin's Press, 1973, pp. 6–11.

Some Contradictions of the Modern Welfare State

Claus Offe

The welfare state has served as the major peace formula of advanced capitalist democracies for the period following the Second World War. This peace formula consists, first, in the explicit obligation of the state apparatus to provide assistance and support (either in money or in kind) to those citizens who suffer from specific needs and risks which are characteristic of the market society; such assistance is provided as legal claims granted to the citizens. Second, the welfare state is based on the recognition of the formal role of labour unions both in collective bargaining and the formation of public policy. Both of these structural components of the welfare state are considered to limit and mitigate class conflict, to balance the asymmetrical power relation of labour and capital, and thus to overcome the condition of disruptive struggle and contradiction that was the most prominent feature of pre-welfare state, or liberal, capitalism. In sum, the welfare state has been celebrated throughout the post-war period as the political solution to societal contradictions.

Until [the 1970s], this seemed to be the converging view of political elites both in countries in which the welfare state is fully developed (e.g. Great Britain, Sweden) as well as in those where it is still an incompletely realized model. Political conflict in these latter societies, such as the USA, was centred not on the basic desirability and functional indispensability, but on the pace and modalities of the implementation of the welfare state model.

This was true, with very minor exceptions, up to the mid-1970s. From that point on we see that in many capitalist societies this established peace formula becomes itself the object of doubts, fundamental critique and political conflict. It appears that the most widely accepted device of political problem-solving has itself become problematic, and that, at any rate, the unquestioning confidence in the welfare state and its future expansion has rapidly vanished. It is to these doubts and criticisms that I will direct my attention in the following remarks. The point to start with is the observation that the almost universally accepted model for creating a measure of social peace and harmony in European post-war societies has itself become the source of new contradictions and political divisions in the 1970s.

Historically, the welfare state has been the combined outcome of a variety of factors which change in composition from country to country: Social Democratic reformism, Christian socialism, enlightened conservative political and economic elites and large industrial unions. They fought for and conceded comprehensive compulsory insurance schemes, labour protection legislation, minimum wages, the expansion of health and education facilities and state-subsidized housing, as well as the recognition of unions as the legitimate economic and political representatives of labour. These continuous developments in Western societies were often dramatically accelerated in a context of intense social conflict and crisis, particularly under war and post-war conditions. The accomplishments, which were won under conditions of war and post-war periods, were regularly maintained; added to them were the innovations that could be introduced in periods of prosperity and growth. In the light of the Keynesian doctrine of economic policy, the welfare state came to be seen not so much as a burden imposed upon the economy, but as a built-in economic and political stabilizer which could help to regenerate the forces of economic growth and prevent the economy from spiralling downward into deep recessions. Thus, a variety of quite heterogeneous ends (ranging from reactionary pre-emptive strikes against the working class movement in the case of Bismarck, to socialist reformism in the case of the Weimar Social Democrats; from the social-political consolidation of war and defence economies, to the stabilization of the business cycle) adopted identical institutional means which today make up the welfare state. It is exactly its multi-functional character, its ability to serve many conflicting ends and strategies simultaneously which made the political arrangement of the welfare state so attractive to a broad alliance of heterogeneous forces. But it is equally true that the very diversity of the forces that inaugurated and supported the welfare state could not be accommodated forever within the institutional framework which today appears to come increasingly under attack. The machinery of class compromise has itself become the object of class conflict.

The Attack from the Right

The sharp economic recession of the mid-1970s [gave] rise to a renaissance of neo-*laissez-faire* and monetarist economic doctrines of equal intellectual and political power. These doctrines amount to a fundamental critique of the welfare state, which is seen to be the illness of which it pretends to be the cure. Rather than effectively harmonizing the conflicts of a market society, it exacerbates them and prevents the forces of social peace and progress (namely the forces of the market place) to function properly and beneficially. This is said to be so for two major reasons. First, the welfare state apparatus imposes a burden of taxation and regulation upon capital which amounts to a *disincentive to investment*. Second, the welfare state grants claims, entitlements and collective power positions to workers and unions which amount to a *disincentive to work*, or at least to work as hard and productively as they would be forced to under the reign of unfettered market forces. Taken together, these two effects lead into a dynamic of declining growth and increased expectations, of economic demand over-load (inflation) as well as political demand overload (ungovernability) which can less and less be satisfied by the available output.

The reactionary political uses of this analysis are obvious, but it may well be that the truth of the analysis itself is greater than the desirability of its practical conclusions. Although the democratic left has often measured the former by the latter, the two deserve at least a separate evaluation. In my view, at least, the above analysis is not so much false in what it says as in what it remains silent about.

To take up the first point of the conservative analysis: isn't it true that under conditions of declining growth rates and vehement competition on domestic and international markets, individual capitalists (at least those firms which do not enjoy the privileges of the monopolistic sector) have many good reasons to consider the prospects for investment and profits bleak, and to blame the welfare state, which imposes social security taxes and a great variety of regulations on them, for reducing profitability even further? Isn't it true that the power position of unions, which in turn is based on rights they have won through industrial relations, collective bargaining and other laws, is great enough as to make an increasing number of industrial producers unprofitable or to force them to seek investment opportunities abroad? And isn't it also true that capitalist firms will make investment (and hence employment) decisions according to criteria of expected profitability, and that they consequently will fail to invest when long-term profitability is considered unattractive by them, thus causing an aggregate relative decline in the production output of the economy?

No one would deny that there are causes of declining growth rates and capitalists' failure to invest which have nothing to do with the impact of the welfare state upon business, but which are rather to be looked for in inherent crisis tendencies of the capitalist economy such as overaccumula-tion, the business cycle or uncontrolled technical change. But even so, it still might make sense to alleviate the hardship imposed upon capital and therefore, by definition, upon the rest of society (within the confines of a capitalist society), by dropping some of the burdens and constraints of the welfare state. This, of course, is exactly what most proponents of this argument are suggesting as a practical consequence. But after all, as the fairly compelling logic of the argument continues, who benefits from the operation of a welfare state that undermines and eventually destroys the production system upon which it has to rely in order to make its own promises come true? Doesn't a kind of 'welfare' become merely nominal and worthless anyway if it punishes capital by a high burden of costs and hence everyone else by inflation, unemployment or both? In my view, the valuable insight to be gained from the type of analysis I have just described is this: the welfare state, rather than being a separate and autonomous source of well-being which provides incomes and services as citizen rights, is itself highly dependent upon the prosperity and continued profitability of the economy. While being designed to be a cure to some ills of capitalist accumulation, the nature of the illness is such that it may force the patient to refrain from using the cure.

A conceivable objection to the above argument would be that capitalists and conservative political elites exaggerate the harm imposed upon them by the welfare state arrangements. To be sure, in the political game they have good tactical reasons to make the welfare state burden appear more intolerable than it really is. The question boils down then to what we mean, and how we measure 'reality' in this context. In answering this question we must remember that the power position of private investors includes the power to *define* reality. That is to say, whatever they *consider* an intolerable burden *is* an intolerable burden which will *in fact* lead to a declining propensity to invest, at least as long as they can expect to effectively reduce welfare-state-related costs by applying such economic sanctions. The debate about whether or not the welfare state is 'really' squeezing profits is thus purely academic because investors are in a position to *create* the reality and the effects of 'profit squeeze'.

The second major argument of the conservative analysis postulates that the effect of the welfare state is a disincentive to work. 'Labour does not work!' was one of the slogans in the campaign that brought Mrs Thatcher into power. But again, the analytical content of the argument must be carefully separated from the political uses to which it is put. And again, this analytical argument can, often contrary to the intention of its proponents, be read in a way that does make a lot of empirical sense. For instance, there is little doubt that elaborate labour protection legislation puts workers in a position to resist practices of exploitation that would be applied, as a rule, in the absence of such regulations. Powerful and recognized unions can in fact obtain wage increases in excess of productivity increases. And extensive social security provisions make it easier, at least for some workers for some of the time, to avoid undesirable jobs. Large-scale unemployment insurance covering most of the working population makes unemployment less undesirable for many workers and thus partially obstructs the reserve army mechanism. In sum, the welfare state has made the exploitation of labour more complicated and less predictable. On the other hand, as the welfare state imposes regulations and rights upon the labour-capital exchange that goes on in production, while leaving the authority structure and the property relations of production untouched, it is hardly surprising to see that the workers are not, as a rule, intrinsically motivated to work as productively as they possibly can. In other words, the welfare state maintains the control of capital over production, and thus the basic source of industrial and class conflict between labour and capital; but it by no means establishes anything resembling 'workers control'. At the same time, it strengthens workers' potential for resistance against capital's control, the net effect being that an unchanged conflict is fought out with means that have changed in favour of labour. Exploitative production relations coexist with expanded possibilities to resist, escape and mitigate exploitation. While the *reason* for struggle remained unchanged, the *means* of struggle increased for the workers. It is not surprising to see that this condition undermines the work ethic, or at least requires more costly and less reliable strategies to enforce such ethic.

My point so far has been that the two key arguments of the liberal-conservative analysis are valid to a large extent, contrary to what critics from the left have often argued. The basic fault in this analysis has less to do with what it explicitly states than with what it leaves out of its consideration. Every worthwhile political theory has to answer two questions: first, what is the desirable form of the organization of society and state, and how can we demonstrate that it is at all workable, i.e. consistent with our basic normative and factual assumptions about social life? This is the problem of defining a consistent *model* or goal of transformation. Second, how do we get there? This is the problem of identifying the dynamic forces and *strategies* that could bring about the transformation.

The conservative analysis of the welfare state fails on both counts. To start with the latter problem, it is extremely hard today in Western Europe to conceive of a promising political strategy that would aim at even partially eliminating the established institutional components of the welfare state, to say nothing about its wholesale abolition. That is to say, the welfare state has, in a certain sense, become an irreversible structure, the abolition of which would require nothing less than the abolition of political democracy and the unions, as well as fundamental changes in the party system. A political force that could bring about such dramatic changes is nowhere visible as a significant factor (right-wing middle-class populist movements that occasionally spring up in some countries notwithstanding). Moreover, political opinion research has shown that the fiercest advocates of *laissez-faire* capitalism and economic individualism show marked differences between their *general* ideological outlook and their willingness to have *special* transfers, subsidies and social security schemes abandoned from which they *personally* derive benefits. Thus, in the absence of a powerful ideological and organizational undercurrent in Western politics (such as a neo-fascist or authoritarian one), the vision of overcoming the welfare state and resurrecting a 'healthy' market economy is not much more than the politically impotent daydream of some ideologues of the old middle class. This class is nowhere strong enough to effect, as the examples of Mrs Thatcher and Ronald Reagan demonstrate, more than marginal alterations to an institutional scheme that they had to accept as given when taking office.

Even more significant, however, is the second failure of the conservative analysis, its failure to demonstrate that advanced capitalism *minus* the welfare state would actually be a workable model. The reasons why it is not, and consequently why the neo-*laissez-faire* ideology would be a very dangerous cure, *if* it could be administered, are fairly obvious. In the absence of large-scale state-subsidized housing, public education and health services, and extensive compulsory social security schemes, the working of an industrial economy would be inconceivable. Given the conditions and requirements of urbanization, large-scale concentration of labour power in industrial production plants, rapid technical, economic and regional change, the reduced ability of the family to cope with the difficulties of life in industrial society, the securalization of the moral order, and the quantitative reduction and growing dependence of the propertied middle classes, all of which are well known characteristics of capitalist social structures, the sudden disappearance of the welfare state would leave the system in a state of exploding conflict and anarchy. The embarrassing secret of the welfare state is that, while its impact upon capitalist accumulation may well become destructive (as the conservative analysis so emphatically demonstrates), its abolition would be plainly disruptive (a fact that is systematically ignored by the conservative critics). The contradiction is that while capitalism cannot coexist *with* the welfare state, neither can it exist *without* the welfare state. This is exactly the condition to which we refer when using the concept 'contradiction'. The flaw of the conservative analysis is in the one-sided emphasis it puts on the first side of this contradiction, and its silence about the second one.

This basic contradiction of the capitalist welfare state could of course be thought to be a mere dilemma which then would be solved or managed by a circumspect balancing of the two components. This, however, would presuppose two things, both of which are highly uncertain: first, that there *is* something like an 'optimum point' at which the order-maintaining functions of the welfare state are preserved while its disruptive effects are avoided; and second, if so, that political procedures and administrative practices will be sufficiently 'rational' to accomplish this precarious balance. Before I consider the prospects for this solution, let me first summarize some elements of the contending socialist critique of the welfare state.

The Critique from the Socialist Left

Although it would be nonsensical to deny that the struggle for labour protection legislation, expanded social services, social security and union recognition which has been led by the working-class movement for over a century now, and which has brought substantial improvements to the living conditions of most wage earners, the socialist critique of the welfare state is nevertheless a fundamental one. It can be summarized in three points which we will consider in turn: the welfare state is said to be (1) ineffective and inefficient, (2) repressive and (3) conditioning a false ideological understanding of social and political reality within the working class. In sum, it is a device to stabilize rather than a step in the transformation of capitalist society.

In spite of the undeniable gains in the living conditions of wage earners, the institutional structure of the welfare state has done little or nothing to alter the income distribution between the two principal classes of labour and capital. The huge machinery of redistribution does not work in a vertical direction but in a horizontal direction, namely *within* the class of wage earners. A further aspect of its ineffectiveness is that the welfare state does not *eliminate the causes* of individual contingencies and needs (such as work-related diseases, the disorganization of cities by the capitalist real estate market, the obsolescence of skills, unemployment, etc.) but *compensates for* some of the *consequences* of such events (by the provision of health services and health insurance, housing subsidies, training and retraining facilities, unemployment benefits and the like). Generally speaking, the kind of social intervention most typical of the welfare state is always 'too late', and hence its *ex post facto* measures are more costly and less effective than a more 'causal' type of intervention would allow them to be. This is a generally recognized dilemma of social policy making, the standard answer to which is the recommendation to adopt more 'preventive' strategies. It is also recognized that effective prevention would mean interference with the prerogatives of investors and management, i.e. the sphere of the market and private property which the welfare state has only very limited legal and *de facto* powers to regulate.

A further argument pointing to the ineffectiveness of the welfare state emphasizes the constant threat to which social policies and social services are exposed due to the fiscal crisis of the state, which in turn is a reflection of both cyclical and structural discontinuities of the process of accumulation. All West European countries [...] experienced a sharp economic recession in the mid-1970s, and we know of many examples of social policy expenditure cuts in response to the fiscal consequences of this recession. But even if the absolute and relative rise of social policy expenditures continues uninterrupted as a percentage of GNP, it is by no means certain, as Ian Gough and others before him have argued, that increases in the expenditures are paralleled by increases in real 'welfare'. The dual fallacy, known in technical literature as the 'spending service cliché', is this: first, a marginal increase in expenditures must not necessarily correspond to a marginal increment in the 'output' of the welfare state apparatus; it may well be used up in feeding the bureaucratic machinery itself. Second, even if the output (say of health services) *is* increased, a still larger increase in the level of risks and needs (or a qualitative change of these) may occur on the part of the clients or recipients of such services, so as to make the net effect negative.

The bureaucratic and professional form through which the welfare state dispenses its services is increasingly seen to be a source of its own inefficiency. Bureaucracies absorb more resources and provide less services than other democratic and decentralized structures could. The reason why the bureaucratic form of administering social services is maintained in spite of its inefficiency and ineffectiveness must therefore have to do with the social control function exercised by centralized welfare bureaucracies. This analysis leads to the critique of the *repressiveness* of the welfare state, its social control aspect. Such repressiveness, in the view of the critics, is indicated by the fact that in order to qualify for the benefits and services of the welfare state, the client must not only prove his or her 'need', but must also be a 'deserving' client, that is, one who complies to the dominant economic, political and cultural standards and norms of the society. The heavier the needs, the stricter these requirements tend to be defined. Only if, for instance, the unemployed are willing to keep themselves available for any alternative employment (often considerably inferior to the job they have lost) that is made available to them by employment agencies, are they entitled to unemployment benefits; and the claim for welfare payments to the poor is everywhere made conditional upon their conformity to standards of behaviour which the better-to-do strata of the population are perfectly free to violate. In these and other cases, the welfare state can be looked upon as an exchange transaction in which material benefits for the needy are traded for their submissive recognition of the 'moral order' of the society which generates such need. One important precondition for obtaining the services of the welfare state is the ability of the individual to comply with the routines and requirements of welfare bureaucracies and service organizations, an ability which is often inversely correlated to need itself.

A third major aspect of the socialist critique of the welfare state is its *politico-ideological* control function. The welfare state is seen not only as the source of benefits and services, but at the same time the source of false conceptions about historical realities which have damaging effects on working-class consciousness, organization and struggle. The welfare state creates the false image of two separated spheres of working-class life. On the one side is the sphere of work, the economy, production and 'primary' income distribution. On the other is the sphere of citizenship, the state, reproduction and 'secondary' distribution. This division of the socio-political world obscures the causal and functional links that exist between the two, and thus prevents the formation of a political under-standing of society as a coherent totality to be changed. That is to say, the structural arrangements of the welfare state tend to make people ignore or forget that the needs and contingencies which the welfare state responds to are themselves constituted, directly or indirectly, in the sphere of work and production. The welfare state itself is materially and institutionally constrained by the dynamics of the sphere of production, and a reliable conception of social security does therefore presuppose not only the expansion of citizen rights, but of workers' rights in the process of production. Contrary to such insights, which are part of the analytical starting-points of any conceivable socialist strategy of societal transforma-tion, the inherent symbolic indoctrination of the welfare state suggests the ideas of class co-operation, the disjunction of economic and political struggles, and an ill-based confidence in an ever continuing cycle of economic growth and social security.

The Welfare State and Political Change

What emerges from this discussion of the analysis of the welfare state by the right and the left are three points on which the liberal conservative and the socialist critic exhibit somewhat surprising parallels.

First, contrary to the ideological consensus that flourished in some of the most advanced welfare states throughout the 1950s and 1960s, the welfare state is no longer believed to be the promising and permanently valid answer to the problems of the socio-political order of advanced capitalist economies. Critics in both camps have become more vociferous and fundamental in their negative appraisal of welfare state arrangements. Second, neither of the two approaches to the welfare state could or would be prepared, in the best interests of their respective clientele, to abandon the welfare state, as it performs essential and indispensable functions both for the accumulation process as well as for the social and economic well-being of the working class. Third, while there is, on the conservative side, neither a consistent theory nor a realistic strategy about the social order of a non-welfare state (as I have argued before), it is evident that the situation is not much better on the left where one could possibly speak of a consistent theory of socialism, but certainly not of an agreed upon and realistic strategy for its construction. In the absence of the latter, the welfare state remains a theoretically contested, though in reality firmly entrenched fact, of the social order of advanced capitalist societies. In short, it appears that the welfare state, while being contested both from the right and the left, will not be easily replaced by a conservative or progressive alternative.

[...]

Note

From *Critical Social Policy*, 2, 2, 1982, pp. 7–14.

The Power Resources Model
Walter Korpi

Walter Korpi argues that most modern social scientific accounts of social structure and change have relied upon one of three models: a 'pluralist-industrial' model which emphasizes the emergence in developed industrial societies of a plurality of competing interests and social groupings whose relations are mediated through largely consensual societal institutions; a 'Marxist-Leninist' model which insists that Western societies are still essentially riven by those forms of class struggle originally identified by Marx and in which the state acts in the interests of capital; and a neo-corporatist account in which certain (economically defined) interests have privileged access to the state and in which collective action is negotiated at an elite level between the state and these privileged social actors. Here he offers his own alternative account of a 'power resources model'. (Eds)

Power Resources

The stability implied in the pluralist industrial model of society rests on the assumption that the distribution of power resources between various groups and collectivities in the capitalist democracies is potentially equal. Schmitter's assumption of relative stability of neo-corporatist arrangements appears to imply an unequal yet fairly stable distribution of power resources. The Leninist interpretation of Marx similarly implies an unequal but stable power distribution in the capitalist democracies. Such assumptions must be questioned. One way of elucidating the distribution of power is to analyse what instruments and resources of power different groups and collectivities in society have at their disposal in the interaction which takes place between them over long periods of time.

What, then, are power resources? Power resources are characteristics which provide actors – individuals or collectivities – with the ability to punish or reward other actors. These resources can be described in terms of a variety of dimensions. Power resources can thus vary with regard to domain, which refers to the number of people who are receptive to the particular type of rewards and penalties. They can also differ in terms of scope – the various kinds of situation in which they can be used. A third important dimension is the degree of scarcity of a power resource of a particular type. Furthermore, power resources can vary in terms of centrality; i.e. they can be more or less essential to people in their daily lives. They also differ with regard to how easily they are convertible into other resources. The extent to which a power resource can be concentrated is a crucial dimension. Of relevance are also the costs involved in using a power resource and in its mobilization, i.e. in making it ready for use. Power resources can furthermore differ in the extent to which they can be used to initiate action or are limited to responses to actions by others.

It is important to realize that power resources need not be used or activated in order to have consequences for the actions of other people. An actor with the ability to reward or punish need thus not always do so to influence others. Since every activation of power resources entails costs, it actually lies in the interests of power holders to increase efficiency in the deployment of power resources. This can be achieved through what we may call the investment of power resources. Thus, power resources can be invested through the creation of structures for decision-making and conflict regulation, whereby decisions can be made on a routine basis and in accordance with given principles. Investments of power resources can be made in institutions for conflict resolution such as laws, ordinances and bureaucracies, in technologies, in community and national planning, and in the dissemination of ideologies.

Some types of power resource can be described as basic in the sense that they in themselves provide the capacity to reward or to punish other actors. Through processes of investment, from basic power resources actors can derive new types of power resource. These derived power resources, however, ultimately depend on the basic power resources for their effectiveness. The distinction between basic and derived power resources is not easy to make but appears fruitful. It indicates, for instance, that power resources such as ideologies can be seen as ultimately based on resources which provide the capability to apply positive or negative sanctions.

Let us now look briefly at the characteristics of some of the more important basic power resources in Western societies. Among resources familiar to students of power, means of violence have traditionally been considered important. In terms of the aforementioned dimensions, means of violence have a large domain, wide scope and high concentration potential, as well as a relatively high convertibility. Although the legit-imate use of violence is typically reserved for the state, resources for violence are not scarce. Their essential drawback is the high costs asso-ciated with their use.

Two types of power resource are central and their dimensions important for the theoretical controversy between pluralists and Marxist social scientists. The first type of power resource consists of capital and control over the means of production. The second type is what economists often call 'human capital', i.e. labour power, education and occupational skills. The pluralist approach assumes that persons possessing control over capital and the means of production do not have appreciably greater power resources at their disposal than persons with only human capital. Yet in terms of the aforementioned dimensions, capital and control over the means of production are power resources which differ drastically from human capital, making parity between them extremely pro-blematic.

As power resources, capital and the means of production have a large domain, wide scope and high concentration potential, as well as high scarcity and convertibility. The costs involved in mobilizing and using these resources are relatively low. Furthermore, control over the means of production has high centrality, since it affects people's livelihood. Capital is also typically used to initiate action.

When regarded as a power resource, human capital is characterized by serious limitations. Usually it has a fairly small domain and narrow scope. Since everybody has some of it, human capital is generally not a highly scarce resource. Where labour power is offered on the labour market, its value depends on demand from capital, and its ability to initiate action is limited. Human capital has low convertibility and a low concentration potential. In an era of mass education, formal training beyond a certain level can at times yield diminishing returns. To be effective, the human capital of various individuals and groups must therefore be co-ordinated on a broad basis. This requires investments in organizations for collective action and hence fairly large mobilization costs.

In Western countries, most human capital is utilized in the labour market. Economists often discuss the labour market as one of supply and demand where commodities are bought and sold. But human labour power is a very special commodity, since it is inseparable from its owner. Thus it cannot be sold; that would be slave trade. Labour can be hired only for a certain time, and the buyer acquires the right to make use of the seller's labour capacity during hours of work. Once the employment contract has been concluded, the owner of human capital cannot shed it like an overcoat but must deliver his labour power at the workplace, and on the job must personally subordinate himself to the directives of management. Thus the system of wage labour creates relationships of authority and subordination among people and the basis for a division into classes.

The possibility of increasing the effectiveness of the power resources of individuals through collective action provides a rational explanation for the origin of unions to promote the interests of wage-earners in disputes with employers. It also offers an explanation of why wage-earners organize themselves into political parties. As the growth of 'juristic persons' and corporate actors during the past centuries indicates, other actors also have organized for collective action to increase the efficiency of their power resources. Alongside capital and control over the means of production, organizations to co-ordinate wage-earners' actions – primarily trade unions and political parties – belong to the strategically important power resources in the capitalist democracies.

Are, then, either of these types of strategic power resources – on the one hand control over capital and the means of production, and on the other hand control over human capital co-ordinated through the organizations of wage-earners – dominant in the capitalist democracies? Let us look more closely at the clearest confrontation between them, viz. at the workplace. Control over the means of production forms the basis of management's right of command over labour. It is capital which hires labour, not labour which hires capital. The subordination of labour is, however, a matter of degree inasmuch as the prerogatives of the representatives of capital have been restricted by legislation and by collective bargaining, the effectiveness of which in turn is influenced by the market situation. The prerogatives of management still confirm that, in terms of power resources, the wage-earners in these societies are in a position of inferiority *vis-à-vis* capital. The maintenance of a system of authority and subordination based on control over the means of production is a major problem confronting the dominant groups in the capitalist democracies.

I agree with the pluralist view on power distribution in the capitalist democracies to the extent that in these societies power is probably more widely shared than in other contemporary societies with different political and economic systems. However, I object to the next and crucial step in pluralist thought: that the assumed equal opportunities to mobilize power has generated a distribution of power resources in these societies that is sufficiently equal to no longer warrant our attention. If we view the development of wage-earners' collective organizations as essential for the effectiveness with which their 'human capital' can be applied in the conflicts of interest with capital, it appears evident that the distribution of power resources in Western societies can vary considerably over time as well as between countries. Once we drop the assumptions of the distribution of power resources implicit in the pluralist, neo-corporatist and neo-Leninist models, a host of interesting questions concerning distributive processes, social consciousness and patterns of conflict, as well as institutional functioning and stability, come to the fore.

Social Change

In Western societies variations in the difference in power resources between labour and business interests, along with their allied groups, can be expected to have a variety of consequences. This difference can influence:

1 the distributive processes in the society;
2 the social consciousness of the citizens;
3 the level and patterns of conflicts in the society; and
4 the shaping and functioning of social institutions.

The processes of distribution in society can be viewed as exchange relations where, for example, the right to control labour power is exchanged for wages. These exchanges, however, need be neither in accordance with principles of equity nor mutually balanced. Instead, we must assume that the distribution of power resources influences the outcomes of the exchange processes and consequently the degree of inequality in society. Stronger groups thus will often get the 'lion's share' of what is to be distributed. Power resources, which can be regarded as stocks of values, thus influence the flow of values between individuals and collectivities.

But the distribution of power resources is also critical for the social consciousness and levels of aspiration of citizens as well as for the way in which they define their interests. Perceptions of what is just, fair and reasonable *vis-à-vis* other groups of citizens are largely dependent upon the power relations between these groups. Weak groups often learn, or are taught to accept, circumstances which stronger groups would consider unjust. Strong actors also tend to develop more long-range definitions of their interests than weaker groups.

The distribution of power resources is of major importance for the levels and patterns of conflict in society. Even if a weak group feels that an exchange relationship is unjust, the group may have to accept the terms of exchange because it lacks better alternatives and opposition may lead to reprisals of various kinds. But when the power resources of actors increase, they can offer resistance in situations which they previously had to accept. They can also attempt to change conditions which they find unjust. The distribution of power resources and its changes thus influences the levels of conflicts in society. Since changes in the distribution of power resources also affect the alternatives for action open to the actors, they can be expected to influence the actors' strategies of conflict and thus the pattern of conflict between them.

From this perspective, changes in the distribution of power resources between different collectivities or classes can thus be assumed to be of central importance for social change. Such changes will affect the levels of aspiration of the actors and their capacity to maintain or to change existing social structures. Social change can be expected to emerge from various types of bargaining, but will sometimes involve manifest conflicts. Since open conflicts are costly to all parties, it is in the interests of the actors to limit their length and frequency. Through settlements following bargaining and/or manifest conflicts, the terms of exchange between the parties are thus moulded.

Where parties are involved in long-term interactions, settlements between them generally tend to involve different types of compromise. Such compromises may lead to the creation of new social institutions or changes in the functioning of existing institutions. Social institutions and arrangements related, for example, to processes of distribution and decision-making can thus be seen as outcomes of recurrent conflicts of interest, where the parties concerned have invested their power resources in order to secure favourable outcomes. Such institutions thus need not be viewed as neutral or objective arrangements for conflict resolution. Instead, the ways in which they were created and function reflect the distribution of power in society. When the distribution of power resources is altered, the form and functioning of such institutions and arrangements are also likely to change.

The distribution of power resources between the major collectivities or classes in society will thus shape people's actions in a variety of ways. These actions, in turn, will affect social structure as well as the distribution of power. A continuous interplay between human action and the structure of society arises. The approach outlined here comes close to the perspective of Marx, according to which structural change is the result of people, through co-operation or conflict, seeking solutions to what they define as important social problems. The definitions of social problems are, however, not objectively given but depend largely on the distribution of power resources in society. The alternative solutions considered and ultimately chosen are also affected by the power distribution.

In this perspective the state can be conceived of as a set of institutional structures which have emerged in the struggles between classes and interest groups in a society. The crucial aspect of this set of institutions is that they determine the ways in which decision-making on behalf of the whole society can legitimately be made and enforced. The state must not, however, be seen as an actor in itself, or as a pure instrument to be used by whichever group that has it under its control. While the institutional structures and the state can be used to affect, for example, distributive processes in the society, these structures also affect the way in which power resources can be mobilized and are, in turn, affected by the use of power resources.

Conflicts of interest between different groups or collectivities continuously generate bargaining, manifest conflicts and settlements. At some points, however, the settlements are the outcomes of important changes in the distribution of power resources and are of such a nature that they significantly affect institutional arrangements and strategies of conflict for long periods of time. In connection with such settlements or 'historical compromises', the patterns and conceptions of 'normal politics' change.

In the capitalist countries, the acceptance of the wage-earners' right to organize in unions and parties and to participate in political decision-making via universal and equal suffrage are examples of such historical settlements. The winning of political democracy was the result of a decrease in the disadvantage of working-class power resources brought about through organization and often through alliances with middle-class groups. It limited the legitimate use of means of repression by the state and opened up legitimate avenues for the citizens to participate in the decision-making of state organs. In many Western countries, the historical settlements concerning political democracy came around the First World War. These institutional changes significantly affected the patterns of interest conflicts in the years to come.

Societal Bargaining

With the exception of setbacks in countries like Italy, Germany and Spain, during the inter-war period the strength of the unions and working-class parties increased in the Western nations. In the period after the Second World War this trend has by and large continued. Through increasing levels of organization the wage-earners have considerably strengthened their bargaining position in the distributive conflicts in the capitalist democracies. This has affected strategies of conflict and patterns of institutional arrangements. It is my hypothesis that the tripartite 'neo-corporatist' institutional arrangements largely reflect the compromises and settlements generated by the decreasing differences in the distribution of power resources between wage-earners and representatives of capital and allied groups in these countries. The decreasing disadvantage in wage-earner power resources has generated institutional arrangements and practices in reaching settlements involving major interest groups, which we can describe as 'societal bargaining'. The notion of bargaining implies that the outcome of the interaction cannot be predetermined.

The choice of the term 'societal bargaining' to describe arrangements and practices which others have termed 'corporatism' is made not only to avoid a word which many have found hard to swallow. In my view, societal bargaining of the tripartite type that was developed in some countries of Western Europe during the post-war period clearly differs from traditional corporatist arrangements. It is therefore misleading to regard the two as more or less functional equivalents in the way several writers on neo-corporatism have done.

Traditional state corporatism, for example in Italy, Germany and Spain, must be seen as a successful attack on the working class and its organizations in a situation where the power gap between classes was very large. State corporatism was used to widen that gap. The institutional arrangements of societal bargaining, however, have come about in situations where the disadvantage in power resources of the wage-earners is much smaller than where the traditional 'state corporatist' solutions have been practised. Societal bargaining involving the organizations of the wage-earners must, by and large, be seen as reflecting an increasingly strongly organized working class. Whether societal bargaining benefits the wage-earners or not is an empirical question, which cannot be settled through definitions. We must assume, instead, that its long-term as well as the short-term outcomes can vary and are dependent on the distribution of power resources between the parties. From the power resource perspective the institutional arrangements of societal bargaining (i.e. the 'neo-corporatist' institutions) appear as intervening variables between, on the one hand, the distribution of power resources in society and, on the other hand, the pattern and outcome of distributive conflicts.

The spread of societal bargaining in Western nations during the post-war period is the result of an important shift in the lines separating decision-making through markets and politics. Since the breakthrough of political democracy, the relative importance of these two forms of decision-making has been largely dependent on the contest between two different types of power resource: the (at least in principle) equally distributed political resources, and the highly unequally distributed power resources in the markets. By using their votes, wage-earners have been able to encroach upon and to limit the sphere of operations of the markets, where they are more often at a disadvantage. An example of the shift from markets towards politics is the decision-making determining levels of unemployment. Where Keynesian ideas have been accepted, the level of unemployment has come to be seen as a responsibility of the political authorities, and no longer to be left only to market processes. Also, distributive processes have been affected, for example through social policy and taxation.

A Democratic Class Struggle?

I have suggested above that, in the capitalist democracies, it is fruitful to view politics as an expression of a democratic class struggle, i.e. a struggle in which class, socio-economic cleavages and the distribution of power resources play central roles. In contemporary social science, this view will be challenged from different directions. From a pluralist point of view the primacy which this interpretation gives to class cleavages will be questioned. While accepting the importance of class, those who lean towards the Leninist interpretation of Marxism tend to argue that the major organized interest groups, which presently are the main actors in these conflicts, do not actually represent the interests of the working class. Many writers on neo-corporatism also share such a view. Let us look briefly at the concepts concerned and the counter-arguments made.

The class concept is of relevance, *inter alia*, in attempts to explain social conflict, the distribution of goods and social change. This concept should therefore sensitize us to the many fissures and rents in the social fabric, which may become cleavages delineating the bases upon which citizens will organize themselves into collective action in the conflicts of interest in society. According to my reading of Marx and Weber, the two dominant figures in the theory of class, they both view the class concept in this perspective. Marx no less than Weber recognized a multitude of potential cleavages on the basis of which citizens can combine themselves for collective action. The two differ, however, in the relative importance which they ascribe to different types of bases of cleavage.

Marx assumed that, in the long run, the conflicts of interest rooted in the sphere of production and especially in the economic organization of production would come to dominate over the other potential cleavages, such as those based on market resources and status. Contrary to what is often assumed, the class theory of Marx is not a one-factor theory. Its basic hypothesis is instead that, among the multitude of lines of cleavage and conflicts of interest, the relative importance of those arising from the economic organization of production will increase in the long run.

Weber, however, places class, market resources and status on an equal footing as potential bases for cleavages and assumes that over time their importance will tend to oscillate. The class theory of Weber has also often been misinterpreted, not least by those who regard him as their intellectual standard-bearer. Weber explicitly argued that power must be seen as the generic concept of social stratification, the threefold expressions of which are class, status and party. Yet, pluralist writers have often conceived of power as a separate 'dimension' of social stratification, parallel to, but not included in, 'class' and 'status'. In contrast to Weber's stress on power as the basic independent variable behind social stratification, pluralist writers have therefore tended to conceive of power as restricted to the realm of the political order. While Weber saw 'property' and 'the lack of property' as the basic characteristics of all class situations, the institution of property has received scant attention in pluralist and functionalist analyses of industrial societies.

[...]

The Marxian hypothesis that, in the development of capitalism, the relative importance of class will increase at the expense of other possible bases of cleavages has been attacked by generations of social scientists. A recent challenger, Frank Parkin, develops a self-professed bourgeois critique, based on a neo-Weberian approach to stratification which puts power and conflict in a central place. In contrast to the Marxian class theory, which he interprets to be a one-factor theory of distributive conflict, focused exclusively on the positions in the productive system, Parkin argues for a multi-dimensional approach where control over productive resources, race, ethnicity, religion, sex and so on are viewed as equally important bases for cleavages and the formation of conflict groups. Against the background of developments during the 1960s and 1970s, for example in Northern Ireland, Belgium and the United States, Parkin maintains that, in contrast to Marxian predictions, not class but rather 'racial, ethnic, and religious conflicts have moved towards the centre of the political stage in many industrial societies', and that therefore 'any general model of class and stratification that does not fully incorporate this fact must forfeit all credibility'.[1] Parkin thus explicitly denies the primary role of the sphere of production as a basis for conflict of interest.

Another challenge to the centrality of class in modern Western societies has been made by students of electoral behaviour, who have analysed the relative importance of different bases for party cleavages. While some of them stress the importance of socio-economic factors, others argue that religion and language are more important. Thus in a study of party choice in Belgium, Canada, the Netherlands and South Africa, Lijphart comes to the following conclusions: 'Social class is clearly no more than a secondary and subsidiary influence on party choice, and it can become a factor of importance only in the absence of potent rivals such as religion and language.'[2]

It goes without saying that language, religion and race are easily and frequently seen as introducing a communality of interests and therefore often become bases for collective action. In fact, language and religion are so important bases of cleavages that over the centuries they have helped to generate decision-making units, i.e. states, which tend to be more or less homogenous with respect to these characteristics. Class divisions, on the contrary, occur within decision-making units. In this sense, then, cleavages based on language, religion and ethnicity can be seen as primary to class.

However, a different picture emerges when we look at the cleavages within the present nation-states. Parkin's claim that race, language and religion are of equal or greater importance than the sphere of production in generating social cleavages in industrial society appears to be based on the extent to which different cleavages have generated open or violent conflicts. This, however, is a rather superficial reading of the evidence. While conflicts based on religion, race, ethnicity and also on environmental issues clearly have been the most violent ones during these decades, this fact tells us little about the importance of different cleavages as bases of collective action, which is what is here in question. The power distribution approach outlined above indicates that the extent of manifest conflicts primarily reflects changes in the distribution of power resources between groups or collectivities.

To evaluate the relative importance of different bases of cleavages, we must primarily look not only at the violent conflicts, dramatic as they may be, but also at the more institutionalized conflicts and, above all, at the extent to which these cleavages have served as bases for organizations of interest. In this perspective class organizations in the sphere of production, i.e. unions and employers' (or business) organizations, emerge in the central roles. These organizations have been the key participants in the societal bargaining which has emerged in the Western nations during the post-war period. Only rarely have religious or ethnic groups figured in such contexts. Socio-economic cleavages also remain central bases for the party structures in most Western nations.

As indicated above, many neo-corporatist writers have assumed a major 'goal-displacement' within the organizations purporting to represent the interests of the working class. In neo-corporatism these organizations are assumed to serve largely the interests of the organizational leaderships and to control their members on behalf of the dominant groups in society. Schmitter assumes that this holds for labour unions while, for example, Panitch and Jessop acquit unions and place social democratic parties in the central controlling roles.

While 'goal displacement' within interest organizations is a clear possibility, it is an empirical question to what extent this has occurred in the wage-earner organizations. Assuming rational actors, a high level of voluntary union membership and party support can support the assumption that the union or party furthers the interests of the actors as perceived by them. The claim that unions in the Western nations have largely ceased to represent the interests of their members appears difficult to substantiate. In view of the fact that union members have daily opportunities to evaluate the consequences of leadership decisions at the place of work, such an assumption strikes me as rather absurd.

As far as the left parties are concerned, the variations between them would appear to be greater. Since they are rooted largely in the continuum of social stratification, political parties have a more flexible basis than unions, which reflect class divisions. Therefore goal displacements may occur more easily in left parties than in labour unions. The policy which a left party comes to represent when in government is affected by many factors, and such a party may come to choose a strategy which severely compromises working-class interests. The extent to which this has occurred probably varies considerably between countries. If we assume that unions tend to represent working-class interests more closely than the parties on the left, the closeness of the relationship between a left party and the union movement can be seen as one indicator of the type of policy which the party stands for.

My general hypothesis is that the presence of reformist socialist parties in the government can bring public policies closer to wage-earner interests. Also in this context, the distribution of power resources in society is of crucial importance. In the tripartite societal bargaining between the state, labour and capital, the distribution of power resources and the political composition of the government can affect the pattern of coalition formation in this triad and the outcomes of the bargaining. The smaller the disadvantage in power resources of the labour movement and the stronger the left party hold over the government, the more likely are state representatives to side with labour in the tripartite bargaining. Accordingly, the compromises resulting from societal bargaining can be expected to be more to the favour of wage-earners. There are considerable differences in the power position of the wage-earners between the Western nations.

Notes

From W. Korpi, *The Democratic Class Struggle*, London, Routledge and Kegan Paul, 1983, pp. 14–25.
1 F. Parkin, *Marxism and Class Theory*, New York, Columbia University Press, 1979.
2 A. Lijphart, 'Language, Religion, Class and Party Choice', in R. Rose, *Electoral Participation*, Beverly Hills, CA, Sage, 1980.

Responses from the Right

The Meaning of the Welfare State

Friedrich von Hayek

[...]

Unlike socialism, the conception of the welfare state has no precise meaning. The phrase is sometimes used to describe any state that 'concerns' itself in any manner with problems other than those of the maintenance of law and order. But, though a few theorists have demanded that the activities of government should be limited to the maintenance of law and order, such a stand cannot be justified by the principle of liberty. Only the coercive measures of government need be strictly limited. [...] There is undeniably a wide field for non-coercive activities of government and [...] a clear need for financing them by taxation.

Indeed, no government in modern times has ever confined itself to the 'individualist minimum' which has occasionally been described,[1] nor has such confinement of governmental activity been advocated by the 'orthodox' classical economists.[2] All modern governments have made provision for the indigent, unfortunate and disabled and have concerned themselves with questions of health and the dissemination of knowledge. There is no reason why the volume of these pure service activities should not increase with the general growth of wealth. There are common needs that can be satisfied only by collective action and which can be thus provided for without restricting individual liberty. It can hardly be denied that, as we grow richer, that minimum of sustenance which the community has always provided for those not able to look after themselves, and which can be provided outside the market, will gradually rise, or that government may, usefully and without doing any harm, assist or even lead in such endeavours. There is little reason why the government should not also play some role, or even take the initiative, in such areas as social insurance and education, or temporarily subsidize certain experimental developments. Our problem here is not so much the aims as the methods of government action.

References are often made to those modest and innocent aims of governmental activity to show how unreasonable is any opposition to the welfare state as such. But, once the rigid position that government should not concern itself at all with such matters is abandoned – a position which is defensible but has little to do with freedom – the defenders of liberty commonly discover that the programme of the welfare state comprises a great deal more that is represented as equally legitimate and unobjectionable. If, for instance, they admit that they have no objection to pure-food laws, this is taken to imply that they should not object to any government activity directed toward a desirable end. Those who attempt to delimit the functions of government in terms of aims rather than methods thus regularly find themselves in the position of having to oppose state action which appears to have only desirable consequences or of having to admit that they have no general rule on which to base their objections to measures which, though effective for particular purposes, would in their aggregate effect destroy a free society. Though the position that the state should have nothing to do with matters not related to the maintenance of law and order may seem logical so long as we think of the state solely as a coercive apparatus, we must recognize that, as a service agency, it may assist without harm in the achievement of desirable aims which perhaps could not be achieved otherwise. The reason why many of the new welfare activities of government are a threat to freedom, then, is that, though they are presented as mere service activities, they really constitute an exercise of the coercive powers of government and rest on its claiming exclusive rights in certain fields.

The current situation has greatly altered the task of the defender of liberty and made it much more difficult. So long as the danger came from socialism of the frankly collectivist kind, it was possible to argue that the tenets of the socialists were simply false: that socialism would not achieve what the socialists wanted and that it would produce other consequences which they would not like. We cannot argue similarly against the welfare state, for this term does not designate a definite system. What goes under that name is a conglomerate of so many diverse and even contradictory elements that, while some of them may make a free society more attractive, others are incompatible with it or may at least constitute potential threats to its existence.

We shall see that some of the aims of the welfare state can be realized without detriment to individual liberty, though not necessarily by the methods which seem the most obvious and are therefore most popular; that others can be similarly achieved to a certain extent, though only at a cost much greater than people imagine or would be willing to bear, or only slowly and gradually as wealth increases; and that, finally, there are others – and they are those particularly dear to the hearts of the socialists – that cannot be realized in a society that wants to preserve personal freedom.

There are all kinds of public amenities which it may be in the interest of all members of the community to provide by common effort, such as parks and museums, theatres and facilities for sports – though there are strong reasons why they should be provided by local rather than national authorities. There is then the important issue of security, of protection against risks common to all, where government can often either reduce these risks or assist people to provide against them. Here, however, an important distinction has to be drawn between two conceptions of security: a limited security which can be achieved for all and which is, therefore, no privilege, and absolute security, which in a free society cannot be achieved for all. The first of these is security against severe physical privation, the assurance of a given minimum of sustenance for all; and the second is the assurance of a given standard of life, which is determined by comparing the standard enjoyed by a person or a group with that of others. The distinction, then, is that between the security of an equal minimum income for all and the security of a particular income that a person is thought to deserve. The latter is closely related to the third main ambition that inspires the welfare state: the desire to use the powers of government to ensure a more even or more just distribution of goods. Insofar as this means that the coercive powers of government are to be used to ensure that particular people get particular things, it requires a kind of discrimination between, and an unequal treatment of, different people which is irreconcilable with a free society. This is the kind of welfare state that aims at 'social justice' and becomes 'primarily a redistributor of income'. It is bound to lead back to socialism and its coercive and essentially arbitrary methods.

Though *some* of the aims of the welfare state can be achieved *only* by methods inimical to liberty, *all* its aims *may* be pursued by such methods. The chief danger today is that, once an aim of government is accepted as legitimate, it is then assumed that even means contrary to the principles of freedom may be legitimately employed. The unfortunate fact is that, in the majority of fields, the most effective, certain and speedy way of reaching a given end will seem to be to direct all available resources towards the now visible solution. To the ambitious and impatient reformer, filled with indignation at a particular evil, nothing short of the complete abolition of that evil by the quickest and most direct means will seem adequate. If every person now suffering from unemployment, ill health or inadequate provision for [...] old age is at once to be relieved of his [or her] cares, nothing short of an all-comprehensive and compulsory scheme will suffice. But if, in our impatience to solve such problems immediately, we give government exclusive and monopolistic powers, we may find that we have been short-sighted. If the quickest way to a now visible solution becomes the only permissible one and all alternative experimentation is precluded, and if what now seems the best method of satisfying a need is made the sole starting-point for all future development, we may perhaps reach our present goal sooner, but we shall probably at the same time prevent the emergence of more effective alternative solutions. It is often those who are most anxious to use our existing knowledge and powers to the full that do most to impair the future growth of knowledge by the methods they use. The controlled single-channel development towards which impatience and administrative convenience have frequently inclined the reformer and which, especially in the field of social insurance, has become characteristic of the modern welfare state may well become the chief obstacle to future improvement.

If government wants not merely to facilitate the attainment of certain standards by the individuals but to make certain that everybody attains them it can do so only by depriving individuals of any choice in the matter. Thus the welfare state becomes a household state in which a paternalistic power controls most of the income of the community and allocates it to individuals in the forms and quantities which it thinks they need or deserve.

In many fields persuasive arguments based on considerations of efficiency and economy can be advanced in favour of the state's taking sole charge of a particular service; but when the state does so, the result is usually not only that those advantages soon prove illusory but that the character of the services becomes entirely different from that which they would have had if they had been provided by competing agencies. If, instead of administering limited resources put under its control for a specific service, government uses its coercive powers to ensure that men are given what some expert thinks they need; if people thus can no longer exercise any choice in some of the most important matters of their lives, such as health, employment, housing and provision for old age, but must accept the decisions made for them by appointed authority on the basis of its evaluation of their need; if certain services become the exclusive domain of the state, and whole professions – be it medicine, education or insurance – come to exist only as unitary bureaucratic hierarchies, it will no longer be competitive experimentation but solely the decisions of authority that will determine what men shall get.[3]

The same reasons that generally make the impatient reformer wish to organize such services in the form of government monopolies lead him also to believe that the authorities in charge should be given wide discretionary powers over the individual. If the objective were merely to improve opportunities for all by supplying certain specific services according to a rule, this could be attained on essentially business lines. But we could then never be sure that the results for all individuals would be precisely what we wanted. If each individual is to be affected in some particular way, nothing short of the individualizing, paternalistic treatment by a discretionary authority with powers of discriminating between persons will do.

It is sheer illusion to think that when certain needs of the citizen have become the exclusive concern of a single bureaucratic machine, democratic control of that machine can then effectively guard the liberty of the citizen. So far as the preservation of personal liberty is concerned, the division of labour between a legislature which merely says that this or that should be done[4] and an administrative apparatus which is given exclusive power to carry out these instructions is the most dangerous arrangement possible. All experience confirms what *is* clear enough from American as

> well as from English experience, that the zeal of the administrative agencies to achieve the immediate ends they see before them leads them to see their function out of focus and to assume that constitutional limitations and guaranteed individual rights must give way before their zealous efforts to achieve what they see as a paramount purpose of government.[5]

It would scarcely be an exaggeration to say that the greatest danger to liberty today comes from the men who are most needed and most powerful in modern government, namely, the efficient expert administrators exclusively concerned with what they regard as the public good. Though theorists may still talk about the democratic control of these activities, all who have direct experience in this matter agree that (as one [...] English writer put it) 'if the Minister's control ... has become a myth, the control of Parliament is and always has been the merest fairy tale'.[6] It is inevitable that this sort of administration of the welfare of the people should become a self-willed and uncontrollable apparatus before which the individual is helpless, and which becomes increasingly invested with all the *mystique* of sovereign authority – the *Hoheitsverwaltung* or *Herrschaftstaat* of the German tradition that used to be so unfamiliar to Anglo-Saxons that the strange term 'hegemonic'[7] had to be coined to render its meaning.

Notes

From F. A. von Hayek, *The Constitution of Liberty*, London, Routledge, 1959, pp. 257–62.

1   Cf., e.g., Henry Sidgwick, *The Elements of Politics*, London, 1891, ch. 4.
2   See on this particularly Lionel Robbins, *The Theory of Economic Policy*, London, 1952.
3   Cf. J. S. Mill, *On Liberty*, ed. R. B. McCallum, Oxford, 1946, pp. 99–100: 'If the roads, the railways, the banks, the insurance offices, the great joint stock

companies, the universities, and the public charities, were all of them branches of the government; if, in addition, the municipal corporations and local boards, with all that now devolves on them, became departments of the central administration; if the employés of all these different enterprises were appointed and paid by the government, and looked to the government for every rise in life; not all the freedom of the press and popular constitution of the legislature would make this or any other country free otherwise than in name. And the evil would be greater, the more efficiently and scientifically the administrative machinery was constructed – the more skilful the arrangements for obtaining the best qualified hands and heads with which to work it.'

4   Cf. T. H. Marshall, *Citizenship and Social Class*, Cambridge, 1958, p. 59: 'So we find that legislation . . . acquires more and more the character of a declaration of policy that it is hoped to put into effect some day.'

5   Roscoe Pound, 'The Rise of the Service State and its Consequence', in *The Welfare State and the National Welfare*, ed. S. Glueck, Cambridge, MA, 1952, p. 220.

6   P. Wiles, 'Property and Equality', in *The Unservile State*, ed. G. Watson, London, 1957, p. 107.

7   See L. von Mises, *Human Action*, New Haven, 1949, pp. 196ff.

The Two Wars against Poverty

Charles Murray

[...]

When news reports cite percentages of 'people living in poverty', they are drawing from the official definition of the 'poverty line' established in 1964 by a task force in the Social Security Administration. The poverty line is, in effect, set at three times the cost of an adequate diet, and is adjusted for inflation, a variety of family characteristics and one's location (rural or non-rural).

This measure has been attacked as niggardly by some and as overly generous by others. Almost everyone agrees that it fails to capture the important differences in the quality of life between a family living at the poverty line in the South Bronx, for example, and a family with the same income that lives in a less punishing environment. But this measure of poverty has its merits nonetheless. It is widely known, it takes family size and inflation into account, and it provides a consistent measure for examining income over time. I will use it to discuss the history of three different 'types' of poverty: official poverty, net poverty and latent poverty [...].

The most widely used measure of poverty is the percentage of people with cash incomes that fall beneath the poverty line before taxes, but after taking cash income transfers from government into account. We shall call it *official poverty* because it is the measure reported by the Bureau of the Census.

Conventional wisdom has it that, at least according to this one measure, the 1960s and 1970s brought economic progress for the poor. The most widely shared view of recent events is that the United States entered the 1960s with a large population that had been bypassed during the prosperity of the Eisenhower years. The rich and the middle class gained but the poor did not. Then, after fits and starts during the Kennedy years, came the explosion in the number and size of social programmes under Johnson. The programmes were perhaps too ambitious, it is widely conceded, and perhaps some of the efforts were misdirected, but at least they put a big dent in the poverty problem; this can be seen, it is said, in the large reduction in poverty that occurred during LBJ's administration and thereafter. The Great Society reforms were seen to have produced results that Eisenhower's 'trickle-down' economics had not.

The essential assertion of this view is that poverty decreased during the War on Poverty and had not been decreasing as rapidly before this period. It is a simple assertion, for which the data are a matter of historical record, and it is only half right.

Poverty did indeed fall during the five Johnson years, from 18 per cent of the population in 1964 to 13 per cent in 1968, his last year in office. Yet this was scarcely an unprecedented achievement. Between 1949 and 1952, poverty had already begun to fall from 33 to 28 per cent. Under Eisenhower it fell to 22 per cent. Under Kennedy and Johnson it dropped to 18 per cent by 1964. In short, the size of the official 'impoverished' population dropped by twenty percentage points in twenty years, of which the five Johnson years accounted for precisely their fair share, five points.[1]

Then, after two decades of reasonably steady progress, improvement slowed in the late 1960s and stopped altogether in the 1970s. A higher percentage of the American population was poor in 1980, in terms of cash income, than at any time since 1968. The percentage dipped as low as 11.1 per cent in 1973, but by 1980 it stood at 13 per cent and was heading upward.

When this history of the official poverty level is placed alongside the history of social welfare expenditures, a paradox appears. Social welfare expenditures had been increasing at a steady rate through the Eisenhower, Kennedy and early Johnson years. But it was not until the budgets of 1967 and 1968 that the Johnson programmes were reaching enough people to have a marked impact on the budget; it was then that social welfare expenditures started to take off. So just at the time when the reforms of the mid-1960s were being implemented, progress in reducing poverty began grinding to a halt!

The paradox is even more pronounced when we remember what it is we are measuring. If the measure were of chronic joblessness, for example, the flattening curve [...] would be understandable: it often is harder to fix the last 10 per cent of a problem than the first 90 per cent. But it this case, 'official poverty' is simply a measure of cash income *after* taking government transfers into account. To eliminate official poverty, all we need do is mail enough cheques with enough money to enough people. Starting in the late 1960s, the number of cheques, the size of the cheques and the number of beneficiaries all began to increase. Even if we ignore increased in-kind expenditures such as housing, food stamps and medical care (which are not included in this definition), and discount administrative costs and the effects of inflation, the federal government increased its real cash-benefit payments for income maintenance programmes by more than two-thirds during the 1970s.

Furthermore, the anti-poverty programmes of the 1970s had a much smaller target population than those of earlier, smaller budgets. In 1950 there were an estimated forty-six million people living beneath the poverty line (as it was subsequently defined); in 1960 there were 40 million, and in 1970 only 25 million. Given these conditions – more money and fewer people – progress begun during the 1950s and 1960s should have accelerated in the 1970s instead of slowing, stopping and then reversing.

Net Poverty

The official poverty statistic is based only on cash income. In-kind assistance – food programmes, housing, medical care – is not included. Yet this assistance has been the fastest-growing component of the social welfare budget, rising from $2.2 billion in 1965 to $72.5 billion in 1980. If the dollar value of these benefits is computed and added to cash income, this new measure may be called *net poverty*: the percentage of the population remaining beneath the poverty level after all resources – cash and in-kind, earned and unearned – are taken into account.[2]

In 1950, in-kind transfers were quite small, so the percentage of official poor (30 per cent) was nearly identical to the percentage of net poor. This situation continued into the early 1960s as net poverty decreased at roughly the same rate as official poverty. By 1968, the gap between official poverty (12.8 per cent) and net poverty (10.1 per cent) was quite small.

Unlike changes in official poverty, however, large decreases in net poverty continued into the early 1970s. Then, from 1972 until 1980, the trendline flattened, just as that for official poverty had a few years earlier. In 1980, net poverty stood at 6.1 per cent of the population, compared with 6.2 per cent in 1972, despite the fact that expenditures on in-kind assistance had tripled (in constant dollars) during the 1970s.

The concept of net poverty is ambiguous. Taken by itself, 6.1 per cent represents a near victory over poverty; it is a very small proportion of the population. But a citizen who lives in a black or Hispanic ghetto, for example, may be forgiven for arguing that poverty has not come within 6.1 percentage points of vanishing. We must consider what it really means to live at or near the poverty level through in-kind support.

It means, to begin with, living in housing projects or other subsidized housing. Given their cost, most of these units ought to provide decent, comfortable housing, but in practice public housing is among the most vandalized, crime-ridden and least livable housing in the country. It means relying on food stamps. In theory, food stamps can purchase the foods necessary for a nutritious diet, but in practice they can be misused in other ways. It also means paying for medical care through Medicaid or Medicare, which have concrete value only if the recipient is sick.

In short, having the resources for a life that meets basic standards of decency is not the same as actually living such an existence. Whether this is the fault of the welfare system or the recipient is not at issue; it is simply a fact that must be kept in mind when interpreting the small, encouraging figure of 6.1 per cent.

But the economic point remains: as of 1980, the many overlapping cash and in-kind benefit programmes made it possible for almost anyone to place themselves above the official poverty level. If the ultimate criterion of social welfare policy is eliminating net poverty, the War on Poverty has very nearly been won.

Latent Poverty

Of course, eliminating net poverty is not the ultimate criterion. Lyndon Johnson undertook the War on Poverty to end the dole, to enable people to maintain a decent standard of living by their own efforts. As he signed the initial anti-poverty bill he sounded the theme that formed the basis of the consensus for the Great Society:

> We are not content to accept endless growth of relief or welfare rolls. We want to offer the forgotten fifth of our population opportunity and not doles.... The days of the dole in our country are numbered.[3]

Johnson was articulating a deeply shared understanding among Americans as to how the welfare system is supposed to work – 'a hand, not a handout' was the slogan. Throughout American history, the economic independence of the individual and the family has been the chief distinguishing characteristic of good citizenship.

To measure progress along these lines we must calculate yet a third statistic. The poverty statistic with which I began, the one used by the government in its analyses, is cash income *after* the cash transfers from the government have been counted. Then I added the value of the non-cash, in-kind transfers in order to measure net poverty. Now I must ask: what is the number of poor before the cash and in-kind transfers are taken into account? How many people *would be* poor if it were not for government help? These may be called the *latent poor*. For practical purposes, they are the dependent population, those who were to be made independent as we eliminated the dole.

Latent poverty decreased during the 1950s. We do not know the precise level of decline, because 1965 is the first year for which the number of latent poor [was] calculated.[4] But we do know that the number of latent poor (pre-transfer poor) can be no smaller than the number of post-transfer poor; therefore, since the number of post-transfer poor stood at 30 per cent of the population in 1950, the percentage of latent poor had to have been somewhat larger (a conservative estimate is 32 per cent). As of 1965, the latent poor were 21 per cent of the population – a drop of about one-third. Put another way, dependency decreased during the years 1950–65. Increasing numbers of people were able to make a living that put them above the poverty level and progress was being made on the long-range goal of eliminating the dole.

The proportion of latent poor continued to drop through 1968, when the percentage was calculated at 18.2, but this [. . .] proved to be the limit of our success in the war against economic dependence. At some point during 1968–9, progress stopped; the percentage of latent poor then started to grow. It was 19 per cent by 1972, 21 per cent by 1976, and 22 per cent by 1980.[5] Once again, as in the case of official poverty, the shift in the trendline coincided with the advent of the programmes that were to eliminate poverty.

Again, how could it be that progress against official poverty and net poverty slowed or stopped when so much more money was being spent for cash and in-kind transfers? The data on latent poverty provide one of the most important answers: because latent poverty was increasing, it took more and more money in transfers just to keep the percentage of post-transfer poor stable. The social welfare system fell into the classic trap of having to run faster and faster to stay in the same place. The extremely large increases in social welfare spending during the 1970s were papering over the increase in latent poverty.

The three measures of poverty – official poverty, net poverty and latent poverty – reveal a pattern from 1950 to 1980 that has important implications for the American welfare state. For example, it explains a major element in the budget crisis. As of 1980, roughly the same proportion of people remained above the poverty line through their own earned incomes as did in the early 1960s. But in the early 1960s, our legislated spending obligations to those who earned less than that amount were comparatively small. Whether or not one approves of the spending obligations taken on since then, they cannot be sustained indefinitely in the face of increasing latent poverty. Latent poverty must be turned around, or the obligations must be slashed, or both.

Rising Tide, Sinking Ships

The poverty trendlines [...] are not widely publicized. Because it has not been recognized that the implementation of the Great Society reforms coincided with an end to progress in reducing poverty, there has been no debate over why this should be the case.

The best place to begin the debate is to examine the common view that the bright hopes of the 1960s dimmed in the 1970s due to a slowdown in the economy. According to this view, inflation and dislocations brought on by the Vietnam War, along with the revolution in energy prices, made the economy go sour. As the expansionist environment of the 1960s vanished, strategies and programmes of the War on Poverty had to be put aside. It is good that the entitlements and income transfer programmes were in place, runs this line of argument, or else the troubles in the economy would have been even more devastating on the poor.

What, if anything, do the data suggest about the merits of this economic explanation? As in the discussion of poverty, I must start with the simplest, most widely used measure of the state of the economy, growth in the GNP, and examine its relation to changes in the number of people living in poverty. The answer – perhaps surprisingly to those who have ridiculed 'trickle-down' as a way to help the poor – is that changes in GNP have a very strong inverse relation to changes in poverty. As GNP increases, poverty decreases. (The simple correlation coefficient for the period 1950–80 is –.69[6].) The effects of economic growth did indeed trickle down to the lowest economic levels of the society. Economic growth during the 1950s and 1960s was strong, during the 1970s it was weak – and progress in reducing poverty ceased.

So it can be said that the fortunes of the economy explain recent trends in poverty. But the flip side of this finding is that social welfare expenditures did *not* have an effect on poverty. *Once the effects of GNP are taken into account, increases in social welfare spending do not account for reductions in poverty [since the 1950s].* The same analysis that supports the economic explanation for the failure in the 1970s gives scant support to remedies that would boost social welfare spending [...].

Conservatives generally recognize the role of economic growth in reducing poverty, but some feel this is not a sufficient explanation for the failures of the 1970s. It is not just that the social welfare reforms were ineffective in reducing poverty, they argue, but that the reforms actually made matters worse by emasculating the work ethic and creating 'work disincentives'. As people became less inclined to take low-paying jobs, hold onto them, and use them to get out of poverty, they became dependent on government assistance. The academic treatment of poverty has generally dismissed this conservative explanation out of hand. It has understandably been mistaken for curmudgeonly, mean-spirited and occasionally racist rhetoric. But the trendline for latent poverty – the key indicator of how people are doing without government help – offers a solid reason for concluding that the Great Society reforms exacerbated many of the conditions they sought to alleviate.

It is important to emphasize that the trend in latent poverty did not reverse direction when the economy went bad; it did not even wait until the official poverty and net poverty figures stabilized. Latent poverty started to increase while the other two measures of poverty were still going down. Most strikingly, progress on latent poverty stopped in 1968 while the economy was operating at full capacity (unemployment stood at 3.5 per cent in 1968–9, the lowest rate since the Korean War).

Welfare and Labour-Force Participation

The second half of the 1960s was a watershed in other ways as well. A number of social indicators began showing strange and unanticipated shifts during those years, and the onset of these changes had no discernible relation to the health of the economy. Together, the evidence is sufficiently provocative to make the conservative interpretation worth looking into.

One such indicator is *participation in the labour force*. By definition, participation in the civilian labour force means either being employed or intending to work, given the opportunity. Among the poor, participation in the labour force 'should' be very high, approaching 100 per cent, for able-bodied adults without child-care responsibilities. Conservatives argue that such participation has dropped because welfare benefits have become more extensive and more easily available. The statistics on labour-force participation – a standard measure calculated by the Bureau of Labor Statistics – are readily available, and they conform quite well to conservative expectations.

Consider the record of two populations of immediate comparative interest: black males, who are disproportionately poor relative to the entire population, and white males, who are disproportionately well off. In 1948 (comparable data for 1950 are not available), the participation rate for both groups was 87 per cent. This equivalence – one of the very few social or economic measures on which black males could claim parity with whites in the 1950s – continued throughout the decade and into the early 1960s. As late as 1965, only a percentage point separated the two groups. But by 1968, a gap of 3.4 percentage points in participation had opened up between black males and white males. By 1972, the gap was 5.9 percentage points. In 1980, 70.5 per cent of black males participated in the labour force compared with 78.6 of white males; the gap had grown to

8.1 percentage points. To put it another way, during the period 1954–67, 1.4 black males dropped out of the labour force for every white male who dropped out; from 1968 to 1980, 3.6 black males dropped out for every white male who did.

The abrupt drop in the labour-force participation of black males cannot easily be linked to events in the economy at large. One of the most commonly cited popular explanations of why poor people drop out of the labour force is that they become discouraged – there are no jobs, so people quit looking. But the gap first opened up during the boom years of 1966–8, when unemployment was at a historic low. The 'discouraged worker' argument cannot be used to explain the drop-out rate during this period. Nor can the opposite argument be substituted: black males did not stop dropping out when the Vietnam boom cooled and unemployment rose. Whether unemployment was high or low, until 1967 black males behaved the same as whites; after 1967 they did not.

One may ask whether this is a racial phenomenon; it is nothing of the kind. Using the 1970 census data, participation for 1970 may be broken down by both race and economic status, and doing so reveals that the apparent racial difference is artificial. For males at comparable income levels, labour-force participation among black males was *higher* than among white males. The explanation of the gap is not race, but income. Starting in 1966, low-income males – white or black – started dropping out of the labour force. The only reason it looks as though blacks were dropping out at higher rates is that blacks are disproportionately poor. If trendlines are examined showing participation rates by income rather than race, the 1970 census data strongly suggest that middle- and upper-income males participated in the labour force at virtually unchanged rates since the 1950s, while the participation rate for low-income males decreased slowly until 1966, and plummeted thereafter.

This phenomenon needs explanation, for it was a fundamental change in economic behaviour – participation in the labour market itself. Once explanations based on unemployment fail, and once the racial discrepancy is shown to be artificial, the conservative hypothesis has considerable force. Without a doubt, *something* happened in the mid-1960s that changed the incentives for low-income workers to stay in the job market. The Great Society reforms constitute the biggest, most visible, most plausible candidate.

Welfare and Family Breakup (Revisited)

A second social indicator which links increases in latent poverty to the Great Society reforms is the decline in the intact husband–wife family unit, especially among blacks.

A racial difference in family composition has existed since statistics have been kept, but by the middle of this century the proportions for whites and blacks, while different, were stable. As of 1950, 88 per cent of white families consisted of husband–wife households, compared with 78 per cent of black families. Both figures had remained essentially unchanged since before the Second World War (the figures for 1940 were 86 and 77 per cent, respectively). In the early 1950s, the black proportion dipped slightly, then remained between 72 and 75 per cent until 1965. The figures for white families stayed in the 88 to 89 per cent range between 1958 and 1965, never varying by more than two-tenths of a percentage point from year to year.

The years 1966 and 1967 saw successive drops in the percentage of black husband–wife households, even though it remained in the 72–5 per cent range. Then, in a single year (1968), the percentage dropped to 69, the beginning of a steep slide that has not yet been arrested. By the end of 1980, the proportion of black husband–wife families had dropped to 54 per cent – a drop of 19 percentage points since 1965. The figure for whites dropped by four percentage points in the same period, from 89 to 85 per cent.

From a demographic perspective, a change of this magnitude is extra-ordinary, nearly unprecedented in the absence of war or some other profound social upheaval. Much is made of the social changes that swept America during the 1960s and 1970s, and discussions of the change in black family composition have discounted the phenomenon as a slightly exaggerated manifestation of this broader social transformation. But the data do not permit such an easy dismissal. In the rest of society the changes in family composition were comparatively modest.

As in the case of labour-force participation, we are witnessing a confusion between race and income, though not as severe. When husband–wife families are examined on the basis of income (using the 1970 census), the percentage of husband–wife families among blacks above the poverty level is found to be 82 per cent, very close to the overall rate for whites. This indicates that data based on income may be expected to show that the precipitous drop in intact families is concentrated among the low-income population, not exclusively (perhaps not even disproportionately) among blacks.

Why did low-income families start to disintegrate in the mid-1960s while higher-income families did not? As in the case of participation in the labour force, there is no obvious alternative to the conservatives' hypothesis: namely, during precisely this period, fundamental changes occurred in the philosophy, administration and magnitude of social welfare programmes for low-income families, and these changes altered – both directly and indirectly – the social risks and rewards, and the financial costs and benefits, of maintaining a husband–wife family. It should surprise no one that behaviour changed accordingly.

This hypothesis is not 'simplistic', as has been charged. It is plausible that the forces which changed welfare policy could have affected family composition even if welfare policy had not been changed. Those forces were surely various and complex. Still, these forces are not enough to explain the extraordinary change in family composition. If in the early 1960s one had foreseen the coming decade of sweeping civil rights legislation, an upsurge in black identity and pride, and a booming economy in which blacks had more opportunities than ever before, one would not have predicted massive family breakup as a result. The revolutionary change in black family composition went *against* the grain of many contemporaneous forces. Casual assertions that 'it was part of the times' are inadequate.

A Pyrrhic Victory?

The effect of the decline in labour-force participation, and of the breakup of the husband–wife family, were tragic and severe. In the case of the labour market, the nature of the effect is obvious: when low-income males drop out of the labour force and low-income females do not enter it, the size of the latent poor population will grow. This alone could explain why the proportion of latent poor increased even as the proportions of official poor and net poor were still declining.

The effects of family breakup are less obvious, but no less noteworthy. An analysis by the Bureau of the Census indicates that changes in family composition accounted for two million additional poor families in the 1970s.[7] For example, the analysis shows that if black family composition had remained the same as in 1971, the poverty rate for black families would have been 20 per cent in 1980 instead of 29 per cent. Other findings all lead to the same conclusion: the changes in family composition that started in the mid-1960s have raised poverty significantly above the levels that 'would have' prevailed otherwise. The Bureau's analysis actually *understates* the overall effect of the change in family composition on poverty – by 1971, the baseline for the analysis, much of the deterioration had already occurred.

These are some of the reasons behind the paradox of our failure to make progress against poverty in the 1970s despite the enormous increases in the amount of money that the government has spent to do so. There are other reasons as well – the large proportion of the social welfare budget spent on people above the poverty level being perhaps the most notable – but the preceding few will serve to convey a point that is too often missed in the debates over budget cuts in social welfare programmes. It is genuinely an open issue – intellectually as well as politically – whether we should be talking about spending cuts, or whether we should be considering an overhaul of the entire welfare system as conceived in the Great Society. If the War on Poverty is construed as having begun in 1950 instead of 1964, it may fairly be said that we were winning the war until Lyndon Johnson decided to wage it.

Notes

From *The Public Interest*, 69, 1982, pp. 4–16.
1   Data for 1959–79 are taken from the figures published annually in the *Statistical Abstract of the United States*. Figures for 1949–58 are taken from 'Economic Report to the President: Combating Poverty in a Prosperous Economy', January 1969, reprinted in US Department of Health, Education and Welfare, *The Measure of Poverty*, ed. M. Orshansky, Technical Paper I, vol. 1 [n.d.], p. 349, chart 10. The percentage for 1980 was obtained directly from the Poverty Statistics Section of the Bureau of the Census.
2   The figures are taken from Timothy M. Smeeding, *Measuring the Economic Welfare of Low-Income Households and the Antipoverty Effectiveness of Cash and Noncash Transfer Programs*, PhD diss., Department of Economics, University of Wisconsin-Madison, 1975; Smeeding, 'The Antipoverty Effectiveness of In-Kind Transfers', *Journal of Human Resources*, 12, 1977, pp. 360–78; and Smeeding, 'The Anti-poverty Effect of In-Kind Transfers: A 'Good Idea Gone Too Far?', *Policy Studies Journal*, 10, 3, 1982 pp. 499–522.
3   Quoted in the *New York Times*, 21 August 1964, p. 1.
4   The figures for 1965–78 are taken from Sheldon Danziger and Robert Plotnick, 'The War on Income Poverty: Achievements and Failures', in *Welfare Reform in America*, ed. P. Sommers, Hingham, MA, Martinus Nijhoff, 1982, table 3.1, p. 40.
5   It should be noted that the measure of latent poverty excludes social security income. Since families headed by persons over the age of sixty-five make up nearly half of those in latent poverty, the percentages reported here may somewhat exaggerate the extent of the problem among those able to work. (Unfortunately, no figures on this point prior to 1976 have been published.) But even if it were possible to include social security – or exclude the elderly – in calculations over this period, this adjustment would not affect the steep *rise* in latent poverty we have observed. [. . .]
6   The variables are the first difference in real GNP per household and the first difference in percentage of population under the poverty line using the official measure of poverty.
7   Gordon Green and Edward Welniak, 'Measuring the Effects of Changing Family Composition during the 1970s on Black–White Differences in Income', unpublished manuscript, Bureau of the Census, 1982.

The New Politics of the New Poverty

Lawrence M. Mead

The poverty of today's underclass differs appreciably from poverty in the past: underclass poverty stems less from the absence of opportunity than from the inability or reluctance to take advantage of opportunity. The plight of the underclass suggests that the competence of many of the poor – their capacity to look after and take care of themselves – can no longer be taken for granted as it could in the past.

The changing nature of poverty has also ushered in a fundamental change in our politics, which formerly focused on class but now emphasizes conduct. Prior to the 1960s, in what I call the era of progressive politics, the overriding issue was how to help ordinary working Americans advance economically. The solutions of liberals and conservatives differed greatly, but both groups agreed that available opportunities would be seized by the poor. They disagreed in locating the barrier to opportunity: liberals blamed the unregulated economy, and conservatives blamed the government. As a result, liberals favoured greater government intervention, while conservatives hoped to reduce it. At issue were class inequalities and the need for economic redistribution: was the inequality meted out by the marketplace acceptable? How desirable were regulations of wages, hours and working conditions, along with the creation of social-insurance programmes to benefit workers and their families?

Anti-poverty strategy and politics differ greatly today, because poverty is rarely found among workers but is common among non-workers. In the new era, characterized by what I call dependency politics, the leading issue is how to handle the disorders of inner-city non-workers: conservatives usually want to enforce civilities, which liberals resist doing. For the most part, we spend less time debating whether the income of the working poor should be larger than we do discussing whether and how we can transform poor non-workers into workers.

Recent disagreements over tax hikes and budget cuts suggest that redistributive conflicts over the economy remain very much with us; economic inequality has increased, and Kevin Phillips's prediction of heightened conflict between rich and poor received much attention [in 1990]. Nevertheless, in the absence of economic collapse serious class conflict is unlikely. The politics of conduct, which focuses on dependency and disorder, is simply more salient than the politics of class. The problems of rising crime, welfarism, homelessness and declining schools (and the tax increases imposed to pay for them) are what chiefly concern most Americans; they worry far less about the income gap separating them from their employers. Most Americans doubt government's ability to solve the new social problems that confront us. Unless government better responds to them, it will receive no new mandate to tackle the older problem of unequal fortunes.

The public's focus on dependency and disorder has obviously damaged the American left, which is more comfortable dealing with issues of economic redistribution. The public's conservatism on social (as opposed to economic) issues largely explains why Republicans have controlled the White House and the national agenda for most of a generation. Democrats in presidential politics have paid a high price for their perceived softness on the question of 'values'. In the 1988 election, Michael Dukakis proposed new benefit programmes of the kind that used to win elections for Democrats. The Bush campaign easily defeated him by speaking of crime and Willie Horton.

But despite its electoral advantages, the anti-government right – like the redistributionist left – is uncomfortable with dependency politics. When the poor behave badly, bigger government becomes indefensible, because many of its beneficiaries are 'undeserving'. But smaller government is also questionable, because many believe that the poor could not cope without the many benefits and services that they receive. Distrust of the dysfunctional poor defeated the most ambitious plans to expand government during the Great Society. But concern for these same poor helps explain why Ronald Reagan was unable significantly to reduce the size of domestic government.

Working Class to Underclass

This political change was brought about by the appearance of an intractable type of poverty in American cities in the 1960s and early 1970s. Ironically, the same era witnessed the last great victories of old-style progressive politics. The victories were achieved by the civil-rights and feminist movements, which were largely composed of working people seeking expanded economic opportunities. Their demands, like those made in earlier decades by distressed farmers and organized labour, sought to increase the income of workers.

But in the same era, welfare rolls more than doubled, crime soared and riots broke out in the ghettos of major cities. These developments raised issues of order and propriety much more sharply than the earlier movements. By the end of the 1960s, the closely linked problems of poverty, welfare and the inner city dominated the domestic agenda. Since then, the claims of broader groups, including minorities and women, have not gone unnoticed, but they no longer command centre stage. Social-reform efforts now focus on welfare, education and criminal justice, not the economy. Even the recessions of the 1970s and early 1980s, the most serious since the Depression, failed to inspire major new efforts to help workers. Issues of dependency and dysfunction, not opportunity, now preoccupy us.

Some might say that dependency politics is not new, in that controversies about the 'undeserving' poor, and what to do about them, have often marked American history. But if the themes of dependency politics are not new, its prominence as 'welfare politics' before 1960 was largely a local affair. At the national level, the arena was always dominated by groups that were not dependent and were usually employed. Only in the recent era have dependent, mostly non-working groups captured the nation's political attention.

The employment issue, like no other, marks the boundary between the old politics and the new. The movements of the progressive era had weight above all because their members worked, or at least had a job history. The aggrieved might have been destitute, but they could make claims on the basis of desert. The recent poor seldom can do this. They are controversial, above all, because they usually do not work. Only 40 per cent of poor adults had any earnings at all in 1987, and only 9 per cent worked full-time year-round. That initially was why most of them were poor. Work effort among the poor has also dropped sharply. Only 47 per cent of the heads of poor families worked at all in 1987, down from 68 per cent in 1959.

Of course, only about half the poverty population is working-aged, and only about half remains in poverty for more than two years. The underclass, consisting of the poor with the most severe behavioural problems, is quite small: it includes no more than eight million people by various estimates. Yet persistent poverty is highly visible in cities, and it is central to all major urban problems – not only welfare, crime and homelessness, but troubled schools and a decaying economic base. So it gets more policy-making attention than the affairs of the vastly larger working and middle classes.

This new poverty created a new politics because the old politics found no answer to it. Neither of the traditional, competing progressive-era remedies – increasing or decreasing government intervention in the economy – seems an appropriate response to the passive poverty of the inner city. It is true that analysts wedded to progressive-era assumptions – whether liberal or conservative – continue to try to trace passive poverty to some social barrier that must be eliminated: liberals say that poor adults cannot earn enough to make work worthwhile, cannot find jobs or child care, or are barred from jobs by racial bias; conservatives claim that welfare 'pays' dependents not to marry or work. But the hard evidence mostly undercuts these explanations. Liberal claims notwithstanding, jobs usually are available to the unskilled; taking these jobs would generally move families in which both parents worked above the poverty line. The flood of new immigrants entering the job market is one clear sign that opportunity still exists. Working mothers can usually arrange child care informally and cheaply, and discrimination in any overt form has disappeared. But conservative claims notwithstanding, welfare disincentives are also too weak to explain the collapse of the family or the very low work levels typically found in the inner city today.

I do not mean that barriers are totally absent. Differences of opportunity certainly exist in America. Better-educated people, for example, are more likely to succeed. [Since the 1970s] the income disparity between low-skilled and high-skilled workers has increased. The progressive-era debate over whether and how to narrow these differences in wages remains alive.

Unequal opportunities, however, chiefly explain why some workers earn more than others. They usually do not explain the failure of non-workers to work steadily *at all*, which is in turn the cause of most poverty and dependency among working-aged people. Most Americans have responded to stagnant wages by working *more*; only the poor have worked less. Most Americans refuse to believe that society's failure to expand opportunity causes the poverty of non-workers who do not take and hold available jobs.

To explain most entrenched poverty, we must go back to what used to be called the 'culture of poverty'. Non-working adults apparently want to work, but they seldom do so consistently – some because the pay offered is unacceptable, others because they feel overwhelmed by the practical difficulties of employment. These reactions run strongest in the inner city, because of its isolation from workaday society, and among racial minorities who have traditionally faced discrimination. The greatest cause of today's poverty may simply be that the attempts [...] to equalize opportunity have failed to persuade many blacks and Hispanics that it is worth working.

But if non-work is rooted mostly in the demoralization of the poor, rather than impersonal impediments, then traditional reformism holds no answer for it. Passive poverty has defeated, in turn, the strategies of both larger and smaller governments. The Great Society invented wave after wave of new anti-poverty programmes, only to see the poverty level stagnate and welfare rise. The Reagan administration cut or curbed the growth of these programmes to reinvigorate the economy. But even the longest boom in American history could not reduce poverty below 13 per cent, because the poor are now substantially detached from the economy. Each in its own way, these strategies provided new chances to poor adults, but neither directly addressed the puzzling reluctance of the poor to do more to help themselves.

As a result, social policy has been driven away from structural reforms and towards paternalism. The drift is toward policies that address motivation by seeking to direct the lives of those dependent on government. Public institutions are taking over tutelary functions from weakened families. Social-service agencies are raising children, and schools are organizing the lives of students before and after class as well as during it. Homeless shelters and the criminal-justice system are managing the disordered lives of single men. Above all, recent welfare legislation requires rising numbers of employable recipients to participate in job placement or training on pain of cuts in their grants. Such measures violate the traditional prescriptions of liberals, who want benefits given without conditions, but also those of conservatives, who would prefer to see discipline applied by the private rather than the public sector. But they seem required by the changing nature of the social problem.

These trends are most advanced in the US, but they are appearing in Europe as well. An underclass, largely non-white, has grown up in British cities, while throughout Europe controversy rages over whether immigrants from the Third World are corrupting traditional mores. These racial and ethnic divisions now arouse more passion than the traditional conflicts of labour and business. The behaviour of 'outsiders' is far more controversial than economic claims. Crime, dependency and a failure to learn the national language are at issue, not working-class demands for higher wages and benefits. The West as a whole seems destined for a politics of conduct rather than class.

The New Agenda

Dependency politics and progressive-era politics differ substantially in content, even though there is much overlap in practice. I exaggerate the contrasts here for emphasis:

The old issues were economic; the new ones are social. Progressive-era politics debated the proper organization of society, especially the issue of government control of the economy. Liberals supported higher and more progressive taxation; public regulation of industries; union rights; the minimum wage and other protections for workers; pension, health and unemployment benefits: [...] [The right sought to] weaken or undo all these steps in the belief that only a revivified free market could really generate 'good jobs at good wages'.

In dependency politics, in contrast, the question is how to deal with the problems of basic functioning among the seriously poor. The social, more than the economic, structure of society is at issue. The focus is on troubled individuals or ethnic groups rather than industry, agriculture, or the relations of labour and management. Social problems are no longer seen to stem directly from injustice, nor are they obviously reformable. So social policy must focus on motivation and order rather than opportunity or equality.

Affluence helped produce this shift. Before the 1960s, working-class incomes were still low enough that many people were poor, even though they worked normal hours. That is much less common today, because the poverty line is constant in real terms while real wages have risen. The poor, who used to work more than the better-off, now commonly work less. Inevitably, the focus of the social agenda has shifted from the low wages that used to impoverish workers to the dysfunctions that keep the non-working poor out of the labour force.

In progressive-era politics the issue was government control of the economy; in dependency politics it is government supervision of behaviour. Progressive-era politicians disputed how far government should regulate the free market in the collective interest, how much it should spend on benefit programmes such as Social Security.

In dependency politics, however, the chief question is how far government should control the lives of dysfunctional people in their own interests. Do we require that people stay in school, obey the law, avoid drugs, and so on? Above all, do we require adults to work or prepare for work as a condition of receiving welfare? Proposals to do these things do not much change what government does for people. Rather, they demand that dependants do more for themselves in return.

Formerly it was local authorities who grappled with maintaining social order, while Washington managed the economy. But order issues have become federal, because national programmes are involved in all the key areas – welfare, education and criminal justice. It is now the main domestic challenge of presidents, as of mayors, to reduce crime and dependency and to raise standards in the schools. Presidents Nixon, Carter and Reagan all tried to reform welfare, and George Bush aspired to be an 'education president'.

The old issues concerned adults; the new issues concern children and youth. Progressive-era political claims were on behalf of adults, especially workers. The question was how to reorganize government or the economy so that adults could have influence and opportunity. In the dependency era, however, these issues are less salient than people's problems on the road to adulthood – illegitimacy, educational failure and crime. So dependency politics focuses heavily on the formative years. Reformism aims to improve family, neighbourhood and schools rather than the political or economic structure.

Daniel Patrick Moynihan says that social policy has entered a 'post-industrial' age. The main challenge is no longer to expand economic opportunity but to overcome social weaknesses that stem from the 'post-marital' family and the inability of many people to get through school. The inequalities that stem from the workplace are now trivial in comparison to those stemming from family structure. What matters for success is less whether your father was rich or poor than whether you knew your father at all.

A focus on youth is inevitable once the leading social problem changes from the poverty of workers to dysfunctional poverty. For if the source of poverty is behaviour rather than lack of opportunity, remedies must focus on youth, the stage of life at which behaviour is most malleable. Conversely, reform for adults must be structural because it must take personality largely as given.

The pressures in progressive-era politics arise from self-seeking behaviour; in dependency politics, they arise from passivity. Progressive-era politics debates the freedom that America allows people to make money and get ahead on their own. To conservatives, this prerogative is a right that government may not limit. To the left, it is a licence that government must restrain in the name of a broader social interest.

The poor and dependent, however, are not exploitative but inert. They are controversial mostly because they do so little to help themselves, not because they hurt others in the pursuit of advantage. Even when violent, they are unable to exert themselves effectively. They are not aggressive so much as *passive* aggressive. So in dependency politics, the issue is whether poor people should have to do more to help themselves. The question is how passive you can be and still be a citizen in full standing.

Formerly, the right defended property and the established order against public controls. Now it is the left that defends the status quo, by justifying passivity among the needy, while the right demands greater activity. Recent measures such as workfare or reformed schools are attempts to stimulate the poor, not to curb the rich. The point is to set a floor under self-advancement, not a ceiling above it. The hope is to make the poor more effectively self-seeking than they are.

Claims in progressive-era politics derived from strength; those in dependency politics arise from weakness. The chief players in the progressive era were unions, farmers, businesses and other economic interests that demanded some benefit or protection from government on a basis of desert. They were economically disadvantaged, but their demands were also made from a position of strength, because they had economic and political resources of their own. They could use these resources to get attention from politicians, but they could also survive on their own if rebuffed.

In dependency politics, the claimants usually have no such strength, as they lack any regular position in the economy. They are simply needy. Their main claim is precisely their vulnerability. It is not their own power that gets attention, but politicians' fear of a backlash from the better-off if the needy are left unprotected. Economic groups state their claims by speaking of troubled finances. The very poor state theirs by a disassembly of the personality – by failing to function in embarrassing ways that force society to take responsibility for them.

In dependency politics, the poor claim a right to support based on the injuries of the past, not on anything that they contribute now. Wounds are an asset today, much as a pay cheque was in progressive-era politics. One claims to be a victim, not a worker. The non-white poor, particularly, appeal to historic injustices. Even some policies that aid better-functioning minorities, such as affirmative action, require their beneficiaries to adopt the identity of victimhood to some extent – to exploit an appeal, as Shelby Steele says, based on 'suffering' rather than 'achievements'.

Poverty shifts the agenda from equality to citizenship. The question is no longer what the worst-off members of the community should receive. Now the question is who should be considered a bona fide member of the community in the first place. Who has the moral standing to make the demands for economic redress typically made in the progressive era? When dependency comes to dominate politics, class-oriented issues of equality for workers inevitably move off the agenda, while issues of identity and belonging replace them.

In Europe as well as the US, dependency concerns replaced progressive ones as motives for the reconsideration of the welfare state that began in the 1970s and 1980s. At first, the issues were economic, the fear that excessive spending on income and health programmes was overburdening the economy. Cuts were made to promote economic growth, the step conservatives always recommend in progressive-era politics. [In the 1990s], however, the greater concern has been declining social cohesion, as evidenced by rises in crime, single parenthood and chronic unemployment. The response, in Britain and Sweden as in the US, has been new steps to enforce child support and work effort among the dependent. The shift from the older, redistributive agenda to these new, more behavioural issues ushers in a new political age.

[...]

The Western Tradition

Today's efforts to respond to dependency face serious challenges. They may well not allay our social problems as fully as progressive policies resolved yesterday's economic disputes. The newer, paternalistic social programmes probably will do more to reduce poverty than the less demanding policies of the past: more authoritative schools are producing some results, and workfare programmes have been able to increase work effort (though they have not yet reduced dependency). But it is doubtful that even these programmes can do more than contain the social problem.

Even if they are effective, paternalistic measures raise serious political objections. The new structures reduce disorder, but at a cost to the autonomy of clients. This is particularly true if, as is likely, the chronic poor require direction on an on-going basis, not just temporarily. That is why, even now, government prefers to spend money on the dependent rather than try to tell them how to live. Benefits lack the power of public authority to change behaviour, but they do not violate our notions of a free society.

A more serious problem stems from our political traditions. Anti-dependency policies – and disputes about them – find no basis in the Western political tradition, which assumes that the individuals who compose society are competent to advance their own interests, if not society's. The traditional Western assumption is that politics arises from conflicting interests, as individuals and groups seek economic advantage. Government's task is to resolve these disputes in the general interest. It does not animate society, but rather responds to energy coming from below.

Historically, Western politics has been class-oriented: aristocratic elites, then bourgeois elements, then workers without property have advanced their own conceptions of how government and the economy should be organized. The dominant principles have become more democratic, then more collectivist, as government came to represent the mass of the populace and then to serve its needs. The contending visions may seem radically opposed, but from today's perspective they were remarkably alike: all assumed a working population, competent to advance its own interests.

This tradition is inapplicable to the problems posed by today's dysfunctional poor. But policy makers in [the US] and Europe are prone to respond to these problems by replaying the old scenarios. Today's liberals see history as a grand progression in which the rights of ordinary people have been expanded: first civil liberties, then representative government, then protections against the insecurities of capitalism were attained. Faced with passive poverty, the left can imagine no response other than providing some further entitlement, for example government jobs. The idea that dependants should have to function better seems like an attempt to deny benefits, and is thus anathema.

Anti-government conservatives, for their part, blame poverty on an excess of government, just as the left blames it on the lack of government intervention. They insist that cuts in spending and taxes will somehow liberate the energy of the poor, as they do that of entrepreneurs. The idea that competence is a prior and different problem, requiring perhaps more government rather than less, is unthinkable.

These liberal and conservative responses are doomed to fail. If the seriously poor had the initiative to respond to new opportunities, they would not be poor for very long in the first place. The Great Society and the Reagan era both failed to solve poverty, because each in a different way offered new chances to the poor without confronting the motivation problem. Neither could seriously address competence, because that problem fell outside the Western assumptions underlying their ideas of social reform.

But despite these conceptual failures, government has begun to do something about poverty: a new, paternalistic regime for the poor is emerging. Ronald Reagan's greatest domestic legacy, despite his tax cuts, was not to reduce government; it was to start changing welfare into workfare. But the new regime is accepted grudgingly, if at all. Politicians argue heatedly about the issues of responsibility and competence that it raises, but they seldom do so honestly. They mention the 'underclass' and the need for discipline, but they still talk as if they were offering the poor only 'freedom' or 'opportunity'.

We need a new political language that considers more candidly the questions of human nature that now underlie politics. The political contestants need to defend their positions on a philosophic level, rather than hide behind outmoded theories. Liberals need to show why poor people are blameless, therefore still deserving; conservatives need to show how the poor are competent and why they need to be held accountable, in spite of dysfunction. From such premises they could then erect consistent doctrines of social policy, comparable to the competing theories of economic management that framed the leading issues in the progressive era.

If anyone is writing this theory, it is not philosophers like John Rawls and his critics (who assume a rational economic psychology and thus remain wedded to the competence assumption) but social-policy experts who grapple concretely with poverty. They know too much of the hard evidence about barriers to pretend that nothing has changed. To explain poverty and justify any policy toward it, experts need a psychological doctrine that explains how personal degradation occurs in an affluent and open society.

Differing visions of human nature are what really divide Charles Murray, William Julius Wilson, myself and others. For Murray, poor adults are short-sighted calculators who are tempted into dysfunction by the disincentives of welfare. For Wilson, they are driven into disorder by a changing economy that denies them jobs that could support a family. My own view, articulated in *Beyond Entitlement: The Social Obligations of Citizenship* [1986], is that they are depressed but dutiful, willing to observe mainstream norms like work if only government will enforce them. But none of us has defended these premises in enough depth, or linked them clearly enough to our prescriptions.

Armed with theories like this, the political process might face more squarely the issues raised by dependency politics. It is more important that the positions be candid than that they agree. Progress requires that the fears of both sides be more fully aired, not that one side wins. The debate might finally generate the consensus needed to support the new paternalistic social policy that is already emerging. There could be agreement on the basic civilities that everyone is prepared to enforce. On that basis, the nation could grapple with passive poverty more successfully.

Note

From *The Public Interest*, 103, 1991, pp. 3–20; fuller version in Lawrence M. Mead, *The New Politics of Poverty*, New York, Basic Books, 1992.

Feminism

Feminism and Social Policy

Mary McIntosh

During the 1970s, feminists developed a critique of the welfare system that was both sophisticated and damning. It began in a fragmentary way in the early seventies with specific protests about issues like the 'cohabitation rule' and the 'tax credit' proposals. There was a growing awareness that women figure prominently among the clients of social workers, the inmates of geriatric and psychiatric hospitals, the claimants of supplementary benefits – despite the fact that married and cohabiting women are not eligible for many benefits. There was resentment about the degrading way that women are treated when they need state benefits and state services.

The first responses were articulated most clearly by libertarian feminists, who could express vividly what women know of the conditions under which welfare is granted. They know the queues and the forms, the deference, the anger, the degradation, the sense of invisibility and the loss of autonomy. They see the mean, withholding face of the state and can readily take up the negative cry of 'smash the state!' But the cohabitation campaign also raised deeper issues. It was not just that the 'SS' were 'sex snoopers' who prevented women claimants from drawing their benefit if they were suspected of living with a man. They also tried to force women into prostitutional dependence on the men they slept with. This raised the whole question of women's dependence on men and the fact that women were second-class citizens. The Women's Family Allowance Campaign against the Tory government's 1972 tax-credit proposals focused on the same problems. The family allowance paid directly to a mother was preferable to the same, or even a greater, amount paid in tax credits through a father's pay packet. The model of the couple as a financial unit bore little relation to reality as many women experienced it. In the end, after we had defeated this aspect of the tax-credit scheme, the trade unions' reluctance to accept the loss of the child tax allowance that accompanied the improved child benefit only verified what we already knew: that money in a husband's pay packet was not equivalent to a direct payment to his wife.

In the context of the women's liberation movement, the developing awareness of women's relation to the welfare state was crystallized at the national conference in 1974. Elizabeth Wilson's pamphlet *Women and the Welfare State* (1974) was launched there and a new demand, for 'legal and financial independence', was adopted. The new demand, the fifth to be adopted by the movement, recognized clearly the relevance of the state in solving the problem of women's dependence upon men. The other demands (concerned with equal opportunities in jobs and training, equal pay, nurseries, abortion and contraception) all had a bearing on women's independence in their different ways. But this one, as the paper calling for it to be adopted expressed it, 'highlights the links between the state and the family, and the way in which the state systematically bolsters the dependent-woman family' (Gieve et al., 1974). It saw the relevance of state policy not merely to those categories of women who receive or are denied state benefits of various kinds – not merely to mothers and non-mothers, wives and non-wives, earners and non-earners – but to women as a whole category. For it saw how state policies play a part in constructing that category and in constructing the idea of the family in which it exists. All women suffer from the stereotype of the woman as properly dependent upon a man. But all women also suffer in quite practical terms from the fact that there are few viable alternatives to such dependence. (For an argument against this view, see Bennett et al., 1980.)

Since then, this critique of state policy has been detailed and sustained. Academic articles have been published (especially by Hilary Land, 1976, 1977), and so have pamphlets (for instance, Streather and Weir, 1974; Lister and Wilson, 1976). Many a parliamentary select committee and inter-departmental working party has been told of our views by various women's groups. Wider campaigns, like the rousing but in the end rather abortive one on wives' treatment under income tax, have been mounted. What is disappointing is how little this critique has really affected thinking among other radicals about social policy. Goodwill towards feminism expresses itself in manning the crèche, going on the abortion demo and avoiding sexist styles of behaviour. But how many critics of the DHSS review of Supplementary Benefit [in the late 1970s] – apart from women – argued against the aggregation of the income and resources of husband and wife? Yet separate treatment has been our demand ever since the first feminist critiques of the Beveridge Report in the early 1940s (see, for instance, Abbott and Bompas, 1943; Pierce, 1979).

At the same time as this awareness of how the state constructs dependent women, there was a growing awareness of women as state employees. Both the state bureaucracies and the institutions of health, education and welfare employ enormous numbers of women in their lower ranks; often their clients are women; and often they are engaged in classically 'feminine' types of work both in terms of the contents of their tasks and in terms of the social functions they fulfil. In fact, insofar as previously domestic functions like health care, child care and personal services have become socialized, the social tasks are frequently performed by women just as the private ones were. In struggles to improve social services and nurseries, and in struggles to unionize women workers and advance their position, feminist issues and the question of what women in different situations have in common were fought out time and again. 'The patter of tiny contradictions' was how Val Charlton (1974) described a child-care centre started by some women's liberation groups in London.

All of these critical approaches to social policy were the feminist version of the radical and Marxist critiques of the 1960s and 1970s. The burden of these was that the welfare state is nothing of the kind: that it is not redistributive as between the social classes, but makes the working class pay for its own social casualties, that it does not even eliminate poverty at the bottom end of the scale, that it is not the harbinger of socialist provision according to need – neither in its style nor in its effects – and that it is an instrument of bourgeois control, forcing people to work and imposing standards of morality, decency and household management. To this, feminists add that the welfare state is especially oppressive to women, in that it harnesses them into the team that pulls the whole welfare charabanc along.

What was new, though, was that there was a clear recognition at the same time that women need state provision. Faced with a choice between a chancy dependence on a man on the one hand and dependence on the state or exploitation in waged work on the other, feminists opt for the state and the wage.

Personal dependence carries with it a whole baggage of psychological dependence. Lack of autonomy, deference, the need to manipulate personal relations, all tend to stunt women's potential and make us insecure and unadventurous. Indeed the characteristics of femininity which Juliet Mitchell (1974) has explained in terms of the experience of infancy – passivity, masochism and narcissism – could equally be explained by the adult experience of dependence and the practical need to seek support. This explanation would in fact fit better the reality, which is one of public passivity, based on self-repression and often masking an underlying attitude of cynicism and rebellion, similar to that of Franz Fanon's colonized people.

With all their problems, then, the state and the employer can be fought collectively and unlike modern marriage they are not intrinsically patriarchal. And whenever feminists have formulated the demand for the socialization of housework and of personal care, it has been state provision rather than private commercial provision that they have had in mind.

Feminists in [England] have never been for very long attracted to purely anti-statist positions. Such utopian individualism (or even small-scale collectivism) is a possible dream for men who can envisage a world of self-supporting able-bodied people. But women are usually concerned with how the other three-quarters live. They have argued for new forms of interdependence based in the community and not in the family, and these necessarily involve the state at one level or another.

There have been some interesting debates in the women's movement about the development and provision of feminist services. The question has been: should we provide these ourselves or should we demand state provision and then fight about the form that provision should take? Nurseries, playgroups, health care, advice on contraception and abortion, refuges for battered women, rape crisis centres, legal and welfare rights advice – all clearly fall within the ambit of things that we expect to be provided by state agencies. Yet these are either not available or, when they are, are inadequate and unfeminist in their approach. Setting up services like this is a way both of meeting women's needs and also of developing public awareness of the effects of women's oppression, and providing a base for feminist analysis and agitation around the issue (Flaskas and Hounslow, 1980). In Australia and in the United States there has been a great proliferation of feminist health and welfare services and the results have sometimes been disappointing in that the energies of the women involved have been used up in providing a good service so that the more forward-looking political tasks have been neglected. In England, with the notable exception of the network of Women's Aid refuges for battered women, the tendency has been to set up very few feminist agencies but to concentrate on campaigning for state provision. The more developed social and health services in England have made this a more promising direction to work in. It also seems to me to be the right approach, since it can lead to more long-term and more universal provision than any voluntary efforts are likely to do. The character of such campaigns is also different and in some ways more outgoing politically. Instead of the independent and sometimes rather inward-looking group work involved in establishing and running a feminist service, there is the need to make alliances and work in the existing political arena. The struggle to develop the present services in a feminist direction involves work in the unions and professional bodies of the service workers as well as organizing among clients and users.

Making claims on the state thus involves fruitful political work and agitation at many levels and is far from being confined to the politics of Westminster. So in this respect, as in some others, women have been at the forefront of the rethinking of the rather facile radical libertarianism of the 1960s and early 1970s. (The other thing that feminists questioned was the general assumption that decriminalization, decarceration and de-insti-tutionalization were unambiguously progressive. Sometimes they have gone too far as in calling for exceptionally heavy punishments and the suspension of the usual rights of the accused in cases of rape and of violence against women, and in calling for increased state control over pornography. In some spheres we have not yet gone far enough: we should be mounting a much stronger criticism of present ideas of 'community care' and fighting for new forms of institutional care that avoid the problems earlier radicals have pointed to.)

[...] We have to develop ideas and organizations that enable us to engage with social policy as it forms. And this will mean discussing what sort of welfare state we do want, not just sniping at the existing one and waiting for The Revolution to put everything right.

However, for Marxists this cannot mean a Fabian-style formulation of gradual ameliorative goals and means. It must mean taking a very clear class position and working within the labour movement and all organizations that can take up an anti-capitalist position. It means working out what gains can be made in any given situation and what threats most need defending against, not assuming that social policy makers are people of good will who will see reason when a clear and forceful case is put to them. I suggest that at the most general level there are two key points to remember.

(1) The first is that although the dominant factor affecting state policies will always be the long-term interests of the ruling class and although the central interests of the working class and the capitalist class are antagonistic, it is not necessarily the case that their interests will be opposed on every single issue of social policy. The most fundamental reason for this is that, despite the fact that the wage relation is an antagonistic one, workers' and capitalists' interests coincide in requiring the satisfaction of the workers' basic needs, whether through the wage or by other means. The capitalist requires the reproduction of labour power; the worker requires food and clothing. Of course, they will differ widely over what sort of needs should be met and under what conditions: over what constitutes 'adequate' reproduction of labour power; and this is where struggles over social policy come in. The history of the growth of the welfare state and the growth of collective consumption (Grevet, 1976; Castells, 1978) in general in capitalist societies is thus neither a history of cherries snatched

from the greedy hands of capitalists by a militant working class, nor is it a history of a crafty capitalist plot to control and enfeeble the workers in the interests of guaranteeing the reproduction of labour power and of the relations of production. It is both. The gains and losses have to be figured partly in terms of some felicific calculus and partly in political terms: are we better placed for the next battle? Has morale improved?

(2) The second key point is that we need to keep in mind the limits that are set on social policy by the capital-labour contradiction. In particular, we need to recognize that the wage system is fundamental to capitalist production and that the primary means of the reproduction of labour power will be the wage. Social security provisions and collective consumption will be designed in such a way as to minimize their interference with the labour market and with the existence of a proletariat obliged to sell its labour power in order to survive.

This means that demands for a 'guaranteed minimum income' have no connection with social policy in capitalist society. The 'guaranteed minimum income' is a demand adopted by the Claimants' Union as a radical solution to their degrading experiences at the hands of the social security officials. They see the problems of the means test, the search for a 'liable relative', and the obligation to sign on for employment as ways in which the working class are harassed and controlled. So they demand their abolition, the right of everyone to a guaranteed income regardless of whether or not they are willing to look for waged work. As a Claimants' Union representative argued in one of the workshops at the 'Crisis in the Welfare State' conference [1980]: 'People who don't have jobs need an income as much as those who do; it is hard work just staying alive in capitalist society.' The demand is thus very different from a demand for a minimum wage coupled with improved social security benefits at the same level. It is a demand that the need to sell one's labour power in order to survive should be abolished. So it is nothing less than a demand that socialism be introduced: but a demand ostensibly made of the capitalist state and a demand that socialism should enter through the back door, the relations of distribution; rather than the front door, the relations of production. It is thus, as its proponents are well aware, an unrealizable demand under capitalism, since it negates the wage relation which lies at the heart of capitalism. Any of their supporters who join the ranks because they think they might actually gain the demand have been sadly deceived. But the existence of such demands can have the depressing effect of making all real current struggles over policy look paltry and reformist by comparison.

Feminists have been very aware of this problem in relation to the demand for 'wages for housework', rejected by the women's liberation movement in England in 1972, but still having a small, vocal following.

Effectively this is a demand that women should have a guaranteed minimum income, since the idea that there should be any check on whether they actually do any housework is rejected. It is thus a demand that all women should be lifted out of the proletariat and put on a pension. It, too, can be dispiriting if it has the effect of making current struggles over matters like invalid care allowances or the infamous 'Housewife's Non-Contributory Disability Allowance' seem trivial and reformist.

Though dependence on the wage will continue to be the primary means of support for the working class, we have seen during the twentieth century a notable narrowing of the range of people who are expected to depend upon a wage. A wage-earner is no longer expected to provide the main support for old and disabled relatives, only for his wife and children (or, more rarely, her husband and children). The welfare state has defined whole categories of people out of the labour market – the old, the young, the disabled – enabling the capitalist work process to be intensified and many welfare benefits to be offered unconditionally and apparently benevolently. But there cannot be an infinite extension of such benefits unless the working class is to be de-proletarianized altogether.

These two key points are proposed as basic considerations for the formulation of any socialist strategy for social policy in capitalist societies. But I shall illustrate their importance by looking at the problems of feminist strategy. Women have to consider whether they have gained or lost by the policies accepted by the working class in the past, and how they should relate to working-class political organization for the future. And we have to consider what relation we want women to have to wage labour. Should we become more fully proletarianized or should we seek better conditions of dependence on husbands or on state benefits?

I shall turn now to these more specific questions of feminist strategy. In some ways, the central problem is the same one that has plagued feminism ever since the achievement of the vote left the movement without a central rallying cry. The problem is whether to press for equality with men, usually in terms of legal, political and citizenship rights, or to press for greater support and respect for women in their roles as housewives and mothers: a right to an independent income and a recognition of the importance of their contribution.

The second position was that of the 'new feminists' who emerged after the First World War. So Eleanor Rathbone argued in 1925 that the point had been reached where women could say:

> At least we have done with the boring business of measuring everything women want, or that is offered to them, by men's phraseology. We can demand what we want for women, not because it is what men have got, but because it is what women need to fulfill the potentialities of their own

natures and to adjust themselves to the circumstances of their own lives (Rathbone, 1929, quoted in Lewis, 1973).

The argument against the older equalitarianism took the form of a rejection of male definitions of women's work as inferior and a plea for a new dignity and new measures of protection. In some respects it was more progressive than equalitarianism: it sought to change the world, not merely to give women access to the better places in it. But in the end it was less radical because the changes it sought were too shallow. They were designed to ease the suffering where the shoe pinches rather than build a new shoe on a better last. For modern feminists it is easy to see why Rathbone's mountainous ideal of Family Endowment brought forth the rather ridiculous mouse of Child Benefit and why women's dependence is still a key issue today. As Hilary Land put it: 'Eleanor Rathbone laid much emphasis on the unequal economic relationship between husband and wife but had far less to say about the division of responsibilities for child care and housework' (Land, 1980). A deeper analysis would have led her to see the two as inseparable within any wage-based economy. The problem as it was posed then is that of the impossibility either of the equalitarian ideal – which asks for equal treatment for unequal people – or of the 'new feminist' ideal – which asks for women to be treated as different but equal.

It is interesting to ask whether the difference between these two strategies has been transcended by the more recent feminism of the women's liberation movement. Certainly it is not the basis for the main divisions within the movement at present. And the modern movement is characterized much more by methods that have nothing to do with legal changes or state policies and so may appear to sidestep the problems of equalitarianism: cultural politics, the politics of lifestyle and changing household relationships, self-help and self-defence, support for victims of rape and violence, forming international links and (perhaps most distinctively) developing theoretical analyses of women's oppression.

Yet in many fields of work, the choice between those two strategies remains and continues to pose thorny problems. These tend to be the modern versions of the very issues of law and social policy that exercised our feminist grandmothers. The issue of protective legislation, restricting the hours and conditions of women's work in factories, is a conspicuous example. Feminists have been divided over it ever since it was first introduced during the nineteenth century. At that time equalitarianism was the dominant approach and such feminists as took an interest in the question opposed the legislation on the grounds that it infringed women's liberty and put them at a disadvantage in the labour market – a view which I think is justified by the historical evidence (Barrett and McIntosh, 1980; but for the opposite view, see Hutchins and Harrison, 1911; Humphries, 1977,

1981). Later the 'new feminists' attacked this stance and argued that women's functions of home-making and child-rearing could not be carried out properly if they were forced to work long hours and at night outside the home. This is not, of course, a defence that appeals to women's liberationists today.

However, the situation today is not at all comparable to that in the past. For one thing, we have formulated the goal of transforming the processes of home-making and child-rearing, so that if these are to be done privately we want men's factory hours to be limited as well. For another, while the CBI wants protective legislation ended, the TUC wants it continued and extended to cover men and to cover workers everywhere, not just in factory production. So when the Equal Opportunities Commission (1979) [. . .] recommended abolishing the legislation it was siding with the bosses as well as taking an unhistorical perspective and thinking in terms of immediate equality of treatment (for the unequal) rather than of working to eliminate the underlying inequality.

However, it should be noted that the position that women's liberationists usually adopt on this issue depends upon trusting the TUC. If they are not genuine in their commitment to extend protection to men – or if they have no hope of carrying it through – our position becomes one that simply accepts the present role of women and seeks to protect us from some of its worst penalties. I shall come back later to the questions of political practice that this raises. I want first to say something about strategy in relation to one particular feminist campaign, that for 'disaggregation'. I focus on this campaign because it raises important problems and also because I happen to have been involved in it, rather than because I believe it to be any more or less important than other campaigns. It is obviously just one part of a wider struggle.

Socialist feminists in the women's liberation movement have transcended the old divide in the sense that they have questioned not only masculinity and femininity, not only man's place and woman's place, but also the very existence of social division and difference based on sex. We have firmly located the origin and support for this division in the family. This does not mean that we locate it in individual kin-based households, but in the institution of the family, with its ideology, its imperatives and its constraints, which spread far beyond households themselves and both cause and enable the organization of everything else to be marked by gender division. Women's liberation depends upon the radical transformation of that family. However, although there is much disagreement about the relation of that family system to capitalism, most socialist feminists agree on two things: that the specific character of women's oppression at present is related to the articulation between the family system and the wage system; and that we should start working now towards the transformation of the family system and that it will not automatically arrive along with socialism. Indeed, I would add that the family system is changing and is under great strain at present (and not only because of the resurgence of feminism), so that it is incumbent on us to play a part in determining what form that change takes.

On the whole we choose to campaign for those things that we know will both help the immediate problems of many women and also help to open up possibilities for further and more far-reaching change. The demand for 'disaggregation' in social security, income tax, student grants and so on is a good example. The aggregation of the married couple into a tax unit and into a means-testable unit – however it may be dressed up in unisex clothing – represents women's dependence on their husbands. This is a dependence that is unreliable and degrading when it does exist and which in any case is a less common pattern than is often supposed, since most women are breadwinners (Hamill, 1978). In terms of social security, disaggregation would mean that a married woman who could not get a job could claim supplementary benefit regardless of her husband's income. But it would also mean that a married man would get a single person's benefit with no allowance for the wife; she would have to claim herself and fulfil the usual conditions: unless she was responsible for caring for small children or an invalid or something like that, she would have to sign on for employment.

This is a demand that comes out of our own experience. Several of the group which formulated it had suffered indignities and deprivation at the hands of the social security. Even so, the chief argument for it is not that thousands of women will be better off. It is that all women will have rights to full social security and that all men will lose the right to state back-up for keeping their wives in dependence. We realize that some women, especially older ones who have not had recent experience of going out to work, will be disadvantaged. We realize that forcing women onto the labour-market as it exists for them now is painful. But we believe that married women's dependence is in part responsible for their dreadful position in the labour-market, and the movement is simultaneously fighting for better pay and conditions at work, including the part-time and low-paid jobs that many women are forced to take.

We realize, too, that many who are concerned about poverty will tell us that there are other groups worse off than married women, whose needs should be met first. I think that argument reveals one of the weaknesses of the approach to social policy that focuses on questions of income equality, in terms of the outcome of distributional and redistributional processes, and does not look at the structure of relations involved in producing those outcomes. Our concern is with moving towards a structural change; by unhitching marriage from the social security system we hope to contribute to loosening its ties to the welfare system in general and ultimately to the wage system itself. We do believe that many unemployed married women are in poverty; those who are may benefit from the change. So we think that disaggregation would meet important immediate needs for some women, but more importantly it would help undermine the existing unequal marriage system. (Incidentally, I am not much swayed by the argument that disaggregation would remove one of the few advantages of forming households not based on the heterosexual pair-bond, and so provide another bonus for traditional marriage. For one thing, the argument considers individual types of household rather than the institutions as a whole. But more importantly, it assumes that marriage would be strengthened because more people would be motivated to enter it, or to stay in it, and I doubt whether this would be true for many people.)

In the present situation, the main point of arguing for disaggregation is to get an acceptance of the principle as widely as possible: to get to the point where the chief basis for resistance to it is cost and all the objections on principle have been rejected, both within the labour movement and in official circles. Some of the strongest arguments for it will, of course, be equalitarian ones, not because we want to conceal our real aims, but because equality is indeed an important dimension of the demand and one that people most readily latch on to. [...]

The day-to-day battles, unfortunately, are much more defensive ones against the cuts. But it is important to give these a feminist dimension, which often means one informed by the perspective of disaggregation, so that we recognize and attack cuts that force women further into dependence as well as those that take away their jobs or give them extra unpaid work. Disaggregation and protective legislation are only two examples. Similar strategic decisions have to be made in relation to almost every field. Should we press for a share of the matrimonial home and adequate maintenance for wives on the breakup of marriage? (Law Commission, 1980) Should we press for cohabitant women to be given rights equivalent to those of married women? (Anne Bottomley et al., 1981) These fields need to be linked and seen as part of the overall strategy for women's liberation, which of course goes far beyond the confines of social policy, even in its broadest sense.

The positions that I have argued for here are adopted in the light of the two key points of guidance for socialist social policy that I outlined earlier. They are based on the belief that there can be significant gains for women and for the working class (real gains for women are also gains for working-class unity) within capitalist society, since not every working-class gain is an immediate capitalist loss. And they are based on the belief that the wage system is fundamental to capitalist society, so that despite all the disadvantages of wage work, the way forward must be through furthering the process of proletarianization of women and rescuing women from preproletarian dependence. The struggle to end capitalist wage labour cannot be helped by women opting out and can only be undertaken by a working class that is less divided by male domination than the present one.

I want to end with some remarks about problems of organization in pursuing feminist goals in social policy. I shall not discuss questions of organization for women's liberation in general, though what I shall say clearly reflects certain views on that.

Firstly, I think we have got to develop a feminist presence in all the places where changes in social policy are fought for. This means within the left political parties, within the labour movement, within all the campaigning and lobbying bodies, and as much as possible in the women's organizations. Building up such a presence is often an unattractive activity for contemporary women's liberationists. Once we have experienced the joys and terrors of swimming in structureless movements like the women's liberation movement (if we managed to keep our heads above water), whose favourite forums are the mass meeting in an overcrowded school hall with an inadequate PA system and the small intimate and supportive workgroup, we find it hard even to tread water in the structured world of jockeying for office, juggling agendas and bowing to the constraints of representative democracy. But we cannot bypass those organizations; they exist, and each of them has carved out its own space of power. If we are not to be in constant opposition to them we must work within them as well as working in our own ways outside them. Sometimes this means challenging and transforming their styles of work and approach. Often, though, it means forming alliances where we have only a few points of agreement; and often it means compromises: avoiding taking a line that will lose us the support that we need for other more important battles. The question of protective legislation and the TUC, which I discussed earlier, is a case in point. Above all, it means getting in there and arguing our case in the context of on-going work.

The second remark I want to make is about men's relation to feminist social policy and to the Women's Liberation Movement. I think it may be true to say that there is never an entirely acceptable stance for outsiders towards a movement of liberation. I have experienced this as a white person in relation to the black movement in the 1960s and as a Briton in relation to anti-imperialist movements. It is easy to be caught in the double bind of being told simultaneously that we should not interfere, not impose our ideas, not assume we can escape being oppressors by an act of will, leave the oppressed group to constitute its own autonomous movement. But it is easier still to use that double bind as an excuse for doing nothing to support the cause of liberation for carrying on with our own struggles quite unaffected by those of our neighbours. Many men have used that double bind as a way of getting off the hook in relation to women's liberation. They respect the autonomy of the women's movement, wish it well, and there the matter can rest.

But such an easy benevolence is not appropriate to the case. We aim to overthrow men's dominance and remove their privileges as a gender. Our cause cannot just be added on to the list of radical causes. We are not a newly discovered minority group like dyslexics or people whose homes are threatened by road-widening, because our oppression is built in to the very structure of production and reproduction. So anyone concerned with social policy must decide what stand to take on the issues we raise and must see the question of women as integral to any analysis of social policy. We have been talking and writing for many years now about the inadequacy of existing analyses. Yet those of us who are teachers still find that our well-meaning male colleagues invite us to give a lecture or two on 'women and welfare', 'women and crime', or whatever. This is done with a modest, 'I am only a man; I can't speak for women'. But I sometimes wonder what they think the other eighteen lectures in their course are about: men? neuters? a gender-free society? The welfare system as it stands (or totters) is utterly dependent upon a specific construction of gender. The Department of Health and Social Security is well aware of that and it is time that critics of social policy were as well.

Note

This extract, from *Critical Social Policy*, 1, 1981, pp. 32–42, is based on the author's paper given at the Critical Social Policy Conference, 'Crisis in the Welfare State', November 1980.

References

Elizabeth Abbott and Katherine Bompas, *The Woman Citizen and Social Security: A Criticism of the Proposals Made in the Beveridge Reports as they Affect Women*, London, Mrs Bompas, 1943.

Sandra Allen, et al., eds, *Conditions of Illusion*, Leeds, Feminist Books, 1974.

Michèle Barrett and Mary McIntosh, 'The Family Wage', *Capital and Class*, no. 11, 1980.

Fran Bennett, et al., 'The Limitations of the Demand for Independence', *Politics and Power*, no. 1, 1980.

Anne Bottomley et al., *The Cohabitation Handbook: A Woman's Guide to the Law*, London, Pluto Press, 1981.

Manuel Castells, 'Collective Consumption and Urban Contradictions in Advanced Capitalism', reprinted in Castells, *City, Class and Power*, London, Macmillan, 1978.

Valerie Charlton, 'The Patter of Tiny Contradictions', *Red Rag*, no. 5, reprinted in Allen et al., 1974.

Equal Opportunities Commission, *Health and Safety Legislation: Should we Distinguish between Men and Women?*, London, HMSO, 1979.

Feminism and Social Policy

Carmel Flaskas and Betty Hounslow, 'Government Intervention and Right-Wing Attacks on Feminist Services', *Scarlet Woman* (Australia) no. 11, 1980.

Katherine Gieve, et al., 'The Independence Demand', in Allen et al., 1974.

Patrice Grevet, *Besoins populaires et financement public*, Paris, Editions Sociales, 1976.

Lynn Hamill, 'Wives as Sole and Joint Breadwinners', paper presented to the Social Science Research Council, Social Security Research Workshop, 1978.

Jane Humphries, 'Class Struggle and the Persistence of the Working-Class Family', *Cambridge Journal of Economics*, vol. 1, no. 3, 1977, pp. 241–58.

Jane Humphries, 'Protective Legislation, the Capitalist State and Working-Class Men: 1842 Mines Regulation Act', *Feminist Review*, no. 7, 1981.

B. L. Hutchins and A. Harrison, *A History of Factory Legislation*, London, P. S. King and Son, 2nd edn, 1911.

Hilary Land, 'Women: Supporters or Supported?', in Diana Barker and Sheila Allen, *Sexual Divisions and Society: Process and Change*, London, Tavistock, 1976.

Hilary Land, 'Social Security and the Division of Unpaid Work in the Home and Paid Employment in the Labour Market', in Department of Health and Social Security, *Social Security Research Seminar*, London, HMSO, 1977, pp. 43–61.

Hilary Land, 'The Family Wage', *Feminist Review*, no. 6, 1980.

Law Commission, *Family Law: The Financial Consequences of Divorce: The Basic Policy: A Discussion Paper*, Law Com. no. 103, London, HMSO, Cmnd. 8041, 1980.

Jane Lewis, 'Eleanor Rathbone and the New Feminism during the 1920s', unpublished mimeograph, 1973.

Ruth Lister and Leo Wilson, *The Unequal Breadwinner*, London, National Council for Civil Liberties, 1976.

Juliet Mitchell, *Psychoanalysis and Feminism*, London, Allen Lane, 1974.

Sylvie Pierce, 'Ideologies of Female Independence in the Welfare State: Women's Response to the Beveridge Report', paper given at British Sociological Association Annual Conference, 1979.

Eleanor F. Rathbone, *Milestones: Presidential Addresses at the Annual Council Meetings of NUSEC*, London, 1929.

Jane Streather and Stuart Weir, *Social Insecurity: Single Mothers on Social Security*, Child Poverty Action Group, Poverty Pamphlet no. 16, 1974.

Elizabeth Wilson, 'Women and the Welfare State', *Regd Rag*, no. 2, 1974.

The Patriarchal Welfare State

Carole Pateman

[...]

Theoretically and historically, the central criterion for citizenship has been 'independence', and the elements encompassed under the heading of independence have been based on masculine attributes and abilities. Men, but not women, have been seen as possessing the capacities required of 'individuals', 'workers' and 'citizens'. As a corollary, the meaning of 'dependence' is associated with all that is womanly – and women's citizenship in the welfare state is full of paradoxes and contradictions. [...] Three elements of 'independence' are particularly important for present purposes, all related to the masculine capacity for self-protection: the capacity to bear arms, the capacity to own property and the capacity for self-government.

First, women are held to lack the capacity for self-protection; they have been 'unilaterally disarmed'.[1] The protection of women is undertaken by men, but physical safety is a fundamental aspect of women's welfare that has been sadly neglected in the welfare state. From the nineteenth century, feminists (including J. S. Mill) have drawn attention to the impunity with which husbands could use physical force against their wives,[2] but women / wives still find it hard to obtain proper social and legal protection against violence from their male 'protectors'. Defence of the state (or the ability to protect your protection, as Hobbes put it), the ultimate test of citizenship, is also a masculine prerogative. The anti-suffragists in both America and Britain made a great deal of the alleged inability and unwillingness of women to use armed force, and the issue of women and combat duties in the military forces of the warfare state was also prominent in the [...] campaign [of the 1980s] against the Equal Rights Amendment in the United

States. Although women are now admitted into the armed forces and so into training useful for later civilian employment, they are prohibited from combat duties in Britain, Australia and the United States. Moreover, past exclusion of women from the warfare state has meant that welfare provision for veterans has also benefited men. In Australia and the United States, because of their special 'contribution' as citizens, veterans have had their own, separately administered welfare state, which has ranged from preference in university education (the GI bills in the United States) to their own medical benefits and hospital services, and (in Australia) preferential employment in the public service.

In the 'democratic' welfare state, however, employment rather than military service is the key to citizenship. The masculine 'protective' capacity now enters into citizenship primarily through the second and third dimensions of independence. Men, but not women, have also been seen as property owners. Only some men own material property, but as 'individuals', all men own (and can protect) the property they possess in their persons. Their status as 'workers' depends on their capacity to contract out the property they own in their labour power. Women are still not fully recognized socially as such property owners. To be sure, our position has improved dramatically from the mid-nineteenth century when women as wives had a very 'peculiar' position as the legal property of their husbands, and feminists compared wives to slaves. But today, a wife's person is still the property of her husband in one vital respect. Despite recent legal reform, in Britain and in some of the states of the United States and Australia, rape is still deemed legally impossible within marriage, and thus a wife's consent has no meaning. Yet women are now formally citizens in states held to be based on the necessary consent of self-governing individuals. The profound contradiction about women's consent is rarely if ever noticed and so is not seen as related to a sexually divided citizenship or as detracting from the claim of the welfare state to be democratic.

The third dimension of 'independence' is self-government. Men have been constituted as the beings who can govern (or protect) themselves, and if a man can govern himself, then he also has the requisite capacity to govern others. Only a few men govern others in public life – but all men govern in private as husbands and heads of households. As the governor of a family, a man is also a 'breadwinner'. He has the capacity to sell his labour power as a worker, or to buy labour power with his capital, and provide for his wife and family. His wife is thus 'protected'. The category of 'breadwinner' presupposes that wives are constituted as economic dependants or 'housewives', which places them in a subordinate position. The dichotomy breadwinner/housewife, and the masculine meaning of independence, were established in Britain by the middle of the nineteenth century; in the earlier period of capitalist development, women (and children) were wage-labourers. A 'worker' became a man who has an economically dependent wife to take care of his daily needs and look after his home and children. Moreover, 'class', too, is constructed as a patriarchal category. 'The working class' is the class of working *men*, who are also full citizens in the welfare state.

[T. H. Marshall first presented his influential account of citizenship in 1949, at the height of the optimism in Britain about the contribution of the new welfare state policies to social change. He referred specifically to ...] the universal, civil right to 'work', that is, to paid employment. The democratic implications of the right to work cannot be understood without attention to the connections between the public world of 'work' and citizenship and the private world of conjugal relations. What it means to be a 'worker' depends in part on men's status and power as husbands, and on their standing as citizens in the welfare state. The construction of the male worker as 'breadwinner' and his wife as his 'dependant' was expressed officially in the census classifications in Britain and Australia. In the British Census of 1851, women engaged in unpaid domestic work were 'placed ... in one of the productive classes along with paid work of a similar kind'.[3] This classification changed after 1871, and by 1911 unpaid housewives had been completely removed from the economically active population. In Australia an initial conflict over the categories of classification was resolved in 1890 when the scheme devised in New South Wales was adopted. The Australians divided up the population more decisively than the British, and the 1891 Census was based on the two categories of 'breadwinner' and 'dependant'. Unless explicitly stated otherwise, women's occupation was classified as domestic, and domestic workers were put in the dependant category.

The position of men as breadwinner-workers has been built into the welfare state. The sexual divisions in the welfare state have received much less attention than the persistence of the old dichotomy between the deserving and undeserving poor, which predates the welfare state. This is particularly clear in the United States, where a sharp separation is maintained between 'social security', or welfare-state policies directed at 'deserving workers who have paid for them through "contributions" over their working lifetimes', and 'welfare' – seen as public 'handouts' to 'barely deserving poor people'.[4] Although 'welfare' does not have this stark meaning in Britain or Australia, where the welfare state encompasses much more than most Americans seem able to envisage, the old distinction between the deserving and undeserving poor is still alive and kicking, illustrated by the popular bogey-figures of the 'scrounger' (Britain) and the 'dole-bludger' (Australia). However, although the dichotomy of deserving/undeserving poor overlaps with the divisions between husband/wife and worker/housewife to some extent, it also obscures the patriarchal structure of the welfare state.

Feminist analyses have shown how many welfare provisions have been established within a two-tier system. First, there are the benefits available to individuals as 'public' persons by virtue of their participation, and accidents of fortune, in the capitalist market. Benefits in this tier of the system are usually claimed by men. Second, benefits are available to the 'dependants' of individuals in the first category, or to 'private' persons, usually women. In the United States, for example, men are the majority of 'deserving' workers who receive benefits through the insurance system to which they have 'contributed' out of their earnings. On the other hand, the majority of claimants in means-tested programmes are women – women who are usually making their claims as wives or mothers. This is clearly the case with AFDC (Aid to Families with Dependent Children), where women are aided because they are mothers supporting children on their own, but the same is also true in other programmes: '46 per cent of the women receiving Social Security benefits make their claims as wives'. In contrast: 'men, even poor men, rarely make claims for benefits solely as husbands or fathers'.[5] In Australia the division is perhaps even more sharply defined. In 1980–81, in the primary tier of the system, in which benefits are employment-related and claimed by those who are expected to be economically independent but are not earning an income because of unemployment or illness, women formed only 31.3 per cent of claimants. In contrast, in the 'dependants group', 73.3 per cent of claimants were women, who were eligible for benefits because 'they are dependent on a man who could not support them, ... [or] should have had a man support them if he had not died, divorced or deserted them'.[6]

Such evidence of lack of 'protection' raises an important question about *women's* standard of living in the welfare state. As dependants, married women should derive their subsistence from their husbands, so that wives are placed in the position of all dependent people before the establishment of the welfare state; they are reliant on the benevolence of another for their livelihood. The assumption is generally made that all husbands are benevolent. Wives are assumed to share equally in the standard of living of their husbands. The distribution of income *within* households has not usually been a subject of interest to economists, political theorists or protagonists in arguments about class and the welfare state – even though William Thompson drew attention to its importance as long ago as 1825 [in a book entitled *Appeal of One Half the Human Race, Women, against the Pretensions of the Other Half, Men*] – but past and present evidence indicates that the belief that all husbands are benevolent is mistaken. Nevertheless, women are likely to be better off married than if their marriage fails. One reason why women figure so prominently among the poor is that after divorce, as recent evidence from the United States reveals, a woman's standard of living can fall by nearly 75 per cent, whereas a man's can rise by nearly half.[7]

The conventional understanding of the 'wage' also suggests that there is no need to investigate women's standard of living independently from men's. The concept of the wage has expressed and encapsulated the patriarchal separation and integration of the public world of employment and the private sphere of conjugal relations. In arguments about the welfare state and the social wage, the wage is usually treated as a return for the sale of *individuals'* labour power. However, once the opposition breadwinner/ housewife was consolidated, a 'wage' had to provide subsistence for several people. The struggle between capital and labour and the controversy about the welfare state have been about the *family wage*. A 'living wage' has been defined as what is required for a worker as breadwinner to support a wife and family, rather than what is needed to support himself; the wage is not what is sufficient to reproduce the worker's own labour power, but what is sufficient, in combination with the unpaid work of the housewife, to reproduce the labour power of the present and future labour force.

[...]

Women's Work and Welfare

Although so many women, including married women, are now in paid employment, women's standing as 'workers' is still of precarious legitimacy. So, therefore, is their standing as democratic citizens. If an individual can gain recognition from other citizens as an equally worthy citizen only through participation in the capitalist market, if self-respect and respect as a citizen are 'achieved' in the public world of the employment society, then women still lack the means to be recognized as worthy citizens. Nor have the policies of the welfare state provided women with many of the resources to gain respect as citizens. Marshall's social rights of citizenship in the welfare state could be extended to men without difficulty. As participants in the market, men could be seen as making a public contribution, and were in a position to be levied by the state to make a contribution more directly, that *entitled* them to the benefits of the welfare state. But how could women, dependants of men, whose legitimate 'work' is held to be located in the private sphere, be citizens of the welfare state? What could, or did, women contribute? The paradoxical answer is that women contributed – welfare.

The development of the welfare state has presupposed that certain aspects of welfare could and should continue to be provided by women (wives) in the home, and not primarily through public provision. The 'work' of a housewife can include the care of an invalid husband and elderly, perhaps infirm, relatives. Welfare-state policies have ensured in various ways that wives/women provide welfare services gratis, disguised as part of their responsibility for the private sphere. A good deal has been written about the fiscal crisis of the welfare state, but it would have been more acute if certain areas of welfare had not been seen as a private, women's matter. It is not surprising that the attack on public spending in the welfare state by the Thatcher and Reagan governments [went] hand-in-hand with praise for loving care within families, that is, with an attempt to obtain ever more unpaid welfare from (house)wives. The Invalid Care Allowance in Britain has been a particularly blatant example of the way in which the welfare state ensures that wives provide private welfare. The allowance was introduced in 1975 – when the Sex Discrimination Act was also passed – and it was paid to men or to single women who relinquished paid employment to look after a sick, disabled or elderly person (not necessarily a relative). Married women (or those cohabiting) were ineligible for the allowance.

The evidence indicates that it is likely to be married women who provide such care. In 1976 in Britain it was estimated that two million women were caring for adult relatives, and one survey in the north of England found that there were more people caring for adult relatives than mothers looking after children under sixteen.[8] A corollary of the assumption that women, but not men, care for others is that women must also care for themselves. Investigations show that women living by themselves in Britain have to be more infirm than men to obtain the services of home helps, and a study of an old people's home found that frail, elderly women admitted with their husbands faced hostility from the staff because they had failed in their job.[9] Again, women's citizenship is full of contradictions and paradoxes. Women must provide welfare, and care for themselves, and so must be assumed to have the capacities necessary for these tasks. Yet the development of the welfare state has also presupposed that women necessarily are in need of protection by and are dependent on men.

The welfare state has reinforced women's identity as men's dependants both directly and indirectly, and so confirmed rather than ameliorated our social exile. For example, in Britain and Australia the cohabitation rule explicitly expresses the presumption that women necessarily must be economically dependent on men if they live with them as sexual partners. If cohabitation is ruled to take place, the woman loses her entitlement to welfare benefits. The consequence of the cohabitation rule is not only sexually divided control of citizens, but an exacerbation of the poverty and other problems that the welfare state is designed to alleviate. In Britain today

> when a man lives in, a woman's independence – her own name on the weekly giro [welfare cheque] is automatically surrendered. The men become the claimants and the women their dependents. They lose control over both the

revenue and the expenditure, often with catastrophic results: rent not paid, fuel bills missed, arrears mounting.[10]

It is important to ask what counts as part of the welfare state. In Australia and Britain the taxation system and transfer payments together form a tax-transfer system in the welfare state. In Australia a tax rebate is available for a dependent spouse (usually, of course, a wife), and in Britain the taxation system has always treated a wife's income as her husband's for taxation purposes. It is only relatively recently that it ceased to be the husband's prerogative to correspond with the Inland Revenue about his wife's earnings, or that he ceased to receive rebates due on her tax payments. Married men can still claim a tax allowance, based on the assumption that they support a dependent wife. Women's dependence is also enforced through the extremely limited public provision of child-care facilities in Australia, Britain and the United States, which creates a severe obstacle to women's full participation in the employment society. In all three countries, unlike Scandinavia, child-care outside the home is a very controversial issue.

Welfare-state legislation has also been framed on the assumption that women make their 'contribution' by providing private welfare, and, from the beginning, women were denied full citizenship in the welfare state. In America 'originally the purpose of ADC (now AFDC) was to keep mothers out of the paid labor force.... In contrast, the Social Security retirement program was consciously structured to respond to the needs of white male workers.'[11] In Britain the first national insurance, or contributory, scheme was set up in 1911, and one of its chief architects wrote later that women should have been completely excluded because 'they want insurance for others, not themselves'. Two years before the scheme was introduced, William Beveridge, the father of the contemporary British welfare state, stated in a book on unemployment that the 'ideal [social] unit is the household of man, wife and children maintained by the earnings of the first alone.... Reasonable security of employment for the bread-winner is the basis of all private duties and all sound social action.'[12] Nor had Beveridge changed his mind on this matter by the Second World War; his report, *Social Insurance and Allied Services*, appeared in 1942 and laid a major part of the foundation for the great reforms of the 1940s. In a passage now (in)famous among feminists, Beveridge wrote that 'the great majority of married women must be regarded as occupied on work which is vital though unpaid, without which their husbands could not do their paid work and without which the nation could not continue.'[13] In the National Insurance Act of 1946 wives were separated from their husbands for insurance purposes. (The significance of this procedure, along with Beveridge's statement, clearly was lost on T. H. Marshall when he was writing his essay on citizenship and the welfare state.) Under the act, married women paid lesser contributions for reduced benefits, but they could also opt out of the scheme, and so from sickness, unemployment and maternity benefits, and they also lost entitlement to an old age pension in their own right, being eligible only as their husband's dependant. By the time the legislation was amended in 1975, about three-quarters of married women workers had opted out.[14]

A different standard for men and women has also been applied in the operation of the insurance scheme. In 1911 some married women were insured in their own right. The scheme provided benefits in case of 'incapacity to work', but, given that wives had already been identified as 'incapacitated' for the 'work' in question, for paid employment, problems over the criteria for entitlement to sickness benefits were almost inevitable. In 1913 an inquiry was held to discover why married women were claiming benefits at a much greater rate than expected. One obvious reason was that the health of many working-class women was extremely poor. The extent of their ill health was revealed in 1915 when letters written by working women in 1913–14 to the Women's Cooperative Guild were published. The national insurance scheme meant that for the first time women could afford to take time off work when ill – but from which 'work'? Could they take time off from housework? What were the implications for the embryonic welfare state if they ceased to provide free welfare? From 1913 a dual standard of eligibility for benefits was established.[15] For men the criterion was fitness for work. But the committee of inquiry decided that, if a woman could do her housework, she was not ill. So the criterion for eligibility for women was also fitness for work – but unpaid work in the private home, not paid work in the public market that was the basis for the contributory scheme under which the women were insured! This criterion for women was still being laid down in instructions issued by the Department of Health and Social Security in the 1970s.[16] The dual standard was further reinforced in 1975 when a non-contributory invalidity pension was introduced for those incapable of work but not qualified for the contributory scheme. Men and single women were entitled to the pension if they could not engage in paid employment; the criterion for married women was ability to perform 'normal household duties'.[17]

Wollstonecraft's Dilemma

So far, I have looked at the patriarchal structure of the welfare state, but this is only part of the picture; the development of the welfare state has also brought challenges to patriarchal power and helped provide a basis for women's autonomous citizenship. Women have seen the welfare state as one of their major means of support. Well before women won formal citizenship, they campaigned for the state to make provision for welfare, especially for the welfare of women and their children; and women's organizations and women activists have continued their political activities around welfare issues, not least in opposition to their status as 'dependants'. In 1953 the British feminist Vera Brittain wrote of the welfare state established through the legislation of the 1940s that 'in it women have become ends in themselves and not merely means to the ends of men', and their 'unique value as women was recognised'.[18] In hindsight, Brittain was clearly overoptimistic in her assessment, but perhaps the opportunity now exists to begin to dismantle the patriarchal structure of the welfare state. In the 1980s the large changes in women's social position, technological and structural transformations within capitalism, and mass unemployment mean that much of the basis for the breadwinner/dependant dichotomy and for the employment society itself is being eroded (although both are still widely seen as social ideals). The social context of Hegel's two dilemmas is disappearing. As the current concern about the 'feminization of poverty' reveals, there is now a very visible underclass of women who are directly connected to the state as claimants, rather than indirectly as men's dependants. Their social exile is as apparent as that of poor male workers was to Hegel. Social change has now made it much harder to gloss over the paradoxes and contradictions of women's status as citizens.

However, the question of how women might become full citizens of a democratic welfare state is more complex than may appear at first sight, because it is only in the current wave of the organized feminist movement that the division between the private and public spheres of social life has become seen as a major *political* problem. From the 1860s to the 1960s women were active in the public sphere: women fought not only for welfare measures and for measures to secure the private and public safety of women and girls, but for the vote and civil equality; middle-class women fought for entry into higher education; and the professions and women trade unionists fought for decent working conditions and wages and maternity leave. But the contemporary liberal-feminist view, particularly prominent in the United States, that what is required above all is 'gender-neutral' laws and policies, was not widely shared. In general, until the 1960s the focus of attention in the welfare state was on measures to ensure that women had proper social support, and hence proper social respect, in carrying out their responsibilities in the private sphere. The problem is whether and how such measures could assist women in their fight for full citizenship. In 1942 in Britain, for example, many women welcomed the passage in the Beveridge Report that I have cited because, it was argued, it gave official recognition to the value of women's unpaid work. However, an official nod of recognition to women's work as 'vital' to 'the nation' is easily given; *in practice*, the value of the work in bringing women into full membership in the welfare state was negligible. The equal worth of citizenship and the respect of fellow citizens still depended on participation as paid employees. 'Citizenship' and 'work' stood then and still stand opposed to 'women'.

The extremely difficult problem faced by women in their attempt to win full citizenship I shall call 'Wollstonecraft's dilemma'. The dilemma is that the two routes toward citizenship that women have pursued are mutually incompatible within the confines of the patriarchal welfare state, and, within that context, they are impossible to achieve. For three centuries, since universal citizenship first appeared as a political ideal, women have continued to challenge their alleged natural subordination within private life. From at least the 1790s they have also struggled with the task of trying to become citizens within an ideal and practice that have gained universal meaning through their exclusion. Women's response has been complex. On the one hand, they have demanded that the ideal of citizenship be extended to them, and the liberal-feminist agenda for a 'gender-neutral' social world is the logical conclusion of one form of this demand. On the other hand, women have also insisted, often simultaneously, as did Mary Wollstonecraft, that *as women* they have specific capacities, talents, needs and concerns, so that the expression of their citizenship will be different-iated from that of men. Their unpaid work providing welfare could be seen, as Wollstonecraft saw women's tasks as mothers, as women's work *as citizens*, just as their husbands' paid work is central to men's citizenship.

The patriarchal understanding of citizenship means that the two demands are incompatible because it allows two alternatives only: either women become (like) men, and so full citizens; or they continue at women's work, which is of no value for citizenship. Moreover, within a patriarchal welfare state neither demand can be met. To demand that citizenship, as it now exists, should be fully extended to women accepts the patriarchal meaning of 'citizen', which is constructed from men's attributes, capacities and activities. Women cannot be full citizens in the present meaning of the term; at best, citizenship can be extended to women only as lesser men. At the same time, within the patriarchal welfare state, to demand proper social recognition and support for women's responsibilities is to condemn women to less than full citizenship and to continued incorporation into public life as 'women', that is, as members of another sphere who cannot, therefore, earn the respect of fellow (male) citizens.

The example of child endowments on family allowances in Australia and Britain is instructive as a practical illustration of Wollstonecraft's dilemma. It reveals the great difficulties in trying to implement a policy that both aids women in their work and challenges patriarchal power while enhancing women's citizenship. In both countries there was opposi-tion from the right and from *laissez-faire* economists on the ground that family allowances would undermine the father's obligation to support his children and undermine his 'incentive' to sell his labour power in the market. The feminist advocates of family allowances in the 1920s, most notably Eleanor Rathbone in Britain, saw the alleviation of poverty in families where the breadwinner's wage was inadequate to meet the family's basic needs as only one argument for this form of state provision. They were also greatly concerned with the questions of the wife's economic dependence and equal pay for men and women workers. If the upkeep of children (or a substantial contribution toward it) was met by the state outside of wage bargaining in the market, then there was no reason why men and women doing the same work should not receive the same pay. Rathbone wrote in 1924 that 'nothing can justify the subordination of one group of producers – the mothers – to the rest and their deprivation of a share of their own in the wealth of a community'.[19] She argued that family allowances would, 'once and for all, cut away the maintenance of children and the reproduction of the race from the question of wages'.[20]

But not all the advocates of child endowment were feminists – so that the policy could very easily be divorced from the public issue of wages and dependence and be seen only as a return for and recognition of women's private contributions. Supporters included the eugenicists and pronatalists, and family allowances appealed to capital and the state as a means of keeping wages down. Family allowances had many opponents in the British union movement, fearful that the consequence, were the measure introduced, would be to undermine the power of unions in wage bargaining. The opponents included women trade unionists who were suspicious of a policy that could be used to try to persuade women to leave paid employment. Some unionists also argued that social services, such as housing, education and health, should be developed first, and the TUC adopted this view in 1930. But were the men concerned, too, with their private, patriarchal privileges? Rathbone claimed that 'the leaders of working men are themselves subsconsciously biased by prejudice of sex.... Are they not influenced by a secret reluctance to see their wives and children recognised as separate personalities?'[21]

By 1941 the supporters of family allowances in the union movement had won the day, and family allowances were introduced in 1946 as part of the government's wartime plans for post-war reconstruction. The legislation proposed that the allowance would be paid to the father as 'normal household head', but after lobbying by women's organizations, this was overturned in a free vote, and the allowance was paid directly to mothers. In Australia the union movement accepted child endowment in the 1920s (child endowment was introduced in New South Wales in 1927, and at the federal level in 1941). But union support there was based on wider redistributive policies, and the endowment was seen as a supplement to, not a way of breaking down, the family wage.[22] In the 1970s, in both countries, women's organizations again had to defend family allowances and the principle of redistribution from 'the wallet to the purse'.

The hope of Eleanor Rathbone and other feminists that family allowances would form part of a democratic restructuring of the wage system was not realized. Nevertheless, family allowances are paid to women as a benefit in their own right; in that sense they are an important (albeit financially very small) mark of recognition of married women as independent members of the welfare state. Yet the allowance is paid to women as *mothers*, and the key question is thus whether the payment to a mother – a private person – negates her standing as an independent citizen of the welfare state. More generally, the question is whether there can be a welfare policy that gives substantial assistance to women in their daily lives *and* helps create the conditions for a genuine democracy in which women are autonomous citizens, in which we can act *as women* and not as 'woman' (protected/dependent/subordinate) constructed as the opposite to all that is meant by 'man'. That is to say, a resolution of Wollstonecraft's dilemma is necessary and, perhaps, possible.

The structure of the welfare state presupposes that women are men's dependants, but the benefits help to make it possible for women to be economically independent of men. In the countries with which I am concerned, women reliant on state benefits live poorly, but it is no longer so essential as it once was to marry or to cohabit with a man. A considerable moral panic has developed in recent years around 'welfare mothers', a panic that obscures significant features of their position, not least the extent to which the social basis for the ideal of breadwinner/dependant has crumbled. Large numbers of young working-class women have little or no hope of finding employment (or of finding a young man who is employed). But there is a source of social identity available to them that is out of the reach of their male counterparts. The socially secure and acknowledged identity for women is still that of a mother, and for many young women, motherhood, supported by state benefits, provides 'an alternative to aimless adolescence on the dole' and 'gives the appearance of self-determination'. The price of independence and 'a rebellious motherhood that is not an uncritical retreat into femininity'[23] is high, however; the welfare state provides a minimal income and perhaps housing (often substandard), but child-care services and other support are lacking, so that the young women are often isolated, with no way out of their social exile. Moreover, even if welfare state policies in Britain, Australia and the United States were reformed so that generous benefits, adequate housing, health care, child care and other services were available to mothers, reliance on the state could reinforce women's lesser citizenship in a new way.

Some feminists have enthusiastically endorsed the welfare state as 'the main recourse of women' and as the generator of 'political resources which, it seems fair to say, are mainly women's resources'.[24] They can point, in Australia for example, to 'the creation over the decade [1975–85] of a range of women's policy machinery and government subsidized women's services (delivered by women for women) which is unrivalled elsewhere.'[25] However, the enthusiasm is met with the rejoinder from other feminists that for women to look to the welfare state is merely to exchange dependence on individual men for dependence on the state. The power and capriciousness of husbands is being replaced by the arbitrariness, bureaucracy and power of the state, the very state that has upheld patriarchal power. The objection is cogent: to make women directly dependent on the state will not in itself do anything to challenge patriarchal power relations. The direct dependence of male workers on the welfare state and their indirect dependence when their standard of living is derived from the vast system of state regulation of and subsidy to capitalism – and in Australia a national arbitration court – have done little to undermine class power. However, the objection also misses an important point. There is one crucial difference between the construction of women as men's dependants and dependence on the welfare state. In the former case, each woman lives with the man on whose benevolence she depends; each woman is (in J. S. Mill's extraordinarily apt phrase) in a 'chronic state of bribery and intimidation combined'.[26] In the welfare state, each woman receives what is hers by right, and she can, potentially, combine with other citizens to enforce her rightful claim. The state has enormous powers of intimidation, but political action takes place collectively in the public terrain and not behind the closed door of the home, where each woman has to rely on her own strength and resources.

Another new factor is that women are now involved in the welfare state on a large scale as employees, so that new possibilities for political action by women also exist. Women have been criticizing the welfare state in recent years not just as academics, as activists, or as beneficiaries and users of welfare services, but as the people on whom the daily operation of the welfare state to a large extent depends. The criticisms range from its patriarchal structure (and, on occasions, especially in health care, misogynist practices), to its bureaucratic and undemocratic policy-making processes and administration, to social work practices and education policy. Small beginnings have been made on changing the welfare state from within; for example, women have succeeded in establishing Well Women Clinics within the NHS in Britain and special units to deal with rape victims in public hospitals in Australia. Furthermore, the potential is now there for united action by women employees, women claimants and women citizens already politically active in the welfare state – not just to protect services against government cuts and efforts at 'privatization' (which has absorbed much energy recently), but to transform the welfare state. Still, it is hard to see how women alone could succeed in the attempt. One necessary condition for the creation of a genuine democracy in which the welfare of *all* citizens is served is an alliance between a labour movement that acknowledges the problem of patriarchal power and an autonomous women's movement that recognizes the problem of class power. Whether such an alliance can be forged is an open question.

Despite the debates and the rethinking brought about by mass unemployment and attack on the union movement and welfare state by the Reagan and Thatcher governments, there are many barriers to be overcome. In Britain and Australia, with stronger welfare states, the women's movement has had a much closer relationship with working-class movements than in the United States, where the individualism of the predominant liberal feminism is an inhibiting factor, and where only about 17 per cent of the workforce is now unionized. The major locus of criticism of authoritarian, hierarchical, undemocratic forms of organization since about 1970 has been the women's movement. The practical example of democratic, decentralized organization provided by the women's movement has been largely ignored by the labour movement, as well as in academic discussions of democracy. After Marx defeated Bakunin in the First International, the prevailing form of organization in the labour movement, the nationalized industries in Britain and in the left sects has mimicked the hierarchy of the state – both the welfare and the warfare state. To be sure, there is a movement for industrial democracy and workers' control, but it has, by and large, accepted that the 'worker' is a masculine figure and failed to question the separation of (public) industry and economic production from private life. The women's movement has rescued and put into practice the long-submerged idea that movement for, and experiments in, social change must 'prefigure' the future form of social organization.[27]

If prefigurative forms of organization, such as the 'alternative' women's welfare services set up by the women's movement, are not to remain isolated examples, or if attempts to set them up on a wider scale are not to be defeated, as in the past, very many accepted conceptions and practices have to be questioned. [...] Debates [during the 1980s] over left alternatives to Thatcherite economics policies in Britain, and over the Accord between the state, capital and labour in Australia, suggest that the arguments and demands of the women's movement are still often unrecognized by labour's political spokesmen. For instance, one response to unemployment from male workers is to argue for a shorter working week and more leisure, or more time but the same money. However, in women's lives, time and money are not interchangeable in the same way.[28] Women, unlike men, do not have leisure after 'work', but do unpaid work. Many women are arguing, rather, for a shorter working day. The point of the argument is to challenge the separation of part- and full-time paid employment and paid and unpaid 'work'. But the conception of citizenship needs thorough questioning, too, if Wollstonecraft's dilemma is to be resolved; neither the labour movement nor the women's movement (nor democratic theorists) has paid much attention to this. The patriarchal opposition between the private and public, women and citizen, dependant and breadwinner is less firmly based than it once was, and feminists have named it as a political problem. The ideal of full employment so central to the welfare state is also crumbling, so that some of the main props of the patriarchal understanding of citizenship are being undermined. The ideal of full employment appeared to have been achieved in the 1960s only because half the citizen body (and black men?) was denied legitimate membership in the employment society. Now that millions of men are excluded from the ideal (and the exclusion seems permanent), one possibility is that the ideal of universal citizenship will be abandoned, too, and full citizenship will become the prerogative of capitalist, employed and armed men. Or can a genuine democracy be created?

The perception of democracy as a class problem and the influence of liberal feminism have combined to keep alive Engels's old solution to 'the woman question' – to 'bring the whole female sex back into public industry'.[29] But the economy has a patriarchal structure. The Marxist hope that capitalism would create a labour force where ascriptive characteristics were irrelevant, and the liberal-feminist hope that anti-discrimination legislation would create a 'gender-neutral' workforce, look utopian even without the collapse of the ideal of full employment. Engels's solution is out of reach – and so, too, is the generalization of masculine citizenship to women. In turn, the argument that the equal worth of citizenship, and the self-respect and mutual respect of citizens, depend upon sale of labour power in the market and the provisions of the patriarchal welfare state is also undercut. The way is opening up for the formulation of conceptions of respect and equal worth adequate for democratic citizenship. Women could not 'earn' respect or gain the self-respect that men obtain as workers; but what kind of respect do men 'achieve' by selling their labour power and becoming wage-slaves? Here the movement for workplace democracy and the feminist movement could join hands, but only if the conventional understanding of 'work' is rethought. If women as well as men are to be full citizens, the separation of the welfare state and employment from the free welfare work contributed by women has to be broken down and new meanings and practices of 'independence', 'work' and 'welfare' created.

For example, consider the implications were a broad, popular political movement to press for welfare policy to include a guaranteed social income to all adults, which would provide adequately for subsistence and also participation in social life.[30] For such a demand to be made, the old dichotomies must already have started to break down – the opposition between paid and unpaid work (for the first time all individuals could have a genuine choice whether to engage in paid work), between full- and part-time work, between public and private work, between independence and dependence, between work and welfare – which is to say, between men and women. If implemented, such a policy would at last recognize women as equal members of the welfare state, although it would not in itself ensure women's full citizenship. If a genuine democracy is to be created, the problem of the content and value of women's contribution as citizens and the meaning of citizenship has to be confronted.

To analyse the welfare state through the lens of Hegel's dilemma is to rule out such problems. But the history of the past 150 years and the contemporary record show that the welfare of all members of society cannot be represented by men, whether workers or capitalists. Welfare is, after all, the welfare of all living generations of citizens and their children. If the welfare state is seen as a response to Hegel's dilemma, the appropriate question about women's citizenship is: how can women become workers and citizens like men, and so members of the welfare state like men? If, instead, the starting-point is Wollstonecraft's dilemma, then the question might run: what form must democratic citizenship take if a primary task of all citizens is to ensure that the welfare of each living generation of citizens is secured?

The welfare state has been fought for and supported by the labour movement and the women's movement because only public or collective provision can maintain a proper standard of living and the means for meaningful social participation for all citizens in a democracy. The implication of this claim is that democratic citizens are both autonomous and interdependent; they are autonomous in that each enjoys the means to be an active citizen, but they are interdependent in that the welfare of each is the collective responsibility of all citizens. Critics of the class structure of the welfare state have often counterposed the fraternal interdependence (solidarity) signified by the welfare state to the bleak independence of isolated individuals in the market, but they have rarely noticed that both have been predicated upon the dependence (subordination) of women. In the patriarchal welfare state, independence has been constructed as a masculine prerogative. Men's 'independence' as workers and citizens is their freedom from responsibility for welfare (except insofar as they 'contribute' to the welfare state). Women have been seen as responsible for (private) welfare work, for relationships of dependence and interdependence. The paradox that welfare relies so largely on women, on dependants and social exiles whose 'contribution' is not politically relevant to their citizenship in the welfare state, is heightened now that women's paid employment is also vital to the operation of the welfare state itself.

If women's knowledge of and expertise in welfare are to become part of their contribution as citizens, as women have demanded during the twentieth century, the opposition between men's independence and women's dependence has to be broken down, and a new understanding and practice of citizenship developed. The patriarchal dichotomy between women and independence-work-citizenship is under political challenge, and the social basis for the ideal of the full (male) employment society is crumbling. An opportunity has become visible to create a genuine democracy, to move from the welfare state to a welfare society without involuntary social exiles, in which women as well as men enjoy full social membership. Whether the opportunity can be realized is not easy to tell now that the warfare state is overshadowing the welfare state.

Notes

From C. Pateman, *The Disorder of Women*, Cambridge, Polity Press, 1989, pp. 185–9, 192–209.

1 The graphic phrase is Judith Stiehm's, in 'Myths Necessary to the Pursuit of War', unpublished paper, p. 11.

2 See especially F. Cobbe, 'Wife Torture in England', *The Contemporary Review*, 32, 1878, pp. 55–87. Also, for example, Mill's remarks when introducing the amendment to enfranchise women in the House of Commons in 1867, reprinted in *Women, the Family and Freedom: The Debate in Documents*, ed. S. Bell and K. Offen, vol. 1, Stanford, CA, Stanford University Press, 1983, p. 487.

3 D. Deacon, 'Political Arithmetic: The Nineteenth-Century Australian Census and the Construction of the Dependent Woman', *Signs*, 11(1), 1985, p. 31 (my discussion draws on Deacon); also H. Land, 'The Family Wage', *Feminist Review*, 6, 1980, p. 60.

4 T. Skocpol, 'The Limits of the New Deal System and the Roots of Contemporary Welfare Dilemmas', in *The Politics of Social Policy in the United States*, ed. M. Weir, A. Orloff and T. Skocpol, Princeton, NJ, Princeton University Press, 1988.

5 B. Nelson, 'Women's Poverty and Women's Citizenship: Some Political Consequences of Economic Marginality', *Signs*, 10(2), 1984, pp. 222–3.

6 M. Owen, 'Women – A Wastefully Exploited Resource', *Search*, 15, 1984, pp. 271–2.

7 L. J. Weitzman, *The Divorce Revolution*, New York, The Free Press, 1985, ch. 10, esp. pp. 337–40.

8 J. Dale and P. Foster, *Feminists and the Welfare State*, London, Routledge and Kegan Paul, 1986, p. 112.

9 H. Land, 'Who Cares for the Family?', *Journal of Social Policy*, 7(3), 1978, pp. 268–9. Land notes that even under the old Poor Law twice as many women as men received outdoor relief, and there were many more old men than women in the workhouse wards for the ill or infirm; the women were deemed fit for the wards for the able-bodied.

10 B. Campbell, *Wigan Pier Revisited: Poverty and Politics in the 80s*, London, Virago Press, 1984, p. 76.

11 Nelson, op. cit., pp. 229–30.

12 Both quotations are taken from Land, op. cit., p. 72.

13 Cited in Dale and Foster, op. cit., p. 17.

14 H. Land, 'Who Still Cares for the Family?', in *Women's Welfare, Women's Rights*, ed. J. Lewis, London and Canberra, Croom Helm 1983, p. 70.

15 M. Davis, *Maternity: Letters from Working Women*, New York, Norton, 1978 (first published 1915).

16 Information taken from Land, op. cit. (n. 9), pp. 263–4.

17 Land, op. cit. (n. 14), p. 73.

18 Cited in Dale and Foster, op. cit., p. 3.

19 Cited in Land, op. cit. (n. 3), p. 63.

20 Cited in B. Cass, 'Redistribution to Children and to Mothers: A History of Child Endowment and Family Allowances', in *Women, Social Welfare and the State*, ed. J. Goodnow and C. Pateman, Sydney, Allen and Unwin, 1985, p. 57.

21 Cited in ibid., p. 59.

22 Ibid., pp. 60–1.

23 Campbell, op. cit., pp. 66, 78, 71.

24 F. Fox Piven, 'Women and the State: Ideology, Power, and the Welfare State', *Socialist Review*, 14(2), 1984, pp. 14, 17.

25 M. Sawer, 'The Long March through the Institutions: Women's Affairs under Fraser and Hawke', paper presented to the annual meeting of the Australasian Political Studies Association, Brisbane, 1986, p. 1.

26 J. S. Mill, 'The Subjection of Women', in *Essays on Sex Equality*, ed. A. Rossi, Chicago, University of Chicago Press, 1970, p. 137.

27 See S. Rowbotham, L. Segal and H. Wainright, *Beyond the Fragments: Feminism and the Making of Socialism*, London, Merlin Press, 1979, a book that was instrumental in opening debate on the left and in the labour movement in Britain on this question.

28 See H. Hernes, *Welfare State and Woman Power: Essays in State Feminism*, Oslo, Norwegian University Press, 1987, ch. 5, for a discussion of the political implications of the different time-frames of men's and women's lives.

29 F. Engels, *The Origin of the Family, Private Property and the State*, New York, International Publishers, 1942, p. 66.

30 See also the discussion in J. Keane and J. Owens, *After Full Employment*, London, Hutchinson, 1986, pp. 175–7.

Part II

Debates and Issues

Welfare Regimes

Three Worlds of Welfare Capitalism

Gøsta Esping-Andersen

What Is the Welfare State?

Every theoretical paradigm must somehow define the welfare state. How do we know when and if a welfare state responds functionally to the needs of industrialism, or to capitalist reproduction and legitimacy? And how do we identify a welfare state that corresponds to the demands that a mobilized working class might have? We cannot test contending arguments unless we have a commonly shared conception of the phenomenon to be explained.

A remarkable attribute of the entire literature is its lack of much genuine interest in the welfare state as such. Welfare state studies have been motivated by theoretical concerns with other phenomena, such as power, industrialization or capitalist contradictions; the welfare state itself has generally received scant conceptual attention. If welfare states differ, how do they differ? And when, indeed, is a state a welfare state? This turns attention straight back to the original question: what is the welfare state?

A common textbook definition is that it involves state responsibility for securing some basic modicum of welfare for its citizens. Such a definition skirts the issue of whether social policies are emancipatory or not; whether they help system legitimation or not; whether they contradict or aid the market process; and what, indeed, is meant by 'basic'? Would it not be more appropriate to require of a welfare state that it satisfies more than our basic or minimal welfare needs?

The first generation of comparative studies started with this type of conceptualization. They assumed, without much reflection, that the level of social expenditure adequately reflects a state's commitment to welfare.

The theoretical intent was not really to arrive at an understanding of the welfare state, but rather to test the validity of contending theoretical models in political economy. By scoring nations with respect to urbanization, level of economic growth, and the proportion of aged in the demographic structure, it was believed that the essential features of industrial modernization were properly considered. Alternatively, power-oriented theories compared nations on left-party strength or working-class power mobilization.

The findings of the first-generation comparativists are difficult to evaluate, since there is no convincing case for any particular theory. The shortage of nations for comparisons statistically restricts the number of variables that can be tested simultaneously. Thus, when Cutright (1965) or Wilensky (1975) find that economic level, with its demographic and bureaucratic correlates, explains most welfare-state variations in 'rich countries', relevant measures of working-class mobilization or economic openness are not included. Their conclusions in favour of a 'logic of industrialism' view are therefore in doubt. And, when Hewitt (1977), Stephens (1979), Korpi (1983), Myles (1984) and Esping-Andersen (1985) find strong evidence in favour of a working-class mobilization thesis, or when Schmidt (1982, 1983) finds support for a neo-corporatist, and Cameron (1978) for an economic openness argument, it is without fully testing against plausible alternative explanations.

Most of these studies claim to explain the welfare state. Yet their focus on spending may be misleading. Expenditures are epiphenomenal to the theoretical substance of welfare states. Moreover, the linear scoring approach (more or less power, democracy or spending) contradicts the sociological notion that power, democracy or welfare are relational and structured phenomena. By scoring welfare states on spending, we assume that all spending counts equally. But some welfare states, the Austrian one, for example, spend a large share on benefits to privileged civil servants. This is normally not what we would consider a commitment to social citizenship and solidarity. Others spend disproportionately on means-tested social assistance. Few contemporary analysts would agree that a reformed poor-relief tradition qualifies as a welfare-state commitment. Some nations spend enormous sums on fiscal welfare in the form of tax privileges to private insurance plans that mainly benefit the middle classes. But these tax expenditures do not show up on expenditure accounts. In Britain, total social expenditure [grew] during the Thatcher period, yet this is almost exclusively a function of very high unemployment. Low expenditure on some programmes may signify a welfare state more seriously committed to full employment.

Therborn (1983) is right when he holds that we must begin with a conception of state structure. What are the criteria with which we should judge whether, and when, a state is a welfare state? There are three approaches to this question. Therborn's proposal is to begin with the historical transformation of state activities. Minimally, in a genuine welfare state the majority of its daily routine activities must be devoted to servicing the welfare needs of households. This criterion has far-reaching consequences. If we simply measure routine activity in terms of spending and personnel, the result is that no state can be regarded as a real welfare state until the 1970s, and some that we normally label as welfare states will not qualify because the majority of their routine activities concern defence, law and order, administration and the like (Therborn, 1983). Social scientists have been too quick to accept nations' self-proclaimed welfare state status. They have also been too quick to conclude that if the standard social programmes have been introduced, the welfare state has been born.

The second conceptual approach derives from Richard Titmuss's (1958) classical distinction between residual and institutional welfare states. In the former, the state assumes responsibility only when the family or the market fails; it seeks to limit its commitments to marginal and deserving social groups. The latter model addresses the entire population, is universalistic, and embodies an institutionalized commitment to welfare. It will, in principle, extend welfare commitments to all areas of distribution vital for societal welfare.

The Titmuss approach has fertilized a variety of new developments in comparative welfare state research (Korpi, 1980; Myles, 1984; Esping-Andersen and Korpi, 1984, 1986; Esping-Andersen, 1985, 1987). It is an approach that forces researches to move from the black box of expenditures to the content of welfare states: targeted versus universalistic programmes, the conditions of eligibility, the quality of benefits and services, and, perhaps most importantly, the extent to which employment and working life are encompassed in the state's extension of citizen rights. The shift to welfare state typologies makes simple linear welfare state rankings difficult to sustain. Conceptually, we are comparing categorically different types of state.

The third approach is to theoretically select the criteria on which to judge types of welfare state. This can be done by measuring actual welfare states against some abstract model and then scoring programmes, or entire welfare states, accordingly (Myles, 1984). But this is ahistorical, and does not necessarily capture the ideals or designs that historical actors sought to realize in the struggles over the welfare state. If our aim is to test causal theories that involve actors, we should begin with the demands that were actually promoted by those actors that we deem critical in the history of welfare state development. It is difficult to imagine that anyone struggled for spending *per se*.

A Re-specification of the Welfare State

Few can disagree with T. H. Marshall's (1950) proposition that social citizenship constitutes the core idea of a welfare state. But the concept must be fleshed out. Above all, it must involve the granting of social rights. If social rights are given the legal and practical status of property rights, if they are inviolable, and if they are granted on the basis of citizenship rather than performance, they will entail a de-commodification of the status of individuals *vis-à-vis* the market. But the concept of social citizenship also involves social stratification: one's status as a citizen will compete with, or even replace, one's class position.

The welfare state cannot be understood just in terms of the rights it grants. We must also take into account how state activities are interlocked with the market's and the family's role in social provision. These are the three main principles that need to be fleshed out prior to any theoretical specification of the welfare state.

Rights and De-commodification

In pre-capitalist societies, few workers were properly commodities in the sense that their survival was contingent upon the sale of their labour power. It is as markets become universal and hegemonic that the welfare of individuals comes to depend entirely on the cash nexus. Stripping society of the institutional layers that guaranteed social reproduction outside the labour contract meant that people were commodified. In turn, the introduction of modern social rights implies a loosening of the pure commodity status. De-commodification occurs when a service is rendered as a matter of right, and when a person can maintain a livelihood without reliance on the market.

The mere presence of social assistance or insurance may not necessarily bring about significant de-commodification if they do not substantially emancipate individuals from market dependence. Means-tested poor relief will possibly offer a safety net of last resort. But if benefits are low and associated with social stigma, the relief system will compel all but the most desperate to participate in the market. This was precisely the intent of the nineteenth-century Poor Laws in most countries. Similarly, most of the early social-insurance programmes were deliberately designed to maximize labour-market performance.

There is no doubt that de-commodification has been a hugely contested issue in welfare state development. For labour, it has always been a priority. When workers are completely market-dependent, they are difficult to mobilize for solidaristic action. Since their resources mirror market inequalities, divisions emerge between the 'ins' and the 'outs', making labour-movement formation difficult. De-commodification strengthens the workers and weakens the absolute authority of the employer. It is for exactly this reason that employers have always opposed de-commodification.

De-commodified rights are differentially developed in contemporary welfare states. In social-assistance dominated welfare states, rights are not so much attached to work performance as to demonstrable need. Needs-tests and typically meagre benefits, however, service to curtail the de-commodifying effect. Thus, in nations where this model is dominant (mainly in the Anglo-Saxon countries), the result is actually to strengthen the market since all but those who fail in the market will be encouraged to contract private-sector welfare.

A second dominant model espouses compulsory state social insurance with fairly strong entitlements. But again, this may not automatically secure substantial de-commodification, since this hinges very much on the fabric of eligibility and benefit rules. Germany was the pioneer of social insurance, but over most of the [twentieth century] can hardly be said to have brought about much in the way of de-commodification through its social programmes. Benefits have depended almost entirely on contributions, and thus on work and employment. In other words, it is not the mere presence of a social right, but the corresponding rules and preconditions, which dictate the extent to which welfare programmes offer genuine alternatives to market dependence.

The third dominant model of welfare, namely the Beveridge-type citizens' benefit, may, at first glance, appear the most de-commodifying. It offers a basic, equal benefit to all, irrespective of prior earnings, contributions or performance. It may indeed be a more solidaristic system, but not necessarily de-commodifying, since only rarely have such schemes been able to offer benefits of such a standard that they provide recipients with a genuine option to working.

De-commodifying welfare states are, in practice, fairly recent. A minimal definition must entail that citizens can freely, and without potential loss of job, income or general welfare, opt out of work when they themselves consider it necessary. With this definition in mind, we would, for example, require of a sickness insurance that individuals be guaranteed benefits equal to normal earnings, and the right to absence with minimal proof of medical impairment and for the duration that the individual deems necessary. These conditions, it is worth noting, are those usually enjoyed by academics, civil servants and higher-echelon white-collar employees. Similar requirements would be made of pensions, maternity leave, parental leave, educational leave and unemployment insurance.

Some nations have moved towards this level of de-commodification, but only recently, and, in many cases, with significant exemptions. In almost all nations, benefits were upgraded to nearly equal normal wages in the late 1960s and early 1970s. But in some countries, for example, prompt medical certification in case of illness is still required; in others, entitlements depend on long waiting periods of up to two weeks; and in still others, the duration of entitlements is very short. [...] The Scandinavian welfare states tend to be the most de-commodifying; the Anglo-Saxon the least.

The Welfare State as a System of Stratification

Despite the emphasis given to it in both classical political economy and in T. H. Marshall's pioneering work, the relationship between citizenship and social class has been neglected both theoretically and empirically. Generally speaking, the issue has either been assumed away (it has been taken for granted that the welfare state creates a more egalitarian society), or it has been approached narrowly in terms of income distribution or in terms of whether education promotes upward social mobility. A more basic question, it seems, is what kind of stratification system is promoted by social policy. The welfare state is not just a mechanism that intervenes in, and possibly corrects, the structure of inequality; it is, in its own right, a system of stratification. It is an active force in the ordering of social relations.

Comparatively and historically, we can easily identify alternative systems of stratification embedded in welfare states. The poor-relief tradition, and its contemporary means-tested social-assistance offshoot, was conspicuously designed for purposes of stratification. By punishing and stigmatizing recipients, it promotes social dualisms and has therefore been a chief target of labour-movement attacks.

The social-insurance model promoted by conservative reformers such as Bismarck and von Taffe was also explicitly a form of class politics. It sought, in fact, to achieve two simultaneous results in terms of stratification. The first was to consolidate divisions among wage-earners by legislating distinct programmes for different class and status groups, each with its own conspicuously unique set of rights and privilege which was designed to accentuate the individual's appropriate station in life. The second objective was to tie the loyalties of the individual directly to the monarchy or the central state authority. This was Bismarck's motive when he promoted a direct state supplement to the pension benefit. This state-corporatist model was pursued mainly in nations such as Germany, Austria, Italy and France, and often resulted in a labyrinth of status-specific insurance funds.

Of special importance in this corporatist tradition was the establishment of particularly privileged welfare provisions for the civil service (*Beamten*). In part, this was a means of rewarding loyalty to the state, and in part it was a way of demarcating this group's uniquely exalted social status. The corporatist status-differentiated model springs mainly from the old guild tradition. The neo-absolutist autocrats, such as Bismarck, saw in this tradition a means to combat the rising labour movements.

The labour movements were as hostile to the corporatist model as they were to poor relief – in both cases for obvious reasons. Yet the alternatives first espoused by labour were no less problematic from the point of view of uniting the workers as one solidaristic class. Almost invariably, the model that labour first pursued was that of self-organized friendly societies or equivalent union- or party-sponsored fraternal welfare plans. This is not surprising. Workers were obviously suspicious of reforms sponsored by a hostile state, and saw their own organizations not only as bases of class mobilization, but also as embryos of an alternative world of solidarity and justice; as a microcosm of the socialist haven to come. Nonetheless, these micro-socialist societies often became problematic class ghettos that divided rather than united workers. Membership was typically restricted to the strongest strata of the working class, and the weakest – who most needed protection – were most likely excluded. In brief, the fraternal society model frustrated the goal of working-class mobilization.

The socialist 'ghetto approach' was an additional obstacle when socialist parties found themselves forming governments and having to pass the social reforms they had so long demanded. For political reasons of coalition-building and broader solidarity, their welfare model had to be recast as welfare for 'the people'. Hence, the socialists came to espouse the principle of universalism; borrowing from the liberals, their programme was, typically, designed along the lines of the democratic flat-rate, general revenue-financed Beveridge model.

As an alternative to means-tested assistance and corporatist social insurance, the universalistic system promotes equality of status. All citizens are endowed with similar rights, irrespective of class or market position. In this sense, the system is meant to cultivate cross-class solidarity, a solidarity of the nation. But the solidarity of flat-rate universalism presumes a historically peculiar class structure, one in which the vast majority of the population are the 'little people' for whom a modest, albeit egalitarian, benefit may be considered adequate. Where this no longer obtains, as occurs with growing working-class prosperity and the rise of the new middle classes, flat-rate universalism inadvertently promotes dualism because the better-off turn to private insurance and to fringe-benefit bargaining to supplement modest equality with what they have decided are accustomed standards of welfare. Where this process unfolds (as in Canada or Great Britain), the result is that the wonderfully egalitarian spirit of universalism turns into a dualism similar to that of the social-assistance state: the poor rely on the state, and the remainder on the market.

It is not only the universalist but, in fact, all historical welfare state models which have faced the dilemma of changes in class structure. But the response to prosperity and middle-class growth has been varied, and so, therefore, has been the outcome in terms of stratification. The corporatist insurance tradition was, in a sense, best equipped to manage new and loftier welfare-state expectations since the existing system could technically be upgraded quite easily to distribute more adequate benefits. Adenauer's 1957 pension reform in Germany was a pioneer in this respect. Its avowed purpose was to restore status differences that had been eroded because of the old insurance system's incapacity to provide benefits tailored to expectations. This it did simply by moving from contribution- to earnings-graduated benefits without altering the framework of status-distinctiveness.

In nations with either a social-assistance or a universalistic Beveridge-type system, the option was whether to allow the market or the state to furnish adequacy and satisfy middle-class aspirations. Two alternative models emerged from this political choice. The one typical of Great Britain and most of the Anglo-Saxon world was to preserve an essentially modest universalism in the state, and allow the market to reign for the growing social strata demanding superior welfare. Due to the political power of such groups, the dualism that emerges is not merely one between state and market, but also between forms of welfare-state transfers: in these nations, one of the fastest growing components of public expenditure is tax subsidies for so-called 'private' welfare plans. And the typical political effect is the erosion of middle-class support for what is less and less a universalistic public-sector transfer system.

Yet another alternative has been to seek a synthesis of universalism and adequacy outside the market. This road has been followed in countries where, by mandating or legislation, the state incorporates the new middle classes within a luxurious second-tier, universally inclusive, earnings-related insurance scheme on top of the flat-rate egalitarian one. Notable examples are Sweden and Norway. By guaranteeing benefits tailored to expectations, this solution reintroduces benefit inequalities, but effectively blocks off the market. It thus succeeds in retaining universalism and also, therefore, the degree of political consensus required to preserve broad and solidaristic support for the high taxes that such a welfare state model demands.

Welfare State Regimes

As we survey international variations in social rights and welfare-state stratification, we will find qualitatively different arrangements between state, market and the family. The welfare state variations we find are therefore not linearly distributed, but clustered by regime-types.

In one cluster we find the 'liberal' welfare state, in which means-tested assistance, modest universal transfers or modest social-insurance plans predominate. Benefits cater mainly to a clientele of low-income, usually working-class, state dependants. In this model, the progress of social reform has been severely circumscribed by traditional, liberal work-ethic norms: it is one where the limits of welfare equal the marginal propensity to opt for welfare instead of work. Entitlement rules are therefore strict and often associated with stigma; benefits are typically modest. In turn, the state encourages the market, either passively – by guaranteeing only a minimum – or actively – by subsidizing private welfare schemes.

The consequence is that this type of regime minimizes de-commodification effects, effectively contains the realm of social rights, and erects an order of stratification that is a blend of a relative equality of poverty among state-welfare recipients, market-differentiated welfare among the majorities, and a class-political dualism between the two. The archetypical examples of this model are the United States, Canada and Australia.

A second regime-type clusters nations such as Austria, France, Germany and Italy. Here, the historical corporatist-statist legacy was upgraded to cater to the new 'post-industrial' class structure. In these conservative and strongly 'corporatist' welfare states, the liberal obsession with market efficiency and commodification was never pre-eminent and, as such, the granting of social rights was hardly ever a seriously contested issue. What predominated was the preservation of status differentials; rights, therefore, were attached to class and status. This corporatism was subsumed under a state edifice perfectly ready to displace the market as a provider of welfare; hence, private insurance and occupational fringe benefits play a truly marginal role. On the other hand, the state's emphasis on upholding status differences means that its redistributive impact is negligible.

But the corporatist regimes are also typically shaped by the Church, and hence strongly committed to the preservation of traditional family hood. Social insurance typically excludes non-working wives, and family benefits encourage motherhood. Day care, and similar family services, are conspicuously underdeveloped; the principle of 'subsidiarity' serves to emphasize that the state will only interfere when the family's capacity to service its members is exhausted.

The third, and clearly smallest, regime-cluster is composed of those countries in which the principles of universalism and de-commodification of social rights were extended also to the new middle classes. We may call it the 'social democratic' regime-type since, in these nations, social democracy was clearly the dominant force behind social reform. Rather than tolerate a dualism between state and market, between working class and middle class, the social democrats pursued a welfare state that would promote an equality of the highest standards, not an equality of minimal needs as was pursued elsewhere. This implied, first, that services and benefits be upgraded to levels commensurate with even the most discriminating tastes of the new middle classes; and, second, that equality be furnished by guaranteeing workers full participation in the quality of rights enjoyed by the better-off.

This formula translates into a mix of highly de-commodifying and universalistic programmes that, nonetheless, are tailored to differentiated expectations. Thus, manual workers come to enjoy rights identical with those of salaried white-collar employees or civil servants; all strata are incorporated under one universal insurance system, yet benefits are graduated according to accustomed earnings. This model crowds out the market, and consequently constructs an essentially universal solidarity in favour of the welfare state. All benefit; all are dependent; and all will presumably feel obliged to pay.

The social democratic regime's policy of emancipation addresses both the market and the traditional family. In contrast to the corporatist-subsidiarity model, the principle is not to wait until the family's capacity to aid is exhausted, but to pre-emptively socialize the costs of family hood. The ideal is not to maximize dependence on the family, but capacities for individual independence. In this sense, the model is a peculiar fusion of liberalism and socialism. The result is a welfare state that grants transfers directly to children, and takes direct responsibility of caring for children, the aged and the helpless. It is, accordingly, committed to a heavy social-service burden, not only to service family needs but also to allow women to choose work rather than the household.

Perhaps the most salient characteristic of the social democratic regime is its fusion of welfare and work. It is at once genuinely committed to a full-employment guarantee, and entirely dependent on its attainment. On the one side, the right to work has equal status to the right of income protection. On the other side, the enormous costs of maintaining a solidaristic, universalistic and de-commodifying welfare system means that it must minimize social problems and maximize revenue income. This is obviously best done with most people working, and the fewest possible living off social transfers.

Neither of the two alternative regime-types espouse full employment as an integral part of their welfare state commitment. In the conservative tradition, of course, women are discouraged from working; in the liberal ideal, concerns of gender matter less than the sanctity of the market.

[. . .] Welfare states cluster, but we must recognize that there is no single pure case. The Scandinavian countries may be predominantly social democratic, but they are not free of crucial liberal elements. Neither are the liberal regimes pure types. The American social-security system is redistributive, compulsory and far from actuarial. At least in its early formulation, the New Deal was as social democratic as was contemporary Scandinavian social democracy. And European conservative regimes have incorporated both liberal and social democratic impulses. Over the decades, they have become less corporativist and less authoritarian.

Notwithstanding the lack of purity, if our essential criteria for defining welfare states have to do with the quality of social rights, social stratification and the relationship between state, market and family, the world is obviously composed of distinct regime-clusters. Comparing welfare states on scales of more or less or, indeed, of better or worse, will yield highly misleading results.

The Causes of Welfare-State Regimes

If welfare states cluster into three distinct regime-types, we face a substantially more complex task of identifying the causes of welfare state differences. What is the explanatory power of industrialization, economic growth, capitalism or working-class political power in accounting for regime-types? A first superficial answer would be: very little. The nations we study are all more or less similar with regard to all but the variable of working-class mobilization. And we find very powerful labour movements and parties in each of the three clusters.

A theory of welfare state developments must clearly reconsider its causal assumptions if it wishes to explain clusters. The hope of finding one single powerful causal force must be abandoned; the task is to identify salient interaction effects. Based on the preceding arguments, three factors in particular should be of importance: the nature of class mobilization (especially of the working class); class-political coalition structures; and the historical legacy of regime institutionalization.

[...] There is absolutely no compelling reason to believe that workers will automatically and naturally forge a socialist class identity; nor is it plausible that their mobilization will look especially Swedish. The actual historical formation of working-class collectivities will diverge, and so also will their aims, ideology and political capacities. Fundamental differences appear both in trade unionism and party development. Unions may be sectional or in pursuit of more universal objectives; they may be denominational or secular; and they may be ideological or devoted to business unionism. Whichever they are, it will decisively affect the articulation of political demands, class cohesion and the scope for labour-party action. It is clear that a working-class mobilization thesis must pay attention to union structure.

The structure of trade unionism may or may not be reflected in labour-party formation. But under what conditions are we likely to expect certain welfare state outcomes from specific party configurations? There are many factors that conspire to make it virtually impossible to assume that any labour, or left-wing, party will ever be capable, single-handedly, of structuring a welfare state. Denominational or other divisions aside, it will be only under extraordinary historical circumstances that a labour party alone will command a parliamentary majority long enough to impose its will. [...] The traditional working class has hardly ever constituted an electoral majority. It follows that a theory of class mobilization must look beyond the major leftist parties. It is a historical fact that welfare state construction has depended on political coalition-building. The structure of class coalitions is much more decisive than are the power resources of any single class.

The emergence of alternative class coalitions is, in part, determined by class formation. In the earlier phases of industrialization, the rural classes usually constituted the largest single group in the electorate. If social democrats wanted political majorities, it was here that they were forced to look for allies. One of history's many paradoxes is that the rural classes were decisive for the future of socialism. Where the rural economy was dominated by small, capital-intensive family farmers, the potential for an alliance was greater than where it rested on large pools of cheap labour. And where farmers were politically articulate and well organized (as in Scandinavia), the capacity to negotiate political deals was vastly superior.

The role of the farmers in coalition formation and hence in welfare state development is clear. In the Nordic countries, the necessary conditions obtained for a broad red–green alliance for a full-employment welfare state in return for farm price subsidies. This was especially true in Norway and Sweden, where farming was highly precarious and dependent on state aid. In the United States, the New Deal was premised on a similar coalition (forged by the Democratic Party), but with the important difference that the labour-intensive South blocked a truly universalistic social security system and opposed further welfare-state developments. In contrast, the rural economy of continental Europe was very inhospitable to red–green coalitions. Often, as in Germany and Italy, much of agriculture was labour-intensive; hence the unions and left-wing parties were seen as a threat. In addition, the conservative forces on the continent had succeeded in incorporating farmers into 'reactionary' alliances, helping to consolidate the political isolation of labour.

Political dominance was, until after the Second World War, largely a question of rural class politics. The construction of welfare states in this period was, therefore, dictated by whichever force captured the farmers. The absence of a red–green alliance does not necessarily imply that no welfare-state reforms were possible. On the contrary, it implies which political force came to dominate their design. Great Britain is an exception to this general rule, because the political significance of the rural classes eroded before the turn of the century. In this way, Britain's coalition-logic showed at an early date the dilemma that faced most other nations later; namely, that the rising white-collar strata constitute the linchpin for political majorities. The consolidation of welfare states after the Second World War came to depend fundamentally on the political alliances of the new middle classes. For social democracy, the challenge was to synthesize working-class and white-collar demands without sacrificing the commitment to solidarity.

Since the new middle classes have, historically, enjoyed a relatively privileged position in the market, they have also been quite successful in meeting their welfare demands outside the state, or, as civil servants, by privileged state welfare. Their employment security has traditionally been such that full employment has been a peripheral concern. Finally, any programme for drastic income-equalization is likely to be met with great hostility among a middle-class clientele. On these grounds, it would appear that the rise of the new middle classes would abort the social democratic project and strengthen a liberal welfare state formula.

The political leanings of the new middle classes have, indeed, been decisive for welfare state consolidation. Their role in shaping the three welfare state regimes described earlier is clear. The Scandinavian model relied almost entirely on social democracy's capacity to incorporate them into a new kind of welfare state: one that provided benefits tailored to the tastes and expectations of the middle classes, but nonetheless retained universalism of rights. Indeed, by expanding social services and public employment, the welfare state participated directly in manufacturing a middle class instrumentally devoted to social democracy.

In contrast, the Anglo-Saxon nations retained the residual welfare state model precisely because the new middle classes were not wooed from the market to the state. In class terms, the consequence is dualism. The welfare state caters essentially to the working class and the poor. Private insurance and occupational fringe benefits cater to the middle classes. Given the electoral importance of the latter, it is quite logical that further extensions of welfare state activities are resisted.

The third, continental European, welfare state regime has also been patterned by the new middle classes, but in a different way. The cause is historical. Developed by conservative political forces, these regimes institutionalized a middle-class loyalty to the preservation of both occupationally segregated social-insurance programmes and, ultimately, to the political forces that brought them into being. Adenauer's great pension reform in 1957 was explicitly designed to resurrect middle-class loyalties.

Conclusion

We have here presented an alternative to a simple class-mobilization theory of welfare-state development. It is motivated by the analytical necessity of shifting from a linear to an interactive approach with regard to both welfare states and their causes. If we wish to study welfare states, we must begin with a set of criteria that define their role in society. This role is certainly not to spend or tax; nor is it necessarily that of creating equality. We have presented a framework for comparing welfare states that takes into consideration the principles for which the historical actors have willingly united and struggled. When we focus on the principles embedded in welfare states, we discover distinct regime-clusters, not merely variations of 'more' or 'less' around a common denominator.

The historical forces behind the regime differences are interactive. They involve, first, the pattern of working-class political formation and, second, political coalition-building in the transition from a rural economy to a middle-class society. The question of political coalition-formation is decisive. Third, past reforms have contributed decisively to the institutionalization of class preferences and political behaviour. In the corporatist regimes, hierarchical status-distinctive social insurance cemented middle-class loyalty to a peculiar type of welfare state. In liberal regimes, the middle classes became institutionally wedded to the market. And in Scandinavia, the fortunes of social democracy over the past decades were closely tied to the establishment of a middle-class welfare state that benefits both its traditional working-class clientele and the new white-collar strata. The Scandinavian social democrats were able to achieve this in part because the private welfare market was relatively undeveloped and in part because they were capable of building a welfare state with features of sufficient luxury to satisfy the wants of a more discriminating public. This also explains the extraordinarily high cost of Scandinavian welfare states.

But a theory that seeks to explain welfare state growth should also be able to understand its retrenchment or decline. It is generally believed that welfare state backlash movements, tax revolts and roll-backs are ignited when social expenditure burdens become too heavy. Paradoxically, the opposite is true. Anti-welfare-state sentiments [since the 1980s] have generally been weakest where welfare spending has been heaviest, and vice versa. Why?

The risks of welfare state backlash depend not on spending, but on the class character of welfare states. Middle-class welfare states, be they social democratic (as in Scandinavia) or corporatist (as in Germany), forge middle-class loyalties. In contrast, the liberal, residualist welfare states found in the United States, Canada and, increasingly, Britain, depend on the loyalties of a numerically weak, and often politically residual, social stratum. In this sense, the class coalitions in which the three welfare-state regime-types were founded explain not only their past evolution but also their future prospects.

Note

From *The Three Worlds of Welfare Capitalism*, Cambridge, Polity Press, 1990, pp. 18–34.

References

Cameron, D. R., 'The Expansion of the Public Economy: A Comparative Analysis', *American Political Science Review*, 72, 4, 1978, pp. 1243–61.

Cutright, P., 'Political Structure, Economic Development, and National Social Security Programs', *American Journal of Sociology*, 70, 1965, pp. 537–50.

Esping-Andersen, G., 'Power and Distributional Regimes', *Politics and Society*, 14, 1985.

Esping-Andersen, G., 'Citizenship and Socialism', in M. Rein, G. Esping-Andersen and M. Rainwater, *Stagnation and Renewal in Social Policy: The Rise and Fall of Policy Regimes*, New York, Sharpe, 1987.

Esping-Andersen, G. and W. Korpi, 'Social Policy and Class Politics in Post-War Capitalism: Scandinavia, Austria and Germany', in *Order and Conflict in Contemporary Capitalism*, ed. J. Goldthorpe, Oxford, Oxford University Press, 1984, pp. 179–208.

Esping-Andersen, G. and W. Korpi, 'From Poor Relief to Institutional Welfare States: The Development of Scandinavian Social Policy', in R. Erikson et al., *The Scandinavian Model: Welfare States and Welfare Research*, New York, Sharpe, 1986.

Hewitt, C., 'The Effect of Political Democracy and Social Democracy on Equality in Industrial Societies: A Cross-National Comparison', *American Sociological Review*, 42, 1977, pp. 450–64.

Korpi, W., 'Social Policy and Distributional Conflict in the Capitalist Democracies', *West European Politics*, 3, 1980.

Korpi, W., *The Democratic Class Struggle*, London, Routledge and Kegan Paul, 1983.

Marshall, T. H., *Citizenship and Social Class*, Cambridge, Cambridge University Press, 1950.

Myles, J., *Old Age in the Welfare State*, Boston, Little, Brown, 1984.

Schmidt, M. G., 'The Role of Parties in Shaping Macro-Economic Policies', in *The Impact of Parties*, ed. F. Castles, London, Sage, 1982.

Schmidt, M. G., 'The Welfare State and the Economy in Periods of Economic Crisis: A Comparative Study of 23 OECD Nations', *European Journal of Political Research*, 11, 1983, pp. 1–26.

Stephens, J., *The Transition from Capitalism to Socialism*, London, Macmillan, 1979.

Therborn, G., 'When, How and Why does a Welfare State become a Welfare State?', Freiburg, ECPR Workshops, 1983.

Titmuss, R. M., *Essays on the Welfare State*, London, Allen and Unwin, 1958.

Wilensky, H., *The Welfare State and Equality: Structural and Ideological Roots of Public Expenditure*, Berkeley, University of California Press, 1975.

The Real Worlds of Welfare Capitalism

Robert E. Goodin, Bruce Headey, Ruud Muffels and Henk-Jan Dirven

Real lives are not just a jumble of unconnected episodes. Rather, they are temporally extended, as is the impact that welfare regimes have on people's lives. Any serious assessment of welfare regimes needs to take due account of their impact upon people's lives over time, rather than just at one instant.

Existing studies of comparative welfare regimes cannot do that, because they are based on cross-sectional 'snapshots' of one sort or another. The Luxembourg Income Study (LIS), to take the most illustrious example, provides wonderfully rich and reasonably comparable information on what happens to individuals across the Organization for Economic Co-operation and Development (OECD).[1] But LIS surveys are taken at one point in time, and when repeated (every five years or so) they are re-plicated on different samples of individuals each time.[2] In such studies – which until very recently were the very best we had – there was simply no way to track individuals through time, linking up what was happening to someone in the first survey with what was happening to that same person in the second.

Clearly, though, it matters enormously to people how long their poverty lasts. Being 'temporarily embarrassed' (as W. C. Fields might have put it) is undeniably awkward, but the embarrassment is undeniably mitigated by its being only temporary. Far worse to live in grinding poverty, year in and year out, from which you can see no hope of escape.

It also matters to policy makers whether people's poverty is a persistent or a passing phenomenon. Cross-sectional snapshots tell us that every year around 12 per cent of Americans are living below America's (frightfully low[3]) official poverty line. What those snapshots do not – cannot – tell us is whether that is the *same* 12 per cent each year, or whether different people are in poverty in different years. If the former, we would have an underclass which is persistently excluded from the benefits of our society. If the latter, we would have income volatility such that poverty might strike any of us at any time.

The policy prescription differs in those two cases, and so does the potential political constituency behind it. If welfare benefits only those who have always been poor, then anti-poverty policy is of direct material interest only to that beleaguered 12 per cent of the population. If anti-poverty policy potentially benefits many more than just today's poor, then both its political constituency and its moral legitimacy expands accordingly.

It turns out that the latter is the case. Fully a quarter of Americans lived in households which received means-tested welfare benefits for one year between 1969 and 1978. But only about half those receiving benefits in one year continued to receive them in the next year; and fewer than 5 per cent of Americans received welfare benefits for eight out of the same ten years. Those were the pathbreaking findings of the University of Michigan's Panel Study of Income Dynamics, popularized by Greg Duncan's *Years of Poverty, Years of Plenty* and reiterated in Bane's and Ellwood's influential successor, *Welfare Realities.*[4] Such findings could of course only have come through a panel study, reinterviewing the same individuals year after year.

American analysts of the welfare state have enjoyed the benefits of such panel data for quite some time. The Michigan Panel Study on Income Dynamics was established in 1968, in the dying days of the War on Poverty, and it has been following its 'five thousand American families' ever since. The full fruits of that project only began to emerge in the late 1970s, however, when the panel had been running for ten years. Duncan's *Years of Poverty, Years of Plenty* was offered to a wider public on the basis of analysis of that first ten years' worth of panel data. And that timing was not accidental. Ten years is about what it takes for any really conclusive long-term results to emerge from a panel study. The virtue of panels is that they allow us to track individuals through time: the disadvantage is that necessarily takes quite some time.[5]

Rich though the US panel study is, it inevitably pertains to only one country and only one welfare regime. Regime performance, however, can only really be assessed in comparative perspective: single cases are inherently inconclusive. At long last, we are now in a position to attempt a first cut at a truly comparative assessment of the three worlds of welfare capitalism via panel data, tracking individuals in three different countries through ten years.

There are only three countries in the world for which ten years of continuous panel data are available: the US, Germany and the Netherlands.[6] It is just plain good luck that those three countries each represent one of the three basic worlds of welfare capitalism. The US is indisputably a liberal welfare regime, the purest in the world according to the key tables in Esping-Andersen's *The Three Worlds of Welfare Capitalism.*[7] Germany is equally indisputably a corporatist welfare regime, and it is one of the purest representatives of that type in Esping-Andersen's key tables.[8] Taking the Netherlands as an example of a social democratic welfare regime is more controversial; Sweden would have been better. But at least on the tax-transfer side of its operations the Netherlands sits squarely within the social democratic camp.[9] Still, the Netherlands is the only remotely social democratic country for which we have continuous, comparable panel data for anything like ten years.[10] Indeed, in certain key respects those three countries are not only broadly representative of their respective regime types but might even be regarded as the best (biggest and economically most successful) cases of each regime type.[11]

As the German and Dutch panels began only in 1984, we focus on the decade from the mid-1980s to the mid-1990s.[12] The first half of the period corresponded to an economic boom in all three countries, and in the second half all experienced something of an economic downturn – thus providing a test of the comparative performance of these three regimes both in good times and not-so-good.

The Three Worlds Recalled

Let us begin by recalling the basic internal logic of each of the three worlds of welfare capitalism. Under the 'liberal welfare regime', in all its various guises, people are primarily responsible for their own welfare.[13] The state's residual duty is purely to provide for those unable to provide for themselves in the ordinary way, which in modern market society is through market earnings.[14] Under the liberal welfare regime, benefits are both means-tested and meanly calibrated: they are supposed to go to the poor and only the poor; and they are supposed to be sufficient only just to cover bare subsistence needs.

Liberals are anxious for welfare regimes not to create 'disincentives' discouraging people from paid labour. The rigours of the workhouse and the poorhouse were no accidents. Rather, they reflected a deliberate strategy on the part of a previous generation of liberal welfare reformers keen to make living off welfare the most undesirable possible way to earn a living – and thus ensuring that anyone who could secure paid employment would take it instead.[15]

The classically 'corporatist welfare regime', founded in Germany in the 1880s, has contributory social insurance as its cornerstone. That is a quintessentially conservative mechanism, whereby you get what you pay for and you pay for what you get. Furthermore, what insurance pays you when you are unable to work is a direct function, and a large fraction, of what you used to earn when you were in work.

Earnings-related benefits of this classically corporatist sort serve several functions. They provide welcome stability in the earner's own income stream. Not incidentally, they also underwrite the stability of the existing status order. Again not incidentally, tying the household's welfare entitlements to the breadwinner's earnings in this way, where breadwinners are predominantly male, also helps to reinforce the gender order. All that is to the good, from the conservative-corporatist point of view.

The final world of welfare capitalism is the social democratic welfare regime, which had its fullest flowering in Scandinavia in the post-war years. Representing the culmination of the political mobilization of organized labour, the social democratic welfare regime is strongly egalitarian in its ethos and distinctively universalist in its policy style.

Not content merely to eradicate poverty, social democrats actually strive to promote social equality more generally. Full employment policies are, for social democrats, more than just a necessary adjunct to financing generous schemes of redistribution: they are also an important distributive mechanism in their own right, providing people with jobs (which are themselves important social goods) and generating a more nearly equal distribution of labour market earnings (thus reducing the need to redistribute).

These three sorts of welfare regimes, then, can be characterized as having fundamentally different emphases:

- the residual *liberal* welfare regime assigns priority to *economic growth*, wanting to reduce poverty in a way that impinges minimally on that;
- the conservative *corporatist* welfare regime assigns priority to social *stability*; and
- the *social democratic* welfare regime assigns priority to eradicating *poverty* and minimizing social *equality*.

To say that those are their priorities is not to say that they have absolutely no regard for other values. Social democrats and corporatists might not be so obsessed by economic growth as liberals, but neither can they afford to ignore economic impacts. Neither of those regimes would count itself a particular success if economic growth were *all* that they achieved.

Of course there are a great many other fundamental objectives and a great many intermediate aims involved in each of these welfare strategies. While all of them necessarily have important non-financial aspects, we concentrate here upon financial issues alone. Thus, while 'social stability' more broadly conceived has to do with everything from divorce rates to job losses, in this study we look at it in terms of income stability alone. And while 'social equality' has meanings much broader than income equality alone, that narrower concept forms the focus of this discussion.

Findings

We group our main findings under the headings corresponding to the central concerns of each different type of welfare regime: poverty, income inequality, income instability and economic growth.

Poverty

Let us look first, then, at the extent and duration of poverty in the three countries and the three welfare regimes which they represent. The definition of poverty is contentious. But for purposes of our calculations, we simply accept the convention – now standard among cross-national welfare-state researchers – that people are in poverty if their income is less than half the median income in their country as a whole.[16]

By that standard, poverty rates are much higher in the liberal US welfare regime than they are in the other two. That is not because the US generates more poverty through its labour market. As it happens, all three countries are about the same in that respect: about 20 per cent of the population across all three countries would be poor on the basis of what we call 'pre-government' income.[17] The difference lies almost wholly in how much government transfers do to alleviate poverty in the Netherlands (and to a lesser extent in Germany), compared with how little government transfers do to alleviate poverty in the US. After government transfers and taxes have been taken into account, only around 5 per cent of the Dutch (and around 8 per cent of Germans) are in post-government poverty in any given year, compared with around 18 per cent of Americans as is shown on the left side of figure 1.

Not only does the social democratic welfare regime of the Netherlands do more to alleviate poverty in any given year: its cumulative effect is also greater over time. Here, of course, is where the distinctive strengths of our panel data come into play. Since we can track individuals through time, we can aggregate each individual's earnings over longer periods of time. A person's annual income is just the aggregate of that person's weekly earnings over a year: our longer-term aggregates are an extension of that. A person will be said to be poor on a five-yearly basis if that person's income, aggregated over those five years, is below the annual poverty line (also aggregated over five years, of course) – and similarly for ten years.[18]

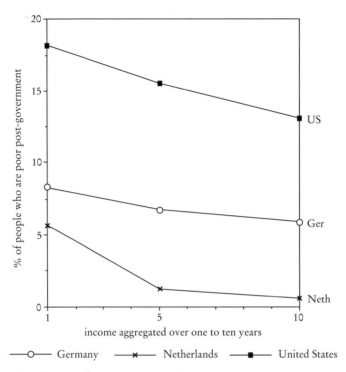

Figure 1 Extent of poverty, post-government
Source: Based on Goodin et al., 1999, Appendix Table A2 (Pov 1A)

Figure 1 shows the percentage of people who are poor in each of these countries on a one-, five- and ten-yearly basis. As stated above, substantially fewer people are poor in the Netherlands than the US on a one-yearly basis. But even poor people's incomes are volatile; and as a result of that volatility five-yearly poverty is lower in all countries than is one-yearly poverty. Ten-yearly poverty is lower again.

What is worth noticing in figure 1, however, is that five-yearly poverty drops off substantially *more steeply* in the Netherlands than in the US. Ten-yearly poverty virtually disappears in the Netherlands (it runs at 0.5 per cent), whereas poverty remains substantial (13 per cent) in the US even on a ten-yearly basis. Germany, again, is in between. But having started near the Dutch on a one-yearly basis, on a ten-yearly basis Germany's performance comes only halfway between the Dutch and American.

The statistics reported in figure 1 pertain to people's 'disposable' income net of government taxes and transfers. (That is why we call it 'post-government income'.) Let us now try to assess the extent to which government transfers, rather than sheer volatility in pre-government

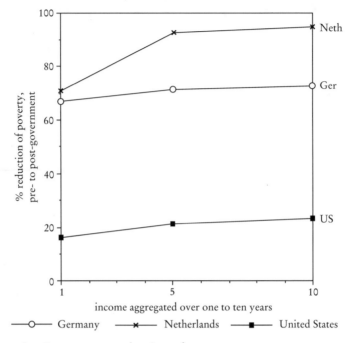

Figure 2   Government reduction of poverty
Source: Based on Goodin et al., 1999, Appendix Table A2 (Pov 5A)

incomes, can be credited with reducing poverty over longer periods. Figure 2 presents statistics, on the same basis as before, on the proportion by which pre-government poverty is reduced by government taxes and transfers.

As shown in figure 2, the liberal US welfare regime does not make much of a dent in poverty. It eradicates only around a fifth of poverty, whether on a one-, five- or ten-yearly basis. Even just on a one-yearly basis, government transfers in both Germany and the Netherlands eradicate substantially more poverty (around two-thirds of it). But whereas the corporatist German welfare regime does virtually no more to eradicate five- or ten-yearly poverty than one-yearly, the social democratic welfare regime of the Netherlands is even more successful in its war on five- and ten-yearly poverty than it is in its attack on one-yearly poverty. The upshot, once again, is striking. Government transfers in the social democratic welfare regime lift out of poverty some 95 per cent of people who would have been poor on the basis of their pre-government income aggregated over ten years. The liberal welfare regime, in contrast, leaves over three-quarters of them poor.

The sheer numbers of people who are poor is not the whole story. Not only are *more people* poor in the liberal welfare regime than elsewhere, but they also tend to be *more deeply poor* (there are more people whose incomes fall further below the poverty line; the 'poverty gap' is bigger). They also tend to be *poor more frequently* (the 'recurrence' of poverty is higher) and to *remain poor longer* (their 'poverty spells' last longer).

All those are crucial factors, both in the lives of poor people and in any comparative assessment of welfare regimes. But the latter issues in particular have long remained underanalysed in comparative welfare state studies, because the data were not available. Questions of the recurrence and duration of poverty can be analysed properly only through panels tracking individuals through time.

Figure 2 reports of poverty rates based on incomes aggregated over longer periods, and shows that people are either poorer or poor for longer in the liberal than the corporatist or especially the social democratic welfare regime. We can disaggregate those factors by calculating simple 'hit rates', reflecting the recurrence of poverty. Figure 3 shows what

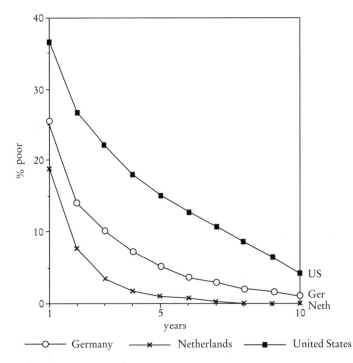

Figure 3   Recurrence of poverty post-government
Source: Based on Goodin et al., 1999, Appendix Table A2 (Pov 4A)

percentage of people in each country were 'hit' by poverty (calculated on a one-yearly basis) in one or more years out of ten, two or more years out of ten, and so on.

Most of the people in each of these three countries were not poor in any of these ten years, of course. That is reflected in the fact that the left intercepts of all three curves in figure 3 are substantially less than 100. But inspecting those left intercepts, we see that these three countries vary considerably in that respect. The proportion of people who were poor in one year or more in the US is substantially higher (over a third) than it is in the Netherlands (under a fifth).

The main thing to note from figure 3, however, is how much larger a fraction of the American population is hit by poverty two, three, four or indeed ten times over these ten years. The proportion of people in the Netherlands who are hit by poverty in two or more years is under 8 per cent. In Germany it is almost twice that, and in the US it is over three times that. The proportion of people in the Netherlands who are hit by poverty in five or more years is under 1 per cent, and in Germany around 5 per cent; in the US it is fully 15 per cent. Thus, once again, the social democratic welfare regime of the Netherlands is best at reducing the recurrence of poverty. And spell analysis would show the same to be true of the duration of poverty as well.[19]

Income Inequality

There are many aspects of inequality, and many different ways of measuring it. Here, we look at income inequality as measured through the Gini coefficient. Gini is a statistic ranging from zero to one, with zero representing perfect equality, and numbers approaching one representing greater inequality. Thus, low Gini coefficients represent the egalitarian ideal.

In assessing how the three welfare regimes do at reducing inequality, we look once again at their comparative performance on a one-, five- and ten-yearly basis. On the basis of one-yearly aggregates, income inequality seems to be virtually identical in Germany and the Netherlands, and it is much lower in both than in the US (whose Gini coefficient is over a third larger than theirs). When we start aggregating over longer periods, people's incomes become more nearly the same; and hence there is a tendency across all countries for measures of five- and ten-yearly income inequality to decline. But as shown in figure 4, that decline in income inequality over time is rather steeper in the Netherlands than in the US; and it is much steeper in the Netherlands than in Germany. Looking at inequality in people's five- or ten-year aggregated income, the gap between the Netherlands and the US has widened further, and on those longer-term bases a

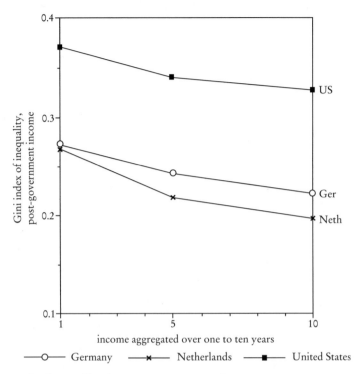

Figure 4   Inequality in post-government income
Source: Based on Goodin et al., 1999, Appendix Table A3 (Eq 1A)

clear difference has emerged between Germany and the Netherlands. In those longer-term views, the social democratic Dutch welfare regime displays decisively less income inequality than either of the other two welfare regimes.

The next question is how to apportion credit for those reductions in income inequality as between government transfers and pre-government income volatility. The statistics showing the proportion of pre-government inequality to have disappeared from the post-government income distribution are presented in figure 5. There we see that, on a one-yearly basis, government transfers eradicate around a third of income inequality in the two European countries (under in the Netherlands, over in Germany). Government transfers in the US are less than half as effective at erasing pre-government income inequality. Furthermore, the US performance is no better on a five- and ten-yearly basis, and Germany's is only a little better. The Dutch, in contrast, perform significantly better over time, reducing income inequality substantially more over longer periods. On a ten-yearly basis, Dutch government transfers are a bit better at reducing income inequality than the German, whereas on a

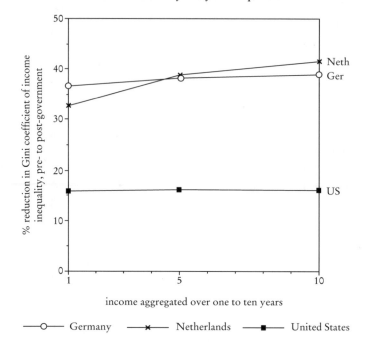

Figure 5   Government reduction in income inequality
Source: Based on Goodin et al., 1999, Appendix Table A3 (Eq 4A)

one-yearly basis they prove worse than the German by about the same margin.

Of course it comes as no surprise that the liberal US welfare regime has most inequality and does least to reduce it. That is simply not one of the priorities of the liberal regime. The relatively strong performance of the corporatist German welfare regime, which does not prioritize social equality either, is rather more surprising. Still, over the longer term, the social democratic regime once again pulls clearly ahead.

Income Instability

Reducing income instability is the classically corporatist concern.[20] There are various ways of assessing the variability of a person's income over time. Statistically most attractive is the 'coefficient of variation' (standard deviation divided by the mean), which tells us whether the person's income in each of ten years is clustered tightly, or dispersed widely, around the average of that person's income over those ten years. The higher the coefficient of variation, the more variable (and hence unstable) the person's income over time.

We calculate the coefficient of variation for each person's income over ten years. Then we find the person in each country whose coefficient of variation is exactly in the middle of that national sample: half the people in the country have incomes that vary more, half less. That median coefficient of variation is then taken as our indicator of the variability of incomes across the country as a whole, and cross-national comparisons simply juxtapose countries' median coefficients of variation.

Our key findings on the issue of income instability appear in figure 6. On the left we show the instability of the median person's pre-government income; on the right, we show the instability of the median person's post-government income. The slope of the line connecting the two represents the contribution that government transfers make toward stabilizing people's incomes in each of those countries.[21]

Figure 6 shows that that the median instability in pre-government income is much lower in the Netherlands than in either Germany or the US. Dutch government transfers, however, make less of a further reduction in pre-government income instability. (The slope of the Dutch line is less steeply downwards than those of the other two countries.) Median post-government income instability turns out to be identical

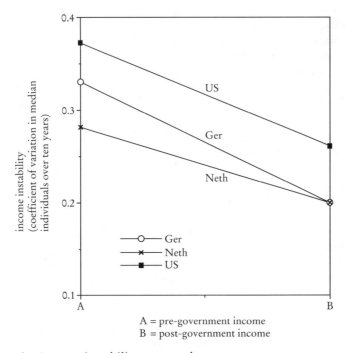

A = pre-government income
B = post-government income

Figure 6 Income instability, pre- and post-government
Source: Based on Goodin et al., 1999, Appendix Table A5 (Stab 3A)

in Germany and the Netherlands (and while higher in the US, much less so).

In short, the social democratic welfare regime starts with relatively stable incomes and keeps them that way, while the corporatist welfare regime starts with less stable incomes but makes them more so. In the end, there seems to be nothing to choose between the two. While the liberal regime reduces income instability, too, it both starts and ends with more income instability than either of the other two regimes.

Economic Growth

All welfare regimes operate against the backdrop of economic constraint. All of them pursue the goals that they do, in the ways that they do, with at least one eye to economic consequences. Thus, a final dimension for assessing comparative welfare regime performance – and one particularly close to the hearts of economic liberals – is in terms of their impact on the macro-economy.

Of course, no one really knows what the impact of any specific policy intervention is on the economy overall. Economists build large and complex models of the economy, wherein a great many things interact in a great many ways to produce or restrain economic growth. All we can do in the present context is to note the economic performance of these three economies over this period.

There are many ways to measure economic performance and many sources of such statistics. The most standard and authoritative is the OECD. A glance at its statistics confirms that economic growth rates, however construed, have been broadly similar across all three of these countries for the period under review. The left-hand column for each country in figure 7 shows, for example, broadly uniform increases in GDP per capita across all three countries over the ten years under study.

Ordinary economic growth rates tell us how well the economy overall is doing, but not necessarily how well people within it are doing. Not all of the growth dividend is necessarily passed on to consumers; and what is passed on is often shared out in a very unequal way.

Ultimately, however, the only reason for worrying how the economy is doing is because we care how well people are doing within it. In the right-hand column for each country in figure 7, we therefore show the percentage increase in the median individual's income over the ten years under study.[22] Judging economic performance in terms of the real equivalent income of median individuals in each country, the Netherlands (and Germany to an only slightly lesser extent) once again are very far ahead of the US. Although all three countries experienced essentially the same growth in per capita GDP, these countries differed dramatically in what

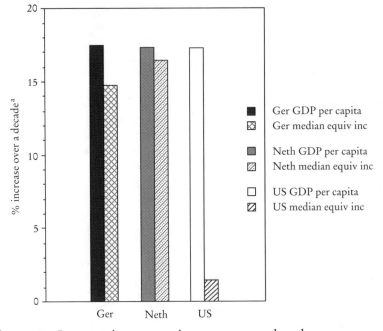

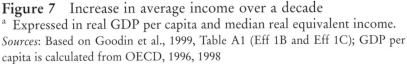

Figure 7   Increase in average income over a decade
[a] Expressed in real GDP per capita and median real equivalent income.
Sources: Based on Goodin et al., 1999, Table A1 (Eff 1B and Eff 1C); GDP per capita is calculated from OECD, 1996, 1998

they did with it. In the Netherlands and to a slightly lesser extent in Germany, the benefits of economic growth were substantially passed on to middle-income people. In the US, they were not.

Not only does the social democratic welfare regime of the Netherlands top the league in terms of all the standard welfare-related goals we ascribe to welfare regime, it also tops the league in terms of economic well-being, most certainly in terms of the economic well-being of the average citizen. Conversely, the liberal welfare regime of the US not only comes bottom of the league in terms of welfare-related goals; it also does far worse at promoting economic well-being for average citizens.

Conclusions

The first conclusion to be drawn from the above is that, when judging welfare regimes, we should 'watch what they do, not what they say'. We should be judging their *performance*, not their protestations, promises or professed priorities.

Taking welfare regimes at their word, we might naturally assume that corporatists should be best at promoting income stability; social democrats should be best at minimizing poverty and income equality; and liberals should be best at reducing poverty while promoting economic growth. That is where their rhetorical emphases fall. That is where their policy priorities point.

But trying is not succeeding. Try as they might, corporatist regimes do not succeed in bettering the social democratic performance when it comes to minimizing income instability. Nor do liberal regimes reduce poverty nearly as well as social democrats, nor do they even succeed in putting nearly as much money into the average person's pocket.

When looking at what welfare regimes do rather than what they say, a second conclusion emerges: the choice among them then becomes far easier than we ever dared to imagine. Whatever it is we want from welfare regimes – whether it is income stability, income equality, low poverty or high economic prosperity – the social democratic welfare regime seems the best on offer. It is at least as good as the other two on all of those dimensions, and far better on some of them. Conversely, the liberal regime is unambiguously the worst on offer, no matter which of those values are prioritized.

Discussions of comparative welfare regimes are rife with talk trade-offs. A monograph on *Equality and Efficiency* (1975) by the Nobel Laureate Arthur Okun is subtitled *The Big Trade-Off*. From the armchair perspective of the necessary truths of micro-economics, it seems that it simply *must* be the case that generous public assistance inhibits work effort and hence economic growth; stabilizing incomes simply *must* preclude redistributing them in a more egalitarian fashion; and so on. Or so it seems from the economist's armchair.

What is true within the realm of some refined micro-economic model is not necessarily true in the real world, however. Our panels suggest that all those familiar trade-offs are not strictly necessary, after all. Far from having to face up to hard choices, we can have it all. Whichever dimension of welfare-regime performance is prioritized, the Netherlands comes out either the clear winner or in shared first place.

Our second conclusion, then, can be encapsulated in the slogan: 'make no gratuitous trade-offs'. It may be a mark of political maturity and intellectual honesty to face up to hard choices, where a choice between mutually incompatible options really is necessary. But fetishizing hard choices is a mistake, too. Trade-offs are something we should avoid if we possibly can.

A final conclusion is simply that, when it comes to welfare states, there is 'something for everyone'. People's economic fortunes fluctuate wildly over time, across all three countries and across virtually all income classes within them. In all three countries, the median person's highest year's pre-government income over this decade was more than twice that person's lowest year's income.[23] (That, mind you, is the median: half the population's pre-government income varied by a factor of more than two!) Even the well-to-do are affected. Everywhere, around one in six of the people who started the decade in the top half of the income distribution dipped into pre-government poverty some time over the course of the next nine years.[24] Thus, everyone – or anyway the vast majority – is seriously at risk of substantially interrupted earnings.[25]

In such circumstances virtually any of us might stand to benefit, some time or another, from welfare state programmes.[26] That is a familiar point to make, *vis-à-vis* old age insurance (a benefit which each of us will someday draw, provided we live long enough). On our evidence, the same might be broadly true of social welfare programmes in general. We are all genuinely at risk of needing them some day. In setting up schemes to help the less well-off, we are also setting up schemes to secure our own future.

Notes

This chapter summarizes themes from our book *The Real Worlds of Welfare Capitalism*, Cambridge, Cambridge University Press, 1999: further details and supporting evidence will be found there, as will a record of our larger debts. For comments on this synopsis specifically, we particularly thank Diane Gibson and audiences at RC 19 of the International Sociological Association and the A. E. Havens Center for the Study of Social Structure & Social Change at the University of Wisconsin, Madison. The views expressed here are our own and may not reflect those of our employers.

1 Atkinson, Rainwater and Smeeding, 1995; Mitchell, 1991.
2 LIS now has a Panel Comparability (PACO) Project; see http://www.ceps.lu.
3 The one we will be using is higher, which accounts for the discrepancy between these PSID poverty statistics for the US and those we report here. On the US poverty line, see Ruggles, 1990.
4 Duncan et al., 1984; Bane and Ellwood, 1994. Bane and Ellwood both served as senior officials in the US Department of Health and Human Services under President Clinton and their 'poverty spell' findings clearly underlie the 'two years and you work' rule written into the 'Personal Responsibility and Work Opportunity Reconciliation Act of 1996', Public Law 104–193 [H.R. 3734], 22 August 1996, 110 Stat. 2105.
5 Of the seven internationally comparable studies contained in the PACO files (see n. 2), only the US files run for more than ten years. There are seven-and eight-year runs for Luxembourg and Germany in the PACO files; the Netherlands does not deposit its panel data to PACO. Eventually the PACO file will be a rich resource, but it is not yet really ready to use. The same is also true of Eurostat's European Community Household Panel, which began in 1994 (and obviously does not include the non-European countries).
6 The US data are from the Panel Study on Income Dynamics run by the University of Michigan. The German is from the German Socio-Economic Panel, starting in 1984 and run by the Deutsches Institut für

Wirtschaftsforschung, Berlin. The Dutch is from the Dutch Socio-Economic Panel Survey, run since 1984 by the Centraal Bureau voor de Statistiek. The US and German data are rendered comparable through the 'matching file' periodically released through the Center for Demography and Economics of Aging at Syracuse University. Ruud Muffels and Henk-Jan Dirven have recast the original Dutch data into the same form as that US-German file for purposes of our book (Goodin et al., 1999); and it is their analyses of those data, the original of which remains held in the CBS, upon which we base the results reported here.

7 Esping-Andersen, 1990, p. 74.

8 Only Austria seems purer (Esping-Andersen, 1990, p. 74).

9 Esping-Andersen, 1990, pp. 52, 74; see similarly LIS results (Mitchell, 1991; Atkinson, Rainwater and Smeeding, 1995). That is to say, its tax-transfer policies are as redistributive as social democratic countries' in general, even though the Netherlands' labour market policy has historically been far less 'active' than those of Scandinavian social democracies, with female labour force participation rates being particularly low. In those latter respects, the Netherlands seems more akin to the other countries of continental Europe (Esping-Andersen, 1996).

10 Swedish panel data are archived at PACO. But whereas the panels cited here were all surveyed at least once a year, the Swedish panel was surveyed only every other year (in 1984, 1986 and 1988) or sporadically (not again until 1991). In the first two waves (1984 and 1986), the Swedish study administered long questionnaires comparable to those used in the other three panel studies we examine. In the latter two waves (1988 and 1991), the Swedish study administered only a very short battery of largely non-comparable questions. Thus it comes as no surprise that the PACO team have been unable to render it sufficiently comparable to incorporate into their PACO database.

11 World Bank, 1996, pp. 18–19. The US and Germany are clearly the biggest liberal and corporatist regimes respectively, judged in terms of population or GDP; and both are among the most successful, judged in terms of economic growth. In terms of population or GDP, the Netherlands is twice the size of Sweden and three times that of Denmark; and it has enjoyed striking economic success in recent years, while the Swedish economy has been unravelling (cf. Hemerijck and van Kersbergen, 1997; Lindbeck et al., 1994).

12 1985–94 for Germany and the Netherlands and 1983–92 for the US, as statistics for years those were the latest available at the time of writing.

13 Cf. Goodin, 1998.

14 Standardly, earnings in the labour market (though rentiers do so through earnings in property or capital markets); standardly, one's own market earnings (though earners' earnings are also used to provide for non-earning dependants within the household). Titmuss' (1974) description of this as a 'residual welfare state' is apt, for the same basic Poor Law mechanisms can be (and historically were) adapted to distinctly pre-liberal, non-market conceptions of the 'ordinary way' in which people are provided for.

15 This is the infamous 'principle of lesser eligibility' (making welfare the least attractive option) written into the New Poor Law in England in 1834 and widely replicated (Checkland and Checkland, 1974; Polanyi, 1944).

16 'Income' is 'equivalent income'. That is calculated by pooling together all the incomes of all members of the household, dividing by an 'equivalence scale' that reflects the economies of scale of larger households (we use the 'square root of the number of members of the household' as our equivalence scale),

and ascribing the resulting income to each member of the household in question.

17 Furthermore, that percentage declines only marginally across all countries over longer time periods: see Goodin et al., 1999, Appendix Table A2 (Pov 1A).

18 The one-year data we present represents the average of two single years: 1987 and 1992 for Germany and the Netherlands, 1985 and 1990 for the US. Those are chosen as the midpoints of our two five-year periods (1985–9 and 1990–94 for the two European countries, 1983–7 and 1988–92 for the US). The ten-year reports thus pertain to the combination of those two five-year periods for each country.

19 Goodin et al., 1999, Appendix Table A2 (Pov 3A).

20 That concern is not confined to corporatists alone, however. Notice that protecting against the risk of interrupted earnings – and providing people with earnings-related benefits to sustain them when their ordinary earnings are interrupted – is the whole point of social insurance, which forms an important component of all welfare regimes worldwide.

21 Note that this is purely an expository device: the independent variable (pre- and post-government instability) does not form an interval scale.

22 These statistics refer to changes in '*real* income', adjusting for inflation. They also refer to '*equivalent* income', adjusting for household size; and the reported increase is that in the income of the *median* individual, not the arithmetic mean across all individuals. All that differs in various respects from the way in which such statistics are standardly reported. But those seem to be the most appropriate ways to report such statistics: what we are interested in is the real standard of living of the average (i.e. the median) person, rather than just statistical artefacts (like means).

23 The ratio is 0.420 in Germany and 0.393 in the US (and only a bit higher, 0.499, in the Netherlands); see Goodin et al., 1999, Appendix Table A5 (Stab 3A). Note that the volatility reported here is not due to the young entering or the old exiting the workforce: this analysis is confined to people who were of prime working age (25–59) in all ten years.

24 Those percentages are nearly half as high even among the most privileged segments of the labour force – prime-aged (25–59) males in the top half of the income distribution, who are white (in the US) or non-guest-workers (in Germany). See Goodin et al., 1999, Appendix Table A2 (Pov 5A).

25 The causes vary, death, incapacity or old age being increasingly augmented by divorce, childbirth or families that are financially dependent upon two earners' incomes.

26 Or would, if government taxes and transfers were arranged in such a way as reliably to help those in pre-government poverty – which in the US they are not, especially for the working poor.

References

Atkinson, A. B., Lee Rainwater and Timothy M. Smeeding, *Income Distribution in OECD Countries: The Evidence from the Luxembourg Income Study (LIS)*, Social Policy Studies no. 18, Paris, OECD, 1995.

Bane, Mary Jo and David T. Ellwood, *Welfare Realities: From Rhetoric to Reform*, Cambridge, MA, Harvard University Press, 1994.

Checkland, S. G. and E. O. A. Checkland, eds, *The Poor Law Report of 1834*, Report from His Majesty's Commission for Enquiring into the Administration and Practical Operation of the Poor Law, Harmondsworth, Penguin Books, 1974 (originally published 1834).

Duncan, Greg J., with Richard D. Coe, Mary E. Corcoran, Martha S. Hill, Saul D. Hoffman and James N. Morgan, *Years of Poverty, Years of Plenty: The Changing Economic Fortunes of American Workers and Families*, Ann Arbor, Survey Research Center, Institute for Social Research, University of Michigan, 1984.

Esping-Andersen, Gøsta, *The Three Worlds of Welfare Capitalism*, Cambridge, Polity Press, 1990.

Esping-Andersen, Gøsta, 'Welfare States without Work: The Impasse of Labour Shedding and Familialism in Continental European Social Policy', in *Welfare States in Transition: National Adaptations in Global Economies*, ed. G. Esping-Andersen, London, Sage for the United Nations Research Institute for Social Development, 1996, pp. 66–87.

Goodin, Robert E., 'Social Welfare as a Collective Social Responsibility', in David Schmidtz and Robert E. Goodin, *Social Welfare and Individual Responsibility*, Cambridge, Cambridge University Press, 1998, pp. 97–194.

Goodin, Robert E., Bruce Headey, Ruud Muffels with Henk-Jan Dirven, *The Real Worlds of Welfare Capitalism*, Cambridge, Cambridge University Press, 1999.

Hemerijck, Anton and Kees van Kersbergen, 'A Miraculous Model? Explaining the New Politics of the Welfare State in the Netherlands', *Acta Politica*, 23, 1997, pp. 258–80.

Lindbeck, Assar, Per Molander, Torsten Persson, Olof Petersson, Agnar Sandmo, Birgitta Swedenborg and Niels Thygesen, *Turning Sweden Around*, Cambridge, MA, MIT Press, 1994.

Mitchell, Deborah, *Income Transfers in Ten Welfare States*, Aldershot, Avebury, 1991.

Okun, Arthur, *Equality and Efficiency: The Big Trade-Off*, Washington DC, Brookings Institution, 1975.

Organization for Economic Co-operation and Development (OECD), *National Accounts, 1960–94*, vol. 1: *Main Aggregates*, Paris, OECD, 1996.

Organization for Economic Co-operation and Development (OECD), *National Accounts, 1960–96*, vol 2; *Main Aggregates*, Paris, OECD, 1998.

Polanyi, Karl, *The Great Transformation*, New York, Rinehart, 1944.

Ruggles, Patricia, *Drawing the Line: Alternative Poverty Measures and their Implications for Public Policy*, Washington, DC, Urban Institute, 1990.

Titmuss, Richard M., *Social Policy*, London, Allen and Unwin, 1974.

World Bank, *World Bank Atlas 1996*, Washington, DC, World Bank, 1996.

A European Welfare State?

Towards a European Welfare State?

Stephan Leibfried

[...]

The Four Social Policy Regimes in the European Community (EC)

[...] 'Social cohesion' is not built into the present structure of the EC. There is no EC welfare state (outside of agriculture). If we look at the different existing welfare systems in Europe may we then realistically expect that a 'Social Europe' will come about by an 'organic' merging of such systems from the bottom up? Positive integration at the EC level would then be a by-product of on-going European economic and political integration. Or are the social and poverty policy regimes of the EC so contradictory that an organic merging from below is not possible and 'harmonization' will necessarily have to come 'from above', i.e. it will have to be synthesized and implemented by an authorized EC bureaucracy? Such a European welfare state would, most likely, presuppose a historical North–South compromise within the EC and, surely, a reformulation of the Rome Treaties, partly already achieved in Maastricht. Without an EC welfare state, in the long run, regional, national welfare regimes will be in atrophy: their economic and legitimatory bases would slowly erode with the completion and further development of the Common Market – just as they eroded in the USA with the realization of its 'common market' inter-state commerce (Peterson and Rom, 1990).

Whether Social Europe might come about via merging from the 'bottom up' can be examined by reviewing typical EC poverty regimes. My attention will centre on the interfaces between poverty, social insurance and poverty policy. The different consequences that the introduction of a *basic income* scheme under each regime might have will be outlined.[1] This is one way to illustrate the practical importance of the differences between these regimes.

Though the discussion of welfare-state regimes usually focuses on those policy areas that quantitatively dominate the welfare state – i.e. the social insurance systems (cf. Schmidt, 1988) – I concentrate on the margins of the welfare state; it is here that the limits – and the contents – of social citizenship are tested, and it is here that any differences in European social policy will be most obstructive.

In the following, I will distinguish four different social policy regimes – four 'worlds of welfare capitalism':[2] the Scandinavian welfare states; the 'Bismarck' countries; the Anglo-Saxon countries; and the 'Latin rim' countries.

The Scandinavian Welfare States

Since the First World War, the welfare states of Scandinavia[3] have stressed the right to work for everyone and have centred their welfare-state policy on this issue and not on compulsory income transfer strategies. Scandinavia fits the type 'modern welfare state'. Universalism reigns, though not primarily through income redistribution outside the sphere of work. Here, the welfare state is *employer of first resort* (mainly for women). Subsidizing 'entry' into – or non-exit from – the labour market is the welfare-state strategy which conveys the institutionalized notion of social citizenship.

In Scandinavian countries, the basic income debate is likely to be used only as an additional argument for the support of a universalist 'work-centred society'. The debate might be of some use for improving 'income packaging' in the Scandinavian welfare state (see Rainwater et al., 1986). Broad-scale issue-specific redistribution, like child allowances, might be improved. Or the rather residual, truly marginal welfare systems there might be improved in such a way that they match the standards of 'Bismarck' countries. But basic income is unlikely to develop into a strong option; to opt out of 'work society' as a general strategy will not be condoned.

The 'Bismarck' Countries

For a century, Germany and Austria have relied on a strategy of 'paying off' social problems, of subsidizing 'exit' from the labour market or even 'non-entry' while pursuing a strong policy of economic development only. These countries might be characterized as 'institutional welfare states'. Here, 'compensatory strategies' which substitute a right to social security for a right to work are prominent, and a basic income debate would be most likely to radicalize the present focus on compensation and exit (or non-entry). The welfare state is not the employer but the *compensator of first resort*, and the institutionalized notion of social citizenship is biased accordingly. Though there is no explicit tradition of universalism in these countries, the 'institutionalized full employment promises' and private labour market 'practices' (of the 1950s to the early 1970s) have created a fragile tradition of virtual universalism (for an overview cf. Leibfried and Voges, 1992).

The basic income debate here amplifies the pre-existing focus on non-entry or easing-exit from the labour market. Perhaps in the Bismarck countries this debate could lead to something like a universalized non-residual needs approach which might become less and less restrictive in terms of means testing and might also develop towards an individual instead of a household orientation.

The Anglo-Saxon Countries

The English-speaking countries have always emphasized the 'residual welfare model' (see Titmuss, 1987: 262), especially in income transfers.[4] They did not accent, as the Scandinavian countries did, the welfare state as the major employer in a 'work society'; rather, they conceived of the welfare state as a work-enforcing mechanism (see Lodemel, 1989). The USA, Australia, New Zealand and also the UK best exemplify the type of 'residual welfare state' (Titmuss, 1987: 367). 'Entry' into the labour market was facilitated more by pure force than by subsidization or by training and qualification policy. Here, selectivism reigns as the principal approach of social policy, making the welfare state rather a *compensator of last resort*. The distance of the Anglo-Saxon model from a 'compensatory regime' or from a Scandinavian 'work society regime' is equally great. Thus 'social citizenship' has remained more of an academic issue in these countries.[5]

The basic income debate in the Anglo-Saxon countries is rather far away from institutionalizing an 'opting out of work society'; it may support the development of a 'normal welfare system' in the Northern European sense. However, the development is not likely to go any further than this. A normal welfare system in the Anglo-Saxon context would mean (especially in the case of the USA) introducing a universal instead of a 'categorical' welfare system (treating each category differently), combining this welfare system with a more prominent role for a public jobs

Table 1 Types of European welfare states

	Scandinavian	Bismarck	Anglo-Saxon	Latin Rim
Type of welfare regime	Modern	Institutional	Residual	Rudimentary
Characteristics	Full employment; welfare state as *employer of first resort* and compensator of last resort	Full growth; welfare state as *compensator of first resort* and employer of last resort	Full growth; welfare state as *compensator of last resort* and tight enforcer of work in the market place	Catching up; welfare state as a semi-*institutionalized promise*
Right to:	Work	Social security	Income transfers	Work and welfare proclaimed
	Backed up by an institutionalized concept of social citizenship		No such back-up	Implemented only partially
Basic income debate	Marginal, but may improve income packaging	May somewhat radicalize decoupling of work and income	May support development of 'normal' welfare system	May support development of 'normal' welfare system

programme that aims at integration into the primary labour market (somewhere between the German and the Scandinavian model), and having adequate ('fair share') and nationally standardized (again especially in the case of the USA) 'welfare' rates.

The 'Latin Rim' Countries

The southern countries of Western Europe, some of them integrated into the EC only in the 1980s, seem to constitute a welfare state regime of their own. This league comprises Spain, Portugal, Greece, to some extent (southern) Italy and, least of all, France.[6] This type could be characterized as 'rudimentary welfare state'. In Portugal, Spain, Italy and Greece, not even a right to welfare is given. In some respects, these states are similar to the Anglo-Saxon countries, *de facto* stressing residualism and forced 'entry' into the labour market. But in these countries, older traditions of welfare (connected to the Catholic Church) seem to exist on which the Anglo-Saxon model and most northern countries cannot build. Moreover, in these countries certain social security programmes serve as basic income measures, although they were not designed as such (the disability pensions in southern Italy seem to have worked out this way; see Ascoli, 1986: 113f., 122). In addition, labour market structures are radically different and often reveal a strong agricultural bias, combined with a 'subsistence' economy which provides a different – non-Northern European – 'welfare'-state background. Finally, these countries do not have a full employment tradition – in particular, one that also fully applies to women – as do some of the Scandinavian countries. But many of these countries have made strong promises pointing towards a 'modern welfare state' in their constitutions; it is the legal, institutional and social implementation which seems to be lacking in the 'Latin rim', the welfare state of *institutionalized promise*. It is hard to gauge the effect of a basic income debate in these countries. The development of 'normal welfare systems' seems most likely – normal in the sense of the Northern European or German welfare model.

These four types of welfare state are summarized in table 1. Modern, institutional, residual and rudimentary welfare states start from rather different, in some cases contradictory, goals and are built on quite disparate intervention structures; and they do not share a common policy (and politics) tradition that could serve as a centripetal force. In any case, this divergence of regimes does not lend support to the notion that a European welfare state might grow via automatic harmonization, building from the national towards the EC level. A 'bottom up' strategy for EC 'social integration' policy seems stillborn.

Whither European Welfare Policy?

'Europeanization' from the 'Top Down' or 'Americanization' from the 'Bottom Up'?

What may be the influence of a continuous Europeanization of economic and representational policy on social, especially poverty, policy? Since automatic harmonization of European social policy, building from the national towards the EC level, is not likely, two alternatives remain:

1 Policy disharmony in welfare policy may either prevail as a permanent underside of European integration or, worse, be transformed into a process of automatic disharmonization at the bottom. National politics may be 'Balkanized' as the European Common Market solidifies, especially when a common currency is achieved. This process resembles what happened to American poverty policy as the New American national state was built, starting at the turn of the twentieth century.

2 Policy disharmony may also provoke – in particular when confronted with more potent pressures for European 'social cohesion' – a Caesarian reaction of European institutions. This might prompt a comprehensive European policy frame for poverty policy – or for all social benefits – primarily tied to social citizenship. In the context of currency union some such non-incremental development is likely [. . .].

Towards 'Americanization' of European Poverty Policy?

In this part, I will concentrate on 'Americanization' as one alternative. Since this path is closest to the given EC situation, I will show how it corresponds with present EC welfare legislation, which is mainly procedural and not substantive (see table 2 below). The development of EC legislation again fits in with the historic model of evolution of poverty policy in European nation-states (see table 3 below).

In my view, European development will most likely leave all poverty and welfare policy at the local or state – that is at a sub-European – level. It is hard to start from a common European denominator. The easy common ground is missing on which a European welfare regime could be built.

Table 2 Status, EC residence permit and poverty support in Germany

	Residence permit	Right to welfare
Self-employed:	For economic activity within EC treaty framework (freedom of services and capital movement); otherwise, see 'Others'	Yes; only take-up of welfare parallel to economic activity is legitimate; otherwise, take-up results in loss of right to residence and in possible deportation
Employed Pre-employed:	For job search in due time (according to EC law, three months)	Yes; beyond due time, take-up of welfare results in loss of right to residence and possibly in deportation[a]
In employment:	Even in the case of sub-poverty-level of remuneration	Yes; parallel take-up of welfare is legitimate
Unemployed:	cf. pre-employed; for the involuntarily unemployed, permit expires as 'availability for work' is denied[b]	Yes; when permit expires, take-up of welfare results in loss of right to residence and possibly in deportation
Not employed[c] Students:	If registered for study and insured in event of sickness	Only temporarily; costs may be recovered from 'home state' of recipient[d]
Pensioners:	If insured in event of sickness and in receipt of sufficient (old age, accident, disability) pension to avoid take-up of welfare	Yes; but take-up of welfare results in loss of right to residence and possibly in deportation
Others:	If insured in event of sickness and in receipt of sufficient resources to avoid take-up of welfare	Yes; but take-up of welfare results in loss of right to residence and possibly in deportation

[a] Section 10, para. 1, no. 10, Ausländergesetz (Alien Bill) stipulates that foreigners may be deported if they cannot support themselves without the take-up of welfare.
[b] Section 103, AFG (Employment Bill).
[c] In the following, I refer to legislation proposed by the Commission (see *Amtsblatt der Europäischen Gemeinschaften*, 28 July 1989, Nr. C. 191/2–6; KOM(89) 275 endg.-SYN 199, 200; 89/C 191/02–04). The Council of Ministers agreed to these somewhat modified proposals on 22 December 1989 (cf. FAZ 23 Dec. 1989). As yet, the 'Not employed' have no mobility rights which are Community protected.
[d] Such recovery, though, would contradict section 4 of the European Convention on Social and Medical Assistance, ratified by all twelve EC member countries.

In contrast to poverty policy, some work-centred social policies – 'health' and 'work safety' issues – would be much easier to 'Europeanize' or to 'harmonize', since these policies are structured in a fairly comparable way to begin with and since the European institutions have a stronger mandate there. Needs-centred social policies are rather difficult to standardize and will have no strong thematic lobby in the European context – unless some poor 'Latin rim' states make it a 'state issue' – and such policies will have a hard time finding a mandate. Thus, the most likely outcome is that needs-centred social policies are least likely to be protected by European development.

One might therefore predict that the 'Europe to be', in terms of social policy and especially in terms of poverty policy, will look much more like the USA did before the 1930s, or like it does today, than like any of the Northern European welfare regimes. Europe after 1992, as far as poverty policy is concerned, might lead to a shift towards the Anglo-Saxon welfare model; at least, it is likely to lead to a welfare state 'Balkanization' quite similar to that in the USA. If 'integration' in poverty policy comes about within these limits it will be of a negative sort, allowing each member state to have its own regime and creating only procedural rules, perhaps also about how to proceed with 'foreign' recipients and with the re-exportation of their burden to their 'home' countries.[7]

What is the current state of EC welfare policy? The few EC rules on welfare that do exist are meaningful only in 'national welfare contexts', where they are meant to become operational. Therefore, I will discuss them in a national – in this case, the 'welfare state generous' German – setting.

At present the situation, as it is captured in table 2, is still at a level where receiving welfare leads to the classic 'poor law' remedial procedures: ship the poor back to their place of origin (in the EC). The EC, therefore, compares with the evolution of poverty policy in European nation-states – still bound to the first of four historical and logical levels of integration of poverty policy, as shown in table 3.

A second, more refined stage of social policy development is realized when a person is permitted to stay in the country granting him or her welfare but the costs of support are charged back to his or her place of origin (table 3). To channel transfers from many national sources through one national agency is a regular feature of social security networks established in bilateral agreements; for example, when pensions are paid to an aged migrant worker. Community law allows for this possibility in welfare policy exclusively for 'students', a most temporary status (see table 2: 'Not employed, Students'). An internal administrative shifting of costs is still rare between national poverty bureaucracies. At the moment, such a solution seems not to be envisioned for the aged (see table 2: 'Not employed, Pensioners') – though they are closest to pensioners, where this

Table 3 Steps in integration of poverty policy

Step	Characteristics
1	'Shipping the poor back home'
2	Shifting only the costs of poor support to the locality of origin
3	Treatment of EC citizens as national (or local) citizens in each country (or community)
4	Creation of European substantive and procedural welfare standards

solution already exists within social insurance. An aged person moving from Germany to Spain, therefore, has to prove to the Spanish authorities that he or she has sufficient resources not to be in need of welfare. Nevertheless, a solution similar to that for 'students' may have to come about for pensioners who did move to another EC country, stayed there for a long time, and then needed long-term care arrangements that they could not afford without welfare co-payments. Rather than destroy the new, last social roots at the place of retirement by insisting that these pensioners return to their country of origin in the EC, it would seem more desirable to recover outlays from that country.

A third step in the evolutionary ladder (see table 3) is taken when take-up of welfare in Germany – or for that matter in any other EC country which grants a right to welfare – becomes as legitimate for EC citizens as it is for German citizens, or for the citizens of any respective EC country. This is the case only in connection with employment (see Zuleeg, 1987); most extremely in the case of low-wage employment (see table 2: 'Employed, In employment'), less in the case of joblessness ('Unemployed') and least in the case of non-employment (job search, 'Pre-employed').

The European Court decided in the cases of Levin and Kempf that it is only relevant under European law that a person be gainfully 'employed' and 'active in wage or salaried employment', independent of whether he or she is earning less than the state-defined subsistence minimum (Zuleeg, 1987: 344f.). For the residence permit of an EC citizen 'it is irrelevant whether such income ... is increased by other income up to this minimum or whether the person is satisfied with his [or her] below-poverty income, as long as he [or she] is truly active in wage or salaried employment' (European Court Reports 1986, 1749ff.). This interpretation does not hinge on what the country concerned defines as 'employment'; it thus holds universally in the EC.

Thus German social security law – Section 8 of the fourth book of the SGB, the Welfare Law Code – levies no pension contributions on 'insignificant employment', defined as being below fifteen hours per week or earnings less than 470 DM (parameters as of 1 January 1990).[8] Looking at the hours only, Kempf – the plaintiff in the European Court case – would not have been considered 'employed' according to German law. But according to superior EC law he is considered 'employed' in Germany, and thus has a right of residence and access to all social benefits in Germany, which includes a right to welfare.

Independent of what a national 'standard employment relationship' is, the EC and its courts set their own Europe-wide principles. A broad interpretation of 'employment' through the Court has been one of the avenues of moving towards 'social citizenship' under the constraints of an employment-oriented concept of freedom and European integration (see, most extensively, Steinmeyer, 1990). The same solution obtains in the case of self-employment that does not provide sufficient resources for self-support (see table 2: 'Self-employed'). Again, welfare may be legitimately used as a supplementary benefit for EC citizens. In this case, however, there is no 'pre' and 'post' protective status as it relates to the employment situation (job search, unemployment). Self-employment is thus less shielded in an EC social policy context against the risk of poverty. But there is also less of a necessity to shield it: empirically, these cases are not very significant; and legally, a Gestalt-switch of the 'self-employed' into the status of 'employed, searching for work' can easily be orchestrated by the person concerned.

The four steps in integration of European poverty policy have been summarized in table 3. [At the time of writing], Step 1 is still the norm, and Steps 2 and 3 are the exception. Step 4, which aims more at a European poverty regime, is entirely out of reach. If the European Court of Justice were to take up the challenge of the Maastricht revisions of the EC Treaty, this might catapult the EC's social and poverty policy immediately to Step 3 and would do away with all present residential and financial restrictions discussed above. Why? Because until now European citizenship has been limited to the migrant worker and – *through* him or her – to the family. But at the Maastricht summit, to demonstrate at least some headway in political and social union, it was agreed 'to strengthen the protection of the rights and interests of the nationals of its Member States through the introduction of a citizenship of the Union. The agreement reads:

> Citizenship of the Union is hereby established. Every person holding the nationality of a member state shall be a citizen of the Union. Every Union citizen shall have the right to move and reside freely within the territory of the Member States [and to receive consular support. No explicit fiscal preconditions seem to be set.] Union citizens resident in the Member States of which they are not nationals will have the right to vote and stand as candidates in municipal and European elections.[9]

This agreement may just seem symbolically gratifying. But it could actually imply for Europe what two basic Supreme Court decisions, Edwards

v. California and Shapiro v. Thomson,[10] achieved for the USA: a right to travel, even when the aim is just to attain better special social benefits.[11] Edwards was arrested for bringing his brother-in-law, an indigent, from Texas to California. To grasp the European analogy let me quote some of the Supreme Court's reasoning in 1941. While California pleaded that other states, like Texas, should not be able 'to get rid of their poor...by low relief and insignificant welfare allowances and drive them into California to become our public charges' (168), the Supreme Court focused on the limits which a federal union places on state power:

> And none is more certain than the prohibition against attempts on the part of any single state to isolate itself from difficulties common to all of them by restraining the transportation of persons and property across its borders....[T]he peoples of the several States must sink or swim together, and...in the long run prosperity and salvation are in union and not in division. (174)

Central to that Supreme Court decision was an underlying assumption, an 'assumed *national* responsibility to address the problem of poverty' (Garth, 1986: 100). The Supreme Court notes a 'growing recognition that in an industrial society the task of providing assistance to the needy has ceased to be local in character. The duty to share the burden, if not wholly to assume it, has been recognized not only by State governments, but by the Federal government as well' (175). From a federal point of view it does not matter whether poverty is in Texas or in California. Does it matter from an EC point of view whether poverty is in Portugal or in Germany, in Ireland or in England? The EC with its new competency *vis-à-vis* 'social exclusion' (*Financial Times*, 12 December 1991), with its new unconditional citizenship and its old general responsibility to deal with 'regional inequality' (Structural Funds), could grasp this opportunity for member states to swim instead of to sink together, if 'social citizenship' were to become a focus for a continuous rights-building exercise at the EC level from the 1990s onwards.

'Europeanization' of Poverty Policy

European institutions could also define European standards of poverty policy, 'social rights' for European citizens 'from the top down' – in a Bismarckian, Napoleonic fashion. These standards could be designed to bring the top – the more generous welfare systems – down or to bring the bottom – the more miserly welfare systems – up. These standards could rely on a European formula (for example, 40 per cent of the average national wage income to be used as the basic welfare rate of each nation) which could still allow for variance between the different nations. As yet I do not see how the political and juridical base for a beneficial European standardization might be forthcoming. However, if the EC may not set standards that inform a European right to welfare, it might still subsidize national poverty policy systematically; for example, in underdeveloped or peripheral regions (cf. on the different strategies, Hauser, 1983, 1987).

With social security 'harmonized' – or not (see Schmähl, 1989: 47) – at the national level and not institutionalized at the European level, it would be a rather peculiar situation to have poverty policy partly centralized supranationally at the EC level. The 'showcase' effect *vis-à-vis* the poor produced at the Community level might even surpass the national 'parading of the poor' so well known from the US social policy scene in AFDC (Aid for Families with Dependent Children).

The Europeanization of poverty policy might also take quite a different angle: it may be that certain risks (the 'deserving poor') will be Europeanized; for example, the 'poverty of the aged' and, much less likely, the poverty of the unemployed. Here, there might be an agreement among all nations for a rather positive means-tested solution. Thus, the 'deserving' categories of the poor, which are already 'privileged' in many of the EC member countries (see Schulte, 1991), could be Europeanized. All the other poor might be left to be dealt with at the state or local level according to diverging national traditions. This filtering of the poor might permit a cultural construction of an 'underclass' at the national level, a stratum against which prejudice might then be better directed.

If such a development were to come about, it would lead to another Anglo-Saxonization (in the sense of the US model) of the European welfare context: the 'categorical' approach to welfare will be imported and the universal approaches which are dominant in Northern European states will be slowly subverted. The USA, with its fixation on single mothers' welfare (AFDC), is the most prominent example of the categorical approach – which Germany had already discarded in the 1920s. Also, if the EC decides partly to subsidize minimum income developments, then control devices of special revenue sharing, as they have evolved in the US residual welfare policy regime (especially in AFDC), are likely candidates for Europeanization. Once the benefits of means-tested income transfers cannot be targeted at nationals only, such transfers may either slowly wither away or have to be delivered directly at the European level or nationally in a strongly harmonized way.

Since European Community law at present (some changes are under way) makes national solutions of the categorical sort difficult unless these nations allow 'transfer exports' to other European countries – the economic benefits of such transfers may not be sheltered nationally (Zuleeg, 1989) – there is a political and economic incentive for a straightforward European categorical solution.

That a more radicalized version of a basic income might become the EC approach seems, at this time, rather unlikely – though the discussion of these issues in a European context may be beneficial for a push towards more generous traditional 'welfare' solutions at the European level.

Conclusion

A unified European poverty regime is no 'all-purpose weapon'. Surely, Europe should develop its own perspectives on a 'War on Poverty' and its standards for a fair distribution of income. Poverty, though, is not limited to the income dimension alone but concerns all sorts of resources – be it education, qualifications or other means of social integration (see Friedrich et al., 1979: 11– 47). But to focus first on absent income may be the easiest way to make deprivation and marginalization visible ('social reporting'; see Leibfried and Voges, 1990) at the European level and to politicize them, using it as an eye-opener for wider poverty issues.

Access to the road from a common market to a Social Europe, a European welfare state, has barely been gained. It will be a long road – but with monetary union on the books it may have to be travelled speedily (Eichengreen, 1990). Germany's first unification at the end of the nineteenth century led to the creation of the national welfare state. This state was built on a then timely concept of social citizenship – for workers. The founding of a United Europe depended mainly, if not totally, on the 'four freedoms': the free movement of persons, goods, capital and services. Thus 'economic citizenship', which does contain some civil aspects of 'social citizenship', is at the fore. Political as well as social citizenship have, until now, been marginal in the process of European unification. For this reason, European unification reminds one more of the unification of the USA – a process in which political citizenship was pertinent from the beginning and has been complemented by social citizenship only since the 1930s, if at all.

The citizenship on which a unifying Europe might come to rest seems primarily an economic or civil notion, secondarily a political one, and only lastly a social one (see Marshall, 1964: 78 ff.). This pattern repeats British and American precedents and is not anchored well either in Germany or in Scandinavian history. Unity in such a restrictive frame would turn into a unity of 'possessive individualism', a unity of markets only. It will not be the unity of an enlightened 'Social Europe' synthesizing its traditions of democracy and solidarity, of civil and social rights, and building on its traditions of merging the citizen and the social state. But, maybe, steps taken towards European citizenship at Maastricht in 1991 will allow the metamorphosis of the 'market citizen' (1957–91) into the 'full-fledged' EC

citizen – a new synthesis which includes a European welfare state trajectory, building on universal rights?

The coming of such an enlightened 'Social Europe' also depends on the
challenges provided and the escapes offered by its 'environment'. Japan
and the USA do not offer the EC a better model for social integration.
'Social Europe' might lose much of its impetus if Eastern Europe – at least
being perceived as 'social' pressure in the days of 'systems competition'[12]
– were to turn into 'less Central Europe than *Zwischeneuropa*...a
dependent intermediate zone of weak states, national prejudice, inequality, poverty, and *Schlamassel*' (Ash, 1990: 22).

Notes

This paper is reproduced in edited and revised form, by permission of Campus
Verlag of Frankfurt a.M. and Westview Press of Boulder, Colorado, from
the volume *Social Policy in a Changing Europe*, edited by Szusza Ferge and Jon
Eivind Kolberg, published May 1992 in the series 'Public Policy and Social Welfare'.

I am grateful to Lutz Leisering, Chiara Saraceno, Bernd Schulte, Peter Townsend
and several participants at the 1990 annual conference of the Social Policy Association in Bath for comments and critical remarks. Hannah Brückner, Marlene
Ellerkamp, Peter Klein, Jutta Mester and Gitta Stender were helpful in completing
this paper. It appeared, with revisions, in *Social Policy in a Changing Europe*. This
extract from C. Jones, ed., *New Perspectives on the Welfare State*, London,
Routledge, 1993, pp. 139–56. The analysis of the effects of European integration
on national welfare states has been developed further in: Stephan Leibfried and
Paul Pierson, eds, *European Social Policy: Between Fragmentation and Integration*, Washington, DC: Brookings Institution Press 1995; a concise and updated
overview is to be found in: Stephan Leibfried and Paul Pierson, 'Social Policy', in
Helen and William Wallace, eds, *Policy-Making in the European Union*, 4th ed.,
Oxford, Oxford University Press 2000 (in preparation).

1 On the structure of 'Basic Income Security' in former West Germany see
  Leibfried, 1990.
2 I add another category ('Latin rim' countries) to Esping-Andersen's (1990)
  three worlds of welfare capitalism. I have studied potential trajectories of *'top
  down'* development of a European welfare state elsewhere (Leibfried, 1992;
  Leibfried and Pierson, 1992).
3 In fact, the Scandinavian model is essentially a Swedish model, which holds for
  Norway, Denmark and Finland only with important modifications.
4 If one took in-kind transfers into account, the prominent UK example of the
  NHS would highlight the taxonomy in a different way.
5 This is, historically speaking, more so in the USA than in the UK, though
  England has moved visibly towards the US in the last decade.
6 In France (see Haupt, 1989: 271 ff.) the strong family focus of all social policy
  (and concomitantly of wage policy) probably leads to a special sort of welfare
  state regime.
7 Outside of building social insurance institutions against poverty in old age or
  with regard to invalids and the sick, this was the traditional pattern of poverty
  policy integration in the building of the German Reich from 1871 to the First

World War. The '*Unterstützungswohnsitzgesetz*' basically left all substantive poverty law to the states or local governments and was concerned only with issues of 'free mobility'.

8 The same holds true for health insurance. Blue-collar workers working less than ten hours a week have no right to continued wage payments in the event of sickness. Then again, unemployment insurance does not reach out to certain 'part-time employed'. For instance, it covers only people working eighteen hours and more per week.

9 *Financial Times*, 12 December 1991: 6.

10 394 US (1969). The Supreme Court dealt here with statutes which limited welfare benefits to persons who had resided for at least one year in the respective state. Justice Brennan: 'State may no more try to fence out those indigents who seek higher welfare benefits than it may try to fence out indigents generally' (631).

11 'Social tourism' is the not so benign label in the negative political discourse that is characteristic of Northern Europe looking south (and lately east).

12 The necessity to 'outcompete' East Germany in social policy was behind much of West German social reform in the 1950s. On this 'struggle of principles' see Hockerts (1980). This necessity has now withered away. In its stead 'functional equivalents', internal mechanisms, will have to be developed which serve as forcing mechanisms for social innovation in the future.

References

Ascoli, U., 'The Italian Welfare State between Incrementalism and Rationalization', in *Time to Care in Tomorrow's Welfare Systems: The Nordic Experience and the Italian Case*, ed. Laura Balbo and Helga Nowotny, Vienna, Eurosocial, 1986, pp. 107–41.

Ash, T. G., 'Eastern Europe: The Year of Truth', *New York Review of Books*, 15 February 1990, xxxvii (2), pp. 17–22.

Eichengreen, B., 'One Money for Europe? Lessons from the US Currency Union', *Economic Policy*, 10, 1990, pp. 117–87.

Friedrich, H. et al., *Soziale Deprivation und Familiendynamik*, Göttingen, Vandenhoeck and Ruprecht, 1979.

Garth, B. G., 'Migrant Workers and Rights of Mobility in the European Community and the United States: A Study of Law, Community and Citizenship in the Welfare State', in *Europe and the American Federal Experience, Vol. I: Methods, Tools and Institutions, Book 3: Forces and Potentials for a European Identity*, ed. Mauro Cappelletti, Monica Secombe and Joseph Weiler, Berlin, de Gruyter, 1986, pp. 85–163.

Haupt, H. G., *Sozialgeschichte Frankreichs seit 1789*, Frankfurt am Main, Suhrkamp, 1989.

Hauser, R., *Problems of Harmonization of Minimum Income Regulations Among EC Member Countries*, Frankfurt am Main, sfb 3, Working Paper no. 118, 1983.

Hauser, R., *Möglichkeiten und Probleme der Sicherung eines Mindesteinkommens in den Mitgliedsländern der Europäischen Gemeinschaft*, Frankfurt am Main, sfb 3, Working Paper no. 246, 1987.

Hockerts, H. G., *Sozialpolitische Entscheidungen im Nachkriegsdeutschland. Allierte und deutsche Sozialversicherungspolitik 1945 bis 1959*, Stuttgart, Klett-Cotta, 1980.

Leibfried, S., 'Soziale Grundsicherung – Das Bedarfsprinzip in der Sozial und Gesellschaftspolitik der Bundesrepublik', in *Strukturwandel der Sozialpolitik. Lohnarbeitszentrierte Sozialpolitik und soziale Grundsicherung*, ed. Georg Vobruba, Frankfurt am Main, Suhrkamp, 1990, pp. 182–225.

Leibfried, S. 'Social Europe, Welfare State Trajectories of the European Community', in *How to Organise Prevention*, ed. Hans-Uwe Otto and Gabi Floesser, Berlin, de Gruyter, CeS-Working Paper No. 10/91, 1992, pp. 17–60.

Leibfried, S. and P. Pierson, 'The Prospects for Social Europe', *Politics & Society*, 20(3), 1992, pp. 333–66.

Leibfried, S. and W. Voges, 'Keine Sonne für die Armut. Vom Sozialhilfebezug als Verlauf ('Karriere') – Ohne umfassende Information keine wirksame Armutsbekämpfung', *Nachrichtendienst des Deutschen Vereins für öffentliche und private Fürsorge*, 70(5), May 1990, pp. 135–41.

Leibfried, S. and W. Voges, *Armut im modernen Wohlfahrtsstaat*, Opladen, Westdeutscher Verlag, 1992.

Lodemel, I., *The Quest for Institutional Welfare and the Problem of the Residuum: The Case of Income Maintenance and Personal Social Care Policies in Norway and Britain 1946 to 1966*, London, LSE, Department of Social Science and Administration, June 1989.

MacDougall Report, *Report of the Study Group on the Role of Public Finance in European Integration, Vol. 1: General Report, Vol. 2: Individual Contributions and Working Papers*, Brussels, Commission of the European Communities, Economic and Financial Series A 13, 1977.

Marjolin Report, *Report of the Study Group 'Economic and Monetary Union 1980'*, Brussels, EC, March 1975.

Marshall, T. H., 'Citizenship and Social Class', in T. H. Marshall, *Class, Citizenship and Social Development*, essays by T. H. Marshall, with an introduction by Seymour Martin Lipset, Chicago, IL, University of Chicago Press, 1964, pp. 71–134.

Peterson, P. E. and M. C. Rom, *Welfare Magnets*, Washington, DC, Brookings Institution, 1990.

Rainwater, L., M. Rein and J. Schwartz, *Income Packaging in the Welfare State: A Comparative Study of Family Income*, Oxford, Clarendon Press, 1986.

Schmähl, W., 'Europäischer Binnenmarkt und soziale Sicherung: Einige Aufgaben und Fragen aus ökonomischer Sicht', *Zeitschrift für die gesamte Versicherungswirtschaft*, 1989, pp. 29–50.

Schmidt, M. G. *Sozialpolitik: Historische Entwicklung und internationaler Vergleich*, Opladen, Leske and Budrich, 1988.

Schulte, B., 'Das Recht auf Mindesteinkommen in der europäischen Gemeinschaft: Nationaler status quo und supranationale Initiativen', *Sozialer Fortschritt*, 40(1), 1991, pp. 7–21.

Steinmeyer, H. D., 'Freizügigkeit und soziale Rechte in einem Europa der Bürger', in *Das Europa der Bürger in einer Gemeinschaft ohne Binnengrenzen*, ed. Siegfried Magiera, Baden-Baden, Nomos, 1990, pp. 63–80.

Taylor, Paul, *The Limits of European Integration*, New York, Columbia University Press, 1983.

Titmuss, R. M., 'Developing Social Policy in Conditions of Rapid Change: the Role of Social Welfare', in *The Philosophy of Welfare: Selected Writings of Richard M. Titmuss*, ed. Brian Abel-Smith and Kay Titmuss, London, Allen and Unwin, 1987, pp. 254–68 (first published 1972).

Zuleeg, M., 'Die Zahlung von Ausgleichszulagen über die Binnengrenzen der Europäischen Gemeinschaft', in *Deutsche Rentenversicherung*, 10, 1989, pp. 621–9.

Zuleeg, S., 'Zur Einwirkung des Europäischen Gemeinschaftsrechts auf die Sozial-hilfe nach dem Bundessozialhilfegesetz', *Nachrichtendienst des Deutschen Ver-eins für öffentliche und private Fürsorge*, 67(10), 1987, pp. 342–7.

Is the European Social Model Fragmenting?

John Grahl and Paul Teague

Introduction

This article presents an overview of the European social model, which is understood as a specific combination of comprehensive welfare systems and strongly institutionalized and politicized forms of industrial relations. The main argument is that this model is in serious crisis, primarily as a result of general economic developments which have undermined its economic functionality. It is suggested, however, that it is too early to write off the European model or to rule out the possibility of its successful reform. Although there are as yet few convincing signs of effective modernization of institutions or practices, influential political forces exist which reject the dismantling of the model and are likely to inspire continuing efforts at its reconstruction. An important index of the strength of these forces will be the progress made in the project of European integration.

A key methodological problem in any survey of European developments as a whole is how to deal with the marked differences across countries, both in existing institutions and in patterns of change. Any account which ignores these differences must seem excessively simplistic; on the other hand, a purely comparative approach may make too much of them. The present argument rests on the following hypotheses. First, convergence towards a common model was a prominent feature of the period of rapid growth in Western Europe from the late 1940s to the early 1970s. This convergence was both positive (national social models became more similar to each other) and normative (a roughly similar model came to be accepted as desirable). Second, the disruption of the model is above all the result of general economic forces which can be detected in all

Western European countries and, indeed, on a global scale. Third, this general crisis is, however, not expressed in uniform patterns of change but rather in widening disparities. Finally, these disparities are attributed not to different strategies of adaptation but to differences in initial conditions: the same disruptive forces have been at work throughout the countries of the European Union (EU), but they have been slowed down or accelerated according to the relative strengths of the economies concerned and the differing degrees of stability of their inherited institutions.

A Common Model

Any discussion of the development of European social policy must deal with the question of diversity. To what extent can the social policy regimes of the different states be usefully regarded as versions of a common social model? Those commentators who are most suspicious of generalization tend to emphasise the diversity of European political cultures as a key factor of differentiation.[1] The definition and representation of interests is profoundly conditioned by diverse traditions; the legacy of past divisions – religious and political – continues to influence the very perception of social problems. Nevertheless, the broad assumption will be made here that a European social model can be identified which has general validity – both descriptive and normative – for the countries of Western Europe. At its origin lie many forces which have shaped social developments on a scale transcending national frontiers. This seems to be true even for the 'invention of the social'[2] – that is, the definition, in the course of nineteenth-century industrialization, of the condition of the new, wage-earning population as a political issue, and the way in which churches and political movements with important transnational dimensions questioned the outcome of economic modernization.

Similarly, many general forces were at work in the period when more or less comprehensive social policy regimes were installed, in a process which can, without excessive distortion, be described as a Europe-wide settlement.[3] The common catastrophe of war, the division of the continent into Eastern and Western blocs, the subsequent process of rapid economic growth and urbanization were all general features of Western European social development, tending to limit the scope of national particularities. Indeed, the social situation in Western Europe has perhaps tended to become more homogeneous over recent decades. Partly this is the result of the working of common economic forces which have gradually narrowed the scope for voluntarist strategies at a national level; partly, it follows from the slow emergence of Union-wide political and social relations which have made national policy debates increasingly open to comparison and contrast with neighbouring countries.

The content of the European social model[4] can be defined first by its scope – it covers *both* social welfare and employment relations – which is clearly wider than in the USA, for example. Thus every aspect of the economic situation of the population can be an object of social policy. It follows from what has been said about diversity that national welfare regimes and industrial relations practices vary more in form than they do in substance. Welfare provision tends towards universality in its coverage and a high standard in the degree of protection, although the institutional structures through which provision is made can be either state agencies or nominally independent associations. Employment conditions and the balance between managerial and employee interests are explicitly political issues, although forms of representation and regulation procedures also exhibit wide variations. The model has most descriptive validity in the wealthier countries of Northern Europe but has been seen by the Mediterranean countries as an objective of reform and development.

The values underpinning the social model vary both across and within countries, but, nearly everywhere, refuse legitimacy to purely market outcomes in the social sphere and accept the rationality of both collective bargaining and collective welfare provision. In spite of diversity in structures and philosophies, the substantive aspects of the social model – social insurance, retirement provision, regulated working conditions, socialized health care – displayed marked tendencies to convergence within EU member countries, at least until the economic slowdown of the 1970s. (For example, health-care systems varied a great deal in their financing mechanisms, the role played by the state versus that of civil agencies, the formal status of health service workers and so on; despite such persisting variations, there were strong common trends in the substantive services provided – towards universal coverage and increasingly comprehensive insurance of health risks.) Of course, this kind of summary is a simplification, but the assumption here is that it is not so simplified as to be a caricature.

A Common Crisis

To assert that there is a common European social model is necessarily to argue that European countries tended to converge on a certain type of social regime. The convergence was certainly incomplete: in Southern European countries, in particular, it remained a partially achieved objective. Nevertheless, there seems to be evidence of such convergence between the 1950s and the 1970s – both in employment relations and in systems of welfare provision. Indicators of the first would include membership trends of trade unions; of the second, the growth of welfare-related state expenditures. On the other hand, to assert that European social regimes face a common *crisis* does not (as suggested by Traxler, for example[5]) imply any homogeneous pattern of development. Crises are selective, differentiated processes. It is certainly not suggested here that there has been anything like a uniform pattern of change in social regimes [since the 1970s]. What is claimed is that the pressures – essentially economic in nature – which have called into question the previous con- vergence trend are universal in scope, although they have differed greatly in intensity. In particular, there are no grounds for accepting the most extreme case of departure from the previous model – that of Britain – as in any way exemplary, in either positive or normative terms. On the con- trary, it will be suggested below that British developments since 1979, which have been in the direction of US models of market-determined employment relations and minimal social protection, do not represent a successful adaptation to the new pressures and, in a way, intensify the social crisis by demonstrating that one clearly defined strategy ends in an impasse.

However, it is by now hard to deny the generality of the forces which disrupted what [in the 1970s] seemed a relatively clear pattern of advance towards ever higher standards of welfare provision and increasing socio- political control over employment relations. It can be observed, first, that macro-economic disturbances have become much more correlated across European countries. Until the late 1960s the economic cycles in large European countries were relatively independent of each other. Since then, both recessions and recoveries have become much more synchron- ized: the inflationary expansion of the early 1970s and the recessions of 1974–5, 1980–81 and 1991–2 testify to a common exposure of the Euro- pean economies to overall variations in business conditions. It is clear that European economic integration and the increasing importance of trade, investment and financial linkages on a global scale have greatly reduced the room for autonomous national economic strategies. The two most ambitious experiments in voluntaristic national economic policy – those of France in 1981–3 and of Sweden until 1989 – both failed to control external pressures and establish alternative growth paths. Behind the synchronization of conjunctural disturbances, the same growth of eco- nomic interdependence has led to the emergence of quite general trends across European economies. Clearly, the trends most relevant for the European social model are those in unemployment and public finance.

Each of the three major recessions which struck Western Europe led to substantial increases in unemployment in all economies, with Sweden and some other Nordic countries as temporary exceptions. These step increases in unemployment were only partly reversed in subsequent recoveries, although the latter, again quite generally, produced substantial gains in real income for those fortunate enough to maintain secure jobs. Obviously there are huge quantitative divergences in unemployment –

between Spain and West Germany, for example. But in qualitative terms many of the key developments in labour markets are again general. For example, increases in unemployment are closely linked to the performance of the industrial sector.[6] Unemployment everywhere bears most heavily on unskilled and young workers; it has become increasingly long-term and dissociated from the process of wage-formation; and there is everywhere a widening mismatch between the skills and qualifications demanded by employers and those in supply.

It is equally true that fiscal disequilibria vary enormously in numerical terms. But again there are striking common patterns and trends. Partly these result from the fact that government deficits are financed on increasingly interlinked capital markets. Thus the problem hardly existed until the 1980s. Through the period of rapid growth most countries maintained a rough balance, while the exceptions such as Spain or Ireland could use inflation as a form of taxation without this provoking severe problems; into the late 1970s low interest rates on world capital markets shielded European governments from financial pressure. In the 1980s quite general forces, expressed through rising real interest rates on increasingly interconnected financial markets, made debt interest payments – *everywhere* – the fastest growing component in public expenditure and led to a common preoccupation with fiscal stabilization. Obviously, there are important differences, for instance between Italy's debt ratio of 115 per cent of GDP and France's 45 per cent. But there are no European countries where public finance is on a clearly sustainable path and they all seem constrained to a long-run search for significant expenditure savings.

Behind these macro-economic trends there are structural changes with important implications for the European social model. But even if we consider, as a first approximation, only the movements of these aggregates, it can be argued that a general crisis of the model is manifest. Unemployment calls into question the efficiency (and the justice) of European employment relations while it intensifies pressure on systems of social insurance. The fiscal crisis rules out any major use of public expenditure to secure better employment outcomes while exposing welfare systems to unremitting pressure for economies.

A Loss of Functionality

It is necessary, however, to combine macro-economic and micro-economic considerations to perceive the full dimensions of the social policy crisis in Europe. The point can perhaps be made by referring to educational and training systems, which are exceptional in that they remain key priorities for expansion in most European countries despite the need to stabilize public finance (and where EU competencies, on the basis of the implications for labour mobility, have been expanding). This is surely because the quality of education and vocational preparation is seen as making an indispensable contribution to economic adaptation at the micro-economic level – in terms of the balance between the skills required by companies and those available in the active population. In the cases of employment relations and social welfare, on the other hand, micro-economic arguments seem to reinforce the impression of dysfunctionality derived from macro-economic disequilibria. Thus, established systems of wage determination have permitted a growing imbalance between aggregate labour supply and demand; but they are also seen as imposing high costs at enterprise level through the constraints that are placed on company strategies. In particular, the perceived need for close involvement of core employees and their enhanced responsibility for company performance are seen as incompatible with standardized forms of bargain.

Similar considerations apply to welfare systems. In macro-economic terms these are seen as increasingly costly and unable to transform the unemployed into a source of labour mobility or wage discipline. But there is concern also about the demobilizing effects of established forms of welfare provision on individuals. No concessions need be made here to crude interpretations of welfare benefits as disincentives; such discourse always comes near to blaming the victims of economic and institutional disorganization. Some of the worst aspects of contemporary welfare arise from the repression which is regarded as necessary to maintain incentive structures. It remains true, however, that core systems of welfare provision give (partial) compensation to those who lose most from economic change; they do little to re-equip them to secure more favourable outcomes for themselves.[7] Even some of the most dynamic recent welfare interventions are exposed to such criticisms: for example, the widespread use of early retirement to control youth unemployment in Germany may have been desirable in human terms, but it has a counterproductive aspect in that it redistributed and compensated a decline in labour demand which was not in itself reversed. As with unemployment compensation, so with retirement pensions. Here it can be argued that established systems are not well adapted to the increasing proportion of old people in European populations and that their lack of funding passes up the opportunity to achieve a substantial increase in the savings ratios which [...] declined in the 1980s almost everywhere.

In both cases what is at stake is a *loss* of functionality, thanks essentially to developments of the productive system, not to some sort of intrinsic inefficiency. This is an important point because, if it is not recognized, the way is opened to *laissez-faire* projects of an extremely utopian kind. European social policy regimes were functional in maintaining macro-economic stability and lowering micro-economic organization and transaction costs. That their functionality is impaired (not destroyed) is the result of changes in economic structure. The latter are expressed in competitive processes but have to do with such factors as the increasing complexity of products, the switch from manufacturing to service-based employment, the intensity of international trade and investment flows and the rapidity of technical change.

Both employment relations and welfare systems within the previous European model relied on relatively centralized decision-making and a high degree of standardization. It seems to be these aspects above all which can lead to dysfunctionality in micro-economic terms. The differentiation of both production processes and individual circumstances has increased; as it does so, standardized agreements and provisions become more costly and less able to control externalities. In addition, the macro-economic payoffs from the previous model seem to have declined as its micro-economic costs have increased. External competitive constraints are today direct and rapid; the objective of internal stabilization to which the social model contributed is given less emphasis. At the same time it becomes harder to aggregate interests in a corporatist manner because of the same underlying process of differentiation.[8] Macro-economic stabilization has thus become a much more difficult task while the contribution which social regimes could make to it has declined.

At both macro-economic and micro-economic levels, then, there are great uncertainties, more focus on cost reduction relative to output expansion and a reduction in the time horizons for which strategies are developed.[9] The social model has now itself become a source of uncertainty, unable either to limit the insecurity facing individuals or to stabilize the employment relations of the enterprise.

Divergence and Decentralization

It was argued above that European social policy faced quite general pressures. In other words, the dynamic forces for change are similar everywhere. This is not to claim, however, that the outcomes of social policy change are the same in every country. In fact, divergences in outcome are quite apparent. Nevertheless, this differentiation seems to relate mostly to initial conditions, differences in the economic and political strength of the various countries, rather than the pursuit of genuinely different paths of reform.

Two factors, in particular, seem responsible for many differences in the extent and speed of change. The first is economic and, above all, industrial performance. To the extent that enterprises have succeeded in adaptation and avoided emergency rationalizations the pressures transmitted from goods markets to labour markets have been smaller and the destabilization of employment relations less dramatic. It is industrial failure which explains the severity of the Spanish employment crisis,[10] just as continuing industrial success had, until the shock of unification, moderated labour market tensions in Germany. Second, political factors have been a direct constraint on the nature and speed of change. The social preferences expressed by electorates confronted with declining economic performance have varied widely and modified the pace and character of social policy reform. Nevertheless, clear general patterns can be detected and these will be illustrated by reference to two polar extremes in European social relations – the advanced social corporatist democracies of Scandinavia and the crisis-struck countries of the post-socialist world.

In the Swedish case, political factors have significantly affected the pace of change in the social model, without, in the end, altering its general direction. Developments in Sweden are of particular importance as they seemed, in the past, to define a line of advance towards the comprehensive socialization of income formation and high levels of social protection. However, the functionality of the Swedish model (centred on wage bargains of the Rehn-Meidner type) disappeared long before the recent crisis which saw the emergence of large-scale unemployment. The fragmentation of employee interests, the determined push of employers towards a decentralization of industrial relations,[11] problems of incentives (for example, mass absenteeism, concern about educational standards[12]) had all undermined the *economic* effectiveness of the model by, at the latest, the early 1980s. The high *political* priority accorded to full employment could then only be made effective by interventionist expedients – devaluations, increases in state expenditure – which exacerbated economic uncertainties and widened disequilibria.

Just because much of the old model had already been dismantled, it would be a mistake to attribute the recent economic disorganization only to its effects. In fact, there were serious errors in the process of economic liberalization in Sweden: the property boom and bust which led commercial banks into insolvency was a by-product of financial deregulation; the attempt to base a counter-inflationary monetary policy on a peg to the DM ended in debacle. To some extent Sweden is now suffering, like other European countries, not simply from the dysfunctionality of the old model but from the absence of any clear alternative to it. However, the signs are that Swedish exceptionalism is at an end. Entry into the EU symbolizes the end of ambitions for a purely national solution to economic and social problems, while the transnational status of key employers will place limits on divergence in employment relations. This (forced) trajectory towards European norms does not imply that policy experiments in individual countries will cease, or that there is any rule which excludes differentiation in national performances. But it does signal that a particular experiment – the attempt to resolve problems of the old model by a *fuite en avant*, by the reinforcement of social corporatist structures – has met with apparently insuperable obstacles.[13]

It is a big step from the advanced democracies of Scandinavia to the crisis-racked transitional economics of Central Europe, but a brief consideration of the latter may help to indicate the generality and the strength of the forces at work. It is becoming clear that the ex-socialist countries are not as exceptional as was first thought. Initial interpretations of their reform agenda, as essentially a change of economic mechanism, have proved to be too abstract.[14] In fact, these new democracies confront, in a particularly acute form, the same problems of economic structure and social integration which face their more fortunate Western neighbours. Modernization and rationalization of industrial sectors point to the same dislocation of employment relations as in the West, although, of course, to a much higher degree.

The objectives, and even the functioning of Eastern social models were not wholly dissimilar from those in the West. Stabilization, redistribution, individual security were not understood in completely different ways. A key peculiarity of the Eastern system was its *unitary* nature: in Western countries it is easy to distinguish the sphere of employment relations, which involved politically conditioned compromises between employers and employees, from that of social insurance and welfare, which was essentially a state function. In the centrally planned economics the two subsystems coalesced in the state-owned enterprise, characterized by vertical and horizontal integration, which assumed responsibility for both employment conditions and the provision of social services and social protection. Hence the particularly acute nature of the Eastern social crisis, where the restructuring of enterprises amounts to an immediate dismantling of the social policy regime and makes the strategic articulation of economic and social reform programmes almost impossible.[15]

It is a key constraint on the Eastern reform process that the Western models, which inevitably provide the standards and objectives of transition, are themselves in disarray. Practices and procedures are adopted which are necessary concomitants of economic liberalization but at the same time generate negative externalities and delays in modernization. Thus there has been widespread recourse to quasi-corporatist wage stabilization, despite the fact that Western experience gives little indication of how such emergency measures might lead to economically functional systems of employment relations in the longer term. In a similar way the acute employment crisis has necessitated the hasty introduction of welfare relief systems organized by the public authorities outside the enterprise, but the demobilizing and disincentive effects of these expedients cannot be easily addressed in the absence of functional Western comparators which might indicate an appropriate line of reform. In these circumstances, massive fiscal crisis and political resistance from the actual and potential victims of transition certainly threaten social dislocation of a different order of magnitude from anything experienced so far in the West. Nevertheless, when due allowance is made for differences in their socio-political development to 1990, the Eastern countries seem to represent an extreme case, and an intensification, of the Western social crisis and not simply an external constraint on its resolution. In effect, the restoration of economic functionality to European social regimes becomes more urgent in view of the reintegration of East and West, but the nature of the dilemma is essentially unchanged.[16]

Once again, it can be emphasized that the discussion of these examples, which could be multiplied, is not intended to support a reductionist 'convergence' thesis which would see all European countries necessarily moving to a common destination – disorganized employment relations and minimalist systems of social protection. On the contrary, the destabilization deriving from present economic and social changes makes divergent outcomes more probable. Convergence was rather a feature of the more stable and predictable growth patterns of the past. The generality of these destabilizing forces can be emphasized without suggesting that they work towards homogeneous outcomes. But the opposite mistake is also possible, and not absent from contemporary discussion: the very generality of the social crisis intensifies the search for exceptions. This search will only be fruitful, however, if it distinguishes between, on the one hand, variations in the rhythm and intensity of the crisis and, on the other, reforms and adaptations with a genuine potential for social renewal.

The Fate of the Unions

Labour unions played a key role in the process of convergence towards a common European social model in the 1950s and 1960s. As civil associations, at least in juridical terms, they made it possible for employment relations to retain the form of private contracts while, in practice, making for a substantial politicization of bargaining outcomes. The widespread, although never universal, use of the law to extend collective agreements to employers and workers who were not directly party to them indicated the ambivalence of the unions' role – on the one hand, private interest groups; on the other, agents of an administered social policy. Such a dual role was rendered feasible by the economic functionality of collective bargaining systems. Given the highly standardized nature of industrial processes and the rapid expansion of the semi-skilled workforce, aggregation across employees could achieve major reductions in transactions costs without causing serious market distortions. At the same time, industry-wide wage agreements seemed to be compatible with prevailing oligopolistic processes of inter-firm competition centred on physical productivity and the pursuit of scale economies. Innovations were less likely to trigger dislocative price reductions but rather influenced industrial structures through the more rapid expansion of the most successful enterprises. Functionality, never complete but often significant, can also be found at the macroeconomic level – a high measure of centralization and standardization in employment relations permitted, to varying degrees, exercises in the corporatist stabilization of income growth. Finally, labour unions made a critical contribution to social stability; under their auspices millions of newly urbanized workers were initiated into the disciplines of industrial life. The anti-capitalist ideologies which were adopted by much of the European labour movement – always more a question of rhetoric than of practice – were perhaps a necessary symbolic cover for this essentially system-preserving role.

As with other features of the European model, economic slowdown and instability had the most obvious consequence of undermining the convergent patterns of the long prosperity. For many observers, in particular those who emphasize the methodology of comparative studies, this *differentiation* of national experience in the field of industrial relations is the most salient characteristic of recent developments.[17] The view taken here, however, is that widening national differences are the paradoxical outcome of a general process of disruption and decline: once again, crises are selective processes; for example, it is the extremely adversarial industrial relations systems of France and Britain which were the earliest victims of changing economic structures. This does not mean, however, that the more consensual or organized systems of Scandinavia or Germany have escaped the process of decline – far from it. In this respect, comparative studies can be positively misleading if they direct attention away from the general forces at work.

A relatively superficial view of general decline can be derived in the first instance from membership data.[18] The picture is one of decline at different speeds. Even those few countries, such as Denmark, where stable union membership is observed may not represent true exceptions: the role of Danish unions in distributing unemployment benefits makes it convenient for many workers to retain membership, even when unions have little influence over wages or working conditions. Structural change is everywhere adding to the erosion of union coverage. Although, of course, the impact on membership of such factors as workforce feminization, atypical employment contracts, the switch of employment from industrial to service activities and so on differs as much from country to country as these processes do themselves, there are *no* convincing examples of the successful penetration and organization of the most rapidly growing sections of the European workforce.[19]

Behind these quantitative factors of membership and coverage, one can detect – again in differentiated form – a full-blown crisis of union representation. Stagnant or volatile output markets make for fierce resistance to wage demands; unemployment weakens the discipline of union memberships; the increasing importance of individual companies as loci of economic decision-making tends to break up economy-wide bargaining structures; the elimination of highly standardized tasks and the increased significance of individual performance undermines the mechanical solidarity of the industrial union. It is naturally possible to find wide divergencies within this pattern – from the aggressive de-unionization, *à l'américaine*, favoured by some British employers to situations of near stability in Belgium or Germany. But what is much harder to find are convincing examples of positive union adaptation to economic restructuring or signs of a renewed dynamic in the world of organized labour, rather than more or less successful resistance to employer strategies or the more or less stubborn defence of inherited practices and institutions. Thus attempts (for example, by Robert Boyer[20]) to construct optimistic scenarios of union renaissance on the basis of observed differences in national trajectories fail to see the wood for the trees. (As is argued below, the development of a certain structure of employee rights in the framework of the European Union hardly changes this position.)

Lean Production and Social Adaptation

It has been argued so far that the destabilization of European social models results from economic developments which have undermined their functionality.[21] It is now necessary to specify that there is no automatic mechanism which would adapt employment relations or welfare systems to restore their compatibility with the altered productive economy.

In making this point it is useful to draw on the work of the French *régulation* school which, in spite of the schematic nature of some of its formulations, offers a wide and complete account of the disjunction between the economic and the social.[22] These writers explain the dynamism of the post-war European economy by the congruence of its production structures (the 'accumulation regime') with the processes of control and stabilization (the 'mode of regulation') which include, beside patterns of price formation and industrial finance, industrial relations procedures and the forms of state intervention. They see this congruence, however, not as the result of any spontaneous adaptation of the two spheres, but as historically contingent, the outcome of conflicts and compromises which have finally released productive potentials from the obstruction of inherited institutions and obsolete economic mechanisms.

One aspect of contingency was the combination, in Western Europe, of imported, essentially US, industrial systems, and more original, indigenous regulation processes. The former are seen as centred on the mass production of standardized consumer products, above all automobiles, through intensely disciplined and subdivided labour processes. (These are the productive methods which Gramsci characterized as 'Americanism' meaning by this the combination of Fordism – in technologies – and Taylorism – in management and work organization; he argued with prescience that these were developments of universal significance.[23]) Within Europe, these revolutionary production systems were co-ordinated and stabilized in ways which perhaps went further than in the USA itself towards dynamic efficiency. Far-reaching social settlements within each country won a secure share of rising output for the industrial working class as a whole. Industrial systems could generate ever greater scale economics in an environment which guaranteed the provision of corresponding infrastructures, the stable growth of consumer demand and the acceptability of working conditions.

It is the need for profound modification of these industrial structures which renders the existing social model dysfunctional. Quality and variety of output are increasingly important considerations; these do not make mass production obsolete (as some romantics wish to believe) but they do require a revised view of standardization. The rapid performance of specific detail functions – the role of the semi-skilled operative – becomes an obsolete criterion of working efficiency which now depends on the more responsible involvement of workers in widely defined tasks; thus tertiarization is more an employment phenomenon, linked to worker functions, than a pattern of development on output markets.[24] Highly centralized, and standardized, industrial relations tend to become inefficient and incompatible with appropriate incentives. Income maintenance systems are less efficient from a macro-economic point of view; since movements of aggregate demand are not reliably distributed across enterprises, it is more difficult to control the general level of activity by manipulations of aggregate demand; at the same time these systems impose an inefficient uniformity of treatment on individuals in widely different circumstances, whose actual reintegration into employment requires a variety of strategies. Such, in the briefest outline, are some of the emergent dysfunctions of the social model.

Now it appears more simple to identify effective economic adaptations by enterprises than to envisage a set of social reforms which would at the same time enhance overall economic co-ordination and address the most pressing problems of unemployment and social exclusion. Business strategy is a buoyant and optimistic discipline; social policy a troubled and uncertain one. Once again, external models exist for enterprises, though today they draw on the super-productive industrial systems of Japan as well as on practice in the USA. In fact, certain forms of productive organization, which can be denoted here as 'lean production', are diffusing rapidly in Western Europe.[25] Nothing guarantees, however, that a conformable (efficient and socially legitimate) set of welfare and regulatory institutions will develop in response.

The Limits to Flexibility

The myth of spontaneous conformity to changing economic fundamentals underlies more extreme neo-liberal approaches to social policy reform, so that it is relevant at this point to address the case of Britain. Since 1979 British governments have been the champions of the labour flexibility drive, which works, in essence, for a market-led adaptation of employment relations to economic developments. The strategy has taken somewhat different forms in Britain and continental Europe: trade union reform was one of the most important elements in Britain, although there has also been labour market deregulation and the exposure of previously sheltered public sector employees to competitive pressures: elsewhere, regulatory change has been the most important instrument, especially in relation to dismissals and fixed-term contracts. The political basis of the strategy in Britain is questionable, as such thorough-going change only came about because electoral factors made it possible to implement reforms without a broad consensus. On the other hand, there can be no doubt that employers throughout Europe welcomed such moves, which responded to their perception of regulatory constraints on business strategy. It can be argued that, in fact, employers came to define the content of the strategy: in abstract terms 'labour flexibility' might denote many things – from the macro-economic response of wage rates to unemployment, through geographical and occupational mobility, to the more flexible use of labour by individual enterprises. In practice, however, it has been the last of these – the attempt to render labour a more plastic resource in financial, numerical and functional terms for individual employers – which has dominated reform agendas. In this connection the US experience was explicitly, and frequently, invoked: to a certain extent labour market flexibility represents a purposeful shift towards a US model of employment relations and this is perhaps another reason for the fact that it has been pushed furthest in Britain, where juridical and political traditions are closest to those in the USA.

Assessment of the outcome raises complex issues, but it has certainly not been a sufficient condition for economic revival in Britain. There are important interactions with welfare systems – to what extent can the 'flexible workforce' (part-timers, those on short-term contracts, the self-employed) be covered by European systems of social protection? In Britain, and to a lesser extent elsewhere, reductions in social insurance cover are increasingly seen as necessary to increase the competitive pressure in labour markets. Thus a move towards the US model of employment relations would be complemented by a similar move in the field of social welfare.

Two summary judgements are here. First, labour market deregulation on its own, although it has an obvious economic rationale, by no means represents an effective response to the problem of social exclusion, which it may indeed aggravate. Insecurity and low wages bear most heavily on the weakest sections of the working population: there is little social rationale in transforming the problem of long-term unemployment into that of the working poor, although even this shift can only be partially achieved by such means.

Second, the flexibility agenda also results in serious *economic* malfunctions.[26] On the one hand, failures of social integration can increase transactions costs by eroding relations of trust: this is surely a possibility if it is always less qualified workers who are most subject to insecurity and most exposed to immediate market pressure. Employers themselves can, of course, choose to give priority to integration and commitment by paying efficiency wages. But an employer who decides not to do so may generate for the most part external costs if cynical and opportunistic attitudes are then encouraged in the 'flexible' workforce as a whole. On the other hand, and more seriously for the flexibility agenda, it now seems quite inadequate in its own terms; that is to say, flexibility fails as a model of labour market competition. The most dramatic evidence of this comes from Spain, where major labour market reforms have hardly dented the massive unemployment total, but there is no reason to doubt that the mechanisms involved are quite general in their operation.[27] Flexibility intensifies labour market segmentation and aggravates the insider–outsider divide which is central to dysfunctional patterns of wage-setting. This is because no enterprise can rely on flexible workers alone. The very nature of the enterprise, as was long ago shown by the seminal work of Coase, requires at least some employment to be based on long-term commitments by both parties.[28] Now the core workers who benefit from these long-term relations cannot be exposed to direct competitive pressures in the same way as the 'flexible' periphery. As a result, the very growth of precarious (short-term, subcontracted or self-employed) forms of work acts to insulate the more privileged employees from external labour market conditions. Aggregate wage determination may then become more dysfunctional and less responsive to variations in demand. Unconstrained micro-flexibility becomes macro-rigidity.

Co-ordinated Decentralization?

None of these considerations eliminates the rational core of the flexibility programme which can be summed up as the imperative of decentralization. Since this imperative arises from the on-going transformation of productive systems, it is quite inescapable, and voluntaristic attempts to maintain highly centralized control over employment contracts have everywhere proved increasingly costly. Corporatist bargaining may still be resorted to as an emergency measure – as recently in Italy, for example[29] – to accelerate the absorption of inflationary shocks. The value of this recourse should not be minimized, but there is no reason to doubt the general assessment that, as a strategic programme for the resolution of employment issues, neocorporatism is moribund – defeated on the ground by the actual evolution of employment relations before reluctant abandonment by its academic proponents. (This last judgement may itself require some differentiation according to the size of countries and thus to the scale of corporatist arrangements. Scale is an essential factor because we are dealing with the relative transaction costs of centralized and decentralized bargains; it is certainly the case that in small countries there has in general been less pressure on national labour market institutions, which is as one would expect. We would argue, however, that even in smaller countries there has been a decisive move away from centralized control and from the classical corporatism which assigns governmental powers and corresponding legal recognition to aggregated private interests. The much looser arrangements that one finds today in Ireland, for example, focus on voluntary provisions with a maximum of discretion accorded to the individual enterprise.[30])

It follows that the future of the European social model hinges on the legal, social and political context of decentralization. The search is for institutional frameworks and policy initiatives which can reconcile productive decentralization with social cohesion and thus achieve social objectives in ways which contribute funtionally to economic modernization. The divergencies which matter most in the debate are the national and regional experiments which promise some advance in these directions. This is certainly what lies behind the fascination with the Italian industrial districts, for example.[31] Regini, for example, draws on this Italian experience to indicate the possibility of introducing decentralized mechanisms for the control of externalities, but his very optimistic assessment of the scope for such measures must be regarded as tentative.[32] The recent identification of 'organized decentralization' in Denmark may prove to be of similar significance.[33] In the field of social security, the same decentralizing imperative has led to an interesting revaluation of the informal, family- or community-based, mechanisms of social protection which were in the past too easily dismissed as archaic or paternalistic.[34]

Of particular importance here is German experience. The 1970s and 1980s saw important industrial restructuring which maintained Germany's international competitiveness while avoiding extreme pressure on employment relations or the (comprehensive and well-funded) welfare state. Unions remained influential; unemployment did rise substantially in the 1980s but was under better control than in most European countries; the economy was strong enough to permit the huge undertaking of assimilating [the former] East Germany to the economic and social norms of the Federal Republic. The most positive assessments of German experience stress the existence of strong associations among economic agents which permit the decentralization of decisions without the disorganization and dysfunctionality to which the weakening of central institutions has led elsewhere. In employment relations, for example, wage rates are agreed at the level of the industry and with strong price-leadership from the engineering workers' union, IG-Metall. These settlements are sufficiently co-ordinated to avoid the most damaging bargaining externalities; on the other hand, they remove conflict from individual enterprises where advanced and non-adversarial employee participation seems to have facilitated industrial adaptation. In another frequently cited example, vocational training systems, in which employers' associations play a key role, have attacked the skills mismatch and at least limited the mass social exclusion of younger workers.[35] Do we have here the flexible corporatism that would square the circle of economic adaptation without social regression? The opposite evaluation would argue from industrial success to social stability rather than the other way round: a strong industrial performance has so far reduced pressure on social institutions, such as industry-wide bargaining and generous unemployment compensation, but these institutions are showing signs of age and radical reform (in a market-orientated, decentralizing, public-expenditure-reducing direction) cannot be long delayed. The fiscal imbalance resulting from unification requires substantial cuts in the West: enterprises dependent on public support must be allowed to fail; unemployment relief must reflect the actual devaluation of obsolete human capital; wage differentials must widen to price less qualified workers into jobs.[36]

No attempt can be made here to adjudicate between these rival accounts of German reality.[37] Even the more critical view recognizes that Germany is uniquely well placed to benefit from the transformation of Eastern Europe. The reintegration of Germany's own Eastern *Länder*, despite the political frictions to which it gives rise, testifies to the strength of both industrial systems and social policy regimes in the Federal Republic. The 'Rhenish' form of stakeholder capitalism which has evolved in Germany supports coalitions of interest which facilitate economic adaptation while preserving social cohesion.[38] At the same time the continuing internationalization of economic relations and the imperative of competitiveness in export-orientated industry create pressures, here as elsewhere, towards more differentiated economic outcomes. In particular, co-ordinated wage-bargaining according to the formula of *Tarifautonomie*, which gives almost legislative power to organized private interests, may be increasingly difficult to sustain.[39] And, of course, the German version of the social model, like all the others, is conditioned by national traditions and cultural specificities which rule out anything like a direct transplant to other countries. Social achievements are impressive (though not uniquely so – every Western European country can point to exemplary features of its social policy) and forms of enterprise governance suggest principles by which new 'modes of regulation', complementary to developing productive systems, might be constructed. To a great extent, however, this is still a challenge for the future.

Social Policy and the European Union

There are at least two reasons for examining the potential contribution of EU structures to the resolution of European social policy problems. The first can be described as the principle of collective defence. It has been emphasized that the pressures which have dislocated national social systems are general and pervasive; the huge scale of the Union and the immense interests behind it may offer some possibilities for the control of forces which can no longer be mastered by individual nations. It should be pointed out in this context that, even with a minimal, 'pre-Federal' budget, the Union has been able to redistribute resources which make a significant difference to some of the poorest countries and regions – Ireland and Greece, for example. It is a positive feature of these interventions that they usually take a developmental form even when their basic political role is to affect transfer payments. Actual spending programmes always attempt to promote adaptation and modernization – through infrastructural investment, training promotion, the encouragement of small enterprises and so on. It is at least conceivable that more ambitious defensive measures might become possible, particularly in the context of monetary union; some of these are indicated below.

There is also an interest in the EU as a constructive agent for social policy reform, and it is this role which is the main focus of interest here since it bears most directly on the future of the European model.[40] To what extent can EU measures support a positive adaptation of employment relations and welfare systems? Two key constraints on the EU's role must be recognized if a realistic assessment is to be made. The social policy of the Union is a superstructure on what are, and will remain, essentially national systems. This is obviously true for social welfare, where the Union's competence is basically restricted to the guarantee of reciprocal access to welfare protection for workers outside their own countries. *De facto*, it applies also to employment relations, in spite of the competencies transferred by the Treaty of Rome, the Single European Act and, for all except Britain until the election of a Labour government, the Social

Protocol of the Maastricht Treaty. Very generous doses of 'subsidiarity' were needed to make the Social Protocol acceptable and as a result it is not possible for the Union to impose detailed or highly prescriptive reforms on national employment relations. This is itself is a recognition of the new imperative of decentralization in the social sphere. To some extent, Britain has constituted an exception to these general statements, since British labour market deregulation has been so forceful as to create conflicts between national practice and even the weak requirements of EU social legislation; thus the majority of judgements in the EU's Court of Justice against national regimes have concerned Britain. Even in this case, however, competence remains preponderantly at national level and both Britain's former opt-out and the modesty of EU legislative proposals will limit future conflict.

Second, the EU is completely implicated in the general dislocation of the social model and the lack of a clear direction of advance to which this has led. Thus, until the 1980s, European Community initiatives could be seen as aimed at the generalization and completion of the Northern European practices which were regarded as setting the standard for all member states. There was an obvious corporatist element in many of the consultative bodies which were established and a readiness to impose quite specific regulatory constraints on a Community-wide basis. This kind of strategy survived into the Delors presidency, although increasing resistance, led by Britain and employers' organizations, prevented it from being implemented during the 1980s. Hence most of the small number of labour market and employment directives which have actually been passed date from the 1970s.[41] The British opt-out on social issues at Maastricht unblocked the legislative process, but the Commission and Council are now much more circumspect in formulating employment law on a Union-wide basis. The recent Works Council Directive, for example, offers an immense range of institutional possibilities through which its central objective of employee consultation might be achieved in transnational companies: consultation and information structures may be either enacted by national legislation or agreed through collective bargaining; representative processes may take a wide variety of forms.[42] In practice, few new constraints will be imposed on the large companies at which the legislation is aimed. Similar caution seems likely to mark the next projected directive – on parental leave.

It seems probable, then, that the Union will avoid, for the foreseeable future, any ambitious legislative proposals.[43] Rather, EU social policy will rely on specific interventions to promote experimentation in national policy and seek to encourage the diffusion of programmes which have achieved some success. This is a co-ordinating and communicational role, rather than a governmental one in the narrow sense. The new direction of the Commission's strategy is shown by the recent White Paper on employment and competitiveness.[44] The object here was not to define an employment strategy which member states would be compelled to follow but to move the issue of employment up the political agenda. A variety of measures were suggested in fields as diverse as infrastructural investment and tax reform where the EU has few legal competencies but where it hopes to encourage and co-ordinate national initiatives. None of this is negligible – there could be significant mobilizing effects on member-state governments – but it does not shift the primary responsibility for social policy reform away from the national level.

One can now turn back to the strategic economic issues facing the EU. These are not in any direct sense questions of social policy, but they must have an important effect on the macro-economic constraints facing national governments. There is still no certainty as to when or whether the Maastricht programme for monetary union will be carried out, but the Commission is trying to co-ordinate a Union-wide reduction in government deficits as a preparation for EMU. Widely differing interpretations are possible. In the most pessimistic view, national governments are losing control over fiscal policy in circumstances which will compel them to compete with each other in the reduction of social expenditures;[45] from the Commission's standpoint, on the other hand, fiscal stabilization appears more as a necessary correction of the macro-economic policy stance – a tightening of fiscal policy, which is in any case necessary to preserve the solvency of national governments, can become the occasion for a less restrictive monetary policy, thus avoiding the kind of credit squeeze which precipitated recession in 1991–2. So far at least, this more optimistic view seems reasonable, although no strong predictions are possible. The Union does try to limit negative-sum games among national governments in particular fields such as locational and industrial subsidies; but this is a long way from an effective co-ordination of fiscal policies which would internalize the externalities resulting from member-state competition. One strategic issue of direct significance for the future of the social model is the taxation of mobile factors – the most qualified types of labour, liquid financial resources and 'dematerialized' forms of productive capital such as transferable technical knowledge. The process of economic modernization in open economies has made such wealth extremely difficult to tax because it can be readily transferred to other countries. In consequence, member states are put into competition with each other to attract mobile resources by reducing the taxes imposed on them, but this exacerbates inequalities since ownership of the factors concerned is highly concentrated. The Union as a whole is large and powerful enough to achieve some correction, and the German government has been ready to compromise with French views on the question, though as yet the wider political conditions for this do not exist. Nevertheless, in general, we must conclude that the Union is an important but secondary player in a reform process which is still situated within member states. Monetary union, if successful, would almost certainly force a revision of this judgement.

Conclusion

A French study of social policy admits that 'France, consciously or not, has chosen unemployment'.[46] The judgement seems admirable in its candour and applicable to the European Union as a whole. How else can one assess twenty years which have seen a 50 per cent increase in incomes at the same time as eight million EU citizens have been condemned to long-term unemployment? The European social model has a future only if a conscious choice is made to reverse this process. Nothing guarantees such an outcome: it is certainly conceivable that economic modernization will be pursued through the continued erosion of social institutions which are now, correctly, perceived as obstacles to market-led adaptation; that social innovations will be too timid and half-hearted to protect a growing mass of 'new poor' from insecurity and marginalization; and that the only response to social exclusion through unemployment will be the multiplication of low-paid, unskilled and precarious employment, sold to electorates as the lesser of two evils.

This would, in a sense, represent the Americanization of Europe's social model. But it would replicate the weakness of the US social economy without its key strengths – the unity of culture and the associated mobility of labour that subjects, however incompletely, advantaged regions and enterprises to continual competitive challenge.[47] The dissolution of the European model would be characterized by extreme national differentiations, amounting to a hierarchy of privilege among national labour forces, some of which would enjoy much of the security of the past while others – above all in the East – would have access only to the most minimal forms of social protection. The EU itself might gradually be threatened by such a development. Although the financial, commercial and industrial interests in European integration are so colossal as to exclude any sudden challenge to existing EU structures, even these interests might be unable to counter the steady erosion of political legitimacy and the rise of regional particularisms which this choice, or refusal to choose, would make possible. Nor would economic renewal, in the aggregate, necessarily be purchased even by this sacrifice. On any balanced view, the economic success of Europe in the 'golden age' of post-war expansion was supported by social settlements – in a variety of national forms – which gave legitimacy to political and economic leaderships and aligned the vast majority of citizens with their strategic decisions.

The feasibility of a different choice – to reconstruct the European model – rests, in the first place, on political values – on the social democratic, Christian democratic and allied traditions which seek to marry respect for individual autonomy with a view of community and social solidarity as the essential conditions for individual development. No single strategy, and no national model, opens the path to successful reform in this direction, which will require a determined assertion of political priorities combined with the most sober economic realism. The latter has many aspects. For instance, it must embrace fiscal stabilization as the price of effective public agency, while rejecting economic and political auctions, which would simply erode the public sector. The reduction of taxes and social security charges on lower-paid employment is a key priority in such an optic, with compensatory increases on higher incomes, on the use of environmental resources and on consumer expenditure. The redistribution implied by this shift cannot be diluted beyond a certain point without, in effect, opting for poverty wages.

However, the key economic challenge is, perhaps, to accept the logic of decentralization (and the more intense competition which this implies) while adapting the instruments of social policy to combat exclusion in this new context. One promising formula here is the notion of organized decentralization. Here the downward shift of decision-making power is conceived as *delegation*: wherever possible individual enterprises, local political-administrative units and civil associations must take responsibility for social integration and the active requalification of those who lose from economic and industrial change. Employment relations can be increasingly determined at enterprise level, within framework agreements which identify general objectives while leaving open the substantive means by which they are pursued. As a complement to this approach one can propose the reinforcement of the citizenship status of individuals, a bottom-up strategy only superficially inconsistent with the top-down procedures of delegation. Both the entitlements and the obligations of individual citizens would be recast in a reassertion of status relations which could both constrain and facilitate the play of contractual forces on decentralized labour markets. The right and duty to retrain is a case in point; as is also a redistribution of employment rights towards the outsiders.[48]

In short, if the continued fragmentation of the social model is a real possibility, so also is its reconstruction and reform. Even in Britain, where dismantlement has been taken much further than elsewhere, there are living projects for the reassertion of social cohesion, which may well form the basis of a new consensus.[49] The political forces which identify with the underlying values of the European social model are numerically strong everywhere. It remains to be seen whether they are capable of moving onto the offensive, of passing from the stubborn defence of inherited institutions to the construction of new forms of social solidarity compatible with the bewildering complexity of modern economic life.

Notes

From *New Political Economy*, 2, 3, 1997, pp. 405–26. Our thanks to Erika Szyazc-zak, and to two anonymous referees, for comments; and to Eilis Rafferty, of Queen Mary and Westfield Library, for bibliographic assistance.

1 See, in particular, Colin Crouch, *Industrial Relations and European State Traditions* (Oxford, Clarendon, 1993) for industrial relations; and Gøsta Esping-Andersen, *The Three Worlds of Welfare Capitalism* (Cambridge, Polity Press, 1990) for an analogous account of differentiation among welfare states.

2 See Jacques Donzelot, *L'invention du social* (Paris, Fayard, 1984), cited in Daniel Lenoir, *L'Europe sociale* (Paris, La Découverte, 1994), p. 5.

3 See, for example, Philip Armstrong, Andrew Glyn and John Harrison, *Capitalism since 1945* (Oxford, Blackwell, 1991), part 1.

4 For a survey of the European social model, see Michael Emerson, *What Model for Europe?* (Boston, MIT Press, 1988).

5 Franz Traxler, 'Farewell to Labour Market Associations? Organised versus Disorganised Decentralisation as a Map for Industrial Relations', in *Organised Industrial Relations in Europe: What Future?*, ed. Colin Crouch and Franz Traxler, (Aldershot, Avebury, 1995).

6 Andrew Glyn and Bob Rowthorn, 'The Diversity of Unemployment Experience since 1973', *Structural Change and Economic Dynamics*, vol. 1, no. 1 (1992), pp. 57–89.

7 For a version of this argument, which is completely unrelated to free-market optimism, see Claus Offe, *Contradictions of the Welfare State*, ed. John Keane (London, Hutchinson, 1982).

8 Wolfgang Streeck, 'The Rise and Decline of Neocorporatism', in *Labour and an Integrated Europe*, ed. Lloyd Ulman, Barry J. Eichengreen and William T. Dickens (Washington, DC, Brookings Institution, 1993), pp. 80–101.

9 For a discussion of the impact of higher interest rates on company strategies and the consequent importance of cash flow as against long-run market shares, see Jean-Paul Fitoussi and Edmund Phelps, *The Slump in Europe: Reconstructing Open Economy Theory* (Oxford, Blackwell, 1988).

10 Samuel Bentolila and Juan J. Dolado, 'Labour Flexibility and Wages: Lessons from Spain', *Economic Policy*, no. 18 (1994), pp. 53–99.

11 Victor A. Pestoff, 'Towards a New Swedish Model of Collective Bargaining and Politics', in Crouch and Traxler, op. cit.

12 Assar Lindbeck, Per Molander, Torsten Persson, Olof Peterson, Agnar Sandmo, Birgitta Swedenborg and Niels Thygesen, 'Options for Economic and Political Reform in Sweden', *Economic Policy*, no. 17 (1993), pp. 219–63.

13 For what has turned out to be a valedictory appreciation of Scandinavian social corporatism, see *Social Corporatism: A Superior Economic System?*, ed. Jukka Pekkarinen, Matti Pohjola and Bob Rowthorn (Oxford, Clarendon, 1992).

14 For a critique of 'naturalism', that is the assumption that Western economic mechanisms are natural expressions of economic forces, see Claus Thomas-berger, 'Monetäre Stabilisierung, das Problem der Fremdwährungsversorgung

und Konvertibilität', in *Wirtschaftliche Entwicklung und institutioneller Wandel, Vol. 2: Bedingungen ökonomischer Entwicklung in Zentralosteuropa,* ed. Jens Hölscher, Anke Jacobsen, Horst Tomann and Hans Weisfeld (Metropolis-Verlag, 1994), pp. 137–64.

15 Nicholas A. Barr, ed., *Labour Markets and Social Policy in Central and Eastern Europe: The Transition and Beyond* (Oxford and New York, Oxford University Press/International Monetary Fund, 1994).

16 John Grahl and Paul Teague, 'Industrial Relations and Economic Citizenship in a Wider Europe', paper presented to the UACES conference, *Integration in a Wider Europe,* Birmingham, September 1995.

17 For the most impressive example of such a comparative study, see *Industrial Relations in the New Europe,* ed. Anthony Ferner and Richard Hyman, (Oxford, Blackwell, 1992).

18 Organization of Economic Co-operation and Development, 'Trends in Trade Union Membership', *OECD Employment Outlook* (1991), pp. 95–113.

19 Richard Disney, Amanda Gosling and Stephen Machin, 'What has Happened to Union Recognition in Britain?', *Economica,* vol. 63, no. 249 (1996), pp. 1–18.

20 Robert Boyer, 'The Future of Unions: Is the Anglo-Saxon Model a Fatality, or will Contrasting National Trajectories Persist?', *British Journal of Industrial Relations,* vol. 33, no. 4 (1995), pp. 545–56.

21 A more fully theorized and, in consequence, more realistic assessment of comparative data can be found in Richard Locke, Thomas Kochan and Michael Piore, 'Reconceptualising Comparative Industrial Relations: Lessons from International Research', *International Labour Review,* vol. 134, no. 2 (1995), pp. 139–61; it should be noted that this study suggests that unions have not yet arrived at an adequate response to the challenges they face.

22 For a recent statement, see Robert Boyer and Jean-Pierre Durand, *L'Après-fordisme* (Syros, 1993).

23 Antonio Gramsci, 'Americanism and Fordism', in *Selections from the Prison Notebooks of Antonio Gramsci,* ed. Quintin Hoare and Geoffrey Nowell Smith (New York, Lawrence and Wishart, 1971).

24 Jonathan I. Gershuny and Ian D. Miles, *The New Service Economy: The Transformation of Employment in Industrial Societies* (London, Pinter, 1983).

25 Marino Regini, *Uncertain Boundaries: The Social and Political Reconstruction of European Economics* (Cambridge, Cambridge University Press, 1995); James P. Womack, Daniel T. Jones and Daniel Roos, *The Machine that Changed the World: Based on the Massachusetts Institute of Technology 5-million-dollar 5-year Study of the Future of the Automobile* (Boston, Rawson Associates, 1990).

26 For a critique of the flexibility drive, see *The Search for Labour Market Flexibility: The European Economics in Transition,* ed. Robert Boyer (Oxford, Clarendon, 1988).

27 Bentolila and Dolado, op. cit.

28 Ronald H. Coase, *The Firm, the Market and the Law* (Chicago, University of Chicago Press, 1988).

29 Michele Salvati, 'The Crisis of Government in Italy', *New Left Review,* no. 213 (1995), pp. 76–95.

30 Martin Rhodes, 'Globalisation, Labour Markets and Welfare States: A Future of Competitive Corporatism', mimeo, Robert Schuman Centre, European University Institute, 1997.

31 For a seminal contribution, see Sebastiano Brusco, 'The Emilian Model: Productive Decentralisation and Social Integration', *Cambridge Journal of Economics*, vol. 6, no. 2 (1982), pp. 167–84; for a recent survey of regional policy in this context, see John Grahl, 'Macro-economic Constraints and Regional Citizenship in the European Union', *International Journal of Urban and Regional Research*, vol. 20, no. 3 (1996), pp. 480–97.

32 Regini, op. cit.

33 J. Due, J. S. Madsen, L. K. Petersen and C. S. Jensen, 'Adjusting the Danish Model: Towards Coordinated Decentralisation', in Crouch and Traxler, op. cit.

34 P. Hespanha, C. Ferreira and S. Portugal, 'The Welfare Society and the Welfare State in Portugal', mimeo, University of Coimbra, 1995.

35 David Soskice and Ronald Schettkat, 'West German Labour Market Institutions and East German Transformation', in Ulman, Eichengreen and Dickens, op. cit. pp. 102–7.

36 For details of this agenda, see Henning Klodt, Jürgen Stehn et al., *Standort Deutschland: Strukturelle Herausforderungen im neuen Europa* (X J. C. B. Mohr, 1994).

37 For a detailed discussion, see Wendy Carlin and David Soskice, 'Shocks to the System: The German Political Economy under Stress', *National Institute Economic Review*, no. 159 (1997), pp. 57–76.

38 Michel Albert, *Capitalism against Capitalism* (Whurr, 1993).

39 Wolfgang Streeck, 'Pay Restraint without Incomes Policy: Institutionalised Monetarism and Industrial Unionism in Germany', in *The Return to Incomes Policy*, ed. Ronald Dore, Robert Boyer and Zoe Mars (London, Pinter, 1994), pp. 118–40.

40 For a detailed survey of EU social policies, see European Commission, *Green Paper: European Social Policy – Options for the Future* (European Commission, 1993).

41 For full details of EU employment directives, see *The Social Dimension: Employment Policy in the European Community*, ed. Michael Gold (London and Basingstoke, Macmillan, 1993).

42 Gerda Falkner, 'Testing the Maastricht Social Agreement: The Case of the European Works Council Directive', mimeo, University of Essex (Department of Government)/University of Vienna (Institüt für Staats- und Politikwissenschaft), 1995.

43 See Erika Szyazczak, 'Future Directions in European Social Policy Law', *Industrial Law Journal*, vol. 24, no. 1 (1995), pp. 19–32; Szyszczak, although attaching more significance to past directives than do the present writers, admits that in retrospect the attempt to 'concretise a social dimension' through legislation may appear as a transient episode.

44 European Commission, *Growth, Competitiveness, Employment: The Challenges and Ways Forward into the 21st Century* (European Commission, 1994).

45 Frederick van der Ploeg, 'Macro-economic Policy Coordination Issues during the Various Phases of Economic and Monetary Union in Europe', *European Economy*, special edition no. 1 (1991), pp. 136–64.

46 Commissariat Général du Plan, *La France de l'An 2000: Rapport au Premier Ministre* (Paris, Odile Jacob/Documentation Française, 1994).

47 On the issue of mobility, see Barry Eichengreen, 'Should the Maastricht Treaty be Saved?', *Princeton Studies in International Finance*, no. 74 (1992).

48 John Grahl and Paul Teague, 'Economic Citizenship in the New Europe', *Political Quarterly*, vol. 65, no. 4 (1994), pp. 379–96.
49 Commission on Social Justice, *Social Justice: Strategies for National Renewal* (London and New York, Vintage, 1994); Ralf Dahrendorf et al., *Report on Wealth Creation and Social Cohesion in a Free Society* (London, Commission on Wealth Creation, 1995).

Competitiveness and Globalization: Economic Challenges to the Welfare State

Social Welfare and Competitiveness

Ian Gough

Introduction

The relationship between social welfare and competitiveness is a perennially topical issue in both political and academic debate. From the mid-1970s the view was advanced that welfare states undermine the competitiveness of advanced economies. This view was developed by a variety of schools of thought including supply-siders, monetarists, theorists of institutional sclerosis, quasi-moral critics of welfare dependency and so on. In these and other ways the welfare state was implicated in the allegedly deteriorating performance of certain, usually European, nations.

However, in the earlier post-war years the opposite view was commonplace: that the welfare state was a necessary element in an efficient and competitive capitalist economy. In the 1990s this older view [...] gained new adherents.

[...]

There are five possible relationships between the two variables:

1 Incompatibility: more extensive social policy undermines national competitiveness.
2 Compatibility: more extensive social policy enhances national competitiveness.
3 Neither: social policy has little impact on national competitiveness.
4 Both: different aspects of social policy have different and opposite effects.

5   Contingency: the relationship between the two is contingent on one or other or both of (at least) the following: (a) other national economic, social and political institutions; (b) the position of the nation-state in the world economy.

Number 4 may be regarded as a form of number 5, while number 3 is best regarded as a residual relationship if all else fails. This leaves me with three theses to consider and evaluate: incompatibility, compatibility and contingency.

[...]

Incompatibility and Compatibility: A Selective Survey of Theories and Evidence

The fundamental neo-classical case against the welfare state is that deliberate alteration of market prices and wages – with a view to redistributing income or achieving some other social goal – weakens or perverts both the signalling and incentive functions which prices perform in market economies. This reduces efficiency in the allocation of resources and the supply of savings and labour. In Okun's phrase, there is a trade-off between equality and efficiency. Redistribution takes place in a 'leaky bucket': the poor will not receive all the money that is taken from the rich. This line of argument has a long history in economic thought.[1]

Leading exponents of the compatibility thesis include Polanyi, Myrdal, Barr and human capital theorists.[2] It is apparent that this group varies between institutional-historical sociologists at one extreme and economists working within the neo-classical paradigm at the other extreme.[3]

Table 4 displays a matrix of links between social welfare and competitiveness. Vertically, it distinguishes between three dimensions of 'social welfare': as input (levels of social expenditure and taxation), as policy output (sets of social programmes) and as outcome (final states of welfare). Horizontally, it distinguishes the three mediating variables through which they can influence structural or underlying competitiveness: the supply of capital, the supply of labour and the productivity of capital and labour. If changes in natural resources are excluded from our consideration (a reasonable assumption), then these mediating variables are exhaustive. Of course, each, particularly the second and third, can be disaggregated in turn. The supply of labour will be affected by changes in both the quantity and quality of labour. Productivity will be affected by either or both of (a) the internal efficiency of firms and (b) the efficiency by which resources are allocated between firms and sectors.

Thus there are nine basic ways in which our independent variable, social welfare, can influence our dependent variable, national competitiveness. Each of these can, in principle, be positive or negative in direction: in table 4 negative or incompatibility effects are shown in roman type and positive or compatibility effects are shown in italics. Let me now comment briefly on those relationships listed in table 4 in three stages, beginning at the top. To save space I shall not cite the large number of primary studies, but only selected secondary or tertiary surveys.

The Impact of State Welfare Effort

One effect on the supply of capital arises if rapidly growing social expenditures are financed by government borrowing which then 'crowds out' private capital investment. Bacon and Eltis hypothesized a direct crowding-out effect, when expansionary government activity is offset, wholly or partially, by reductions in private sector spending.[4] However, this is generally discredited and attention now focuses on financial crowding-out when governments run deficits financed by bond sales. A thorough survey by Saunders and Klau concluded that the effect of fiscal stimulus on long-term interest rates is mediated by monetary policy.[5] If this accommodates to the stimulus then crowding-out is weak, but if it remains unchanged then the threat is real. Again, according to a McKinsey Group Report, global capital markets are becoming more sensitive to the risks of highly indebted governments which are being forced to pay bigger risk premiums.[6] Thus government borrowing could indirectly raise the costs of capital and reduce its supply. However, these factors need not necessarily reduce aggregate investment – if the increment in government spending is on capital goods and the decrement of private spending is on consumption.

Capital supply could also be undermined, it is argued, by high social charges on enterprises as a consequence of an extensive and expensive welfare state. For example, tax and social security charges account for more than 40 per cent of overall labour costs in the EU, much higher than in the USA (30 per cent) and Japan (20 per cent).[7] As well as exacerbating unemployment, these levels could encourage firms to locate production activity outside the EU where labour costs are lower with adverse effects on both performing and underlying competitiveness. However, cutting back on social programmes and expenditure is only one of five policies which can correct for this and improve performance competitiveness. The others are: reducing direct labour costs, reducing other costs, redistributing the costs of welfare statism from enterprises to households, and devaluing the currency.[8] The choice between these is basically a matter of societal preference though each will have other economic consequences.

Table 4 Incompatibility and compatibility

	Supply of capital	Supply of labour	Productivity of capital and labour
Expenditure/ taxation	1.1 Borrowing crowds out investment 1.2 Social security charges encourage export of capital *1.4 Macro-economic stabilization effects*	1.3 Direct taxes reduce labour supply	
Social programmes	2.1 Pay-as-you-go pensions reduce savings	2.2 Pensions reduce labour supply	2.5 Public sector social services have lower internal efficiency
		2.3 Unemploy-ment and/or sickness benefit reduces labour supply	
		2.4 Minimum wages, employment protection pose barriers to hiring	*2.6 Market failures, e.g. unemployment insurance, chronic health services*
	2.7 Deregulation of housing leads to equity withdrawal and rising consumption	*2.8 Support for women's employment*	*2.9 Human capital improvements via education and training*
Welfare outcomes			Redistribution undermines price mechanism
	3.3 Crime deters investment	*3.2 Reduced costs of ill health*	*3.1 Welfare enhances flexibility via greater trust and reduced transaction costs*
		3.3 Crime harms child education	*3.4 Enforcement costs of inequality*

High taxation and social security contributions could also react adversely on the supply of labour.[9] All direct and indirect taxes insert a wedge between the cost of labour to an employer and the value of the goods workers can buy with their wages. However, the effect of this on the supply of labour depends on other considerations. The fact that the substitution and income effects of taxes on labour supply offset each other makes the overall outcome theoretically indeterminate, but this does not stop many commentators from asserting that taxes, specifically direct taxes, dampen labour supply, motivation and effort. An OECD survey showed that income taxation had no significant effect on the labour supply of men but some negative effect on women. However, this is swamped by the impact of other government programmes and the system of taxation of couples.[10] A recent compilation study of the effects in high-tax European countries came to similar conclusions: small negative effects of tax levels on aggregate labour supply, except for married women and lone parents in certain countries and circumstances, which are outweighed by tax structure factors. For example, if the German system of income-splitting for married couples were to be changed to the Swedish system of separate taxation, it is estimated that this would raise the labour force participation rate of German women by 8–10 percentage points – an effect which dwarfs the impact of other features of their respective tax systems.[11]

Against these macro-economic dangers must be set the Keynesian, demand-side argument for the efficiency effects of extensive and redistributive welfare systems. This contends that high and redistributive social spending will contribute to economic stability because social programmes such as unemployment benefit are counter-cyclical in their effects; because poorer people will spend money on consumption more steadily than richer people; and because the balance of payments constraint on macro-economic policy is relaxed if, as is usually the case, the consumption basket of poorer people and public infrastructure spending has a lower import content than the private consumption expenditure of the better-off.[12]

Cross-national evidence.   Respectable theoretical arguments can thus be advanced for both the compatibility and the incompatibility theories and isolated pieces of evidence can be cited in support of both. I consider here some aggregate-level research which tries to test the overall effect of 'welfare state effort' on economic performance. This can take the form of time-series studies of one country or cross-national studies or both. The most common measures of welfare state effort are the shares in GDP of taxation, social security spending and total social expenditure. The only study to try to directly measure competitiveness, to my knowledge, is our own, which included measures of performance and underlying competitiveness for OECD countries for the 1970s and early 1980s.[13] However, we ran only correlation tests and did not use regression or other sophisticated modelling techniques.

Taking the growth rate of manufactured exports 1980–86 as our measure of performance competitiveness, we found no significant correlation with the share of social spending in 1979 or with the change in this share 1973–9. We did find that social spending in 1973 exhibited a significant negative relationship with the change in export shares in the subsequent period 1973–9 (R2 = −0.54). On the other hand, a synthetic measure of welfare statism combining social spending and full employment revealed no significant correlation. Turning to structural competitiveness, we used growth of manufacturing productivity (real value added per employed person in manufacturing) as our main measure. This revealed a series of weak negative correlations with the above measures of welfare statism. These were stronger (and still negative) when countries were ranked according to the 'competitiveness scoreboard' established by the European Management Forum.[14] Lastly, we correlated our social measures against economic growth and found a series of rather high negative associations between social spending levels in 1979 and economic growth rates 1980–87 (R2 = −0.63).

This suggests that state welfare was becoming more incompatible with competitiveness in the 1980s. However, like other studies, we found that the inclusion or exclusion of specific countries makes a big difference to the association. In particular, the presence or absence of Japan has a profound effect in so many of these exercises.[15] So too can the time period selected, particularly with economic variables affected by the trade cycle. Lastly, correlation exercises cannot take account of the host of other variables which may reasonably affect national competitiveness. More complex modelling is required to take these into account.

Atkinson has reviewed the major empirical studies which have regressed social security transfer spending, as a share of GDP, on economic growth rates.[16] Of the nine studies, four find a negative (incompatibility) relationship, three a positive relationship and two an insignificant relationship. Another survey of studies is undertaken by Esping-Andersen,[17] this time of those using a broader definition of welfare state effort – total levels of social spending as a share of GDP. Again, the studies reveal a mix of positive, negative and insignificant effects on national output. The conclusion of a wide range of macro-level regressions is that there is no consistent support for *either* compatibility *or* incompatibility perspectives. But given the widespread assertion that the modern welfare state undermines growth and competitiveness, these agnostic findings deserve wider dissemination.

Specific Social Programmes

Such indeterminate findings are not really surprising, given the number of problems facing aggregate empirical evidence of this kind.[18] In particular, many of the incompatibility arguments rest on micro-economic foundations which cannot be easily aggregated into macro-level variables. Moreover, so many of the arguments depend on what Atkinson calls the 'fine structure' of particular social programmes. It is time to turn to some of these.

Pay-as-you-go state pension schemes, some economists argue, weaken investment, capital supply and thus structural competitiveness.[19] Assuming a neo-classical growth model with substitution between factors, endogenous technical progress and a model of lifetime savings with a finite lifetime and no bequests, then it can be shown that a state pension scheme financed by a payroll tax will displace all or a large part of private savings. Assuming further that changes in savings translate automatically into changes in investment, then it can be demonstrated that a major feature of all Western welfare states has an adverse impact on the long-run growth rate.

However, several of the assumptions in this model can be questioned. If state pay-as-you-go pensions are replaced by private funded pensions, the institutional structure of capital markets is profoundly affected by the rise of large-scale occupational or private pension funds. These may intensify the take-over constraint facing firms, thus reducing their investments and firm growth rates despite the higher aggregate levels of savings in the economy. The effects of pension schemes on savings, investment and growth cannot be conceptualized independently of institutional structures and their alternatives. There is little empirical support either: an OECD survey of cross-national research found no evidence that state pension schemes reduced household savings.[20]

State pensions can be indicted for their adverse effects on the supply of labour as well as the supply of capital since the enhancement of state pension levels might be expected to reduce the retirement age of workers. Time-series studies, mainly in the USA, do indeed show an inverse relationship between pension levels and the labour supply of older men, but cross-national studies reveal no such relationship. Here, much more depends on the availability of work for older men and the effects of other features of national welfare systems.[21]

Unemployment and sickness benefits may adversely affect labour market behaviour if they provide a high replacement rate. A rise in the benefit replacement rate will reduce the cost of being without a job and thus, it is argued, induce some individuals to quit their jobs and/or prolong periods of unemployment. It could also raise the reservation wage which the unemployed will accept and in this way increase long-term unemployment. An OECD survey of empirical studies suggested that the effect of replacement rates is modest but that the duration of benefit does adversely affect employment rates. The recent compilation study by Atkinson and Mogensen of selected European countries found that both unemployment and sickness benefits in Germany and the UK do not discourage return to work, while those in Denmark and Sweden do generate longer periods of unemployment or work absence. However, the Swedish schemes are found to have positive effects: unemployment insurance results in a higher propensity to stay in the labour market and parental benefits encourage women to participate. Much more consistent is the finding that income-tested benefits discourage entry into the labour force or extra hours of work by imposing high marginal rates of taxation, especially in combination with direct taxation.[22]

McLaughlin argues that the assumptions on which the theory is built are flawed. In particular, women do not face a straight choice between work and leisure but a three-way choice between paid work, unpaid work and leisure, and this will be affected by the conditions attached to the receipt of their partner's and their own benefit. In other words, the relationship between unemployment benefit and labour supply is mediated by the detailed regulations of national schemes. However, Atkinson argues that the incorporation of household production into models of decision-making does not necessarily affect predictions concerning labour supply.[23]

More generally, minimum wage legislation, employment protection laws and product market barriers can create barriers to firms hiring extra workers. The OECD claims that there is powerful evidence for this. Others argue that the effects of benefit generosity are swamped by the commitment of different welfare states to full employment.[24] Gregg et al. have developed a specific criticism of these disincentive arguments.[25] They claim that monopsony power exists in many low-pay labour markets, enabling employers to pay wages below the marginal product of labour. This means that there are some workers who do not find it worthwhile to work at the going wage and have little incentive to improve their skills since this too would not attract a commensurate improvement in wages. Thus both employment and skills levels in the economy are inefficiently low. Minimum wages and labour market regulation, along the lines of the Equal Pay Act, wages councils, racial discrimination legislation and the EU Social Chapter, may in certain circumstances enhance, not diminish, labour market performance and competitiveness.

It is also alleged that state welfare impacts directly on productivity levels because public sector social services exhibit lower internal efficiency than their private sector counterparts. This arises from their frequent monopoly position in supplying the service and/or from the politicization of the decision-making process in the public sector. Reviewing the evidence, Ringen concluded that there is considerable support for this view. However, there are clear exceptions. The excessive costs of privately mediated health care in the USA, and their effects on industrial relations may constitute a competitive disadvantage avoided by those countries relying on lower-cost public provision.[26] Nor is monopoly provision a necessary feature of social policy or of the welfare state; quasi-markets and other forms of welfare pluralism can be designed to obviate these drawbacks.

Turning now to compatibility arguments, there are a range of market failures to take into account alongside state failures. Unregulated markets will fail to provide certain benefits – such as unemployment insurance – and certain services – such as health care for uninsurable risks – because of well-established market failures including information failure, adverse selection in insurance schemes, moral hazard and uncertainty. The implication of this argument is that the internal inefficiency of public provision must be offset against the external inefficiency – thanks to sub-optimal levels – of private provision.[27]

State policies affecting the production, finance and regulation of housing may affect the supply of capital and labour in ways which strengthen the compatibility case. According to Muellbauer, the converse deregulation of the British housing market in the 1980s caused sharper fluctuations in house prices, the phenomenon of negative equity and greater regional inequalities in housing markets.[28] These effects may have exacerbated inflation and inhibited labour mobility between buoyant and depressed areas, though hard evidence is lacking.

Further criticisms of the labour disincentive case against social transfers and support services have been advanced once gender effects and the special labour market position of women (especially women with partners) are recognized. The provision of nursery education and pre-school care together with supportive leave and other social policies enables women (and men) to juggle more effectively the competing claims of paid and unpaid work. By enhancing access to the labour market for all groups, such social programmes may increase overall productivity, even those with clear local costs such as generous sickness benefit schemes. 'What at first glance appears as a work disincentive emerges in the larger picture as a precondition for labour supply. Sickness benefit programs may be costly and high rates of absenteeism may generate production problems for firms; yet they are also a means for (gender) equalisation and for greater national economic output.'[29]

Most contemporary restatements of the compatibility theory focus on the supply side of the economy. Of these, *human capital theory* has the longest pedigree since it is related to (is an economics-based variant of) technical-functional or modernization theories of social development. These argue that modern state education systems contribute to economic development, first, by socializing students to modern values and attitudes and, second, by teaching job-related competencies and skills.[30] Human capital theory relates this to individual efficiency in production by applying the marginal productivity theory of wages to assess the rates of return to different levels of education. The social rate of return typically relates the gross earnings of people with different educational qualifications to the total societal costs of their education, while the private rate compares net, post-tax differences in earnings with the private costs of acquiring that education. A World Bank survey of national studies shows that rates of return to formal education vary considerably across countries from 4 per cent to 24 per cent and that the social rate of return is somewhat lower than private rates, though still positive and rather high (ranging from 5 per cent to 15 per cent in the majority of cases). Evidence from the USA and UK shows that this declined somewhat in the 1970s and early 1980s.[31]

More recent research in this area has focused on training for specific skills and other delimited aspects of the education system. Britain performs relatively poorly in educating the lower half of the ability range at school, in persuading them to stay on after school-leaving age and in providing comprehensive vocational training either in college or with employers. The researches of Prais and others suggest that resulting skill shortages have hindered the expansion of several growth sectors of the economy, including engineering and information technology. Finegold and Soskice see Britain as trapped in a 'low-skills equilibrium, in which the majority of enterprises staffed by poorly trained managers and workers produce low-quality goods and services'. What we have called performance competitiveness in this situation will derive from low productivity and pay and may make further training irrational for individual workers and enterprises. Yet this undermines productivity growth and structural competitiveness, which requires a more extensive education and training policy and one, moreover, which is more closely integrated with other social programmes.[32]

Welfare Outcomes: Equality and Competitiveness

Mention has already been made of the alleged conflict between efficiency and equality, with its corollary that state redistribution harms those groups it is designed to help. The opposite view has been recently put in Britain by the Commission on Social Justice:

> Social inequality – low educational levels, unemployment, poor health, high crime – holds back economic growth. It does so directly through the costs to government (higher spending on benefits, low revenue from taxes) and also to business (higher spending on security and on training workers in basic English and arithmetic). It does so indirectly by deterring investors from whole parts of our cities and regions, depressing the demand for goods and services.[33]

Other goals of the welfare state are distinguished by Barr; they include income security or the protection of one's accustomed standard of living, equity and social solidarity.[34] Welfare policies – insofar as they contribute to these goals – may have a competitive pay-off. Let me consider some of the specific ways in which they may be related.

From an institutional economics paradigm, the most general argument concerns the way inequality 'obstructs the evolution of productivity-enhancing structures for the governance of transactions'.[35] More equal societies may be capable of supporting levels of co-operation and trust unavailable in more economically divided societies; they thus assist the development of co-operative or negotiated forms of co-ordination along-side competition and command forms.[36] This in turn can reduce transaction costs and improve incentive structures. Some sociologists also argue that the move towards a post-Fordist quality-based production system requires greater social solidarity and integration, which in turn requires a social infrastructure of collective goods.[37]

Katzenstein has contributed to this thesis from within a political science perspective.[38] He shows how the small open European states have developed democratic corporatist structures as an alternative to protectionism and extensive economic interventions. An important feature of the bargained consensus which results, especially in the 'social corporatist' countries, is advanced welfare policies. Building on this, Leibfried and Rieger contend that, in the face of globalizing pressures, even the biggest states wield a diminished range of economic policy instruments.[39] A near-universal welfare state is now more relevant to economic performance. Acting as a 'filter and buffer', the security which it provides reduces opposition to change and flexibilization among workers and other groups and staves off social disintegration and political upheaval. This is a return to Bismarck's case for the legitimizing role of the welfare state and to the productivist arguments for the Swedish welfare model, both adjusted to the new situation of globalization.[40] It is a theme of the [1994] EU White Paper on European Social Policy: 'Many believe that productivity is the key to competitiveness and that high labour standards have always been an integral part of the [European] competitive formula.'[41]

Let me turn now to specific mechanisms by which these effects may be transmitted. Poor health can indirectly disrupt economic production through sickness absence as well as impose direct costs on the health services. Wilkinson makes a case for a strong form of compatibility here – arguing that absolute levels of health are influenced by relative, not absolute, standards of living.[42] If so, then a redistributive welfare state would help reduce such costs, quite apart from the contribution which a citizenship-based health service could make to the health levels, notably of the worst-off.

Welfare states may also have both direct and indirect effects on crime. Econometric studies have identified various forms of relationship between economic indicators, including unemployment and inequality, and crime rates.[43] Income support, training and employment provision can play a direct role in mediating the link between economic conditions and crime levels, particularly among young people. Welfare systems may also have strong indirect effects on crime rates through their mediation of processes of individual and community marginalization – by reducing the segregation and concentration of vulnerable people and families.

This still leaves open the links between crime and economic performance on which, outside the USA, less research has been conducted.[44] Businesses operating in high crime areas must pay excessive insurance costs or may be refused cover altogether: over twenty years ago 'insurance red-lining', whereby firms in zip-code areas regarded as high risk were refused insurance cover, was recognized as a significant disincentive to investment in deprived areas of US cities.[45] More generally, crime, poverty and social dislocation may stunt children's cognitive and emotional development with long-term harmful consequences for their education and acquisition of skills. I am unaware of any research in this area, but this could be the most important cost of inequality to competitiveness in the long term.

Lastly, there is the diversion of resources towards enforcing law and order and away from more productive uses. One estimate of the more general 'enforcement costs of inequality' has been made by Bowles and Gintis, who calculated expenditures on work supervision, security personnel, police, prison guards and so on.[46] They estimate that in the USA, a highly inegalitarian society, these categories of 'guard labour' constituted over one quarter of the labour force in 1987. If high crime and low trust are correlated with inequality, a redistributive welfare state can reduce these costs.

Cross-national evidence.   Some comparative investigations have been carried out on the relationship between levels of inequality and economic performance. All of these show a positive link between degree of equality and economic growth rates across nations. Kenworthy also finds a positive link between egalitarian income distributions and healthy trade balances, one measure of performance competitiveness. What comparative evidence there is supports the compatibility theory.[47]

Conclusion

It is striking that incompatibility arguments predominate where the concern is with aggregate levels of government spending and taxation. Despite the micro-economic foundations on which many of these arguments rest, they have frequently and promiscuously been generalized to aggregate relationships at the level of the economy. Yet, partly for this reason, there is no empirical consensus on the direction of the relationship between welfare state effort and economic competitiveness. When we look at the imputed outcomes of welfare statism, much theory and some aggregate evidence can be adduced to support the compatibility case. These findings suggest that cost-effective welfare programmes directed at improving the supply of capital and labour and at egalitarian redistribution are an essential component of a policy for national competitiveness. On the other hand, expensive programmes focused on non-egalitarian transfers and non-productive expenditures are likely to burden the national economy, especially in the current epoch of globalization.

However, the bulk of research concerns the effects of specific national programmes, and here no such general conclusions can be drawn. When our attention is turned to the 'fine structures' of individual social programmes, it is the contingency of these relationships which is most noticeable. Does this mean that no more general conclusions can be drawn about the relationship between welfare systems and competitiveness? I now consider whether the concept of welfare regimes provides a more systematic framework to investigate my third conceptual position – that the effect of social welfare systems on competitiveness is contingent on other national institutions and practices.

Contingency Theories

At the end of his survey of the economic impact of welfare states, Esping-Andersen concluded:

> The effects of a welfare state cannot be understood in isolation from the political-institutional framework in which it is embedded ... there may exist a trade-off between equality and efficiency in countries where the welfare state is large and very redistributive but in which the collective bargaining system is incapable of assuring wage moderation and stable, nonconflictual industrial relations. Thus, in concrete terms, a Swedish, Norwegian or Austrian welfare state will not harm growth, while a British one will (even if it is smaller).[48]

This is related to a second conclusion: that the economic impact will differ according to the type of welfare state and, more broadly, welfare regime. In other words, the effect of social policy on competitiveness is *contingent* on the institutions of the nation-state and its place in the global economy. I turn now to an elaboration of this perspective, though there is considerable overlap in practice with what has gone before.

Following Esping-Andersen's book the notion of 'welfare state regimes' has become commonplace. 'To talk of a regime is to denote the fact that in the relation between state and economy a complex of legal and organizational features are [sic] systematically interwoven.'[49] According to Kolberg and Uusitalo, modern capitalism is characterized by increasing functional integration; the goal now is to study national 'institutional complexes' relating together the family, welfare state and labour market.[50]

Esping-Andersen's model of the three worlds of welfare capitalism is too well known to require much elaboration. He distinguishes three welfare regimes according to their policy outputs, their welfare effects on 'de-commodification' (the extent to which a person can maintain a livelihood without reliance on the market), and their feedback effects on systems of stratification. The *liberal* regime, whose exemplar is the United States, places greater reliance on social assistance and residual state welfare alongside private provision; it exhibits low de-commodification; and it fosters a dualistic class system in which the better-off have an incentive to exit from the state welfare system. The *social democratic* regime (exemplar: Sweden) provides generous, universal state benefits in cash and in kind; generates high redistribution and de-commodification; and fosters solidaristic class relations. Esping-Andersen's innovative third regime type, the *conservative* or *corporativist* or *Christian democratic*, whose exemplar country is Germany, is characterized by classic social insurance schemes which tie benefits to labour market performance; achieves moderate levels of de-commodification; and reinforces both existing status differences in society and middle-class support for state welfare.

A body of comparative research suggests that the three regime types are broadly linked to various welfare outcomes, including employment/labour market participation, gender relations and equality. For example, welfare state strategies for managing deindustrialization can be grouped into three: cheapen labour (the USA, UK, New Zealand), reduce labour supply (the EU countries) and expand employment through combined demand and supply-side policies (Scandinavia, Japan). Some studies of gender relations distinguish between (the majority of) 'strong male breadwinner states' and moderate and weak male breadwinner states. Though the link with welfare regimes is not perfect – France and Germany are similar regimes with different gender outcomes – many are agreed that the change in gender relations and life cycle has progressed farthest in Scandinavia and that this is linked to the form of welfare state.[51] Studies of income distribution find growing divergence among countries since the 1970s between liberal and corporatist economies (the latter encompassing conservative-corporatist and social-democratic regimes). Inequality rose rapidly in the USA and Britain but changed little in the other countries (the only exception to this pattern was Canada which showed no change).[52] There is thus considerable support for the idea that national welfare regimes have a salient effect on a wide range of *welfare* outcomes.

Do they affect *economic* outcomes and in particular competitiveness? Evidence is beginning to accumulate that these regime differences impact on some aspects of economic performance. Calmfors and Driffill rated OECD countries according to the degree of centralization of wage-bargaining structures and discovered a U-shaped relationship between this and employment growth.[53] Both liberal, unregulated labour markets, such as that in the USA, and highly centralized systems, like the Scandinavian, performed well in creating jobs, but the in-between nations, notably the EU member states, performed poorly. Rowthorn takes this further and relates it to wage dispersion and the welfare system.[54] The US expansion of jobs occurred alongside growing wage inequality, whereas that in Scandinavia and Japan combined with much narrower inequality.

Further evidence is provided by Weisskopf in a time-series analysis of eight countries to investigate the effect of 'worker security' (a combination of full employment and the social wage) alongside other control variables on growth of labour productivity.[55] He also finds a divergent relationship. Annual increases in worker security reduced productivity growth in the UK and Italy, but improved it in Japan, France, Sweden and Germany. This supports both the compatibility theory – that worker security and co-operative capital-labour relations will improve innovation and productivity growth – in the latter group of countries and the incompatibility theory – that worker security will have disincentive effects – in the former group. The effect of welfare statism on competitiveness will depend on the broader institutional and group relations in society. However, there is little other work in this area.

I shall conclude by outlining a comparative framework for a contingent analysis, one which is heavily indebted to writings of the 1990s by Esping-Andersen.[56] This develops the insights of his original analysis of welfare regimes, by relating state welfare systems to labour market systems and family/household structures to show how they interrelate and reinforce each other within distinct regimes. I shall build on the survey of research findings above to suggest links between these regime types and issues surrounding competitiveness. In particular, I shall speculate about how each regime type generates a different set of *problems* for or *threats* to national competitiveness, how these generate different recommended *policy solutions*, but how these in turn may generate further *dilemmas* or *contradictions*. This section is much more speculative. What is proposed is really a framework for undertaking further research.

In liberal welfare regimes, such as the USA and, in the [1990s], the UK and New Zealand, the dominant welfare threats to competitiveness are not those of disincentives, crowding-out, state redistribution, regulation and other leading issues in current debates. The dominant threat is of inequality and its effects: instability in demand, a poor quality educational base and social disintegration. In the USA low wages and low benefits have stimulated a high rate of job creation; in the UK they coexist with a high but falling level of unemployment. The policy solution almost universally advocated is investment in education and training to improve the skills base and enhance high-productivity sectors of the economy. The dilemma which this may pose is that high quality education cannot coexist with long-term poverty, a growing 'underclass' or major community disintegration. These regimes may well need to increase all forms of social expenditure – on infrastructure, social services and social transfers – in order to realize these gains in competitiveness. The absence of major incompatibility threats provides the economic leeway for this to happen, but the interest coalitions fostered within liberal welfare regimes militate against this solution.

The problems facing conservative welfare regimes, characteristic of the original six members of the European Community and newer continental member states, are very different. They are high and rising social transfers and their effects: high social security charges and non-wage labour costs which cannot always be compensated for by high productivity; discouragement of new service sectors with resulting low employment participation rates, especially among women and young people; labour market inflexibility and an extensive hidden economy which undermines tax revenues; and public sector deficits and rising debt.[57] It is in these countries that several of the predictions of incompatibility theorists bear fruit. The recommended solutions are to deregulate the labour market, to cap insurance benefits, particularly future pensions as in Italy, and to divert social spending towards more productivist ends. The dilemma is that these solutions threaten the interests of the powerful organized sector of the economy and the breadwinner/familist model of welfare which underpins this.

In social democratic welfare regimes, such as Sweden and Denmark, state spending is high on both transfers and social services; unemployment was low (until the 1990s in Sweden) and participation rates particularly for women remain very high; and inequality and poverty are low. The twin threats to this regime today are high rates of taxation and high non-wage labour costs threatening domestic capital supply. The recommended solutions include some cuts in benefits and extension of quasi-markets and private provision. Compared with the previous two regime types many of the policies are in place for a productivist welfare state – indeed the idea was developed in Sweden. The dilemma which remains is that, to free resources for further investment in human capital, further cuts may be necessary in social transfers; these may undermine the corporatist institutions and consensual policy making on which the system partly rests.

Japan and the dynamic new market economies of East Asia such as Taiwan, Hong Kong, Singapore and Korea, may represent a fourth welfare regime (though Esping-Andersen disagrees[58]). They combine low levels of state social spending with developed functional alternatives in the corporation, the family and the private market. A high degree of employment security, a relatively equal distribution of income and low tax levels permit or encourage high levels of savings, which contribute to economic security and growth. The basic threats to this apparently successful system stem from the effects of growth on women's employment, family care functions and the birth rate. A growing double burden on women, especially as the supply of 'grandmother welfare' declines, may create pressure for more state services. At the same time, the falling birth rate is creating a rapidly ageing population, placing greater demands on social transfers. Again the solution points to a more productivist orientation for state policy, but this will require higher taxes which may undermine the self-financing nature of present forms of private welfare.

Three conclusions flow from this admittedly brief and speculative sketch. First, different welfare regimes exhibit different configurations of effects on performance and structural competitiveness. A problem in one may be a solution in another. Second, and despite this contingency, the general goal to which all need to direct themselves is a welfare state which gives due weight to 'productivist' considerations. In this sense the Scandinavian welfare pattern still comes closest to a rational resolution of these dilemmas. Third, in all regimes powerful interest coalitions will resist measures to adapt their welfare systems to the competitive requirements of nations in the new globalized economy.

Notes

From *New Political Economy*, 1, 2, 1996, pp. 209–32. Thanks to David Collard, Mike Dietrich, Chris Heady, Alan Jacobs, Valerie Karn, Yuen-wen Ku, Jane Millar, David Piachaud, Steve Webb, Paul Wilding and contributors to the ESRC Seminar on Social Welfare Systems for useful comments on earlier drafts. The usual disclaimer applies.

1 A. M. Okun, *Equality and Efficiency: The Big Trade-Off* (Washington, DC, Brookings Institution, 1975). See also, for example, A. Fisher, *The Clash of Progress and Security* (London, Macmillan, 1935); and G. Gilder, *Wealth and Poverty* (New York, Basic Books, 1981). Strictly speaking, Okun's trade-off applies only to allocative efficiency, not to technical efficiency.

2 K. Polanyi, *The Great Transformation* (Boston, Beacon Press, 1944); G. Myrdal, *Beyond the Welfare State* (New Haven, Yale University Press, 1969); and N. Barr, *The Economics of the Welfare State* (London, Weidenfeld and Nicolson, 1987).

3 Different writers within Marxist political economy have expounded both compatibility and incompatibility positions. For a model which tries to integrate the two, see I. Gough, *The Political Economy of the Welfare State* (London, Macmillan, 1979), especially ch. 6 and appendix B.

4 R. Bacon and W. Eltis, *Britain's Economic Problem: Too Few Producers* (London, Macmillan, 1976).

5 P. Saunders and F. Klau, *The Role of the Public Sector: Causes and Consequences of the Growth of Government*, OECD Economic Studies no. 4 (Paris, OECD, 1985).

6 *The Economist*, 5 November 1994.

7 Commission of the European Communities, *White Paper on Growth, Competitiveness, Employment* (EC, 1994).

8 A. Pfaller, I. Gough and G. Therborn, eds, *Can the Welfare State Compete?: A Comparative Study of Five Advanced Capitalist Countries* (London and Basingstoke, Macmillan, 1991), p. 7.

9 Again, we need to recognize that modern levels of taxation stem from all activities of government, not just its welfare activities. However, given that welfare spending is the largest and most dynamic part of state activity, and that social security contributions are linked to part of social expenditure, there is a case for including the effect here.

10 Saunders and Klau. op. cit.

11 A. B. Atkinson and G. V. Mogensen, eds, *Welfare and Work Incentives: A North European Perspective* (Oxford, Clarendon Press, 1993), ch. 8.

12 D. Corry and A. Glyn, 'The Macroeconomics of Equality, Stability and Growth', in *Paying for Inequality: The Economic Cost of Social Injustice*, ed. A. Glyn and D. Miliband (London, Rivers Oram Press, 1994).

13 A. Pfaller and I. Gough, 'The Competitiveness of Industrialised Welfare States: A Cross-Country Survey', in Pfaller, Gough and Therborn, op. cit.

14 European Management Forum, *Report on International Industrial Competitiveness* (EMF, 1996).

15 P. Saunders 'What Can We Learn from International Comparisons of Public Sector Size and Economic Performance?', *European Sociological Review*, vol. 2, no. 1 (1986), pp. 52–60.

16 A. B. Atkinson, *The Welfare State and Economic Performance*, Welfare State Programme Discussion Paper 109, STICERD, LSE, May 1995. He points out the necessity to distinguish Levels equations, in which country levels of GDP are the dependent variables, from Growth Rate equations, in which it is the rate of growth of GDP that is to be explained.

17 G. Esping-Andersen, 'Welfare States and the Economy', in *The Handbook of Economic Sociology*, ed. N. J. Smelser and R. Swedberg (Princeton, NJ, Princeton University Press, pp. 711–32.

18 Atkinson, op. cit.

19 G. Saint-Paul, 'Fiscal Policy in an Endogenous Growth Model', *Quarterly Journal of Economics*, vol. 107 (1992), pp. 1243–59.

20 Saunders and Klau, op. cit., pp. 143–6. See also Atkinson, op. cit.

21 Esping-Andersen, op. cit.

22 Saunders and Klau, op. cit., ch. 4C; Atkinson and Mogensen, op. cit.

23 E. McLaughlin, 'Employment, Unemployment and Social Security', in Glyn and Miliband, op. cit.; A. B. Atkinson, 'Work Incentives', in Atkinson and Mogensen, op. cit., p. 37.

24 OECD, *The OECD Jobs Study: Facts, Analysis, Strategies* (Paris, OECD, 1994); Esping-Andersen, op. cit.

25 P. Gregg, S. Machin and A. Manning, 'High Pay, Low Pay and Labour Market Efficiency', in Glyn and Miliband, op. cit.

26 S. Ringen, *The Possibility of Politics: A Study in the Political Economy of the Welfare State* (Oxford, Clarendon Press, 1987), ch. 5; D. Brailer and R. Van Horn, 'Health and the Welfare of US Business', *Harvard Business Review*, March–April (1993), pp. 125–32.

27	N. Barr, 'Economic Theory and the Welfare State: A Survey and Interpretation', *Journal of Economic Literature*, vol. 30 (1992), pp. 741–803.

28	J. Muellbauer, *The Great British Housing Disaster and Economic Policy* (London, 1990).

29	Esping-Andersen, op. cit., p. 722. See also Atkinson and Mogensen; Commission on Social Justice, *Social Justice: Strategies for National Renewal* (London and New York, Vintage, 1994).

30	R. Rubinson and I. Browne, 'Education and the Economy', in Smelser and Swedberg, op. cit., pp. 587–99.

31	Saunders and Klau, op. cit., pp. 124–8. An alternative method is to enter educational and other human capital qualities into an aggregate production function to identify their contribution to average annual rates of growth of the economy. Using this method for the 1950s, E. F. Denison, *Accounting for Slower Economic Growth* (Washington, DC, Brookings Institution, 1979) and M. J. Bowman, 'Education and Economic Growth: An Overview', *Education and Income*, World Bank Staff Working Paper 402, 1980, pp. 1–71, show that education contributed between 0.25 per cent and 0.75 per cent to economic growth, and health and nutrition up to 0.3 per cent. However, this methodology has been subject to several criticisms. See Rubinson and Browne, op. cit.

32	S. Prais and K. Wagner, 'Educating for Productivity', *National Institute Economic Review*, vol. 119 (1987), pp. 40–56; G. D. Worswick, *Education and Economic Performance* (Aldershot, Gower, 1985); D. Finegold and D. Soskice, 'The Failure of British Training: Analysis and Prescription', *Oxford Review of Economic Policy*, vol. 4, no. 3 (1988), p. 22. To my knowledge, there is little comparative analysis in this area. For the beginnings of one, see J. Allmendinger, 'Educational Systems and Labour Market Outcomes', *European Sociological Review*, vol. 5, no. 3 (1989), pp. 231–50. The OECD, in *Literacy, Economy and Society: Results of the First International Adult Literacy Survey* (Paris, OECD, 1995), has [...] published an interesting comparative study on the effects of levels of literacy on competitiveness.

33	Commission on Social Justice, op. cit., p. 97.

34	Barr, op. cit.

35	S. Bowles and H. Gintis, 'Efficient Redistribution in a Globally Competitive Economy', paper prepared for *Colloquium on Social Justice and Economic Constraints* at the Université Catholique de Louvain, 3 June 1994.

36	I. Gough, 'Economic Institutions and the Satisfaction of Human Needs', *Journal of Economic Issues*, vol. 28, no. 1 (1944), pp. 25–65.

37	J. Rogers and W. Streeck, 'Productive Solidarities: Economic Strategy and Left Politics', in *Reinventing the Left*, ed. D. Miliband (Cambridge, Polity Press, 1994).

38	P. Katzenstein, *Small States in World Markets* (Ithaca, NY, Cornell University Press, 1985).

39	S. Leibfried and E. Rieger, 'The Welfare State and Globalisation', 2ES Working Paper, Centre for Social Policy Research, University of Bremen.

40	J. Stephens, 'The Scandinavian Welfare State: Achievements, Crisis and Prospects', in *Welfare State in Transition*, ed. G. Esping-Andersen (London, Sage, 1996).

41	Commission of the European Communities, *White Paper on European Social Policy*, Com (94)333 (EC, 1994), p. 31.

42	R. Wilkinson, 'Health, Redistribution and Growth', in Glyn and Miliband, op. cit.

43 Council of Europe, *Crime and Economy*, reports presented to the 11th Criminological Colloquium, 1994.

44 J. Hagan, 'Crime, Inequality and Efficiency', in Glyn and Miliband, op. cit.

45 US Department of Housing and Urban Development, *Insurance Crisis in Urban America* (HUD-FIA-315, 1978).

46 Bowles and Gintis, op. cit.

47 T. Persson and G. Tabellini, 'Is Inequality Harmful for Growth?', *American Economic Review*, vol. 84 (1994). pp. 600–21; Glyn and Miliband, op. cit.; Esping-Andersen, op. cit.; L. Kenworthy, 'Equality and Efficiency: The Illusory Tradeoff', *European Journal of Political Research*, vol. 27 (1995).

48 Esping-Andersen, op. cit., p. 725.

49 G. Esping-Andersen, *The Three Worlds of Welfare Capitalism* (Cambridge, Polity Press, 1990), p. 2.

50 J. Kolberg and H. Uusitalo, 'The Interface between the Economy and the Welfare State: A Sociological Account', in *Social Policy in a Changing Europe*, ed. Z. Ferge and J. Kolberg (Campus / Westview, 1992).

51 J. Lewis, ed., *Women and Social Policies in Europe: Work, Family and the State* (Aldershot, Edward Elgar, 1993); J. Lewis and J. Ostner, *Gender and the Evolution of European Social Policies* (Zentrum fur Sozialpolitik, University of Bremen, 1994). See also S. Duncan, 'Theorizing European Gender Systems', *Journal of European Social Policy*, vol. 5, no. 4 (1995), pp. 263–84.

52 F. Green, A. Henley and E. Tsakalotos, 'Income Inequality in Corporatist and Liberal Economies', *International Review of Applied Economics*, vol. 8, no. 3 (1994), pp. 303–31.

53 L. Calmfors and J. Driffill, 'Bargaining Structure, Corporatism and Macroeconomic Performance', *Economic Policy*, no. 6 (1988).

54 R. Rowthorn, 'Centralisation, Employment and Wage Dispersion', *Economic Journal*, vol. 102 (1996), pp. 506–23.

55 T. Weisskopf, 'Class Conflict or Class Harmony? A Study of the Effect of Worker Security on Productivity Growth in Eight Advanced Capitalist Countries', unpublished paper. See also T. Weisskopf, 'The Effect of Unemployment on Labour Productivity: An International Comparative Analysis', *International Review of Applied Economics*, vol. 3, no. 2 (1989), pp. 127–51.

56 G. Esping-Andersen, 'Welfare State without Work', paper presented at Research Committee 19 of the International Sociological Association, Pavia, Italy, September 1995; and Esping-Andersen, 'After the Golden Age: Welfare State Dilemmas in a Global Economy', in *Welfare States in Transition*, ed. G. Esping-Andersen (London, Sage, 1996).

57 This scenario applies least well to Germany – Esping-Andersen's archetypical conservative welfare state. It is probable that the maintenance of corporatist structures of interest representation and intermediation account for Germany's continuing good economic performance despite the costs and strains of unification.

58 Esping-Andersen, 'After the Golden Age'.

Negative Integration: States and the Loss of Boundary Control

Fritz Scharpf

[...]

Negative Integration: The Loss of Boundary Control

In the history of capitalism, the decades following the Second World War were unusual in the degree to which the boundaries of the territorial state had become coextensive with the boundaries of markets for capital, services, goods and labour. These boundaries were by no means impermeable, but transactions across them were nevertheless under the effective control of national governments. As a consequence, capital owners were generally restricted to investment opportunities within the national economy, and firms were mainly challenged by domestic competitors. International trade grew slowly, and since governments controlled imports and exchange rates, international competitiveness was not much of a problem. While these conditions lasted, government interest rate policy controlled the rate of return on financial investments. If interest rates were lowered, job-creating real investments would become relatively more attractive, and vice versa. Thus, Keynesian macro-economic management could smooth the business cycle and prevent demand-deficient unemployment, while union wage policy, where it could be employed for macro-economic purposes, was able to control the rate of inflation. At the same time, government regulation and union collective bargaining controlled the conditions of production. But since all effective competitors could be, and were, required to produce under the same regimes, the costs of regulation could be passed on to consumers. Hence the rate of return on investment was not necessarily affected by high levels of regulation and union power; capitalist accumulation was as feasible in the union-dominated Swedish welfare state as it was in the American free enterprise system.

During this period, therefore, the industrial nations of Western Europe had the chance to develop specifically national versions of the capitalist welfare state – and their choices were in fact remarkably different. [...] In spite of the considerable differences between the 'social democratic', 'corporatist' or 'liberal' versions of the welfare state, however, all were remarkably successful in maintaining and promoting a vigorous capitalist economy, while also controlling, in different ways and to different degrees, the destructive tendencies of unfettered capitalism in the interest of specific social, cultural and/or ecological values [...]. It was not fully realized at the time, however, how much the success of market-correcting policies did in fact depend on the capacity of the territorial state to control its economic boundaries. Once this capacity was lost, through the globalization of capital markets and the transnational integration of markets for goods and services, the 'golden years' of the capitalist welfare state came to an end.

Now the minimal rate of return that investors can expect is determined by global financial markets, rather than by national monetary policy, and real interest rates are generally about twice as high as they used to be in the 1960s. So if a government should now try to reduce interest rates below the international level, the result would no longer be an increase of job-creating real investment in the national economy, but an outflow of capital, devaluation and a rising rate of inflation. Similarly, once the territorial state has lost, or given up, the capacity to control the boundaries of markets for goods and services, it can no longer make sure that all competing suppliers will be subject to the same regulatory regime. Thus, if now the costs of regulation or of collective-bargaining are increased nationally, they can no longer be passed on to consumers. Instead, imports will increase, exports decrease, profits will fall, investment decline and firms will go bankrupt or move production to more benign locations.

Thus, when boundary control declines, the capacity of the state and the unions to shape the conditions under which capitalist economies must operate is also diminished. Instead, countries are forced into a competition for locational advantage which has all the characteristics of a Prisoner's Dilemma game [...]. The paradigmatic example of this form of 'regulatory competition' was provided, during the first third of the twentieth century, by the inability of 'progressive' states in the United States to regulate the employment of children in industry. Under the 'negative commerce clause' decisions of the Supreme Court, they were not allowed to prohibit or tax the import of goods produced by child labour in neighbouring states. Hence locational competition in the integrated American market prevented all states from enacting regulations that would affect only enterprises within their own state [...]. In the same way, the increasing transnational integration of capital and product markets, and especially the completion of the European internal market, reduces the freedom of national governments and unions to raise the regulatory and wage costs of national firms above the level prevailing in competing locations. Moreover, and if nothing else changes, the 'competition of regulatory systems' that is generally welcomed by neo-liberal economists [...] and politicians may well turn into a downward spiral of competitive deregulation in which all competing countries will find themselves reduced to a level of protection that is in fact lower than preferred by any of them.

[...]

Note

From G. Marks et al., eds, *Governance in the EU*, London, Sage, 1996, pp. 16–17.

Challenges to Welfare: External Constraints

Martin Rhodes

[...]

The issue of globalization is a controversial one and its effects on the welfare state apparently contradictory. Nevertheless, the interaction of globalization with internal challenges suggests there is a new dynamic at work in the international economy that compounds the problems of the advanced welfare states while also making them more difficult to resolve. 'Europeanization' also has numerous implications for all of the region's welfare regimes, as both a 'subset' of globalization (in creating an unfettered internal market) and the source of new pan-European social policies and programmes.

Globalization

The process of globalization has a number of implications for welfare states. The first of these derive from its impact on inequality and unemployment:

- Relocation to low labour cost countries outside Europe has been occurring at an increasingly rapid pace in manufacturing, especially in sectors where production can easily be separated from production and design and where the market is global. This, and the parallel increase in the growth of manufactured exports from the newly industrialized countries (NICs), has been driven by their growing manufacturing cost advantage and rising productivity. To date, 1997, the major casualties have been unskilled or low-skilled workers in labour intensive manufacturing. In the future, semi-skilled and certain skilled workers will also be threatened by the globalization of information technology to those NICs (mainly in the Asia-Pacific region) that have made massive investments in education and training (Freeman and Soete, 1995).

- Despite the institutional barriers to market forces created by different welfare systems, there is growing evidence that intensified international competition and the changes induced in industry are increasing earnings inequality, in part because the relative wages of more skilled workers are being bid up in Western countries and those of lower skilled workers are falling (Gottschalk and Joyce, 1995).

The second set of implications derives from the impact of globalization on national government autonomy:

- The 'golden age' of the welfare state between the 1950s and 1970s was dependent on internal and external supports (Singh, 1995). The key domestic arrangements included, with varying degrees of success, a compromise on wages and profits between capital and labour and a commitment by the state to a certain level of welfare, living standards and domestic demand. Externally, a stable international monetary and trading regime depended on the support of a hegemonic power – the United States. [...] The relative decline of that power and of the dollar as the monetary bedrock of the system meant that those arrangements could no longer be sustained. The end of the international regime of 'embedded liberalism' – based on fixed exchange rates and capital controls – has witnessed a loss of control by governments over financial transactions as credit and exchange controls have been abandoned.

- In consequence, domestic economies have become hostage to international markets and their demands for 'credibility'. Governments – and especially social democratic ones – have had to shift their priorities away from traditional goals of redistribution, welfarism and full employment towards restraining the expansion of credit and money stock effected by international markets, defending the balance of trade and payments and controlling inflation (Moses, 1995). Meanwhile – and partly in consequence – domestic welfare arrangements have become harder to sustain as corporatist welfare coalitions (between employers and unions – the 'social partners') have been undermined: for increased capital mobility immeasurably strengthens the owners of capital over other groups (Frieden, 1991). The most dramatic example of this shift has been in the Scandinavian model where employers have broken with the long-standing corporatist consensus (Stephens, 1996). Nevertheless, even if it is under stress, corporatist decision-making may prove to be essential in managing welfare retrenchment and change: pension reform, for example, may prove impossible without it in many countries (as revealed [in the 1990s] in France, Germany and Italy).

- Finally, the 'competitive imperative' generated by greater economic interdependence has encouraged the pursuit of policies designed to preserve or create competitive advantage. The main concern is to avoid burdening firms with higher non-wage labour costs or corporate taxes and to alleviate those they currently bear.

Europeanization

Increased integration of the European economy poses a new and parallel set of problems. The critical question is how far the various welfare regimes can retain their diversity in an open trading, finance and, eventually, currency region. The first set of implications relates again to the impact on employment and welfare arrangements. For in a more open European trade area – the single market – a contest may be emerging among the regimes due to their different social costs. There are two dimensions to this phenomenon:

- First, the greater scope created for 'regulatory arbitrage' on the part of firms (i.e. their capacity to choose between locations on the basis of the relative costs of regulation) could lead to 'regime shopping'. Arguably, this is already happening as firms from high-cost jurisdictions such as Germany transfer to lower-cost countries like Britain, where other assets – such as an educated workforce and access to finance – are also in good supply.

- The second, related, prospect is that, if 'regulatory arbitrage' becomes extensive, member-state governments could engage in 'social devaluation, a problem likely to be compounded by progress towards European monetary union (EMU). The austerity policies demanded from countries in preparation for EMU (reductions in deficits and debts, a prioritization of anti-inflation policies) have already had an impact on welfare programmes. Under fully fledged monetary union, reducing wage (and non-wage) labour costs will become the only tool left in the hands of governments seeking to improve the competitiveness of their economies. Those countries able to compete on productivity may be able to sustain existing welfare arrangements; those having to compete on price will be forced to reduce the costs of welfare for firms as well as bidding down real wages. The threat of a further increase in polarization and inequality begins to loom large under these circumstances.

Of course, these aspects of 'negative integration' are the downside of European Union. 'Positive integration' is also occurring as new regulations are put in place to protect the European 'social model'. However, the balance between the positive and negative effects seems strongly biased towards the latter (Scharpf, 1997). Part of the problem lies in the diversity within Europe's 'social model', despite the existence of common principles across the various welfare regimes. Other difficulties derive from the complex, multi-tiered structure of the EU.

[Since the late 1970s] a great deal of political capital has been invested in the so-called European 'social dimension', precisely to prevent 'negative integration' from occurring. However, despite major advances [...], it has failed to live up to the hopes of its promoters (Rhodes, 1995). There are four areas of European policy that can broadly be conceived as 'social': the social security and distributive aspects of the Common Agricultural Policy (CAP); the funds for pan-European transfers – the regional fund, the social funds and the new 'cohesion fund' created at Maastricht; regulations on the environment, product safety and consumer protection; and regulatory policies for the labour market. But none of these, alone or in combination, herald a European welfare state, for the following reasons:

- The Common Agricultural Policy operates in a highly distorted fashion. Because its social policy-like measures are subordinated to its institutional price system they do not discriminate among farmers or rural areas on the basis of *need*. Indeed, its net effect has been to redistribute resources to the more prosperous farmers of the north under its various subsidy and income-maintenance programmes.

- The regional funds are redistributive and inspired by principles of pan-European solidarity. Conceivably, they could provide the basis for a system of inter-regional social transfers and risk insurance, but to do so they would have to be expanded and reoriented towards social inequality and deprivation rather than broad regional disparities.

- While the harmonization of health and safety standards and consumer and environmental protection has made considerable advances – preserving conditions in the workplace and protecting consumers from the market – they do not affect social entitlements or the central, distributive, functions of welfare.

- The same can be said of innovations in European labour market policy. For while the European Commission's action programmes, inspired by the 1989 Social Charter, have begun to have an impact on *workers'* rights and entitlements across the Community – with significant innovations in equal opportunities, working hours' legislation, the rights of women in the workplace and representation in transnational companies

– European policy does not address the issue of *social* citizenship. At the same time, attempts to build a European system of industrial relations are being undermined by the opposition of capital, the weaknesses of employers and union organization at the European level, and the fragility of the European legal basis for institution-building in this area (for further detail, see Rhodes, 1992, 1995).

Beyond these limitations, the strong links between social policy development and political legitimacy mean that multi-tiered institutional systems such as the European Union are vulnerable to *competitive state building* – as revealed by the new centrality of the concept of 'subsidiarity' in European policy discourse and the opposition of the numerous European member states to European social programmes on the grounds of sovereignty. This is not say that sovereignty is not being conceded in this area: indeed, the broad interpretation given by the European Court of Justice to various European social regulations (in pensions and dismissals, for example) have exceeded the limits originally accepted by many member states. But those states are also resisting a significant transfer of fiscal capacity to the European Union and remain protective of their social policy authority (Leibfried and Pierson, 1995). In sum, the role of Europe in defending the European 'social model' will be restricted to general objectives and 'framework' agreements influencing, and being influenced by, existing national diversity. The burden of adjustment of welfare states to the new challenges and constraints will necessarily be shouldered by the national policy makers.

[…]

Note

From M. Rhodes et al., *Developments in West European Politics*, London and Basingstoke, Macmillan, 1997, pp. 66–70.

References

Freeman, C. and L. Soete, *Work for All or Mass Unemployment: Computerised Technical Change in the 21st Century*, London, Pinter, 1995.
Frieden, J. A., 'Invested Interests: The Politics of National Economic Policies in a World of Global Finance', *International Organization*, 45, 4, 1991, pp. 539–64.
Gottschalk, P. and M. Joyce, 'The Impact of Technological Change, Deindustrialization and Internationalization of Trade and Earnings Inequality: An International Perspective', in *Poverty, Inequality and the Future of Social Policy*, ed. K. McFate, R. Lawson and W. J. Wilson, New York, Russell Sage Foundation, 1995, pp. 197–228.

Leibfried, S. and P. Pierson, eds, *European Social Policy: Between Fragmentation and Integration*, Washington, DC, Brookings Institution, 1995.

Moses, J. 'The Social Democratic Predicament in the Emerging European Union', *Journal of European Public Policy*, 2, 3, 1995, pp. 407–26.

Rhodes, M., 'The Future of the Social Dimension: Labour Market Regulation in post-1992 Europe', *Journal of Common Market Studies*, 30, 1, 1992, pp. 23–51.

Rhodes, M. 'A Regulatory Conundrum: Industrial Relations and the Social Dimension', in S. Leibfried and P. Pierson, op. cit., pp. 78–122.

Scharpf, F. W., 'European Welfare States: Negative and Positive Integration', in *A New Social Contract?: Charting the Future of European Welfare*, ed. Y. Meny and M. Rhodes, London, Macmillan, 1997.

Singh, A., 'Institutional Requirements for Full Employment in Advanced Economies', *International Labour Review*, 134, 5, 4/5, 1995, pp. 471–96.

Stephens, J. D., 'The Scandinavian Welfare States: Achievements, Crisis and Prospects', in *Welfare States in Transition: National Adaptations in Global Economies*, ed. G. Esping-Andersen, London, Sage, 1996, pp. 32–65.

National Economic Governance

Paul Hirst and Grahame Thompson

[...]

The Limits of National Economic Governance

There can be no doubt that the combined effects of changing economic conditions and past public policies of dismantling exchange controls have made ambitious and internationally divergent strategies of national economic governance [...] difficult. Also reduced has been the capacity of states to act autonomously on their societies. This is because the range of economic incentives and sanctions at the state's disposal has been restricted as a consequence of this loss of capacity to deliver distinctively 'national' economic policies.

Most obvious is the case of macro-economic management. The case of the current impossibility of ambitious national-level Keynesian strategies hardly needs making, particularly after the failure of the French socialist government's ambitious reflationary programme in the early 1980s. But nationally distinctive monetarist policies of an ambitious nature have proved hardly more viable. Thus the UK was saved from accelerating losses of employment and output in the early 1980s by international impacts that reduced the value of sterling against the dollar and brought down interest rates, but that had nothing to do with national policy.

If macro-economic management is problematic, so too is that supply-side alternative, a centralized state-directed industrial policy. Technologies are currently changing too rapidly for the state, however competent and well informed its officials, to 'pick winners' on a national basis. Moreover, the population of firms that the state would have to bring into such a policy is less stable and easy to interact with than it was in the 1960s. Many major products are now the result of complex inter-firm partnerships. Changed economic conditions favour risk-sharing between firms, diversification and flexibility, and put a premium on specialist and local knowledge. These are factors that traditional state institutions and uniform systems of industrial administration find it hard to cope with.

Despite the foregoing, national governmental policies to sustain economic performance remain important, even if their methods and functions have changed. This is true even when states are part of a supra-national entity. In the EU the free movement of capital, labour, goods and services from the end of 1992, monetary union as provided by the Maastricht Treaty, and greater political integration as envisaged after the next inter-governmental conference [that began] in 1996, must obviously restrict some hitherto important areas of specifically national economic management. But they will make others more important – giving a new significance to non-monetarist fiscal and supply-side policies, for instance.

While national governments may no longer be 'sovereign' economic regulators in the traditional sense, they remain political communities with extensive powers to influence and to sustain economic actors within their territories. Technical top-down macro-economic management is now less important. However, the role of government as a facilitator and orchestrator of private economic actors has become more salient as a consequence. The *political* role of government is central in the new forms of economic management. [...] Neither the financial markets nor the Commission officials in Brussels – to take the case of the most developed supra-national economic association, the EU – can impose or secure the forms of social cohesion and the policies that follow from them in the way that national governments can. National governments can still *compensate* for the effects of internationalization and for the continued volatility of the financial markets, even if they cannot unilaterally control those effects or prevent that volatility.

Before going into more detailed political orchestrational features of national policy, let us look at the more overtly economic character of (non-monetarist) fiscal policy. Fiscal policy has been in the shadow of monetary policy ever since the demise of Keynesianism. During the late 1970s and the 1980s it became very difficult to argue for an 'independent' fiscal policy, one that was both nationally autonomous and independent of monetary policy. However, things may be now about to change.

One thing closer economic and monetary union within Europe (and more generally, the relative 'cooling of the casino' internationally) could do is to help 'disengage' fiscal from monetary policy once again. Take the case of the EU. The closer monetary union becomes, the more individual countries could engage in independent fiscal policies. This does not mean that they will be totally free to do as they wish on the fiscal front. The post-Maastricht guidelines for government fiscal balances, for instance, were quite tight (around 3 per cent of GDP). But these are only meant to be guidelines and in practice they may be quite flexible (more flexible than monetary guidelines for instance, which are to be under the direction of an 'independent' European central bank). Thus, as decisions on monetary policy are increasingly taken elsewhere, i.e. centrally, individual governments will be able to decide their own fiscal policies relatively independently of monetary policy. This could enable some quite innovative fiscal responses as a result. Any new fiscal regime will also be operating in an environment of increasing financial and labour market integration, and this would need to be taken into account by policy makers.

The problem this will pose is how to develop tax systems that minimize both the incentives to avoid individual national taxes and the ability to do so. Broadly speaking the need is to think in terms of factor mobility in relationship to taxation. Capital and money markets will probably integrate most rapidly and thoroughly, so there may be little scope for nationally differential corporation taxes or taxes on savings (via taxes on savings institutions). Nationally differential taxes on domestic consumption may also be difficult, but here it depends upon how internationally mobile purchasers are in the face of tax rates. Will they be prepared to travel long distances just to save tax differences? Thus there may be more scope here. In the case of income taxes again this depends upon how integrated labour markets become. Clearly there are likely to be degrees of integration. A lot of work overseas is temporary. But in general the highest paid and the lowest paid tend to be the potentially most internationally mobile. In the case of indigenous EU workers, cultural and linguistic barriers may still be high in terms of labour mobility, and a lot will depend upon how quickly and efficiently mutual recognition of professional qualifications and standards develops. In general there may still be some scope for differential income taxes before (dis)incentive effects become rife and undermine the effectiveness of these. The most immobile factor is likely to remain property of one kind or another. People cannot just up and away with their houses for instance. Thus there may be some innovative scope for new forms of property taxes as this becomes an increasingly attractive source of tax revenues for governments.

One other significant area where new revenue-raising strategies may be available to national states and to subsidiary governments is energy consumption and environmental pollution (Hewitt, 1990). Taxes on non-renewable energy consumption and the widespread adoption of the 'polluter pays' principle through taxes on industrial emissions, vehicle use, etc. may well be the major sources of revenue of the future. Such taxes have three advantages: they have less of a stigma for international financial markets than direct taxation (mainly because they have not yet been factored into the market-makers' calculations); they appear to be more acceptable to citizens than taxes on income; and they serve the dual purpose of raising revenue and forcing both firms and final consumers to internalize the environmental costs of their actions. Thus energy taxes seem to offer one of the best ways of decoupling fiscal and monetary policy and attaining a measure of autonomy in revenue raising.

Returning to the general theme of the nation-state in regulating the economy, there are three key functions it can perform which stem from its role as orchestrator of an economic consensus within a given community. States are not like markets: they are communities of fate which tie together actors who share certain common interests in the success or failure of their national economies. Markets may or may not be international, but wealth and economic prosperity are still essentially national phenomena. They depend upon how well national economic actors can work together to secure certain key supply-side outcomes. National policy can provide certain key inputs to economic performance that cannot be bought or traded on the market. Markets need to be embedded in social relations. Political authority remains central in assuring that markets are appropriately institutionalized and that the non-market conditions of economic success are present. National governments thus remain a crucial element in the economic success of their societies – providing cohesion, solidarity and certain crucial services that markets of themselves cannot (Hutton, 1995).

The three key functions of states are as follows. First, the state, if it is to influence the economy, must construct a *distributional coalition*: that is, it must win the acceptance of key economic actors and the organized social interests representing them for a sustainable distribution of national income and expenditure which promotes competitive manufacturing performance (among other things). The major components of such a coalition are: the balance of national income devoted respectively to consumption and investment; a broad agreement on the level of taxation necessary to sustain state investment in infrastructure, training and collective services for industry; and a framework for controlling wage settlements, the growth of credit and levels of dividends such that inflation is kept within internationally tolerable limits.

Second, for such a distributional coalition to be possible the state must perform another function, that is, the *orchestration of social consensus*. Such coalitions only work when they emerge from a political culture that balances collaboration and competition and in which the major organized interests are accustomed to bargain over national economic goals, to make on-going commitments to determine policy by such bargaining, and to police their members' compliance with such bargains. Industry, organized labour and the state can be related in various ways, perhaps much less rigidly than the highly structured national corporatism practised in states like West Germany and Sweden into the 1990s. The point is to ensure that the key components of the economic system are in dialogue, that firms co-operate as well as compete, and that different factors of production relate in other than just market terms, i.e. labour and management and capital providers and firms. Such systems will not be devoid of conflict, nor will interests be wholly compatible, but there will be mechanisms for resolving such differences. Such an overall consensus can only work if it is also keyed in with the effective operation of more specific resource allocation mechanisms, such as the system of wage determination and the operation of capital markets.

Third, the state must achieve an adequate balance in the distribution of its fiscal resources and its regulatory activities between the national, regional and municipal *levels of government*. The centralization of EU policy is promoting the increasing importance of effective regional government. The regional provision of education and training, industrial finance, collective services for industry and social services is gaining in importance. Regional governments are more able to assess the needs of industry because they possess more localized, and therefore accurate, information and because they are of a scale where the key actors can interact successfully. Regional government must be seen not as something inherently opposed to national economic management, but as a crucial component of it. It is the national state which determines the constitutional position, powers and fiscal resources of lower tiers of government. Those national states which allow a considerable measure of autonomy to regional governments tend to have the best and most effective supply-side regulation at the regional level. In a European context Germany and Italy offer obvious examples. The most prosperous *Länder*, like Baden-Württemberg and Bavaria, or the most successful Italian regions, like Emilia-Romagna, have achieved a high level of devolution of the tasks of economic management (Sabel, 1989).

The main problem about the ways in which nation-states continue to have a salience as a locus of economic management is that such activities now depend on social attitudes and institutions that are not equally available to all states. The new mechanisms of economic co-ordination and regulation give primacy to the high level of social cohesion and co-operation that the state can both call upon and develop. The new methods of national economic regulation in a more internationalized economy are not, for example, like Keynesianism, that is, a technique of macro-economic management that was in principle available to every substantial and competently administered modern state if it chose to adopt such a strategy. Rather the new methods rest on specific ensembles of social institutions and these are more difficult to adopt or transfer by deliberate choice. States are thus in considerable measure trapped by the legacies of social cohesion that they inherit. Countries like the USA cannot just decide to adopt the more solidaristic and co-ordinative relations between industry, labour and the state that have hitherto prevailed in Germany and Japan (Albert, 1993).

This means that between blocs and within blocs there will be fundamental differences in the ability to respond to competitive pressures and changing international conjunctures. Those societies that have emphasized short-term market performance, like the UK and the USA, are threatened by the competitive pressures of societies that have concentrated on enhancing long-term manufacturing competitiveness and have had the social cohesion to achieve it, like Germany and Japan, and also by newly industrializing societies following similar strategies like South Korea or Singapore. The political process and the interest group culture in societies like the UK and the USA do not favour rapid adaptation in a more co-operative direction: rather they emphasize competition and the dumping of social costs on those who are both least organized or influential and least able to bear them. This tends to push such societies away from effective international or bloc co-operation. The USA, unlike its role between 1945 and 1972, will refuse to bear any substantial level of cost to secure a more stable international environment: it will pursue narrow and short-term considerations of national advantage. The UK will seek to minimize European integration and to trade down standards of social welfare and occupational protection to a lowest common denominator.

It might appear in one sense as if the less solidaristic and more market-oriented societies like the UK or the USA may actually have an *advantage* in a more internationalized economy where national-based economic governance is less effective. British and American firms are used to putting competition before co-operation and to fending for themselves in the face of narrowly self-interested financial institutions. Not only are activist macro-economic management and a centralized state-directed industrial policy increasingly obsolete, but also a range of social and economic changes, and not just the internationalization of major markets, are making national uniform systems of corporatist intermediation more difficult to sustain. Industrial structures and divisions of labour are becoming more complex and differentiated throughout the advanced industrial world. Large, highly concentrated national firms with stable and highly unionized manual workforces are becoming less salient [...]. Thus countries like Japan and Germany will find that their (very different) national systems of corporatist co-ordination are less and less representative of industry and, therefore, less effective.

There is a good deal of truth in this argument, but it does not go to sustain the conclusion that less solidaristic countries will actually *benefit* from the changed conditions. It is difficult to see how the future of complex social systems, including investment in manufacturing, training and public infrastructure, can be left in the hands of firms that compete but cannot co-operate and to the workings of weakly regulated markets alone.

In fact, societies like Japan and Germany will continue to enjoy major competitive advantages even if their national systems of corporatist representation decline, precisely because their forms of non-market economic governance are diverse and multi-layered. In both countries strong patterns of co-operation and solidarity *within* firms and effective forms of governance through regional institutions or patterns of inter-firm co-operation continue to give them advantages in supplementing and sustaining market performance. The general functions performed by political authority in promoting competition and co-ordination remain important, even if some of the means by which they have been delivered heretofore are changing.

Note

From P. Hirst and G. Thompson, *Globalization in Question*, Cambridge, Polity Press, 1996, pp. 143–9.

References

Albert, M., *Capitalism against Capitalism*, London, Whurr, 1993.
Hewitt, P., *Green Taxes*, London, Institute for Public Policy Research, 1990.
Hutton, W., *The State We're In*, London, Cape, 1995.
Sabel, C., 'Flexible Specialization and the Re-emergence of Regional Economies' in *Reversing Economic Decline*, ed. P. Q. Hirst and J. Zeitlin, Oxford, Berg, 1989.

Demographic and Social Change

Social Security around the World

Estelle James

The World Bank study *Averting the Old Age Crisis: Policies to Protect the Old and Promote Growth* (1994) [...] is an empirically based work, drawing on evidence from over one hundred countries. Although its messages are primarily directed toward developing countries (whose populations are aging most rapidly) and transitional socialist economies (where old-age systems are a major current fiscal problem), it also has implications for industrialized countries. Figures 8 and 9 show, for various countries, the percentage of the population over sixty years old in 1990 and 2030 and the number of years required to double that segment of the population from 9 per cent to 18 per cent, respectively.

The World Bank team [...] used two overarching criteria for evaluating old-age programmes. First, such programmes should protect the old. Second, they should promote, or at least not hinder, economic growth, which is good for both elderly and young people. It was found that current systems in many countries fail both tests. They do not always protect elderly people and they have not promoted economic growth; in fact, they have introduced inefficiencies that impede growth. This means that future generations will get lower wages and pensions than they would have otherwise.

[...]

The Problems

Most formal systems of old-age security are mandatory publicly managed schemes financed by payroll taxes, largely on a pay-as-you-go basis,

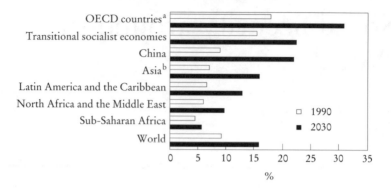

Figure 8   Percentage of population aged over sixty, by region, 1990 and 2030

[a] Including Japan.

[b] Excluding China.

Source: Adapted from the World Bank population database

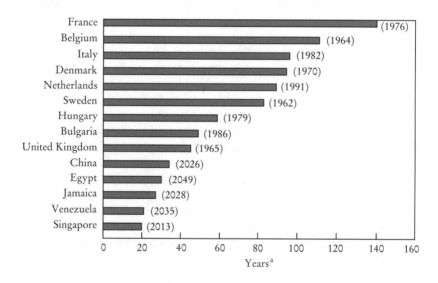

Figure 9   Number of years required to double the proportion of the population older than sixty from 9 to 18 per cent, various countries

[a] Year in which proportion of people over sixty [either] reached or will reach 18 per cent is shown in parentheses.

Sources: B. R. Mitchell, *International Historical Statistics: Europe, 1750–1988*, New York, Stockton Press, 3rd edition, 1990; World Bank database projections

meaning that today's workers pay the pensions of those who have already retired. They combine in one programme the three functions of old-age systems: saving, redistribution and insurance. Almost all existing programmes are in serious trouble, yet countries that are starting new systems are on the verge of making the same mistakes. A list of common problems follows.

High Tax Rates. When populations are young and old-age systems are immature, small contributions from the large number of workers make possible substantial benefits to the few pensioners. As a result, politicians often set up overly generous benefits. However, as populations age and systems mature, these same benefits require high taxes to pay pensions to the growing number of retirees. Payroll taxes for pensions already exceed 25 per cent in Egypt, Hungary, Russia, Kyrgyzstan, Brazil and Italy. They will exceed 30 per cent in many countries over the next thirty years, if pay-as-you-go financing and current benefit schedules are retained. High payroll taxes are regressive and inefficient; they mean lower take-home pay if passed on to workers, and less employment if borne by employers.

Evasion. High taxes that are not closely linked to benefits promote evasion. This is a major problem in developing countries, where tax collection capacities are limited. In many Latin American countries over 40 per cent of the labour force works in the informal sector, in part to avoid payroll taxes for pensions. In Argentina before recent reforms, more than 50 per cent of workers covered by the system evaded their contributions. Workers who evade payroll taxes are either unprotected, thereby defeating the purpose of the old-age system, or they manage to qualify for benefits despite their failure to pay contributions, which undermines the system's financial viability. Evasion hurts the economy, because people who work off the books are often less productive.

Early Retirement. There are many reasons for early retirement, including the availability of public pensions at rates that are not actuarially reduced and, conversely, the imposition of penalties by these plans on those who continue working. In Hungary, more than one-quarter of the population are pensioners, the average retirement age is fifty-four, and the payroll tax is 31 per cent: in Turkey, many workers retire with a generous pension before fifty, or even forty. Over the last two decades the labour force participation rate of men in their fifties and sixties has fallen substantially in almost every OECD country. Early retirees have a twofold impact on social security systems: they stop making contributions and they begin drawing benefits. They also deprive the economy of their experience and work effort.

Increased Burden on the Public Treasury and Misallocation of Public Resources. In 1990 Austria, Italy and Uruguay spent more than one-third of their public budgets on pensions. Given the economic and political limits on taxation, high pension spending can squeeze out government spending on growth-promoting public investments such as infrastructure, education and health services, or can lead to deficit spending that fuels inflation.

Lost Opportunity to Increase Savings. Many countries believe their growth is hampered by inadequate national saving and yet fail to use their old-age systems as a way to induce people to save more. Indeed, some economists believe that existing systems have induced people to save less.

Failure to Redistribute to Lower-Income Groups. Studies of public pension plans in the Netherlands, Sweden, the United Kingdom and the United States have not found much redistribution from the lifetime rich to the lifetime poor, even though these plans are based on seemingly progressive benefit formulas. This is partly because benefit formulas typically pay higher pensions to higher wage workers, and partly because the rich enter the labour force later and live longer, thereby contributing for fewer years and collecting benefits for more years.

Positive Lifetime Transfers to Early Cohorts and Losses to their Children. In general, covered workers who retire in the first twenty to thirty years of a scheme get back more than they contributed, because they pay low payroll tax rates and for only part of their working lives, yet they get full benefits upon retirement. In contrast, their children and grandchildren pay high payroll tax rates and will get back less than they contribute and at lower rates of return than they could have earned elsewhere, as old-age schemes adjust to the demographic transition. In addition, the total GNP may be lower for these future generations than it would have been under another old-age system, because of the effects on long-term savings and labour supply and its allocation, as described previously.

Current Systems are Not Sustainable. In most countries with high coverage, such as OECD and transitional economies, the implicit public pension debt (that is, the present value of pension promises made to old people and workers) far exceeds the conventional debt and comprises more than 100 per cent of GDP. This is illustrated in figure 10. Current contribution rates are not nearly high enough to fulfil these benefit promises. Either pensions or other government spending will have to be cut, or tax rates will have to be raised. Many developing countries have already

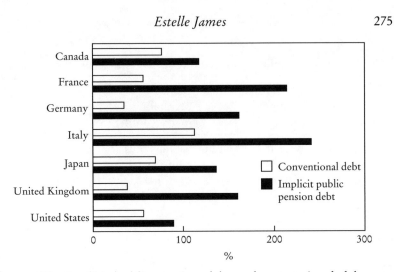

Figure 10 Implicit public pension debt and conventional debt as a percentage of GDP, various countries, 1990[a]

[a] Implicit public pension debt is defined as the present value of pension promises made to old people and workers.

Source: Paul Van der Noord and Richard Herd, 'Pension Liabilities in Seven Major Economies', Working paper, Paris, OECD Economics Department, 1993

reneged on their promises by allowing inflation to take place without indexing benefits. In Venezuela [...] the real value of public pensions fell by 60 per cent during the 1980s, due to inflation.

In these and other ways, current government-run social security systems have hurt the economy and have failed to protect elderly people, or those who will grow old in the future. Not all of these problems are present in every country, but many of them exist in many countries, suggesting that these common problems result from something inherent in the political economy of the systems. A new system is needed that is more immune to these dangers.

The Solution

A good starting point in designing a framework for reform is the three ways in which people can be supported in their old age: saving, redistribution and insurance. The current system in most countries provides all three functions in one dominant, publicly managed, pay-as-you-go, defined benefit system. A reformed system, as shown in table 5, would establish separate administrative and financing mechanisms, or pillars, for redistribution and saving, and would use a mix of public and private management,

Table 5 The three-pillar reformed old-age income security system

Characteristic	Mandatory publicly managed pillar	Mandatory privately managed pillar	Voluntary pillar
Objectives	Redistributive plus coinsurance	Savings plus coinsurance	Savings plus coinsurance
Form	Flat, or means-tested, or minimum pension guarantee	Personal savings plan or occupational plan	Personal savings plan or occupational plan
Financing	Tax-financed	Regulated, fully funded	Fully funded

Source: World Bank, *Averting the Old Age Crisis*, New York, Oxford University Press, 1994, p. 15

full funding and pay-as-you-go tax financing, and defined benefit and defined contribution schemes.

Many social security analysts advocate a multi-pillar system for old-age income security, but unfortunately each analyst means something different by that term. In the system devised by the World Bank study, one mandatory pillar would be fully funded and privately managed. This pillar is ideally suited for handling peoples' savings. But since a privately managed pillar cannot be relied upon to provide a social safety net, a mandatory, publicly managed, tax-financed, redistributive pillar is also needed. And a third, voluntary, pillar would be used by people who wanted additional old-age security.

The pillar for saving is the most controversial. It is envisaged that this pillar would, in part, perform the function of existing public systems; but in such a way as to link benefits closely to contributions (usually through a defined contribution plan) and therefore discourage the evasion and labour market distortions observed in many countries. It would be mandatory for the same reason that current systems are mandatory: because a significant number of people may be shortsighted, may not save enough for their old age on a voluntary basis, and may become a burden on society at large when they grow old.

But the most important characteristics of this saving pillar are that it would be fully funded and privately managed. It should be fully funded, first, because the costs would be clear from the outset and countries would not be tempted to start out by making unrealistic promises that they could not ultimately fulfil. Such promises are difficult to keep, and they are difficult not to keep. By shifting some costs to the early years of a plan, full funding gives a reality check and helps to avoid this dilemma. Second, full funding would prevent dramatically rising contribution rates and large intergenerational transfers, particularly in developing countries with populations that are aging very rapidly. If these countries put in place pay-as-you-go systems or expand their coverage today, they would face a huge increase in the cost of those programmes thirty years from now, and a huge intergenerational transfer. Intergenerational transfers can be justifiable, so long as they are openly discussed and chosen by an informed citizenry. The danger with an unfunded system is that these transfers occur automatically, as a result of the ageing and maturation process, and sometimes in unexpected ways: for example, the largest transfers can go to rich people in the earlier generations. Moreover, the decision to transfer in such a system would have been made by the generation that gained, while younger generations, who would be the losers, would not have participated in this political choice (many of them would not even have been born when the system was set up and expanded). Thus there are serious questions about the procedural fairness of an unfunded system. The third reason in favour of full funding is that it may help build long-term national savings.

In addition, this saving pillar should be privately and competitively managed in order to maximize the likelihood that economic, rather than political, objectives will determine the investment strategy, and thereby to produce the best allocation of capital and the best return on savings. As can be seen from figure 11, throughout the 1980s publicly managed pension reserves earned less than privately managed reserves (based on national averages for countries where data are available) and in many cases lost money. This is not because their managers were incompetent, but because they were required to invest primarily or exclusively in government securities or loans to failing state enterprises, at low nominal interest rates that became negative real rates during inflationary periods. Publicly managed funds may also encourage deficit finance and wasteful spending by the government because they constitute a hidden and exclusive source of funds. Competitively managed, funded pension plans, in contrast, are more likely to enjoy the benefits of investment diversification, including international diversification, that protects them against inflation and other risks, and to spur financial market development, thereby enhancing economic growth. The private managers could be chosen by workers, in the case of personal saving plans, or by employers, in the case of employer-sponsored group plans.

But there are two caveats: countries must have at least rudimentary capital markets before they can establish this funded pillar; and considerable government regulation and regulatory capacity are needed to prevent fraud and excessive risk. Consequently, some countries are not yet ready to handle a funded pillar for mandatory retirement saving.

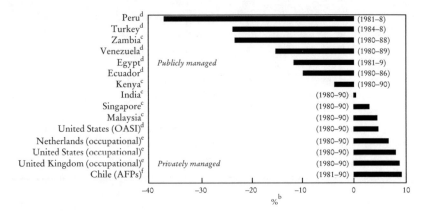

Figure 11 Gross average annual investment returns for selected pension funds, 1980s[a]

[a] Simple averages for countries with at least five years of data, as reflected in parentheses.

[b] Rate of return after inflation.

[c] Malaysia, Singapore, Kenya, India and Zambia are publicly managed provident funds. Rates reported are returns credited to worker accounts.

[d] Peru, Turkey, Venezuela, Egypt, Ecuador and the United States are publicly managed reserves of partially funded pension plans. Amounts reported are gross returns to the funds. In many cases data on administrative costs are not available.

[e] The Netherlands, the United States and the United Kingdom are privately managed occupational plans. Estimated average net returns have been reported by subtracting 1 percentage point from simulated average gross returns. Actual returns and expenses varied by fund.

[f] Actual average net returns, after all administrative expenses, are reported for the Chilean Administradora de Fondos de Pensiones (AFP). Average gross returns were 12.3 per cent; actual returns and expenses varied by fund.

Sources: R. Acuña and A. Iglesias, *Chile: Experienca con un regimen de capitalization, 1981–1991*, Santiago, Economic Conference for Latin America and the Caribbean–United Nations Development Program, 1992; Mukul G. Asher, 'Income Security for Old Age: The Case of Malaysia', National University of Singapore, Department of Economics and Statistics, 1992; E. P. Davis, 'The Structure, Regulation, and Performance of Pension Funds in Nine Industrial Countries', Working paper 1229, Washington, DC, World Bank Policy Research Department, December 1993; India Employees' Provident Fund, *Annual Report 37, 1989–90*, New Delhi Employees' Provident Fund Organization, 1991; Carmelo Meso-Lago, 'Portfolio Performance of Selected Social Security Institutes in Latin America', Discussion paper 139, Washington, DC, World Bank, 1991; Robert Palacios, 'Averting the Old Age Crisis: Technical Annex', World Bank Policy Research Department, Washington, DC, 1994; US Social Security Administration, *Social Security Bulletin*, various issues

Even for countries with the necessary capacities and institutions, it is not enough to rely completely on a privately managed pillar to handle saving; a redistributive pillar is needed to keep old people out of poverty, and this must be publicly managed and financed. Some people who are low-wage earners for most of their working lives will not be able to save enough to keep themselves out of poverty in old age as well. Others may run into a spell of bad returns, despite government regulation of the investment companies. The future is always uncertain, and this applies to capital markets as to all others.

The redistributive pillar that would take care of these problems would resemble existing public pension systems in that it would be publicly managed and tax-financed. However, unlike most current systems, the reformed public pillar would be targeted toward low-income groups, thus providing a social safety net for the old. To accomplish this, benefits could be flat, means-tested or provide a minimum pension guarantee. Because of its limited scope, this pillar could be supported by taxes significantly below current levels.

The third pillar, comprising voluntary saving and annuities, would offer supplemental retirement income for people with the means and inclination to save more, just as voluntary saving does today. This raises an important public policy issue: should governments offer tax incentives for voluntary saving and annuities? The answer depends on whether such incentives are compatible with the country's overall policy toward taxing consumption versus saving. A piecemeal approach runs the risk of being regressive (since voluntary plans are used mainly by upper-income groups) and of shifting retirement saving from taxed to tax-exempt forms, rather than increasing it overall.

All three pillars would coinsure against individual and economy-wide risk, providing better protection to the old than could any single mechanism alone. Risk diversification is especially important given the long time periods and great uncertainty involved. Typically, upper-income people realize this fact and have very diversified sources of retirement income, including privately managed investment income, while lower-income groups are much more heavily reliant on publicly managed pay-as-you-go programmes. The World Bank proposal is founded on the belief that these lower-income groups should also get the benefits of risk diversification and access to income from capital, and that this should be built into a national mandatory plan.

This is not an ivory tower proposal. The key features of this framework – separate mechanisms for redistribution and saving, shared responsibility between the public and private sectors, and a mixture of funded and tax-financed plans – have already been adopted by several countries, including Chile and Argentina, where the funded pillar is based on personal saving plans; Australia and Switzerland, where it is based on mandatory employer-sponsored plans; and Denmark and the Netherlands, where employer-sponsored plans are mandated by widespread collective bargaining, rather than legislation.

[…]

Note

From P. A. Diamond et al., eds, *Social Security: What Role for the Future?*, Washington, DC, Brookings Institute, 1996, pp. 181–90.

On *Averting the Old Age Crisis*

R. Beattie and W. McGillivray

[...]

The Report's Policy Proposals: A High-Risk Strategy

The [World Bank's] policy proposals appear to involve a high degree of risk for all parties concerned: for workers and pensioners, for employers and, last but not least, for the governments who may be induced to adopt them.

Defined Contributions Produce Uncertain Benefits

The degree of risk associated with mandatory savings schemes – advocated by the Bank as the second tier of pension provision – is likely to be significantly greater than the 'political risks' of social insurance schemes. The contributors individually assume the investment risk, and the benefits which people will ultimately receive from such schemes are not defined at all. They depend entirely on how much each person contributes, on the rate of return the fund achieves, on the amount of money that is deducted in the form of charges and commissions, and on the terms which are applied when the accumulated savings are converted into an annuity. People covered by such schemes are faced by enormous uncertainty concerning the income they will enjoy in retirement.

[...] Mandatory savings schemes may thus result in quite excessive replacement rates in some circumstances and very low pensions in others.

For this reason, such schemes cannot by themselves satisfy the ILO Social Security (Minimum Standards) Convention, 1952 (No. 102).

The report claims that under a mandatory savings system, political pressure for public spending to supplement pensions will be absent. However, it is not clear that this would be the case if the general level of pensions resulting from the plan (along with any public benefit) were deemed to be inadequate. Rather than constituting a design failure or inefficiency, the fact that a defined benefit scheme must periodically be modified to take into account emerging socio-economic realities is a recognition of the dynamic nature of social needs and of the national capacity to provide income security to aged persons. Amendments to a defined benefit scheme are based on a national consensus which takes into account the changed circumstances. While this introduces uncertainty, a democratically determined solution will lead to modifications which are acceptable to society. This is preferable to an individual worker assuming risks over which the worker has little or no control, and the implications of which the worker may not even understand.

Under a defined contribution scheme, the conversion of the accumulated contributions at retirement into a pension creates problems. The level of the annuity will be low if the market rate of interest happens to be low at the time that the annuity is purchased. Annuity markets are far from perfect, because insurers have incomplete information on life expectancy; consequently margins tend to be high. Clients have little knowledge or experience of purchasing an annuity and may be easily misled by salespersons who receive large commissions and therefore have an incentive to sell an annuity, whether or not it is in the client's interests. In the absence of mandatory unisex annuity rates (which exist in few countries other than the United States), a woman will receive a lower annuity than a man with the same accumulated savings, other things being equal, as women have much longer life expectancy. The report suggests partial solutions to some of these problems, but in reducing one type of risk, it tends to create another. Paradoxically, the report even suggests that perhaps the public scheme ought to take responsibility for pensioners who live longer than average. The ability of insurers to provide inflation-proofed annuities is also dependent to a large extent on the state issuing indexed bonds.

Investment

Partial funding systems of finance have been adopted for most defined benefit pensions schemes in developing countries. Setting a contribution rate higher than the pay-as-you-go rate has the salutary effect of signalling to participants in the early years of the scheme that there is a real cost and that this cost will increase in the future. The higher contribution rate has created reserves which can be used for development projects. The contribution rate can be set at a level so that the reserves thereby created may be efficiently absorbed by the capital market in the country. This discretion is not possible in a defined contribution scheme, where the contribution rate must be set at a level expected to produce a reasonable benefit, and hence the level of reserves is thereby automatically determined.

The flexibility of a partial funding financial system of defined benefit scheme allows the capacity of the national financial markets and the national economy to absorb investments to be taken into account. Simply having resources to invest does not mean that there will be suitable intermediaries or appropriate projects seeking funds. Financial markets are still rudimentary in most developing countries and, as the report points out, regulatory mechanisms must be established. Investing abroad may be attractive, but in many countries liberalization of the regulations would lead to capital flight. It must be admitted that in a number of cases, where pension systems have accumulated large reserves, the government has absorbed them, either by fiat or by default, with the disastrous consequences which are amply documented in the report. One of the undoubted virtues of pay-as-you-go is that it prevents governments from indulging in such behaviour.

The real rate of return will be affected by changes in the supply of and demand for savings. The report assumes that a mandatory savings system with a contribution rate of about 10 per cent will generate substantial additional savings. This is likely to have a significant effect on rates of return, particularly in cases where a large percentage of the population is covered by the scheme (e.g. in the industrialized countries) or where the capital market is narrow (as in most developing countries and also countries in transition to a market economy). There is a real risk of the domestic capital market becoming saturated. If pension funds invest in overseas assets, international capital markets may also become saturated, leading to a steep fall in the rate of return. The problem is recognized on pages 210–11 of the Report but is dismissed as something which may happen only 'in the very long run'.

The report argues that funded schemes are able to withstand the demographic transition. However, funded systems face the risk that the rate of return on capital may decline as a result of demographic trends: for example, when a smaller proportion of the population is of working age, the bargaining power of labour may well be greater. This will not affect the financial equilibrium of a defined contribution scheme. It will simply leave pensioners worse off and, to the extent that the state offers some minimum guarantee, it may necessitate a substantial increase in public expenditure.

The Inflation Risk

The report says that 'a dominant public pillar increases risk for the old' (p. 236) and uses this argument to support its proposal for funded, privately managed savings schemes. The idea of spreading the risk among different pension arrangements may be intuitively appealing. However, it appears less attractive when in the following sentence it is stated that 'the most common failure occurs when inflation develops'; for it is a well-known fact that in conditions of high inflation, funded schemes typically perform worse than pay-as-you-go schemes. Yet it is this risk of inflation which the report recommends be transferred to workers and pensioners.

Public or Private Management?

In support of private management of pension funds, the report notes that by eliminating information deficiencies, participants in a system which offers a choice of management bodies will have the opportunity to make prudent selections in order to maximize their expectation of return on their defined contribution scheme contributions. Elsewhere, however, the report observes the myopia of pension scheme participants. Access to information does not by itself ensure that participants make informed choices. The choices are complicated, and past investment performance is an uncertain guide to the future. Multiple competing social security investment bodies compete not only on performance but for clients. As the report states, and as recent anecdotal evidence from the United Kingdom concerning the sale of personal pensions indicates, potential contributors must be protected.

It is noteworthy that in both the United Kingdom and the United States, about 35 per cent of the contributions to commercially managed personal pension schemes go in administrative costs and profits, rather than to financing the future pensions.[1] In smaller and less competitive insurance markets, might this figure not be even higher? Other data on administrative costs has recently been obtained by a survey of additional voluntary contribution (AVC) arrangements in the United Kingdom conducted by R. Watson and Sons.[2] The median reduction in yield due to charges (not including commissions) was 5.2 per cent a year for with-profit funds. The calculation was based on a fixed contribution of £20 (US$32) a month for a six-year period. Although AVCs are not the same as the personal pension accounts used for privatized social security arrangements, both provide retirement benefits based on regular contributions. Thus, Spencer concludes, 'in the United Kingdom, which has one of the most competitive markets for the investment of personal pensions, a typical with-profit AVC will have to earn more than 5.2 per cent just to break even'.

On this subject the World Bank report says that 'in principle competition among plan administrators should make regulation of fees and commissions unnecessary' (p. 223). However, the report then adds that because the system will be compulsory and because economies of scale in the pension industry may lead to concentration, companies may end up charging more than they would in a purely voluntary competitive system.

The report takes the view that as mandatory personal savings schemes are likely to be more concentrated than occupational schemes (i.e. there will be fewer plan administrators), they will benefit from greater economies of scale. This is a questionable proposition: the former will have to canvass and sign up individual clients, with all the marketing costs which that entails, and try to retain them as they move from one employer to another; the latter, on the other hand, usually have a captive clientele who are automatically covered by the scheme as part of their conditions of employment, and who are all employed by the same enterprise or group of enterprises. The low rates of compliance in the Chilean system (see 'Special Risks for the Low-Paid' below) reflect the administrative problems that are entailed in trying to control the payment of contributions to a number of different administering institutions.

Once conditions permit it, are decentralization and privatization of the investment function the only solution to more efficient investment of social security funds? Privatization to multiple investment bodies removes the economies of scale, leads to marketing costs and complicates the administration of the schemes, thereby introducing uncertainty. The performance of national provident funds which have some investment independence, such as in Fiji and Malaysia, indicates that public management by a centralized institution can be satisfactory. Whether decentralization and privatization are necessary depends on whether government is prepared to cede control over direction of the investment of social security funds to professional investment managers in the national social security institution. This would not by any means imply that investments would cease to be made in government securities. (In Chile, by 1991, 38 per cent of the investments of AFPs – private pension fund managers – were in government securities (p. 212).) It would mean, however, that investments in these securities were made at the discretion of the investment institution, not solely at the direction of the government.

Given the proportion of national financial assets which a funded social security pension scheme normally commands, it is unlikely that centralized investment management can ever be entirely free of government influence or control, since government fiscal and monetary policy could be thwarted by the scheme's investment activities. Exercise of this government control would be more difficult over decentralized private investment institutions, but in a situation of financial adversity it is difficult to believe that government would not find a method of exerting control over the investments of these institutions.

Problems of Regulating Private Pension Funds

If legislation entrusts the task of providing mandatory pension insurance to private, profit-making entities, then it is vital to have a strong supervisory body which is able and willing to regulate their operations. The sophisticated skills required by regulatory bodies are in very short supply in most countries, especially in the developing world. The risks of the regulators themselves being corrupted by the regulated are immense, particularly as the officials of the supervisory body have precisely the knowledge and qualifications for which the pension funds are willing to pay very high salaries. Thus there is a great risk that regulation will be ineffective unless the necessary skills are in plentiful supply, unless there is a highly developed code of professional conduct among public officials and unless there are strict legal safeguards to prevent conflicts of interest. It is questionable whether these conditions will soon be satisfied in many countries, particularly in those which are criticized by the Bank for corrupt and incompetent administration of social security.

If regulation is inadequate, then pensioners and workers will be exposed to a higher level of risk. However, the risk for the state itself may also be substantial. Any minimum pension guarantees financed by the state may end up costing significantly more than expected if regulation of privately administered mandatory schemes is deficient. Beyond that, the state may be forced by political pressure – or it may even be legally obliged – to compensate people who have suffered losses due to poorly regulated schemes.

State Guarantees

Recognizing the risks inherent in defined contribution schemes, the state may provide certain guarantees. For example, in Chile old people not covered by the mandatory savings scheme may receive a social assistance benefit equal to about 12 per cent of the average wage (the number of the elderly receiving social assistance has quadrupled since the 1970s, but a statutory quota now prevents more than 300,000 receiving assistance at any one time). Old people who have contributed to the scheme for at least twenty years qualify for a minimum pension guarantee of 22 to 25 per cent of the average wage. The state offers two other guarantees in Chile: one limits the extent to which the rate of return provided by one pension fund

(AFP) may fall below that of the AFPs as a whole; the other partially guarantees annuity payments if the insurance company fails (100 per cent of the minimum pension is guaranteed, plus 75 per cent of the rest of the benefit up to a specified limit). None of these guarantees comes near to providing the level of benefits which one would expect from a modest social insurance scheme.

The report recognizes that a minimum pension of 22 to 25 per cent of the average wage is below the poverty line in most countries and that the social assistance of 12 per cent is below the subsistence level. It goes on to suggest that a higher minimum pension could be guaranteed to workers who have contributed for more years, e.g. 12 per cent of the average wage, plus 0.5 per cent for every year of contributing employment, thereby providing a guarantee of 22 per cent after twenty years or 34.5 per cent after forty-five years of employment. Even these guarantees would be very modest and unlikely to meet ILO minimum standards. Furthermore, it is obvious that a guarantee related to years of service will either be less than the poverty level for those with short service or far above that level for those with long service – and of course it would do nothing at all to help those with less than the required period of service.

For any minimum pension guarantee to be administratively feasible, it would be vital that each worker be allowed to have only one personal pension account. However, on page 220 of the report, this rule is described as 'very restrictive and very controversial', since workers are then unable to spread the risk across different investment managers. Thus, if a government were to be more flexible, as suggested by the report, the resulting multiplicity of accounts could well make any minimum pension guarantee provision unworkable.

Special Risks for the Low-Paid

The risk of an inadequate replacement rate is much greater in the case of low-income workers. This is amply shown by experience in Chile, where the proportion of members contributing regularly to the fund is 45–55 per cent in funds catering to lower-paid workers, compared with 80–90 per cent for those with better paid members.[3] Furthermore, charges and commissions tend to weigh much more heavily on the low-paid, as they often include a flat-rate element or minimum amount. The risk of ending up with a very low pension affects not just poor workers themselves but also the state, which may well have to provide social assistance for many of them in their old age.

It has recently been argued by certain economists in Latin America that a fundamental weakness of the Chilean pension system is the fact that the state provides a minimum pension guarantee. Their view is that low-paid workers in precarious jobs prefer to avoid contributing to their mandatory savings account and to rely on the state guarantee instead – particularly as the personal pension they earn may end up being very low in any case. Certainly the high incidence of non-compliance among the low-paid provides some support for this view, although it is difficult to tell whether workers are thereby behaving in an economically rational manner or simply adopting a very short time horizon. What are the policy implications of this argument?

Its proponents may say that the state should provide no guarantee or make it very unattractive through the imposition of stricter conditions. The more socially minded, however, may conclude that the social security system should be redesigned to ensure a much better rate of compliance.

The Double Burden on the Transition Generation

The process of transition from a pay-as-you-go system to a funded system gives rise to a number of particularly intractable problems and risks. For several decades the working generation will be called upon to finance its own (funded) pensions, while at the same time continuing to support members of the older generation who have entitlements under the former pay-as-you-go scheme. This double burden will be borne by workers and employers in the form either of higher contributions or higher taxes. Alternatively, governments may cut back on other public expenditure to finance the transition, but the amounts required are so great that it is extremely unlikely that sufficient cuts could be made without depriving the community of essential services. Governments may borrow, of course, but debts have to be serviced, so that taxpayers will still bear the burden. Another proposal is to use the proceeds from privatization of state assets to finance the transition to a funded pension system. Unfortunately, in countries where this idea has been closely examined, it has turned out that saleable state assets are worth far less than the amounts needed to honour existing pension commitments.

Increased Political Risks if Public Schemes Become Non-Contributory

Pension entitlements under tax-financed public schemes – the type advocated in the report – enjoy significantly less security than those which are contributory in character. As the founders of the United States Social Security system were determined that future governments would not subsequently undo their work, they insisted that it be financed out of contributions. While economists may set little store by the distinction between taxes and contributions, politicians and people in general know better: contributions imply a right to benefit. The major risk with tax-financed schemes is that means tests or income tests may be introduced in order to save money or target resources on those in greatest need. There is also a substantial risk that governments may limit the amount of benefit adjustments to help solve general economic problems or to free resources for other items of public expenditure which they regard as more important. Finally, once most people receive the bulk of their retirement income from private schemes, there will be much less political opposition than at present to cuts in public pensions. Poorer pensioners, wholly or primarily dependent on the public scheme, will be more isolated, and the better-off majority may well be more interested in reducing their tax burden than in defending the level of public pensions.

Savings, Investment and Growth

In view of the risks which have been identified, the pension strategy recommended in the report cannot be justified on social policy grounds. The motivation is indeed to be found elsewhere: it is expected that the introduction of a mandatory savings system in place of a pay-as-you-go public scheme will push up the aggregate rate of saving, that the new savings will be used to finance productive investment and that this investment will lead to increased economic growth from which everyone, including pensioners, will benefit. Whether this agreeable scenario is realistic or not is an open question. It is far from certain, for example, that aggregate savings will rise. In the Chilean case, where the savings scheme was mandatory and the minimum contribution rate quite high at 10 per cent of earnings, this did not happen; the savings rate, which was 21 per cent of GDP in 1980, dipped substantially in the early 1980s and stood at 20 per cent in 1989.[4] Nor can it be taken for granted that entrepreneurs are ready to increase productive investment within the country concerned and that they have simply been prevented from doing so by the shortage of investible funds. It may well be that domestic consumer demand is not sufficient to attract investors and a new mandatory savings scheme could further depress markets.

   Another of the aims of the report is to promote the development of third world stock markets. Yet Stiglitz has argued that the less developed countries should not set their sights on imitating the capital markets of the most developed countries but rather should adapt themselves to the reality that their domestic capital markets will most likely, if not necessarily, work poorly.[5] They must expect, he argues, that firms within their economies will have to rely heavily on bank lending, rather than securities markets, as sources of funds. Similarly, in 1993, Singh concluded that, to the extent that developing countries do have a choice, they should attempt rather to foster bank-based financial systems than to establish and encourage stock markets.[6] Singh refers not only to the special conditions in developing countries but also to the debate in the United States and the United Kingdom about the deleterious role of their stock markets in relation to their competitiveness *vis-à-vis* Germany and Japan, where equity markets have always played a far less significant role.

These are questions which it is not possible to pursue in this article, but which must be considered carefully, since the retirement security of workers and their dependants throughout the world is at stake. Decision-makers must also ask themselves a broader question: is it realistic to expect a pension system not only to provide retirement security but at the same time to solve the problems of underinvestment and low economic growth?

The Way Forward

It is not the purpose of this article to defend the provisions of existing social security pension schemes. The report documents serious design failures and inefficiencies from which many schemes suffer, and it describes the demographic transition and maturation of these schemes. The latter developments have long been recognized, and since the early 1980s schemes have taken steps to address their implications (in Japan, the United Kingdom, the United States and Canada, for example). Pension reform is now and will continue to be on the agenda in many countries. The design failures must be corrected, and the report will perform a useful service if the attention it directs to these failures is translated into action in national schemes.

What this article highlights is that the solution to the 'crisis' which the report claims to have identified, in particular the reliance on a second tier based on defined contribution schemes, does not provide a greater guarantee of pension benefits and in fact holds greater potential risk than a properly designed and administered defined benefit scheme. In any event, as the report notes, in many countries the defined contribution solution would be impractical, given the absence of developed capital markets and of capacity to establish effective regulatory institutions.

It is unfortunate that the issue of pension reform has been mixed up with the wider debate about privatization and the role of government. The application to social policy of principles applicable to general economic activity is not necessarily an illuminating one. Furthermore, it ignores the experience of many of the world's most successful economies, which have for many years operated and continue to operate social insurance pension schemes.

Just as measurement of the effect of funding of social security obligations on savings and competitiveness is inconclusive, so is assessment of the impact of social security on the maintenance of social peace and harmony. Since the Second World War, most Western industrialized countries have witnessed a period of high economic growth, enormous technological change and, recently, lower rates of growth accompanied by persistent high levels of unemployment unprecedented since the 1930s. Throughout this period the social fabric of these countries has remained intact. Intuitively and from anecdotal evidence, the panoply of social security measures, including pensions, has made a positive contribution to the national polity.

A radical restructuring or rejection of the principles on which the present schemes are founded will create uncertainty. It is not at all clear that the pension proposals in the report will result in adequate and acceptable benefits or that they will be viable from technical and administrative points of view. A more efficient and less disruptive approach to the provision of retirement pensions would be to focus efforts on measures to rectify design deficiencies and inequities in existing schemes.

Countries seeking to modify their existing pension schemes should do everything possible to avoid the pitfalls which are illustrated in the report. This will mean taking policy decision only after their long-range financial implications have been thoroughly analysed and understood. In this respect, it is vital to consider not just pensions but social protection as a whole.[7] It will also mean paying far more attention than in the past to questions of governance. As has been emphasized in this article, many of the shortcomings of existing pension systems have little to do with whether they are public or private. They have, however, a great deal to do with the quality of governance, which covers everything from the coherence of decision-making, through good management and sound investment policies, down to the efficient collection of contributions and the timely payment of benefits.

Reform of social security pensions is a national issue. The parties involved in social security in each country – workers, employers, governments, pensioners and other beneficiaries – must evaluate policy advice, and on their own seek to establish a consensus whereby a programme which is efficient and nationally acceptable can be adopted.

Notes

From *International Social Security Review*, 48, 3/4, 1995, pp. 13–22.
1   For the United States, see *Private Pensions and Public Policy* (Paris, OECD, 1992). For the United Kingdom, the same figure has been cited orally by staff of the Department of Social Security and the Government Actuary's Department.

2 Cited in Bruce Spencer, 'Are the Cracks Beginning to Show?', in *IBIS Review*, September 1994.

3 Nicholas Barr, ed., *Labour Markets and Social Policy in Central and Eastern Europe: The Transition and Beyond*, published for the World Bank and the London School of Economics and Political Science (Oxford, Oxford University Press, 1994): ch. 9, 'Income Transfers: Social Insurance', by Nicholas Barr, p. 212.

4 Ibid., p. 213.

5 Joseph E. Stiglitz, 'Financial Markets and Development', in *Oxford Review of Economic Policy*, vol. 5, no. 4, winter 1989.

6 Ajit Singh, 'The Stock-Market and Economic Development: Should Developing Countries Encourage Stock-Markets?', in *UNCTAD Review*, no. 4, 1993.

7 In this regard, see *Social Protection Expenditure in Slovakia: Results of a Quantitative Analysis (Report to the Government of the Slovak Republic)* (Geneva, ILO, 1994), which contains a social budget model [...] developed by the ILO.

Intergenerational Conflict and the Welfare State: American and British Perspectives

Chris Phillipson

Introduction

In 1949 the Royal Commission on Population delivered its report on the long-term future of the population of Great Britain. The background to the work of the Commission was the concern, expressed throughout the 1930s and 1940s, about the possible dangers arising from the ageing of the population. In this debate older people were depicted as a burden on society; a group with the potential for reducing the living standards of the nation and increasing the financial pressures on future generations of workers. The Royal Commission expressed particular anxiety about the conflict of interest between workers and pensioners. The basis for this concern was expressed in the Commission's view that:

> if all the old sit back on their first pensionable birthday and draw a pension with which they compete for consumer goods made by a decreasing section of the population, the standard of life of both generations will inevitably be endangered. (Royal Commission on Population, 1949)

The concept of generations competing over scarce resources was underplayed during the 1950s and 1960s in Britain which, in common with many other industrial societies, fashioned new approaches to the provision of welfare (Lowe, 1993). However, by the 1970s and 1980s, the notion of generational conflict was back on the political agenda and had become a major topic of debate within and beyond the gerontological community (Easterlin, 1978; Clark and Spengler, 1980; Foote, 1982; Longman, 1987; Johnson et al., 1989; Phillipson, 1990; Walker, 1990; Hobman, 1993).

The terms of this more recent debate have not been substantially different from that initiated by the Royal Commission in the late 1940s. For example, in his influential article 'Children and the elderly in the US', the demographer Samuel Preston (1984) raised the possibility of direct competition between young and old over the distribution of economic resources. From a social as well as economic perspective, Preston argued that it was difficult to justify curtailing expenditure on children. Echoing the views of the Royal Commission, Preston argued: 'Whereas expenditure on the elderly can be thought of mainly as consumption, expenditure on the young is a combination of consumption and investment'. And he went to highlight the possibility of increasing polarization in the provision of social policy, concluding:

> If we care about our collective future rather than simply about our future as individuals we are faced with the question of how best to safeguard the human and material resources represented by children. These resources have not been carefully guarded in the past two decades. (Preston, 1984: 49)

[My concern here] is not to review the empirical basis for arguments about 'generational equity' [but] first, to examine the different ways in which the question of generational equity may be approached; secondly, to assess the meaning of key concepts used in the discussion; thirdly, to examine some of the issues raised by the debate for the future organization of the welfare state.

Interpreting the Debate on Population Ageing

How, first of all, do we make sense of the anxieties about population ageing and the question of equity between generations? Clearly, the approach taken by researchers will reflect the concerns and perspectives of their individual disciplines. In respect of the social sciences, Johnson and Falkingham (1992) have usefully detailed three main approaches. From an economic perspective, the concern has been with problems that may arise from the transfer of resources between generations. In a context of declining worker-pensioner ratios, the questions raised by researchers have focused upon the fairness of such transfers and the influence they may have on incentives to work or save. The policy implications have been identified in terms of limiting tax burdens, curbing expenditure on social programmes, and increasing the supply of labour. According to Johnson and Falkingham (1992: 178): 'In most of the economic analysis of population ageing, the welfare of older people in the future appears (if at all) as very definitely subservient to the goal of effective macroeconomic management.'

Secondly, in the case of social policy, the dominant concerns have historically been with the welfare of older people and the development of policies to improve relative living standards. Social policy analysts have also provided a critique of the 'public-burden concept of welfare', claiming that the concern about population ageing has been influenced by ideologically driven policies aimed at reducing the state's role in welfare (Binney and Estes, 1988; Walker, 1990; Minkler and Robertson, 1991). The policy implications of this approach have been to develop a counter-ideology based on the concept of interdependence between generations (Kingson et al., 1986) as well as proposing action to improve the living standards of the present generation of older people (Bornat et al., 1985; Walker, 1990; Estes, 1992).

Thirdly, from a sociological perspective there has been a broader assessment of the transformation in social relationships reflected in an ageing society. Featherstone and Hepworth (1988) have described these changes as part of the modernization of ageing, with factors such as the growth in early retirement, the emergence of distinctive lifestyles among older people, and the renegotiation of relationships between old and young within the sphere of the family. From a policy perspective, these changes are seen to raise fundamental questions about the status of older people and their integration in society. Older people, it is argued, have gained free time and longevity but lead marginal and often trivialized lives (Moody, 1988; Cole, 1992). To challenge this crisis of old age, it is argued that we must reassess both the meanings attached to later life (through, for example, an attack on age discrimination) and increase the power and status of the old within economic, social and cultural institutions (Laczko and Phillipson, 1991; Young and Schuller, 1991).

Finally, we should not also the work of historians such as Cole (1992) and Achenbaum (1974, 1978), who have helped provide a broader perspective on interpretations of demographic change. Cole points out that the late twentieth century is not the first era to turn its disappointments and anxieties into anger against old age. His research suggests that amidst the late nineteenth-century crisis of Victorian morality and the decline of classical liberalism, old age in the USA came to be viewed as an intractable barrier to the limitless accumulation of health and wealth. The theme of the 'obsolescence of old age', to use Achenbaum's (1974) phrase, became widespread and fed into a devaluation of the aged in comparison to the young. One hundred years later, society was again haunted by the 'specter of an ageing society'. Cole argues that:

> In the late twentieth century, old age has again emerged as a lightning rod for the storms of liberal capitalism and of middle-class identity. This time, it is the middle-aged baby boomers who are most susceptible to neo-conservative Cassandras who forecast intergenerational Armageddon and the

bankruptcy of the federal government. Fears about declining fertility and the burden of an ageing population merge with the fiscal and ideological crises of the welfare state. Personal anxieties about growing old are conflated with pessimism about the future. Critics and commentators represent the aging of our social institutions with metaphors of decline, exhaustion, and collapse. (Cole 1992: 235)

These different interpretations of ageing have areas both of complementarity as well as conflict. Taking the former, economists have provided important contributions to evaluating issues relating to dependency ratios, pension provision, and policies for work and retirement (Schulz, 1988). The perspective of social policy is especially important both in highlighting the heterogeneity of the old in terms of income and wealth (Phillipson, 1993), as well as identifying future options for the development of the welfare state (Hills, 1993). The contribution from sociology has helped to highlight the nature of ageing as a reflexive process; that is, its capacity to change social institutions as well as be changed by them. Finally, historians have pointed to the dualism in social images of old age: ageing simultaneously, or at different times, represented as a period of social decay or social progress. At the same time, the areas of conflict between particular disciplines need to be clarified, if not resolved, if the debate on generational equity is to progress. The main focus here is to critically examine the concept of generations and the related issue of generational equity. The discussion will be offered from the perspective of a sociologist using the literature on the nature of generations and the possibilities it offers for re-evaluating the significance of population change.

Generational Change and Conflict

A crucial element in the debate about population ageing has been the use of the concept of generations as a way of explaining both current and potential problems facing the welfare state. Older people have been depicted as a 'selfish welfare generation' (Thomson, 1989) or 'greedy geezers' (*New Republic*, 28 March 1988), in the more direct language of North Americans, soaking the young whilst running up huge public expenditure deficits. In the area of health care, the bio-medical ethicist Callahan (1987) started an intense debate in the USA, following the publication of his book *Setting Limits: Medical Goals in an Aging Society*. His book identified three aspirations for an ageing society: first, to stop pursuing medical goals that combine the features of high costs, marginal gains and benefits (in the main) for the old; secondly, that the old shift their priorities from their own welfare to that of younger generations; and thirdly, that older people should accept death as a condition of life, at least

for the sake of others. Callahan's intervention attracted considerable critical debate and dissension (see, especially, Homer and Holstein, 1990;
Moody, 1992) but it fuelled an already highly charged debate concerning
the divergent interests and attainments of young and old.

Underpinning the debate is a further concern that older people have
begun to mobilize their electoral resources to press the case for additional
benefits. While difficult to argue in the case of Britain (see below), this has
been a popular theme in the USA, where Marmor et al. (1990) note that, if
the tales of journalists are to be believed, congressional representatives live
in fear of arousing the displeasure of the American Association of Retired
Persons (AARP).

All of this literature and research begs some crucial questions about the
issue of generations as a sociological as opposed to economic concept.
Economists are right, within their own terms, to point to the problems
associated with resource transfers across generations. Clearly, important
issues need to be faced regarding how resources are allocated and the
likely impact on different social groups. But the question that must also
be pursued is whether the framing of these issues in generational terms
clarifies or obscures the way in which relations between generations might
develop. From a sociological perspective, the questions that must be asked
include: how reliable is the idea of generations as a predictor of social and
political action? Do people behave as if members of distinctive generations? And if they do, does this point to conflict or co-operation in the
years ahead?

The Problem of Generations

At the heart of our problem is that an economic generation and a sociological generation are two distinct entities. With the former, issues are
presented in terms of discrete groups competing – selfishly or otherwise –
for a fair share of resources. At its most extreme, this model suggests that
generations behave as if on a collision course, with the block votes of the
old threatening to cut off services needed by the young (Longman, 1987),
and the young reconsidering the basis of the welfare contract and supporting threats to dismantle the welfare state (Thomson, 1989). This last point
has been expressed by Thomson in the following way:

> the very nature of aged populations is changing, in ways not comprehended
> in our present debates, and along with this come shifts in relations between
> generations. Members of the welfare generation are now arriving at old age
> with assets, expectations and histories of benefits quite unlike those of their
> predecessors, and it remains to be seen whether the young who are expected
> to make growing transfers to them will feel bound to do so. At the end of the

twentieth century the implicit welfare contract that binds members of successor generations is up for renegotiation – and the aged stand right at the centre of this with a great deal to lose. (Thomson, 1989: 35)

Of course, we might note the point made by Riley et al. (1972) that diverse tendencies do not necessarily become manifest in antagonism nor erupt into organized conflict. They comment: 'The mere fact of inequality among age strata (as is true of other types of stratification also) is not a sufficient condition for age cleavage' (Riley et al. 1972: 443). In reality, the sociological generation will almost certainly behave in a more complex way than suggested by the worker versus pensioner perspective.

What do the sociologists mean when they use the term generations? Abrams (1982), in his classic essay 'Identity and the Problem of genera-tions', used the definition adopted by Heberle, namely, that a generation consisted 'of contemporaries of approximately the same age but for whom age is established not by the calendar of years but by a calendar of events and experiences'. Heberle concluded that: 'A generation is a phenomenon of collective mentality and morality. [The members] of a generation feel themselves linked by a community of standpoints, of beliefs and wishes' (Abrams, 1982: 258). But the identification of people as belonging to a particular generation is a complex process. Abrams himself points out that the cut-off points between generations are often obscure and may develop only gradually as part of a long historical process. And this point has been further developed by the American historian Achenbaum (1986), who suggests that the meaning of the term 'generation' is 'both fuzzy and arbitrary' (Achenbaum, 1986: 93). He argues:

> Less clear cut than the distinction between parent and child, the term may refer with equal plausibility to all people between certain ages, to progeni-tors of any age (as opposed to their progeny), and/or to people who lived through a monumental experience such as the great Depression. The very ambiguity of meaning makes it hard to know who is precisely included or excluded in such a definition. Worse, referring to people as being of a certain generation attributes to them characteristics that they may or may not possess. Who, after all, is a member of the 'gypped generation'? Where and how does one draw the line: on the basis of age? birth order? income? expectations? (Achenbaum, 1986: 93–4)

This last point is of fundamental importance and was central to the position adopted by Mannheim (1952) in his essay 'The Problem of Generations'. Contrary to much of the present speculation about the possible behaviour of generations, Mannheim noted that the characteristic of what he termed 'generational units' was that their location and effec-tiveness in social systems could not be explained adequately on the basis of age alone. Following this, Abrams writes that:

Age is a necessary but not a sufficient condition for their existence. Other factors such as class, religion, race, occupation, institutional setting, in short all the conventional categories of social-structural analysis, must be introduced to explain their unique ability to make something of historical experiences. In other words, the study of generations brings to light consequential differentiations within generations as well as between them. Far from exempting us from the study of social structure any attempt to grapple with the problem of the historical formation of identity forces us in just that direction. The emergence of generation units and their capacity or inability to reconstruct identity can only be explained in those terms. Here as elsewhere historical sociology means more work, not less. (Abrams, 1982: 261–2)

This analysis does help explain some puzzling features of the way generations behave. For example, reference has been to the argument that there is a growing possibility of the old mobilizing against the interests of the young, and the young threatening to break their part of the generational contract (Thomson, 1989). In reality, the evidence for both of these is difficult to find. Wallace et al. (1991) review the former in the American context, suggesting that although older people have been able to influence particular areas of policy and legislation, they have not achieved any enduring pattern of power comparable to that of business or other groups with more focused policy agendas. Wallace et al. (1991) highlight factors that could limit the possibility of a unified movement of older people (see also Binstock, 1991):

> Within a strong capitalist system, the power of the wealthy and big business will continue to take precedence over the power of the elderly. Most importantly, improvements in the lives of the aged will continue to affect classes differently. For example, elders with secure pensions and investments increasingly have the choice of retiring early or working indefinitely. At the same time, low income workers may be increasingly compelled to continue to work through late life because of financial need or to retire early against their will because of ill health. Consequently, the interests of the aged as a group will continue to be subordinated to class interests and 'senior power' will play a secondary role in shaping public policy. (Wallace et al., 1991: 111)

The British case is especially interesting in terms of the welfare generations perspective. Despite the poverty of British pensioners and the government-led campaign against state pensions during the 1980s (Walker, 1993a), the voting record of older people in the 1992 election hardly suggested a pattern of militancy on the part of the elderly people; indeed, quite the reverse. Labour raised hopes of a 'demographic boost' to their chances with the promise of an immediate pensions increase on election and that future rises would once again be pegged to average wage as well as price rises (whichever rose faster). In fact, the Conservative vote among pensioners hardened – Conservative support among women aged sixty-five and over (one of the poorest groups) actually increased by 6 per cent in the period between the 1987 and 1992 election (*Sunday Times*, 12 April 1992). This might be explained in generational equity terms on the basis that a Conservative government would give succour to the deserving old as opposed to the undeserving young. But the argument is tenuous and there is almost certainly a range of factors lying behind this result. For example, it would appear that among men aged twenty-five to thirty-four the Conservative vote remained remarkably steady – 41 per cent voting Conservative in 1987; 40 per cent in 1992. This suggests [. . .] that age may be less important than a range of social factors (such as home ownership, social class, membership of a trade union) in interpreting voter behaviour (Walker, 1986).

More generally, it is difficult to sustain the view that the 1980s was a clear demonstration of the welfare generation rewarding itself at the expense of others. In fact, in key areas such as jobs, income and service provision, the evidence suggests considerable inroads were made during the 1980s into the welfare of the old – precisely at a point where they should have been reaping maximum gains. Older workers experienced greater job losses in this decade than any other age group, and this has almost certainly meant extended years in poverty for a significant proportion (Walker, 1993a).

In terms of income, the defining characteristic of the 1980s was the declining value of the state pension: relative to average (disposable) incomes it reached a peak of 46.5 per cent in 1983, and by 1992 was lower than it had been in 1948. By 1993 the state pension was worth about 15 per cent of average gross male earnings, lower than at any time since 1971 (Hills, 1993). In fact, the most significant feature of the 1980s was not the disparity of incomes between young and old but the growth in inequalities within the older population (Phillipson, 1993), a trend that is likely to reduce further the possibility of unified action by the old against the young.

The 1980s were also important for the extended debate on community care, and the respective merits of home-based and residential care. However, it is difficult to see this area as an example of senior power in action. Indeed, what is significant is how little influence older people (or organizations acting on their behalf) had on legislation such as the National Health Service and Community Care Act 1990. On the contrary, this Act may be seen as an attempt to control the demands of the welfare generation, first, through the 'marketization' of health and social care (Walker, 1993b); secondly, through shifting the burden of care from the formal to the informal sector, with the welfare generation now taking up much of the strain in terms of the provision of personal and social care (Phillipson, 1992).

Finally, there is no clear evidence for the young or young middle age rising in protest either against 'the crushing of youthful expectations' (Thomson, 1989: 53) or the burden of heavy taxation. In the case of Britain, large-scale data sets such as those in the regular series on British Social Attitudes, which have asked the public about priorities for social spending, are consistent in showing a high level of support (across all age groups) for spending on the core welfare services (Taylor-Gooby, 1987, 1991). The 1990 survey confirmed the high level of support for 'much more' government spending in key areas such as health, welfare and education. Rather than a revolt against taxation, the evidence would suggest increased willingness to pay taxes to support an ageing population – confirmation it would appear of a continuing belief rather than rejection of the intergenerational contract.

The argument from Neugarten and Neugarten (1986) is significant here:

> Some young people now believe they will not enjoy as high a material standard of living as their parents, and some point to the federal budget deficits and to demographic changes to support their assertions that they will not receive as much in Social Security benefits when they grow old. But there is no evidence that young people are blaming old people for what they perceive as this deplorable state of affairs. (Neugarten and Neugarten, 1986: 43–4)

The Future of the Generational Contract

If there is limited evidence for open conflict between generations, is it possible to turn the argument around and suggest, instead, that there are signs of mutual interest and solidarity between age groups? The research literature provides at least two examples: one conceptual, and the other empirical. The former starts from the premise that it is more helpful to see generational relations from the standpoint of the life-course as a whole, rather than from a single moment in time (in research terms, taking a longitudinal as opposed to cross-sectional view). This point has been developed by Daniels (1988, 1991) in his concept of the 'prudential life-span account'. This approach allows the development of guidelines for distribution and redistribution between the life-stages under the condition that all individuals can expect the same treatment over their life-course. In the long run, not only would immediate inequalities be compensated, but also the 'prudent' allocation of resources over the life-span would max-imize general well-being. Daniels summarizes his perspective in the following terms:

it tells us we should not think of age groups as competing with each other, but as sharing a whole life. We want to make that life go as well as possible, and we must therefore make the appropriate decisions about what needs it is most important to meet at each stage of life. If we do this prudently, we will learn how fair it is to treat each age group. Instead of focusing on competition, we have a unifying perspective or vision. (Daniels, 1991: 238)

This view is matched, it might be argued, in research on how families behave towards each other. The evidence here is that there is giving and receiving throughout the life-course: both within and across generations. Cheal (1987), for example, notes that within the system of family transfers, older people are not solely, or even largely, the recipients of economic resources. He reviews American research in the 1980s which shows that in fact older people are notable providers of resources for others (to younger generations especially). Cheal comments: 'It is the propensity of the elderly to give, rather than their necessity to receive, that requires sociological explanation at this time' (Cheal, 1987: 141).

In Britain, the work of Finch and Mason (1993) has suggested that it is not so much that 'experiences of giving and receiving help within families were common experiences (though many of them were) but that they were treated as unremarkable experiences by many people who talked with us' (Finch and Mason, 1993; see also Qureshi and Walker, 1989).

[. . .] Other evidence suggests that integrative forces may be at work, identifying points of mutual interest across generations. Hagestad (1986) puts this in the following way (see also Jerrome, 1993):

> There is little doubt that altered mortality and fertility patterns have created a new climate for the building and maintenance of family relationships. Historians and demographers have suggested that under conditions of high mortality, people were reluctant to form strong attachments to particular individuals, knowing that such ties could not be counted upon to endure. Instead, they invested in the security of the family as a group. Today, most people not only take long-term family bonds for granted and invest accordingly in them, but because of reduced fertility rates, there are also fewer individuals within each generation to invest in. As a result, intergenerational relationships are not only more extensive now, but they may also have become more intensive. Such 'intensification of family life' may have gained even further momentum because of the weakening ties between family and community. (Hagestad, 1986: 143–4)

These are all positive views as to how generations may gain the benefit of working with each other, taking a long-term view of the compensations from supporting an individual, group or cohort now, in return for receiving support at a later stage. This may sound idealistic, but it might well be argued that this was roughly how society came to reconstruct itself given the reality of population ageing in the post-war period. For a time at least (and even though expressed in often ageist and barely adequate provision), the response to ageing was viewed in public (i.e. intergenerational) terms. The subsequent break with the generational contract was not the result of conflict between generations. Instead it arose from changes (and conflict) at the level of the state as to how this population change should be assimilated.

From an early stage, the language of the Thatcher government in the 1980s was that of 'talking-up' the possibility of conflict, suggesting that workers were 'reconsidering' how much they should pay in taxes to support pensioners (Phillipson, 1990). The value of this approach – for the Conservative government – was that it reinforced the goal of shifting responsibility and perceptions of ageing as a public/life-course issue, to a private/life-stage problem. People had now to think of their own old age rather than that of others (or other generations), and accept that they must rely upon a different kind of welfare. The implications of this is that if there is conflict over the generational contract, it is of a different kind than that envisaged in the worker versus pensioner perspective. The conflict, it might be argued, is between different types of agencies, and different types of ideas: the agency of the state, on the one hand, and the agency of the family, on the other; the view of the aged as public burden, on the one hand, and the view of the aged as a public benefit, on the other; the view of an ageing population as a sign of exhaustion and decline, on the one hand, and view of ageing as a social achievement, on the other. The historical dualism in social images of ageing – between positive and negative perspectives – has swung backwards and forwards in the post-war period. We now have to consider ways of restoring a more hopeful future: to seek ways of challenging the current impasse.

Conclusion: Towards a New Generational politics

In the 1980s and early 1990s the balance swung towards expressing doubts about the benefits of an ageing population. Despite the radical critique offered by the political economy of ageing (Minkler and Estes, 1991; Myles and Quadagno, 1992), and the activities of groups of older people themselves, the problems of ageing and the welfare state [became] a dominant theme. In the second half of the 1990s, it became clear that we need a period of renewal in terms of generational politics. The basis for this will come from recognizing that presenting social issues in terms of young versus old does not offer a viable way forward – in the key area of economic and social policy. As Heclo (1989) observes:

In an already fragmented society such a framework would be especially unconstructive. It would divert attention from disparities and unmet needs within age groups. It would help divide constituencies that often have a common stake. Above all, a politics of young versus old would reinforce an already strong tendency... to define social welfare in terms of a competitive struggle for scarce resources and to ignore shared needs occurring in everyone's life-cycle. (Heclo, 1989: 387)

Recognition that we are constructing a different type of life-course may also help form the basis for a new generational politics. Here, the worker versus pensioner perspective is especially unhelpful in that it ignores fundamental changes to the distribution of labour through the life-course. The labels 'worker' and 'pensioner' are less easy to define when the stages that separate them are undergoing change. For many (mostly male) workers the predictability of continuous employment is being replaced by insecurity in middle and later life – an experience shared with the majority of women workers (Itzin and Phillipson, 1993). These changes may be seen as part of the reconstruction of middle and old age or the 'modernization of ageing' as defined by Featherstone and Hepworth (1988). The social trends here include: a blurring of the boundaries between different stages of the life-course; the growth of different work categories and statuses in between full-time work and complete retirement; and the convergence of male and female employment trends (Laczko and Phillipson, 1991).

These trends suggest that a new type of language is necessary for describing relations between generations in general, and workers and pensioners in particular. The language here would stress the interdependency of generations facing radical changes to their traditional social and economic foundations. We are entering a postmodern life-course, one in which individual needs and abilities are no longer entirely subordinate to chronological boundaries and bureaucratic mechanisms (Cole, 1992). If the concept of generations has traditionally been elusive and arbitrary, how much more so in a world where the institutions of work and family are being redefined and reshaped.

If we are to take the idea of renewal seriously, the response should not be one of retreat and privatization. Rather, we should acknowledge ageing as a public concern shared equally across the life-course. Above all, we should not 'off-load' the responsibilities for an ageing population to particular generations or cohorts – whether old, young or middle aged. Ageing is an issue *for* generations, but it is also a question to be *solved* with generations. The role of the state and key economic and social institutions will be central in managing an ageing population. Responsibility for this cannot be put aside in the task of developing appropriate policies for the twenty-first century.

Note

From A. Walker, ed., *The New Generational Contract*, London, UCL Press, 1996, pp. 206–20. This chapter draws on material gathered whilst the author was in receipt of a research award, from the University of Keele, which enabled him to have an extended period of study in the USA. Particular thanks are due to the Florida Policy on Aging Exchange Centre at the University of South Florida, Tampa, which provided considerable help and support during the author's three month stay in the USA.

References

Abrams, P., *Historical Sociology*, Shepton Mallet, Open Books, 1982.

Achenbaum, W. A., The Obsolescence of Old Age, *Journal of Social History*, 8(Fall), 1974, pp. 40–52.

Achenbaum, W. A., *Old Age in the New Land*, Baltimore, MD, Johns Hopkins University Press, 1978.

Achenbaum, W. A., 'The Meaning of Risks, Rights, and Responsibility in aging America', in *What Does it Mean to Grow Old?*, ed. T. Cole and S. Gadow, Durham, NC, Duke University Press, 1986, pp. 92–103.

Binney, E. A. and C. L. Estes, 'The Retreat of the State and its Transfer of Responsibility: The Intergenerational War', *International Journal of Health Services*, 18(1), 1988, pp. 83–96.

Binstock, R., 'Aging, Politics, and Public Policy', in *Growing Old in America*, ed. B. Hess and E. Markson, New Brunswick, NJ, Transaction, 1991, pp. 325–40.

Bornat, J., C. Phillipson and S. Ward, *A Manifesto for Old Age*, London, Pluto Press, 1985.

Callahan, D., *Setting Limits: Medical Goals in an Aging Society*, New York, Simon and Schuster, 1987.

Cheal, D., 'Intergenerational Transfers and Life Course Management: Towards a Socio-Economic Perspective', in *Re-Thinking the Life-Cycle*, ed. A. Bryman, P. Allatt and T. Keill, London, Macmillan, 1987, pp. 55–73.

Clark, R. and J. Spengler, *The Economics of Individual and Population Aging*, Cambridge, Cambridge University Press, 1980.

Cole, T. R., *The Journey of Life: A Cultural History of Aging in America*, Cambridge, Cambridge University Press, 1992.

Daniels, N., *Am I my Parents' Keeper?*, Oxford and New York, Oxford University Press, 1988.

Daniels, N., 'A Lifespan Approach to Health Care', in *Aging and Ethics*, ed. A. Jecker, Princeton, NJ, Humana Press, 1991, pp. 227–46.

Easterlin, R. A., 'What Will 1984 be Like? Socio-Economic Implications of Recent Shifts in Age Structure', *Demography*, 15, 1978, pp. 397–432.

Estes, C., 'The Reagan Legacy: Privatization, the Welfare State, and Ageing in the 1990s' in Myles and Quadagno (1992), pp. 59–83.

Featherstone, M. and M. Hepworth, 'Ageing and Old Age: Reflections on the Postmodern Lifecourse', in *Being and Becoming Old*, ed. B. Bytheway, T. Keil, P. Allatt and A. Bryman, London, Sage, 1988, pp. 143–57.

Finch, J. and J. Mason, *Negotiating Family Responsibilities*, London, Routledge, 1993.

Foote, D., *Canada's Population Outlook: Demographic Futures and Economic Challenges*, Ottawa, Canadian Institute for Economic Policy, 1982.

Hagestad, G., 'The Family: Women and the Family as Kin-Keepers', in *Our Aging Society*, ed. A. Pifer and L. Bronte, Ontario, Norton, 1986, pp. 141–60.

Heclo, H., 'Generational Politics', in *The Vulnerable*, ed. T. Smeeding and B. Torrey, Washington, DC, Urban Institute Press, 1989, pp. 381–441.

Hills, J., *The Future of Welfare: A Guide to the Debate*, York, Joseph Rowntree Foundation, 1993.

Hobman, D., ed., *Uniting Generations*, London, Age Concern England, 1993.

Homer, P. and M. Holstein, ed., *A Good Old Age. The Paradox of Setting Limits*, New York, Touchstone, 1990.

Itzin, C. and C. Phillipson, *Age Barriers at Work*, Solihull, METRA, Metropolitan Authorities Recruitment Agency, 1993.

Jerrome, D., 'Intimate Relationships', in *Ageing and Society*, ed. J. Bond, P. Coleman and S. Peace, London, Sage, 1993, pp. 226–54.

Johnson, P., C. Conrad and D. Thomson, *Workers versus Pensioners: Intergenerational Justice in an Ageing World*, Manchester, Manchester University Press in association with the Centre for Economic Policy Research, 1989.

Johnson, P. and J. Falkingham, *Ageing and Economic Welfare*, London, Sage, 1992.

Kingson, E., B. Hirshorn and J. Cornman, *Ties that Bind: The Interdependence of Generations in an Ageing Society*, Maryland, Seven Locks Press, 1986.

Laczko, F. and C. Phillipson, 'Defending the Right to Work', in *Age: The Unrecognised Discrimination*, ed. E. McEwan, London, ACE Books, 1990.

Laczko, F. and C. Phillipson, *Changing Work and Retirement: Social Policy and the Older Worker*, Milton Keynes, Open University Press, 1991.

Longman, P., *Born to Pay: The Politics of Aging in America*, Boston, MA, Houghton Mifflin, 1987.

Lowe, R., *The Welfare State in Britain since 1945*, London, Macmillan, 1993.

Macfarlane, A., *The Origins of English Individualism: The Family, Property and Social Transition*, Oxford, Blackwell, 1978.

Mannheim, K., 'The Problem of Generations', *Essays on the Sociology of Knowledge*, London, Routledge and Kegan Paul, 1952.

Marmor, T. R., J. L. Mashaw and P. L. Harvey, *America's Misunderstood Welfare State*, New York, Basic Books, 1990.

Minkler, M. and C. Estes, *Critical Perspectives on Aging*, New York, Baywood, 1991.

Minkler, M. and A. Robertson, 'The Ideology of Age/Race Wars: Deconstructing a Social Problem', *Ageing and Society*, 11, 1991, pp. 1–23.

Moody, H., *Abundance of Life: Human Development Policies for an Aging Society*, New York, Columbia University Press, 1988.

Moody, H., 'Bioethics and Aging', in *Handbook of the Humanities and Aging*, ed. T. Cole, D. Van Tassell and R. Kastenbaum, New York, Springer, 1992, pp. 395–425.

Myles, J. and J. Quadagno, eds, *States, Labour Markets and the Future of Old-Age Policy*, Philadelphia, Temple University Press, 1992.

Neugarten, B. and D. Neugarten, 'Changing Meanings of Age in the Aging Society', in *Our Aging Society: Paradox and Promise*, ed. A. Pifer and L. Bronte, Ontario, Norton, 1986, pp. 33–52.

Phillipson, C., 'Inter-Generational Relations: Conflict or Consensus in the Twenty-First Century?', *Policy and Politics*, 19, 1990, pp. 27–36.

Phillipson, C., 'Challenging the "Spectre of Old Age": Community Care for Older People in the 1990s', in *Social Policy Review*, 4, ed. N. Manning and R. Page, Canterbury, Social Policy Association, 1992, pp. 111–33.

Phillipson, C., 'Poverty and Affluence in Old Age', in *Poverty, Inequality and Justice*, ed. A. Sinfield, Edinburgh, New Waverley Papers, Social Policy Series 6, 1993.

Preston, S., 'Children and the Elderly: Divergent Paths for America's Dependents', *Demography*, XXI, 1984, pp. 435–57.

Qureshi, H. and A. Walker, *The Caring Relationships: Elderly People and their Families*, Basingstoke, Macmillan/New York, Temple University Press, 1989.

Riley, M., M. Johnson and A. Foner, *Aging and Society 3: A Sociology of Age Stratification*, New York, Russel Sage Foundation, 1972.

Royal Commission on Population, *Report*, London, HMSO, 1949.

Schultz, J., *The Economics of Aging*, Belmont, CA, Wadsworth, 1988.

Taylor-Gooby, P., 'Citizenship and Welfare', in *British Social Attitudes: The 1987 Report*, ed. R. Jowell, S. Witherspoon and L. Brook, Aldershot, Gower, 1987.

Taylor-Gooby, P., 'Attachment to the Welfare State', in *British Social Attitudes: The Eighth Report*, ed. R. Jowell, L. Brook and B. Taylor, Aldershot, Dartmouth Publishing, 1991, pp. 23–42.

Thomson, D., 'The Welfare State and Generation Conflict: Winners and Losers', in Johnson et al., 1989, pp. 33–56.

Thomson, D., *Selfish Generations? The Ageing of New Zealand's Welfare State*, Wellington, NZ, Bridget Williams, 1991.

Walker, A., 'The Politics of Ageing in Britain', in *Dependency and interdependency in Old Age: Theoretical Perspectives and Policy Alternatives*, ed. C. Phillipson, M. Bernard and P. Strang, London, Croom Helm, 1986, pp. 46–53.

Walker, A., 'The Economic "Burden" of Ageing and the Prospect of Intergenerational Conflict', *Ageing and Society*, 10(4), 1990, pp. 377–96.

Walker, A., 'Poverty and Inequality in Old Age', in *Ageing in Society*, ed. J. Bond, P. Coleman and S. Peace, London, Sage, 1993a, 2nd edn, pp. 280–83.

Walker, A., 'Community Care Policy: From Consensus to Conflict', in *Community Care: A Reader*, ed. J. Bornat, C. Pereira, D. Pilgrim and F. Williams, London, Macmillan in association with the Open University, 1993b, pp. 204–26.

Wallace, S., J. Williamson, R. Garson Lung and L. Powell, 'A Lamb in Wolf's Clothing? The Reality of Senior Power', in *Critical Perspectives on Aging*, ed. M. Minkler and C. Estes, Amityville, NY, Baywood, 1991, pp. 95–116.

Young, M. and T. Schuller, *Life after Work: The Arrival of the Ageless Society*, London: HarperCollins, 1991.

Political Challenges to the Welfare State

The New Politics of the Welfare State

Paul Pierson

Why the Politics of Retrenchment is Different

This essay's central claim is that because retrenchment is a distinctive process, it is unlikely to follow the same rules of development that operated during the long phase of welfare state expansion. There are two fundamental reasons for this. First, the political *goals* of policy makers are different; second, there have been dramatic changes in the political *context*. Each of these points requires elaboration.

There is a profound difference between extending benefits to large numbers of people and taking benefits away.[1] [After the Second World War] expanding social benefits was generally a process of political credit claiming. Reformers needed only to overcome diffuse concern about tax rates (often sidestepped through resort to social insurance 'contributions') and the frequently important pressures of entrenched interests. Not surprisingly, the expansion of social programmes had until recently been a favoured political activity, contributing greatly to both state-building projects and the popularity of reform-minded politicians.[2]

A combination of economic changes, political shifts to the right, and rising costs associated with maturing welfare states has provoked growing calls for retrenchment. At the heart of efforts to turn these demands into policy have been newly ascendant conservative politicians. Conservative governments have generally advocated major social policy reforms, often receiving significant external support in their effort, especially from the business community.[3] Yet the new policy agenda stands in sharp contrast to the credit-claiming initiatives pursued during the long period of welfare state expansion. The politics of retrenchment is typically treacherous, because it imposes tangible losses on concentrated groups of voters in return for diffuse and uncertain gains. Retrenchment entails a delicate effort either to transform programmatic change into an electorally attractive proposition or, at the least, to minimize the political costs involved. Advocates of retrenchment must persuade wavering supporters that the price of reform is manageable – a task that a substantial public outcry makes almost impossible.

Retrenchment is generally an exercise in blame avoidance rather than credit claiming, primarily because the costs of retrenchment are concentrated (and often immediate), while the benefits are not. That concentrated interests will be in a stronger political position than diffuse ones is a standard proposition in political science.[4] As interests become more concentrated, the prospect that individuals will find it worth their while to engage in collective action improves. Furthermore, concentrated interests are more likely to be linked to organizational networks that keep them informed about how policies affect their interests. These informational networks also facilitate political action.

An additional reason that politicians rarely get credit for programme cutbacks concerns the well-documented asymmetry in the way that voters react to losses and gains. Extensive experiments in social psychology have demonstrated that individuals respond differently to positive and negative risks. Individuals exhibit a *negativity bias*: they will take more chances – seeking conflict and accepting the possibility of even greater losses – to prevent any worsening of their current position.[5] Studies of electoral behaviour, at least in the United States, confirm these findings. Negative attitudes toward candidates are more strongly linked with a range of behaviours (for example, turnout, deserting the voter's normal party choice) than are positive attitudes.[6]

While the reasons for this negativity bias are unclear, the constraints that it imposes on elected officials are not. When added to the imbalance between concentrated and diffuse interests, the message for advocates of retrenchment is straightforward. A simple 'redistributive' transfer of resources from programme beneficiaries to taxpayers, engineered through cuts in social programmes, is generally a losing proposition. The concentrated beneficiary groups are more likely to be cognisant of the change, are easier to mobilize, and because they are experiencing losses rather than gains are more likely to incorporate the change in their voting calculations. Retrenchment advocates thus confront a clash between their policy preferences and their electoral ambitions.

If the shift in goals from expansion to cutbacks creates new political dynamics, so does the emergence of a new *context*: the development of the welfare state itself. Large public social programmes are now a central part of the political landscape. As Peter Flora has noted, 'Including the recipients of [pensions,] unemployment benefits and social assistance – and the persons employed in education, health and the social services – in many countries today almost 1/2 of the electorate receive transfer or work income from the welfare state.'[7] With these massive programmes have come dense interest-group networks and strong popular attachments to particular policies, which present considerable obstacles to reform. To take one prominent example, by the late 1980s the American Association of Retired People (AARP) had a membership of 28 million and a staff of 1,300 (including a legislative staff of more than 100).[8] The maturation of the welfare state fundamentally transforms the nature of interest-group politics. In short, the emergence of powerful groups surrounding social programmes may make the welfare state less dependent on the political parties, social movements, and labour organizations that expanded social programmes in the first place. Nor is the context altered simply because welfare states create their own constituencies. The structures of social programmes may also have implications for the decision rules governing policy change (for example, whether national officials need the acquiescence of local ones) and for how visible cutbacks will be. 'Policy feedback' from earlier rounds of welfare state development is likely to be a prominent feature of retrenchment politics.[9]

In short, the shift in goals and context creates a new politics. This new politics, marked by pressures to avoid blame for unpopular policies, dictates new political strategies.[10] Retrenchment advocates will try to play off one group of beneficiaries against another and develop reforms that compensate politically crucial groups for lost benefits. Those favouring cutbacks will attempt to lower the visibility of reforms, either by making the effects of policies more difficult to detect or by making it hard for voters to trace responsibility for these effects back to particular policy makers.[11] Wherever possible, policy makers will seek broad consensus on reform in order to spread the blame. Whether these efforts succeed may depend very much on the structure of policies already in place.

[…]

To what extent have welfare states undergone retrenchment? What countries and programmes have been most vulnerable to retrenchment initiatives and why? In this section I address these questions by reviewing the evolution of welfare states in four affluent democracies since the late 1970s. The evidence supports a number of claims. (1) There is little evidence for broad propositions about the centrality of strong states or left power resources to retrenchment outcomes. (2) The unpopularity of retrenchment makes major cutbacks unlikely except under conditions of budgetary crisis, and radical restructuring is unlikely even then. (3) For the same reason, governments generally seek to negotiate consensus packages rather than to impose reforms unilaterally, which further diminishes the potential for radical reform. And (4) far from creating a self-reinforcing dynamic, cutbacks tend to replenish support for the welfare state.

Measuring retrenchment is a difficult task. Quantitative indicators are likely to be inadequate for several reasons. First, pure spending levels are rarely the most politically important or theoretically interesting aspects of welfare states. As Esping-Andersen put it in his analysis of welfare state expansion, 'It is difficult to imagine that anyone struggled for spending per se'.[12] In particular, rising unemployment may sustain high spending even as social rights and benefits are significantly curtailed. Second, spending estimates will fail to capture the impact of reforms that are designed to introduce retrenchment only indirectly or over the long term. Analysis must focus on qualitative and quantitative changes in programmes and on prospective, long-term changes, as well as on immediate cutbacks. My investigation therefore relies on a combination of quantitative data on expenditures and qualitative analysis of welfare state reforms. Rather than emphasizing cuts in spending *per se*, the focus is on reforms that indicate structural shifts in the welfare state. These would include (1) significant increases in reliance on means-tested benefits; (2) major transfers of responsibility to the private sector; and (3) dramatic changes in benefit and eligibility rules that signal a qualitative reform of a particular programme.[13] The selection of countries to investigate was based on the desire to achieve significant variation on what the welfare state expansion literature suggests are the most plausible independent variables. The cases vary widely in the structure of political institutions, the extent of shifts in the distribution of power resources, the design of pre-existing welfare states, and the severity of budgetary crisis.

Beginning with the quantitative evidence, aggregate measures provide little evidence that any of the four welfare states have undergone dramatic cutbacks. From 1974 to 1990 the expenditure patterns across the four cases are quite similar, despite widely different starting-points. As tables 6 and 7 show, social security spending and total government outlays as a percentage of GDP are relatively flat over most of the relevant period. The exception is the recent surge in Swedish expenditures, which will be discussed below. There is a slight upward trend overall, with fluctuations related to the business cycle. Table 8, which tracks public employment, reveals a similar pattern (although the expansion of Swedish public employment from an already high base stands out). For none of the countries does the evidence reveal a sharp curtailment of the public sector.

Table 9 offers more disaggregated indicators of shifts in social welfare spending among the four countries; spending patterns are reported for what the OECD terms 'merit goods' (primarily housing, education and health care) as well as for various income transfers. The figures suggest a bit more divergence among the cases, with the United States and Germany emerging as somewhat more successful in curbing spending. A very few

Table 6 Social security transfers as % of GDP, 1974–90

	Britain	Germany	Sweden	United States
1974	9.8	14.6	14.3	9.5
1980	11.7	16.6	17.6	10.9
1982	14.0	17.7	18.3	11.9
1984	14.0	16.5	17.6	11.0
1986	14.1	15.9	18.4	11.0
1988	12.3	16.1	19.5	10.6
1990	12.2	15.3	19.7	10.8[a]

[a] 1989.

Source: OECD, *Historical Statistics, 1960–1990* (1992), table 6.3

Table 7 Government outlays as % of nominal GDP, 1978–94

	Britain	Germany	Sweden	United States
1978	41.4	47.3	58.6	30.0
1980	43.0	47.9	60.1	31.8
1982	44.6	48.9	64.8	33.9
1984	45.2	47.4	62.0	32.6
1986	42.5	46.4	61.6	33.7
1988	38.0	46.3	58.1	32.5
1990	39.9	45.1	59.1	33.3
1992	43.2	49.0	67.3	35.1
1994[a]	44.8	51.4	70.9	33.9

[a] Projection.

Source: OECD, *Economic Outlook* (December 1993), table A23

Table 8 Government employment as % of total employment, 1974–90

	Britain	Germany	Sweden	United States
1974	19.6	13.0	24.8	16.1
1980	21.1	14.6	30.3	15.4
1982	22.0	15.1	31.7	15.4
1984	22.0	15.5	32.6	14.8
1986	21.8	15.6	32.2	14.8
1988	20.8	15.6	31.5	14.4
1990	19.2	15.1	31.7	14.4[a]

[a] 1989.

Source: OECD, *Historical Statistics, 1960–1990* (1992), table 2.13

Table 9 Government outlays by function as % of trend GDPA[a], 1979–90

	Britain			Germany			Sweden			United States		
	1979	1990	1979–90	1979	1990	1979–90	1979	1990	1979–90	1979	1989	1979–89
Total	44.9	43.2	−1.7	49.9	45.8	−4.1	63.2	61.4	−1.8	33.2	36.9	+3.6
Public goods[b]	9.5	9.7	+0.1	10.0	9.2	−0.8	10.5	8.8	−1.7	8.2	9.3	+1.1
Merit goods	13.6	12.2	−1.4	12.3	10.9	−1.4	15.9	13.4	−2.6	6.1	6.0	−0.1
Education	5.5	5.0	−0.5	5.2	4.2	−1.0	6.6	5.6	−1.0	4.7	4.7	−0.0
Health[c]	4.8	5.1	+0.3	6.3	6.0	−0.3	8.1	6.9	−1.1	0.9	0.9	−0.0
Housing and other	3.4	2.1	−1.2	0.8	0.7	−0.1	1.2	0.8	−0.4	0.5	0.4	−0.1
Income trans.	12.5	13.4	+0.9	20.2	18.5	−1.7	24.6	26.8	+2.2	11.2	11.9	+0.7
Pensions	6.7	6.5	−0.2	12.7	11.2	−1.5	11.0	11.5	+0.4	6.9	7.0	+0.1
Sickness	0.4	0.3	−0.1	0.8	0.7	−0.1	3.4	4.5	+1.2	0.1	0.2	+0.1
Family allowance	1.7	1.6	−0.0	1.2	0.8	−0.4	1.6	1.3	−0.3	0.4	0.4	−0.0
Unemployment	0.7	0.6	−0.1	0.9	1.3	+0.4	0.4	0.5	+0.1	0.4	0.3	−0.1
Other income supports	0.1	0.8	+0.7	1.3	1.6	+0.3	0.1	0.2	+0.1	0.0	0.0	0.0
Admin. and other spending	1.4	1.6	+0.3	2.6	2.4	−0.2	4.9	5.2	+0.3	0.6	0.6	−0.0
Add. transfer	1.4	1.8	+0.5	0.5	0.4	−0.1	3.2	3.7	+0.6	2.7	3.5	+0.8

[a] Numbers may not sum to total due to rounding.
[b] Defence and other public services.
[c] For the US, social security related to health spending is included under 'Additional transfers' below.

Source: OECD, *Economic Outlook* (December 1993), table 21

programme areas – notably British housing and German pensions – experienced significant reductions. Nonetheless, similarities across countries remain more striking than differences. None of the cases show major rises or declines in overall effort, and there are few indications of dramatic change in any of the subcategories of expenditure.

[...]

The New Politics of the Welfare State

Economic, political and social pressures have fostered an image of welfare states under siege. Yet if one turns from abstract discussions of social transformation to an examination of actual policy, it becomes difficult to sustain the proposition that these strains have generated fundamental shifts. This review of four cases does indeed suggest a distinctly new environment, but not one that has provoked anything like a dismantling of the welfare state. Nor is it possible to attribute this to case selection, since the choice of two prototypical cases of neo-conservatism (Britain and the United States) and two cases of severe budgetary shocks (Germany and Sweden) gave ample room for various scenarios of radical retrenchment. Even in Thatcher's Britain, where an ideologically committed Conservative Party [...] controlled one of Europe's most centralized political systems for over a decade, reform [was] incremental rather than revolutionary, leaving the British welfare state largely intact. In most other countries the evidence of continuity is even more apparent.

To be sure, there has been change. Many programmes have experienced a tightening of eligibility rules or reductions in benefits. On occasion, individual programmes (such as public housing in Britain) have undergone more radical reform. In countries where budgetary pressures have been greatest, cuts have been more severe. Over the span of two decades, however, *some* changes in social policy are inevitable; even in the boom years of the 1960s specific social programmes sometimes fared poorly. What is striking is how hard it is to find *radical* changes in advanced welfare states. Retrenchment has been pursued cautiously: whenever possible, governments have sought all-party consensus for significant reforms and have chosen to trim existing structures rather than experiment with new programmes or pursue privatization.

This finding is striking, given that so many observers have seen the post-1973 period as one of fundamental change in modern political economies. A harsher economic climate has certainly generated demands for spending restraint. Additional pressures have stemmed from the maturation of social programmes and adverse demographic trends. Yet compared with the aspirations of many reformers and with the extent of change in fields such as industrial relations policy, macro-economic policy or the privatization of public industries, what stands out is the relative stability of the welfare state.

I have suggested that to understand what has been happening requires looking beyond the considerable pressures on the welfare state to consider enduring sources of support. There are powerful political forces that stabilize welfare states and channel change in the direction of incremental modifications of existing policies. The first major protection for social programmes stems from the generally conservative characteristics of democratic political institutions. The welfare state now represents the status quo, with all the political advantages that this status confers. Non-decisions generally favour the welfare state. Major policy change usually requires the acquiescence of numerous actors. Where power is shared among different institutions (for example, Germany, the United States), radical reform will be difficult.

As the British and Swedish cases show, radical change is not easy even in a situation of concentrated political power. A second and crucial source of the welfare state's political strength comes from the high electoral costs generally associated with retrenchment initiatives. Despite scholarly speculation about declining popular support for the welfare state, polls show little evidence of such a shift, and actual political struggles over social spending reveal even less. On the contrary, even halting efforts to dismantle the welfare state have usually exacted a high political price. Recipients of social benefits are relatively concentrated and are generally well organized. They are also more likely to punish politicians for cutbacks than taxpayers are to reward them for lower costs. Nowhere is there evidence to support the scenario of a self-reinforcing dynamic, with cutbacks leading to middle-class disenchantment and exit, laying the foundation for more retrenchment. Instead, the recurrent pattern in public-opinion polls has been a mild swing against the welfare state in the wake of poor economic performance and budgetary stress, followed by a resurgence of support at the first whiff of significant cuts.

Nor does the welfare state's political position seem to have been seriously eroded – at least in the medium term – by the decline of its key traditional constituency, organized labour. Only for those benefits where unions are the sole organized constituency, such as unemployment insurance, has labour's declining power presented immediate problems, and even here the impact can be exaggerated.[14] The growth of social spending has reconfigured the terrain of welfare state politics. Maturing social programmes produce new organized interests, the consumers and providers of social services, that are usually well placed to defend the welfare state.

The networks associated with mature welfare state programmes constitute a barrier to radical change in another sense as well. As recent research on path dependence has demonstrated, once initiated, certain courses of development are hard to reverse.[15] Organizations and individuals adapt to particular arrangements, making commitments that may render the costs of change (even to some potentially more efficient alternative) far higher than the costs of continuity. Existing commitments lock in policy makers. Old-age pension systems provide a good example. Most countries operate pensions on a pay-as-you-go basis: current workers pay 'contributions' that finance the previous generation's retirement. Once in place, such systems may face incremental cutbacks, but they are notoriously resistant to radical reform.[16] Shifting to private, occupationally based arrangements would place an untenable burden on current workers, requiring them to finance the previous generation's retirement while simultaneously saving for their own.

Over time, all institutions undergo change. This is especially so for very large ones, which cannot be isolated from broad social developments. The welfare state is no exception. But there is little sign that the last two decades have been a transformative period for systems of social provision. As I have argued, expectations for greater change have rested in part on the implicit application of models from the period of welfare state expansion, which can be read to suggest that economic change, the decline in union power, or the presence of a strong state creates the preconditions for radical retrenchment. I find little evidence for these claims.

Notes

From *World Politics*, 48, January 1996, pp. 143–79.
I am grateful to the Russell Sage Foundation for financial and administrative support and to Miguel Glatzer for considerable research assistance, as well as helpful comments.
1 R. Kent Weaver, 'The Politics of Blame Avoidance', *Journal of Public Policy*, 6, October – December 1986.
2 Peter Flora and Arnold J. Heidenheimer, eds, *The Development of Welfare States in Europe and America*, New Brunswick, NJ, Transaction, 1982.
3 As recent research has suggested, it would be wrong to treat business as always and everywhere opposed to welfare state programmes. For illuminating studies of the United States, see, for example, Colin Gordon, *New Deals: Business, Labor, and Politics in America, 1920–1935*, Cambridge, Cambridge University Press, 1994; and Cathie Jo Martin, 'Nature or Nurture? Sources of Firm Preference for National Health Reform', *American Political Science Review*, 89, December 1995. Nonetheless, it is clear that *most* business organizations in all the advanced industrial democracies have favoured – often vehemently – cutbacks in the welfare state over the past fifteen years.
4 Mancur Olson, *The Logic of Collective Action: Public Goods and the Theory of Groups*, Cambridge, MA, Harvard University Press, 1965; James Q. Wilson, *Political Organizations*, New York, Basic Books, 1973, pp. 330–37.
5 Daniel Kahneman and Amos Tversky, 'Prospect Theory: An Analysis of Decision under Risk', *Econometrica*, 47, March 1979; idem, 'Choices, Values and Frames', *American Psychologist*, 39 April 1984.

6   Howard S. Bloom and H. Douglas Price, 'Voter Response to Short-Run Economic Conditions: The Asymmetric Effect of Prosperity and Recession', *American Political Science Review*, 69, December 1975; Samuel Kernell, 'Presidential Popularity and Negative Voting: An Alternative Explanation of the Midterm Congressional Decline of the President's Party', *American Political Science Review*, 71, March 1977; and Richard R. Lau, 'Explanations for Negativity Effects in Political Behavior', *American Journal of Political Science*, 29, February 1985.

7   Peter Flora, 'From Industrial to Postindustrial Welfare State?', *Annals of the Institute of Social Science* (University of Tokyo), special issue 1989, p. 154.

8   Christine L. Day, *What Older Americans Think: Interest Groups and Aging Policy*, Princeton, NJ, Princeton University Press, 1990, pp. 25–6.

9   Gøsta Esping-Andersen, *Politics against Markets: The Social Democratic Road to Power*, Princeton, NJ, Princeton University Press, 1985; Paul Pierson, 'When Effect Becomes Cause: Policy Feedback and Political Change', *World Politics*, 45, July 1993.

10 Weaver, op. cit.; Paul Pierson, *Dismantling the Welfare State? Reagan, Thatcher and the Politics of Retrenchment*, Cambridge, Cambridge University Press, 1994, ch. 1.

11 R. Douglas Arnold, *The Logic of Congressional Action*, New Haven, Yale University Press, 1990.

12 Gøsta Esping-Andersen, *The Three Worlds of Welfare Capitalism*, Cambridge, Polity Press, 1990, p. 21.

13 Establishing what constitutes 'radical' reform is no easy task. For instance, it is impossible to say definitively when a series of quantitative cutbacks amounts to a qualitative shift in the nature of programmes. Roughly though, that point is reached when because of policy reform a programme can no longer play its traditional role (e.g. when pension benefits designed to provide a rough continuation of the retiree's earlier standard of living are clearly unable to do so).

14 Indeed, a cross-national comparison of unemployment programmes provides further support for this analysis. The OECD has measured replacement rates for UI (benefits as a percentage of previous income) over time in twenty countries, with data to 1991. These data thus permit, for one programme, a [...] quantitative appraisal of programme *generosity* rather than simply spending levels. In the majority of cases (twelve out of twenty), replacement rates were *higher* in 1991 than the average rate for either the 1970s or the 1980s, while most of the other cases experienced very marginal declines. Organization for Economic Co-operation and Development, *The OECD Jobs Study: Facts, Analysis, Strategies*, Paris, OECD, 1994, chart 16, p. 24.

15 See Paul David, 'Clio and the Economics of QWERTY', *American Economic Review*, 75, May 1985; and W. Brian Arthur, 'Competing Technologies, Increasing Returns, and Lock-In by Historical Events', *Economic Journal*, 99, March 1989, pp. 116–31. For good extensions to political processes, see Stephen A. Krasner, 'Sovereignty: An Institutional Perspective', in James A. Caporaso, ed., *The Elusive State: International and Comparative Perspectives*, Newbury Park, CA, Sage Publications, 1989; and Douglas North, *Institutions, Institutional Change and Economic Reformance*, Cambridge, Cambridge University Press, 1990.

16 Thus in Germany, Sweden, and the United States the maturity of existing schemes limited policy makers to very gradual and incremental reforms of

earnings-related pension systems. More dramatic reform was possible in Britain because the unfunded earnings-related scheme was far from maturity, having been passed only in 1975. Pierson, '"Policy Feedbacks" and Political Change Contrasting Reagan and Thatcher's Persian-Reform Initiatives', *Studies in American Political Development*, 6, Fall 1992.

Welfare State Retrenchment Revisited

Richard Clayton and Jonas Pontusson

The resilience of the welfare state has emerged as a prominent theme in the scholarly literature of the 1990s, with Paul Pierson's widely cited *World Politics* article of 1996 providing, we think, the clearest and most compelling presentation of the case for welfare state resilience.[1] Using this article as a foil, we seek to examine some of the conventional wisdom in the literature and to sketch an alternative approach to the study of welfare states in transition.

Basing his argument on aggregate OECD statistics as well as on case studies of Germany, Sweden, the UK and the US, Pierson contends that welfare cutbacks and reforms have been strictly limited in scope. At the same time, he observes, 'the power of organized labor and left parties has shrunk considerably in many advanced industrial societies'.[2] Together, these observations pose a challenge for the power-resource model developed by Walter Korpi and others to explain cross-national variations in welfare state development.[3]

The politics of welfare state retrenchment appear to be fundamentally different from the politics of welfare state expansion. Pierson's notion of a 'new politics of the welfare state' yields three specific arguments to explain welfare state resilience. First, 'the welfare state now represents the status quo, with all the political advantages that this status confers'.[4] Especially in countries where different institutions share power, radical reform is inherently difficult. Second, Pierson argues, welfare cutbacks tend to be associated with high electoral costs for the simple reason that basic welfare programmes enjoy widespread popular legitimacy. Third, he attributes resilience to successful mobilization by well-organized groups representing the interests of consumers of welfare benefits (such as retirees), as well as employees of the welfare state. The combination of these factors yields a politics of blame avoidance in which cutbacks can take place only through incremental and surreptitious mechanisms or during moments of extraordinary fiscal stress and political consensus.

The literature on welfare state retrenchment raises the thorny question of how to distinguish radical change from incremental adjustments. For instance, writing about Sweden in the early 1990s, Pierson states that conditions were uniquely favourable to a 'complete overhaul of social policy', but even so 'there was no sign that the welfare state would be radically restructured'.[5] Exactly what, then, would a 'complete overhaul of social policy' or a 'radical restructuring of the welfare state' entail? And should we not allow for some outcomes that are neither 'incremental adjustments' nor 'complete overhauls'? Without resurrecting the crisis rhetoric of the 1970s and its functionalist premises, the following analysis shows that major changes have indeed occurred in the scope and organization of public welfare provision not only in the UK and the US, but across the OECD area more generally.

[...]

This article seeks to broaden the discussion of welfare state retrenchment and, at the same time, to promote a more careful consideration of measurement issues. Exemplified by Pierson's work, the existing literature tends to focus on the efforts by politicians to enact entitlement changes or, more precisely, on the significance of the entitlement changes that have been enacted. This way of thinking about welfare state retrenchment is too narrow. First, recent cutbacks and welfare reforms must be situated in the context of rising social inequality and insecurity. Since the late 1970s the dynamics of advanced capitalism have been undoing some of the post-war achievements of welfare states. Increased welfare effort would have been required to maintain these achievements. Moreover, the rise of mass unemployment and the decline of employment opportunities for unskilled workers affect the way welfare states work, irrespective of whether governments cut or reform social programmes. Even in the Scandinavian welfare states, celebrated for their universalism, the system of social insurance has remained closely tied to employment. Since about the mid-1980s the number of people who do not have access to these universalistic programmes and who must instead rely on means-tested social assistance has increased considerably in proportion to the total population.

We argue in a similar vein that measuring the size of the welfare state in terms of social spending as a percentage of GDP, as virtually all of the literature does, is problematic because such measures fail to take account of changes in societal welfare needs. The alternative measures that we propose show that the rapid growth of social spending in the 1960s and

1970s came to an end in the 1980s and that public services were more affected by the deceleration of growth than transfer programmes. Measuring the welfare state in terms of the absolute size of the public sector labour force, we find quite a few instances of actual welfare state shrinkage in recent years.

By and large, the retrenchment literature tends to ignore the question of changes in the delivery of social services or, in other words, the question of how the public sector is organized. While Pierson does discuss health care, most of the entitlement programmes that he considers are based on transfer payments. At least in Sweden and the UK, however, it is in the realm of public services that we find the most significant cutbacks and market-oriented reforms. Related to this, finally, we argue that summing up changes in individual social programmes does not provide the basis for an adequate assessment of what has happened to welfare states since 1980. We must also consider changes in the overall configuration of welfare spending, that is, how the allocation of resources among individual programmes might have changed. Thus we propose to explore not only the extent of welfare state retrenchment, but also forms of welfare state restructuring.

The importance that we assign to the public sector as a site of service production follows from Gøsta Esping-Andersen's well-known and much-admired comparative analysis of welfare state development.[6] As Esping-Andersen points out, the Scandinavian welfare states are distinguished by their reliance on the direct provision of services. Yet state-produced services constitute a crucial dimension of the public provision of social welfare in virtually all advanced capitalist societies these days. And, to the extent that it involves non-profit production and allocation of output according to political criteria, it is this dimension of the welfare state that most directly contradicts the logic of capitalism.

[...]

Growing Market Inequality

In this section we present evidence to support the propositions that inequality has increased and that security of employment and income has diminished for many wage earners in advanced capitalist societies since 1980. The literature that emphasizes the resilience of the welfare state tends to ignore these trends. Pierson and others seem to take the view that the growth of inequality and insecurity is relevant only to the extent that it is a direct result of spending cuts or reforms of the welfare state. In other words, they confine their discussion to the question of the extent to which the welfare state has become less redistributive or less effective in providing protection against market risks. This view fails to incorporate Esping-Andersen's crucial insight that the activities of the welfare state influence the way that labour markets operate. Moreover, the context of rising inequality and insecurity must be considered when we assess the significance of recent changes in the size and character of welfare states. For example, Swedish governments lowered the replacement rate of unemployment insurance from 90 per cent to 75 per cent in the first half of the 1990s. Had unemployment remained what it had been in the 1980s, these decisions might well have been described as a minor retrenchment of the welfare state. In the context of the dramatic increase of unemployment that occurred in the early 1990s, they take on a different significance.

It is commonplace to measure the distribution of income in terms of the ratio of income at the lower end of the 90th percentile (the lower end of the top 10 per cent of income earners) to income at the upper end of the 10th percentile (the upper end of the bottom 10 per cent). Referring to the earnings of full-time employees, table 10 summarizes recent trends in 90–10 ratios in all OECD countries for which such data are available. For men and women combined, wage inequality increased sharply from the late 1970s to the mid-1990s in the UK as well as in the US. Most other countries experienced increases in the 1–7 per cent range, but a handful of countries, most notably Germany, actually moved in the opposite direction. The trend toward increased inequality becomes more pronounced when we take gender differentials out of the picture and especially when we look at the distribution of earnings among men. The 90–10 ratio for men increased in all but two countries, Belgium and Germany. In the UK and the US, it increased by more than a third, and Italy and New Zealand also registered double-digit percentage increases. In many countries, rising within-gender inequality has been offset by the continuation of the reduction of gender differentials that began in the 1960s or 1970s.[7]

The figures in table 10 capture only part of the tendency since 1980 for market forces to generate more inequality. Several other considerations must be introduced to complete the picture. First, disparities of income from capital have undoubtedly reinforced the effects of these trends in the distribution of wage income. Second, the individual-level trends shown in table 10 have likely been magnified by the pooling of wage income within families. For the US, Gary Burtless shows that the correlation between the incomes of spouses has increased very significantly (well-paid men being increasingly likely to be married to well-paid women) and that this development accounts for a large part of the growth of household inequality.[8]

Third, the figures presented in table 10 understate the rise of inequality because they are restricted to full-time employees. In fifteen out of nineteen OECD countries for which data are available, the incidence of part-time employment increased from 1983 to 1996 and in nine of these countries it increased by more than a third.[9] As women constitute the

Table 10   Percentage changes in wage inequality (90–10 ratios) among full-time wage earners, 1979–95

	Men	Women	Both sexes
Australia 1979–95	7.0	6.7	5.8
Austria 1980–94	5.3[a]	10.7	6.4
Belgium 1985–93	−2.1[a]	−3.9[a]	−4.4[a]
Canada 1981–94	8.0	8.3	5.0
Denmark 1980–90			1.9
Finland 1980–94	3.3	−4.8	−2.8
France 1979–94	1.2	10.0	0.9
Germany 1983–93	−6.3	−14.0	−12.7
Italy 1979–93	14.9	−7.0	−4.4
Japan 1979–94	6.2	1.8	0.0
Netherlands 1985–94			4.0
New Zealand 1984–94	17.6	8.7	5.2
Norway 1980–91			−4.4
Sweden 1980–93	3.8	10.3	3.9
Switzerland 1991–5	4.9	−7.0	−0.4
UK 1979–95	36.6	34.2	21.4
US 1979–95	35.6	28.4	

[a] Based on 80–10 rather than 90–10 ratios.
Source: OECD, *Employment Outlook* (July 1996), pp. 61–2

vast majority of part-time employees in all countries and part-time employees earn less than full-time employees on an hourly basis, the proposition that pay differentials based on gender continued to decline through the 1980s may have to be qualified in light of the growth of part-time employment. Finally, data on the distribution of income from employment fail to capture the impact of unemployment. Because unemployment tends to be concentrated among unskilled, low-paid workers, it correlates negatively with wage inequality as measured in table 10.[10] As the rate of unemployment increases, low-paid workers disappear from the population used to calculate 90–10 ratios and the wage distribution becomes more compressed, but we certainly would not want to conclude from this that unemployment promotes social equality.

[…]

The incidence of poverty provides another obvious indicator of social inequality and insecurity. One common measure of poverty is the percentage of the population living in households with an income of less than 40

Table 11 Percentage of the population living in households with an income of less than 40% of the Median Income, *c.*1980 and 1991

		Before taxes and transfers	After taxes and transfers
Sweden	1981	16.4	6.0
	1992	20.6	3.8
Germany	1978	13.1	2.0
	1989	14.1	2.4
UK	1979	20.0	3.1
	1991	25.7	5.3
US	1979	18.8	10.6
	1991	21.0	11.7

Source: Lane Kenworthy, 'Do Social-Welfare Policies Reduce Poverty', *Social Forces* (forthcoming), pretax/transfer figures for 1978–81 provided directly by Kenworthy

per cent of the median household income. Using this definition and drawing on data from the Luxembourg Income Study, table 11 presents estimates of the incidence of poverty before as well as after taxes and government transfers for Sweden, Germany, the UK and the US around 1980 and 1991. In each of these countries poverty measured in terms of the distribution of 'market income' (that is, the distribution of income before taxes and transfers) increased noticeably over this relatively brief period of time. The fact that the percentage of the population receiving some form of means-tested social assistance increased in fifteen out of eighteen OECD countries from 1980 to 1992 suggests that table 11 captures a general trend, reversing the prior trend toward a reduction of poverty.[11] The pervasiveness of recent inegalitarian trends is indeed striking, especially in view of the strong tendency among students of comparative political economy to emphasize national diversity. We hasten to add that common trends do not necessarily add up to cross-national convergence, for convergence requires that the most egalitarian countries experience the most rapid growth of wage inequality, poverty and so on, and this does not appear to have been the case.

[…]

Measuring Welfare Effort

For the four countries which he surveys, Pierson presents aggregate OECD statistics on the evolution of social security transfers as a

Table 12 Average annual growth of total social spending (at constant prices) per poor person (40% of median income) and real GDP per capita, 1979–92

	Social spending/poor	Real GDP/Capita
Sweden 1981–92	0.66	1.02
Germany 1978–89	0.87	2.11
UK 1979–91	1.63	1.87
US 1979–91	0.81	1.23

Sources: Total social spending as percentage of GDP from OECD, *New Directions in Social Policy in OECD Countries* (Paris, OECD, 1994); and idem, *Social Expenditure Statistics of OECD Member Countries*, Labour Market and Social Policy Occasional Papers (Paris, OECD, 1996); GDP at constant prices from OECD, *National Accounts: Main Aggregates* (Paris, OECD, 1996); poverty rates from Kenworthy (see table 11); population size from OECD, *Labour Force Statistics* (Paris, OECD, various years); and real growth of GDP per capita from OECD, *Historical Statistics* (Paris, OECD, 1996)

percentage of GDP, total government outlays as a percentage of GDP, and government employment as a percentage of total employment. In Pierson's words, the quantitative data show 'a surprisingly high level of continuity and stability', and 'for none of the countries does the evidence reveal a sharp curtailment of the public sector'.[12] This is indeed a judicious assessment of the data presented, but the data are problematic on several counts.

While two of Pierson's time-series end in 1990 and the other ends in 1992, 'total government outlays' is obviously too broad and 'social security transfers' too narrow a measure of the size of the welfare state. More importantly, government spending as a percentage of GDP provides a useful measure of cross-national differences at any point in time, but the GDP denominator of this measure makes it difficult to interpret change over time. In the time-series presented by Pierson, two things are changing – the amount of money spent by the government and the size of GDP – and it is impossible to separate one from the other. Still more importantly, Pierson's quantitative measures do not take socio-economic and demographic changes into account. At any given level of entitlement provisions, an increase in the number of unemployed, poor or retired people automatically generates increased social spending by the government. Indeed, increased spending might be associated with a reduction of entitlements. To use government spending as a proxy for 'welfare effort', we must somehow control for these variables.

Table 12 is the upshot of an alternative approach to the problem of measuring welfare effort or, in a sense, the size of the welfare state. Data available from OECD provide year-to-year observations of total social spending as a percentage of GDP, enabling us to avoid the unhappy choice between total outlays and social security transfers. Using these figures and the amount of GDP, expressed in US dollars at 1990 prices and exchange rates, we can compute the amount of total social spending at constant prices. The poverty rates reported in table 11 in turn allow us to divide this figure by the number of people living in households with a market income of less than 40 per cent of the median household income. Though the figures for total social spending as a percentage of GDP are available for the entire period 1960–93, the availability of poverty data restricts the time period over which we can observe change in this measure. Table 12 reports the annual growth rate of real social spending per poor person in the 1980s for Sweden, Germany, the UK and the US, and compares these figures with the annual growth rate of real GDP per capita. In all four countries the growth of real social spending per poor person failed to keep up with the growth of GDP per capita, and, except for the UK, the differential between these growth rates was quite considerable.

[...]

The Size of the Public Sector

Table 13 summarizes the real growth of final consumption expenditure (that is, the costs of goods and services produced by the public sector) in seventeen OECD countries over the period 1960–94. Like total government outlays, this measure encompasses a range of government activities that have little or nothing to do with the provision of social welfare, but it speaks more directly to the size of the public sector. As noted earlier, services provided by the government represent an important component of the welfare state not only in Scandinavia but across the OECD countries. To conceive this component simply in terms of health care and social services in the narrow sense of the term (as the OECD does for the purpose of computing total social spending) seems unduly narrow. Child care, education, retraining programmes and a great many other services promote social welfare in general, and at least some of these services benefit low-income groups in particular.

In all but two countries the average growth rate of real government final consumption was lower in 1973–9 than in 1960–73 and, again, in all but two countries, the average rate in 1979–89 was lower than in 1973–9. In a handful of countries, the growth of government final consumption rose in

Table 13 Average annual rate of growth of real government final consumption expenditure, 1960–94

	1960–73	1973–9	1979–89	1989–94
Australia	5.8	4.9	3.4	2.8
Austria	3.2	3.9	1.5	2.3
Belgium	5.5	3.7	0.5	0.9
Canada	6.1	3.5	2.5	1.1
Denmark	5.8	4.1	1.5	0.8
Finland	5.4	4.8	3.5	−0.1
France	4.0	3.4	2.3	2.6
Germany	4.5	3.0	1.3	1.7
Italy	4.0	2.7	2.6	0.9
Japan	5.8	4.8	2.7	2.1
Netherlands	2.8	3.5	2.0	1.2
New Zealand	3.6	3.2	1.2	−0.2
Norway	5.9	5.3	3.5	3.1
Sweden	4.9	3.7	1.6	0.9
Switzerland	5.3	1.4	2.7	1.1
UK	2.7	1.8	1.0	1.5
US	2.5	1.7	2.7	0.1
OECD total	3.6	2.8	2.4	1.2

Source: OECD, *Historical Statistics* (Paris, OECD, 1996)

the early 1990s, but all of these countries had comparatively low growth rates in the 1980s. For every single country, the growth rate of 1989–94 was lower than that of 1973–9 and of 1960–73. It would appear that as overall government spending has slowed down while the costs of social assistance and social security entitlements have continued to grow, the service components of the welfare state have been squeezed.

The size of the public sector might also be measured in terms of employment, but we must beware of the denominator problem. From 1990 to 1994 the public-sector labour force in Sweden declined by nearly 12 per cent. As total employment declined even more, however, government employment as a percentage of total employment actually increased slightly. To avoid this problem, table 14 tracks the evolution of the public sector labour force, measured in absolute terms (people) rather than in relative terms (percentage of total employment). For nine of these countries the continuous deceleration story of table 13 becomes a story of outright shrinkage of the public sector. Most remarkably, the size of the public sector labour force declined by nearly 30 per cent in the UK from 1988 to 1994.[13]

Table 14   The size of the public sector labour force, 1960–94

| | Government employees (in thousands) | | | % Change from peak to 1994 |
	1980	Peak	1994	
Australia	1604	1843 (87)	1661	−9.9
Austria	596		837	
Belgium	701	755 (86)	730	−3.3
Canada	2027		2646	
Denmark	708	812 (90)	792	−2.5
Finland	398	550 (91)	514	−6.5
France	3395		5426	
Germany	3843	4329 (92)	4307	−0.5
Italy	3151	3415 (92)	3374	−1.2
Japan	3654		3807	
Netherlands	756	858 (90)	835	−2.7
New Zealand				
Norway	419		613	
Sweden	1299	1425 (90)	1256	−11.9
Switzerland	323		424	
UK	5210	5328 (88)	3789	−28.9
US	16,732		18,049	

Source: OECD, *Labour Force Statistics* (Paris, OECD, various years); and *Historical Statistics* (Paris, OECD, various years)

The Changing Composition of Social Spending

From the analytical perspective of the welfare state literature, summing up changes in individual social programmes hardly provides an adequate basis for assessing the extent to which welfare states have changed, for the central concern of this literature is with relations among social programmes, in other words, with the overall configuration of welfare states. One interpretation of Esping-Andersen's work holds that all welfare states consist of three basic components – a universalistic component providing benefits as a matter of citizen rights, a social-insurance component linking benefits to employment and a means-tested social-assistance component – and that the types of welfare state are essentially distinguished from each other by the relative weight that they assign to these three components. The question becomes whether there have been significant shifts in the mix of welfare state components since the early 1980s. Showing the distribution of total social spending by type of spending in 1980 and 1993, table 15 represents a first stab at this question.

In the Swedish and British cases alike, we observe two important changes: first, a shift of social spending from services to transfer payments and, second, a shift of spending on transfers from social insurance schemes to social assistance. The former shift is particularly pronounced in the Swedish case, and the latter is most pronounced in the British case. In the case of the US, we observe that the relative importance of public health spending rose at the expense of social insurance, suggesting that rising health care costs have been a major factor behind the continued growth of social spending. In a European context the increased relative importance of health spending would represent an increase in the service intensity of the welfare state, but in the US, of course, public health spending primarily takes the form of transfer payments. Consistent with our earlier discussion, Germany stands out in table 15 as a case of remarkable stability.

The spending figures in table 15 do not fit Esping-Andersen's conceptual categories perfectly. While transfer payments may be provided on a universalistic basis rather than being tied to employment, services may be provided on a means-tested basis. Recognizing the limitations of these data, table 13 lends at least some support to the idea that the Swedish welfare state has become institutionally more like the German welfare state and that the British welfare state has become more like the American welfare state. Based on this limited sample of OECD countries, it would appear that universalistic service-based welfare states have undergone more far-reaching changes than social-insurance or residualist

Table 15 The distribution (%) of social spending by type: Sweden, Germany, the UK and the US, 1980, 1993

		Health	Social services	Social assistance grants	Social security transfers
Sweden	1980	27.7	13.0	9.9	49.4
	1993	15.9	16.4	13.1	54.6
Germany	1980	25.4	3.3	12.0	59.3
	1993	26.8	3.1	10.9	59.2
UK	1980	28.4	5.9	19.5	46.3
	1993	25.9	4.7	28.4	41.0
US	1980	25.5	3.1	20.7	50.7
	1993	31.5	1.8	21.8	44.9

Sources: Social services, social security transfers and 1993 health-expenditure data from OECD, *Social Expenditure Statistics of OECD Member Countries*, Labour Market and Social Policy Occasional Papers (Paris, OECD, 1996); 1980 health expenditure data from OECD, *New Directions in Social Policy in OECD Countries* (Paris, OECD, 1994); social assistance figures from OECD, *National Accounts: Detailed Tables* (Paris, OECD, 1996)

welfare states. Yet the trajectory of change in the Swedish and British cases is clearly different, suggesting that partisan politics still matters.

[...]

The fact that the British and Swedish welfare states have become less service-oriented can partly be explained in terms of demographic changes and the maturation of social insurance systems (the extension of full pension benefits to all retired people). In these and other OECD countries final government consumption expenditure continued to grow (in real terms) through the 1980s; it simply grew less rapidly than spending on social security transfers. However, it would also appear to be the case that governments have preferred cutting the public sector to cutting entitlement programmes, and it is first and foremost the service components of welfare states that have been reformed according to market principles. This pattern of retrenchment and restructuring does not seem to accord well with Pierson's assessment of the political risks entailed when politicians challenge entrenched interests, following from the common public choice argument that concentrated interests generally prevail over diffuse interests, for public sector employees constitute the entrenched pro-welfare constituency *par excellence*.

What, then, accounts for the anti-service bias of welfare state retrenchment? Several arguments seem plausible. Consistent with Pierson's emphasis on the politics of blame avoidance, one might argue that the effects of cutting the public sector are less immediate and less tangible (or less visible) than the effects of cutting entitlement programmes. Public sector cutbacks will likely result in a deterioration in quality and this in turn might result in middle-class opt out, but such deterioration will not necessarily be proportionate to spending cuts and no one knows at which point middle-class opt out becomes a serious problem. Even social democratic politicians are likely to find the risks involved here more palatable than those entailed in cutting pension or unemployment benefits.

Second, the popular legitimacy of programmes based on the social insurance principle might be invoked to explain the anti-service bias of recent cutbacks. As Esping-Andersen argues with reference to the welfare states of continental Europe, the consensual manner in which such programmes were developed and the sense of entitlement that the insurance system produces make it very difficult to reform these transfer programmes.[14] Third, the preference for social-insurance welfarism may reflect anxieties about further European integration, insofar as EU legislation outlaws discrimination on the basis of nationality. Since social-insurance benefits are typically based on income from employment, such programmes sidestep the political problem of foreigners taking advantage of generous benefits.[15]

Most importantly perhaps, the patterns of retrenchment we have documented might be seen as a response to political pressure from a cross-class coalition of employers and workers in the export and multinational sectors. Both Peter Swenson and Herman Schwartz argue that with increased openness and intensified international competition, workers and employers in exposed sectors become acutely concerned with containing the upward pressure on domestic costs generated by large public sectors.[16] In this context a new political-economic cleavage between sheltered and exposed sectors opens up and the exposed sector coalition exerts increasing pressure for public sector reform. It is important to recognize that this coalition is based on compromise among its constituent units, rather than on a complete convergence of interests. Left to their own devices, export-oriented employers would probably have favoured across-the-board cuts in the welfare state, but the maintenance of basic social insurance entitlements is a condition for private sector unions to support public sector cutbacks and reforms.

This coalitional account works better for some countries than for others. In the British case electoral support for Thatcherism certainly had a broad cross-class character, but Mrs Thatcher's efforts to restructure the public sector did not involve the co-operation of private sector unions, and business support came mainly from the financial sector rather than from export-oriented manufacturers. The British case would have to be couched in terms of a cross-class coalition centred on financial interests, including the financial interests of working-class homeowners and shareholders, and forged electorally rather than organizationally.

Thinking about public sector restructuring in these terms, it should be noted that market-oriented reforms have had different consequences for different segments of the public sector labour force. In the British case the ratio of median public sector to private sector wages for blue-collar workers fell from 1.05 in 1984 to 0.98 in 1995, but the public-private ratio for white-collar workers remained stable at 1.09–1.10.[17] This divergence of fortunes helps explain why public sector unions were not able to mobilize more effective resistance to market-oriented reforms.

[...]

Whereas Pierson essentially accepts the class-power model associated with Korpi as a valid explanation of post-war welfare state expansion and argues that the politics of the welfare state have fundamentally changed, we believe that the coalitional approach suggested here sheds light on the past as well as the present. Societal interests and coalitional alignments have changed, but there is no need to invent a new set of analytical categories in order to explain current patterns of welfare state retrenchment and restructuring.

Notes

From *World Politics*, 51, 1998, pp. 67–98.

1 Paul Pierson, 'The New Politics of the Welfare State', *World Politics*, 48, January 1996, pp. 143–79; see also extract, pp. 309–19 above. Pierson's article builds on his book *Dismantling the Welfare State?*, New York, Cambridge University Press, 1994, which analyses the Thatcher and Reagan experiments in detail.

2 Pierson, op. cit., p. 150.

3 E.g. Walter Korpi, *The Democratic Class Struggle*, London, Routledge and Kegan Paul, 1983.

4 Pierson, op. cit., p. 174.

5 Pierson, op. cit., p. 171.

6 Gøsta Esping-Andersen, *The Three Worlds of Welfare Capitalism*, Cambridge, Polity Press, 1990. The importance of services relative to transfer payments constitutes the most obvious basis for distinguishing among 'institutional welfare states' (say, between Sweden and the Netherlands). Esping-Andersen's concept of 'de-commodification' partly captures but also blurs this distinction. Scoring very high on Esping-Andersen's de-commodification index, the Scandinavian welfare states have traditionally promoted labour-force participation and strengthened the power of wage earners as sellers of labour power (rather than reducing their dependence on the sale of labour power).

7 Cf. OECD, *Employment Outlook*, Paris, OECD, July 1996, ch. 3; and Pontusson, 'Wage Distribution and Labor-Market Institutions', in *Unions, Employers and Central Banks*, ed. Torben Iversen, Jonas Pontusson and David Soskice (New York, Cambridge University Press, 1999).

8 G. Burtless, 'Widening U.S. Income Inequality and the Growth of World Trade', Manuscript, Washington, DC, Brookings Institution, 1996.

9 OECD, *Employment Outlook* (Paris, OECD, July 1997), p. 177.

10 See David Rueda and Jonas Pontusson, 'Wage Inequality and Varieties of Capitalism', working paper, Institute for European Studies, Ithaca, NY, Cornell University, 1997.

11 See Ian Gough et al., 'Social Assistance in OECD Countries', *Journal of European Social Policy*, 7, February 1997, pp. 24–7. Of course, the percentage of the population receiving social assistance might also increase because of political decisions to broaden the coverage of social assistance programmes or to cut the benefits provided by more universalistic welfare programmes. By the same token, poverty must be measured in terms of market income as well as disposable income in order to distinguish the effects of market forces from the effects of changes in social policy. Finally, it should be noted that the figures in table 12 refer to relative poverty, as distinct from the absolute measures, such as the official US poverty line. The percentage of the US population living in households with a disposable income below the official poverty line fell from 22 per cent in 1960 to less than 12 per cent in 1973–9, and then began to rise, reaching 16–17 per cent in the early 1990s; see Rebecca Blank, *It Takes a Nation*, Princeton, NJ, Princeton University Press, 1997, p. 55.

12 Pierson op. cit., pp. 158–9. Cf. also Esping-Andersen, 'After the Golden Age', in *Welfare States in Transition*, ed. G. Esping-Andersen, London, Sage, 1996, pp. 10–11.

13 As state-owned corporations are not included in the OECD measure of government employment, these figures reflect the government agencies in corporate form but not the privatization of state-owned corporations.

14   Esping-Andersen, 'Welfare States without Work', in G. Esping-Andersen, *Welfare States in Transition*, London, Sage, 1996.

15   Cf. Wolfgang Streeck, 'Neo-Voluntarism: A New European Social Policy Regime?', in *Governance in the European Union*, ed. Fritz Scharpf, Philippe Schmitter and Wolfgang Streeck, London, Sage, 1996.

16   Herman M. Schwartz, 'Small States in Big Trouble: State Reorganization in Australia, Denmark, New Zealand and Sweden in the 1980s', *World Politics*, 46, 1994; and Petet Swenson, 'Labor and the Limits of the Welfare State', in *Bargaining for Change*, ed. Miriam Golden and Jonas Pontusson Ithaca, NY, Cornell University Press, 1992.

17   National Statistical Office, *New Earnings Survey*, London, various editions.

Part III

The Futures of Welfare

High-Risk Strategy

Will Hutton

The British are increasingly at risk. The chances of their jobs disappearing, of their incomes falling, of their homes being repossessed or being impossible to sell, of their families breaking up, of their networks of friendships disintegrating, have not been higher since the war.

There is a new source of inequality abroad. On top of the long-standing concerns about the growing gap between rich and poor, there is an increasing awareness of a new range of risks that are bringing fresh patterns of social distress and exclusion. Unemployment and low pay are no longer the sole measures of inequity and lack of social well-being; with the rise of new forms of casualized, temporary and contract forms of employment, even those on average incomes and above can become the victims of pressures beyond their control. They too can be left partially or completely excluded from their social networks.

The developments in the labour market have led to a new categorization of British society. [As shown in figure 12], there is a bottom 30 per cent of unemployed and economically inactive who are marginalized; another 30 per cent who, while in work, are in forms of employment that are structurally insecure; and there are only 40 per cent who can count themselves as holding tenured jobs which allow them to regard their income prospects with any certainty. But even the secure top 40 per cent know they are at risk; their numbers have been shrinking steadily [since the mid-1970s]. The 30/30/40 society is a proxy for the growth of the new inequality and of the new risks about the predictability and certainty of income that have spread across all occupations and social classes (figure 12).

Each category faces its own dilemmas and crises. For the bottom 30 per cent the risk is that poverty will turn into an inability even to subsist, and that marginalization will change into complete social and economic

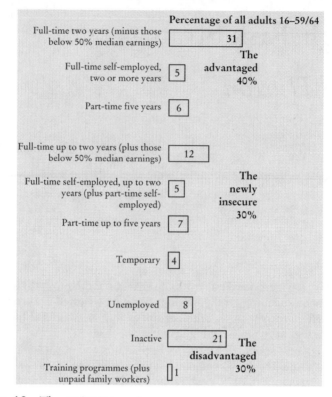

Figure 12   The 30/30/40 society

exclusion. Eight per cent of people are unemployed; 4 per cent have been out of work for more than a year – which means complete social exclusion. The work the unemployed do find is part-time, casualized or insecure, so that their lives consist of unemployment interspersed with periods of insecure semi-employment.

The worrying figure is the 21 per cent of the working population who are now economically inactive – of working age but not making them-selves available for work. [In the mid-1970s] this segment was mostly made up of women voluntarily withdrawing from the labour market to bring up children; now it is largely peopled by men of working age and single parents.

One in four men in Britain of working age is now unemployed or economically inactive. This statistic [rose] inexorably through recession, while the recovery checked its growth [during 1995; . . .] These are the men who have retired early (nearly half the men between fifty-five and sixty-five are now economically inactive); these are the million unskilled men who claim the renamed 'incapacity benefit'. Then there are unemployed women, and, worse, women who would like to work but find themselves trapped in unemployment, because under the social security rules every pound they earn is subtracted from their husbands' income support, leaving the household no better off. In 1979, some 6 per cent of households had neither adult partner working; now, computes Paul Gregg of the LSE (London School of Economics), this is 16 per cent. Life for these people is tough beyond the imagination of most of us.

But it is no bed of roses for the 30 per cent who are newly insecure. More and more risk has accrued on workforces as successive Employment Acts have reduced employee protection and as companies have come under intense and growing pressure from pension fund and insurance company shareholders to deliver the highest financial returns over the shortest period in the industrialized world. Companies can more profitably manage the ebb and flow of demand over the business cycle if they reduce their core staff to a minimum and hire additional workers on contracts which will allow them to be shed quickly if times get tough. The company bears less risk. The risk is borne by their fluctuating labour force. The famous example is of Burger King, where young workers clocked on when customers appeared; this reduced their wages to a derisory level but ensured they were only paid for the *minutes* they were needed.

There has been a marked growth in forms of work that are not 'tenured'. With full-time workers only qualifying for tenure after two years, the recent pick-up in full-time work means little. They can be laid off within two years as easily as they were hired. The rapid growth in the numbers of part-timers without any formal job security, contract workers, workers sacked and then rehired as self-employed, temporary, part-time and agency workers is the true indicator that employment conditions have changed; self-employment alone has doubled [since 1985]. Even those employers who want to hold out against the new trends are forced to conform. If they allow their wage costs to rise above the industry average, they face loss of market share and financial distress.

Here there is a gender effect. Most of the growth in part-time and insecure work has fallen to women, typically less unionized and more compliant. Many married women respond in surveys that they like such work because it allows them to juggle family responsibilities with earning. But as 70 per cent of all *new* part-time jobs are for sixteen hours or less, and so do not attract employment protection or any benefits such as holiday or sickness entitlement, such workers are highly at risk. Such work is becoming essential for family incomes – and women are slowly becoming less content. When the capacity to avoid repossession depends on earnings from an employer who can sack you at will, family stability hangs on a thread.

The last 40 per cent are the advantaged – from the workers still covered by union wage agreements to full-time, tenured employees working in the great organizations in the public and private sectors. The full-time self-employed [. . .] come into this category too. But their numbers are shrinking by 1 per cent a year on average. Market-testing, contracting-out, downsizing and delayering are steadily transferring workers into much less secure work patterns. By the year 2000, full-time tenured employment, around which stable family life has been constructed along with the capacity to service twenty-five-year mortgages, will be a minority form of work. And as the risk of insecure or no employment grows, so the social institutions and systems built up [since the Second World War] to protect against risk are decaying. The welfare state is more threadbare, and eligibility for income support – itself worth less and less in relation to average incomes – ever tougher. Trade unions' capacity to protect against sudden and sharp deteriorations in working conditions has been reduced. The British labour market, reports the OECD, ranks bottom in the league table of industrialized countries.

The individual means to protect against risk are no stronger. With nearly 70 per cent of homes owned by their occupier, one bulwark against financial calamity has been rising house prices. [After 1950], the average British household steadily grew more wealthy on the back of the great house price boom; but the fall in house prices in real terms during the 1990s caused the most savage reverse in personal wealth since the war. The operation of the housing market, with more than a million homeowners having mortgages that exceed the value of their house (negative equity) and every mortgagee paying high real interest rates to own an asset that is falling in value is now a source of insecurity in its own right.

Private insurance companies have become more selective about insuring those whose circumstances indicate that they might claim, making basic protection more expensive, sometimes impossible, to obtain. Millions hold personal pension plans that will pay them a minimal pension in retirement, worth substantially less than the former state earnings-related pension. What financial calamity in the event of unemployment or loss of income really means is captured in one telling statistic from the Institute of Fiscal Studies: half of British households have £450 *or less* in savings. Risk has grown, but the protections have shrunk.

All this has been justified by a narrow conception of 'efficiency'. It is said to be efficient for firms to have lean core workforces; for the provision of welfare to be privatized; for unions to be less powerful. But perversely the promotion of uncertainty, risk and insecurity has made the operation of the economy as a *system* less efficient. It has weakened the growth and stability of demand; it has reduced firms' incentives to invest in their workforces and their infrastructure; it has inflated current public expenditure and reduced the tax base.

One of the features of the recovery has been weak investment growth – with firms repeatedly saying in surveys that they are worried by the need to make high financial returns in the context of uncertain future demand. Consumers have become price-conscious, leery about buying big-ticket items and undertaking long-term commitments. How can they behave otherwise? David Miles, chief economist of Merrill Lynch, calculates that the average variability of income for average workers has grown by half since 1968; we are 50 per cent more likely to have a violent downward swing in our income. The individual firm may find it efficient to reduce its core workforce and displace risk on to part-timers and contract workers; but in aggregate the impact is to make incomes more volatile and individuals more cautious. Demand becomes weaker and more variable. To explain the crisis in the housing market, and the implications for the house-building and construction industries, look no further than the 30/30/40 society.

Nor does it make sense for government finances. Tax revenues this year will undershoot the Treasury's projections by up to £4 billion; low-paid part-timers and short-term contract workers do not generate the same income tax yield as their full-time equivalents, and their spending, biased to subsistence goods that attract no VAT, means that indirect taxation grows less rapidly as well.

Simultaneously social security spending, despite ever tighter eligibility tests, increases as the numbers qualifying for housing benefit assistance and income support rise remorselessly. The freezing of the growing 30/30/40 society would have saved the Chancellor the £3 billion in spending cuts he is searching for this autumn.

The changes make no sense in terms of Britain's wider social structures. The struggle to maintain living standards has meant ever-longer working hours. According to a survey [in October 1995] by recruitment agency Austin Knight, two-thirds of British workers [worked] more than a forty-hour week, while a quarter [worked] more than fifty hours. The rise in stress is marked, and such long hours necessarily reduce the leisure-time that parents can spend with their children or with each other.

Nor is it only parenting that suffers; the capacity to sustain friendships outside work, to become a member of local clubs and societies, to play a part in the local neighbourhood, reduces as hours worked rise. The forty-hour week, along with paid holidays, pensions and sickness benefit, is one of the great social achievements of the twentieth century. It, too, is at risk.

The forces generating the 30/30/40 society could be arrested. A more determined assault on long-term unemployment; extending employment rights to those not in full-time work; relieving companies of the pressure to make sky-high financial returns; constructing more solid systems of social support; placing less emphasis on home ownership as the only form of housing tenure – all would help. To act in this way is supposed to be inefficient. But *not* to act in this way is more inefficient still. In the long run a 30/30/40 society is neither desirable nor sustainable. One day the pendulum will swing back because it must.

Note

Originally published in *The Guardian*, 30 October 1995; this version from *The Stakeholding Society*, Cambridge, Polity Press, 1998, pp. 173–8.

The Implications of Ecological Thought for Social Welfare

Tony Fitzpatrick

Introduction

Social justice and ecological sustainability do not necessarily go together. The objective of redistributing wealth and opportunities is not, in itself, concerned with *how* such goods are generated in the first place, despite the fact that any future success in reducing poverty will be short-lived if anti-poverty strategies are based upon dwindling resources. Equally, it is possible to imagine futures where the price paid for sustainability is a profound social *injustice*, though few at present regard this as either desirable or inevitable.

Many have therefore recognized the need to evolve approaches to social justice which are compatible with ecological sustainability, and vice versa.

[...]

To date, those seeking to understand and contribute to the debate on Green social policy have basically had two starting-points. The first of these was founded by those Green activists and theorists who have considered how welfare institutions should be redesigned to make them consistent with a Green society (Irvine and Ponton, 1988; Kemp and Wall, 1990). Yet the debate here has often been quite general and inter-disciplinary, so that either social policy has been neglected or the discussion has tended to consist of social blueprints and shopping-lists of reforms. The second starting-point has been provided by those social policy researchers who have incorporated ecological perspectives into their work (Ferris, 1991, 1993; Cahill, 1991, 1994, 1995; Weisenthal,

1993). Here, though, pragmatism has dominated to such an extent that this work has revealed little of ecologism's more visionary implications.[1]

In short, ecologism has not achieved the kind of systematic and comprehensive influence upon the academic study of social policy which has been accomplished by feminism, for instance. Consequently, there are even fewer examples of actual Green social policies than there are of feminist ones. The aim of this article is to help rectify that lack of influence.

[...] [W]hat might an ecological *model* of social welfare look like?

The answer which the present article gives to this question is divided into three parts. First, a sketch is given of the main features of the critiques which ecologists direct towards current social welfare provision. Second, the productivist model of welfare to which most social policy institutions, debates and reform proposals might be thought to conform at present is briefly outlined. Finally, an alternative ecological, or non-productivist, model of welfare is presented.

Ecological Critiques

[...]

Associated largely, though not always, with neo-Marxists, the suspicion that the welfare state operates as a system of social control [...] is shared by many ecologists.[2] Even the more de-commodified welfare regimes, such as Sweden, have only provided a highly conditional freedom from the market, the price of which has been the treatment of individuals as the clients of administrative rationality, impersonal bureaucracy and professional expertise (Gould, 1993: 222–33). Left-leaning governments have attempted to socialize capitalism, while leaving intact the very social relations which are inseparable *from* capitalism. [...]

Additionally, though, ecologists share with mainstream democratic socialists and (some) social democrats the notion that social cohesion and an equality of condition are mutually inclusive (Weston, 1986; Ryle, 1988). Without greater equality, the discourse of cohesion and solidarity remains purely rhetorical – a device for loading more burdens, disguised as obligations, upon the poorest. Without some notion of solidarity, however, an equalization of conditions is only a remote possibility: a conception of an overarching common good is needed to secure the legitimacy and popular acceptance of egalitarian social and public policies. And for ecologists, the common good must reflect the necessity of ecological *goods* (O'Neill, 1993).

This emphasis upon a common good sometimes leads social conservatives to make associations between conservatism and ecologism (Naess, 1989; Gray, 1993: 124–77). Philosophically, both are thought to represent an ethic of conservation and nurture, as well as a recognition of the limitations of rationalism and praxis. As such, conservatism and ecologism safeguard the unarticulated lifeworld of trust and empathy which each generation must hand on to the next. Liberals and socialists, meanwhile, are condemned for treating the world as a resource to be appropriated, manipulated and moulded to conform to the conceits of human *hubris*. The function of social policies, therefore, should be to conserve rather than to 'intervene'.

[...]

[E]cologism shares with feminism the recognition that existing social policies are heavily dependent upon two things (Merchant, 1992: 194–200): first, the unpaid activity undertaken, usually by women, in the informal sphere; and second, the low-paid activity performed, mostly by women, in the formal labour market. Consequently, social policies informed by both Green and feminist values require three basic conditions: the emergence of a labour market which is not split between a centre and a periphery; a recognition of the importance of informal activity; and free movement between the formal and informal spheres, which itself requires that wage-earning and income maintenance are decoupled more fully than at present.

But [...] ecological critiques of social welfare bear their own unique features. A principal feature of Green thought is a reaction against what has been called the 'logic of industrialism', a logic to which the above ideologies have subscribed (with the probable exception of feminism). To put it at its simplest, the logic of industrialism says that ever higher levels of economic growth are the necessary, and often the sufficient, condition of social and personal well-being (Pierson, 1991: 92–4). For Greens, however, this is a spurious and untenable correlation to make.

According to this critique, the welfare state is that product of modern industrialization which has done a great deal to humanize the worst aspects of early capitalism. But the price paid for this 'humanization' is the expectation that state welfare would harmonize with, and perhaps even contribute to, industrial and, latterly, post-industrial growth. Consequently, social welfare has become *dependent* upon open-ended economic growth. It is a belief in the necessity of this 'welfare dependency' which characterizes what is perhaps the most important consensus underlying all social policy debates, and it is a consensus which appears to be stronger than ever. Growth for growth's sake has become the leviathan of modern societies: an amoral force which recognizes no constraints beyond its own inexorable dynamic. The general slump in national growth rates since the 1970s has only served to confirm, for many, the *desirability* of the logic of industrialism.

[...]

According to ecologism [...], the logic of industrialism will have to be fundamentally revised, sooner rather than later, since it is neither sustainable nor efficacious. It is not sustainable because there are limits to growth in a finite world (Meadows et al., 1992). A welfare state which depends upon growth, and which largely fuels demands for more, is helping to exhaust the very resources upon which it depends. It is not efficacious because what is created is a *preventative* system of welfare which tends to treat the symptoms rather than the causes of social problems, i.e. it can lighten the stressful demands of too much work, consumption and competition, but does little to prevent such alienating effects from being created in the first place.[3] For a progressive politics the lesson is clear: the radicalism of state welfare has been inseparable from its conservatism, in that it has 'crowded out' other desirable reforms, such as socialization and economic and political decentralization (Pierson, 1991: 94).

The question which must animate attempts to design and implement Green social policies is this: how do we defend, indeed reaffirm, the principles of social welfare while making those principles consistent with Green critiques? The following distinction between a productivist and an ecological model of welfare may shed some light on possible answers to this question.

[...]

A Productivist Model of Welfare

[...]

The productivist model implies three principal elements. [...] First ecologists object to the *indiscriminate* character of growth upon which modern economies depend. [...] Economic indicators such as GNP and GDP are widely regarded as ecologically amoral, if not immoral, formulated as they were to meet the needs of post-war expansion. [...] Ecologists commonly demand that such economic yardsticks be replaced with ones which treat ecological factors as central. Without such a change of emphasis, a universal recognition of the need for an ecologically friendly economy, presumably on a global level, is unlikely to emerge.

[...]

The second element of the productivist model is the *employment ethic* which dominates, to an overwhelming extent, the political and economic debates dealing with social policy. This ethic refers to the fact that wage-earning activity in the formal labour market tends to be valued over all other forms of human activity. Feminists have long highlighted the extent to which the contribution made by domestic labour to social well-being is taken for granted by the bulk of public, economic and social policies. Activities such as child-bearing and child-raising are certainly valued, but the prevalence of the employment ethic ensures that even these are marginalized in importance when it comes to practical decisions about the distribution of resources. The employment ethic derives from two assumptions and is, therefore, embodied in two of the principal 'formations' of modern societies: the sexual division of labour and the wage-contract.

The first assumption, which continues to influence policy making and institutional organization without necessarily corresponding to social reality, insists that social cohesion and continuity through time is almost entirely dependent upon the reproduction of given relations and interactions. To put it simply, the nuclear, heterosexual family is regarded as *the* agency of intergenerational continuity and those family units and households which embody alternative relations are treated with suspicion by commercial, state and welfare institutions.

[...]

In this context, then, the employment ethic may be regarded as the moral flip-side of the sexual division of labour. Domestic labour, in addition to the entire sector of informal care, has been downgraded, and social roles and identities have been organized and distributed around the norm of wage-earning activity. The employment ethic secures, to a considerable extent, the practical and ideological maintenance of the family and the reproduction of existing society.

The second assumption, therefore, is that jobs should be the principal means by which income and status is distributed to the vast majority of people. We have become used to hearing the ecological critique which says that we need to tax less of what we want, i.e. jobs, and more of what we do not want, i.e. pollution. This critique is as much aimed at the human waste of unemployment as it is at natural wastage. Yet it is usually allied to a further insistence, which is far less well known, that jobs no longer be regarded as central to well-being. Unemployment is held to be the consequence of a society addicted to employment, yet unable to satisfy its addiction. Creating jobs by reducing the importance of jobs, e.g. through large-scale working-hour reductions, is held by ecologists to be the *sine qua non* of post-employment welfare.

[...]

The emphasis upon indiscriminate growth and the employment ethic adds up to the notion that welfare equals the material affluence to be earned through observation of, and conformity to, organizational rules and standards. In personal terms, this comes down to the common instinct that our individual worth should be measured against a materialistic yardstick. Given the importance that has just been assigned to wages and jobs, this is hardly surprising. You are what you own, what you drive, what you do for a living and where you go on holiday. This is what I would term the 'accumulative impulse', the last of the productivist model's main ingredients.

[...]

In short, the productivist model of welfare reveals an internal dynamic. Each of the three main elements of the model depend upon and, in turn, perpetuate each of the others. It is against the dynamic force of such productivism that we might see a non-productivist model as having emerged from the work of ecological movements and theorists.

An Ecological Model of Welfare

Each of the three main elements of the ecological model corresponds to each of the elements of the productivist model which I have just outlined.

[...]

There are basically three forms of ecological, *discriminate* growth. First, there is a *negative*, recidivist 'anti-growth'. This envisages a decline in both absolute and relative living standards, and the return to a pre-industrial mode of life, albeit in a post-industrial, low entropy setting.[4] Second, there is *steady-state* growth where we do not extract anything from the earth which is not renewable and where we do not pollute beyond the earth's capacity to absorb such pollution and renew itself (Daly and Cobb, 1990). Third, there is *sustainable* growth which does envisage a depletion of non-renewable resources if sufficient justification can be given and if renewable resources are available as substitutes, e.g. solar, wind and wave energy as eventual replacements for fossil fuels (Pearce, 1993).

I shall assume that negative growth is out of the question for both moral and pragmatic reasons. [...]

So far, it is the 'growth optimists' who have dominated the debate. The conclusions of the Brandt Report (1980) and of the Brundtland Commission (WCED, 1987) envisaged a continuing role for growth, as traditionally conceived, where the present generation can be made better off without making future generations worse off (Solow, 1996: 16). The 'growth sceptics', by contrast, go somewhat further. They agree with the optimists that the scale of economic activity must both alter and be reduced, but they insist that this throws into question the entire efficacy of economic growth itself. So, whereas the optimists favour 'equilibrium' or sustainable growth, the sceptics favour steady-state or zero growth.

[...]

Both optimists and sceptics recognize the need to make room for a redefined, non-economistic conception of welfare, one which could be adapted into a set of economic indicators which are more ecologically friendly than either GDP or GNP. One such measurement of wealth *and* welfare is Ekins's Adjusted National Product which, through sophisticated accounting, would take human capital, natural capital and sustainability into account (Ekins, 1986; Anderson, 1991; Jackson and Marks, 1994). Another alternative is the Index of Sustainable Economic Welfare which, according to its creators, Daly and Cobb (1990), reveals an improvement in social well-being in the 1960s but a decline ever since, due to subsequent increases in private affluence and public squalor.

So, regardless of whether sustainable or steady-state growth is favoured, an important starting-point in resisting the logic of industrialism seems to be the adoption of ecologically biased economic indicators as an instrument for the raising of popular awareness about the need for ecological policies.[5] Such indicators bear obvious implications for social welfare.

The last fifty years of social policy has been dominated by political squabbles over how much is spent and which party spends the most. Arguments centre around public expenditure and, more recently, around efficiency-gains and productivity-gains. And to the extent that attention has moved away from government spending, it has only come to focus upon individualistic issues of lifestyles and behaviour. This twin obsession of expenditure on the one hand and individualism on the other is perhaps inevitable in a political culture which is reluctant to address underlying causes. But according to a thesis which might be termed 'welfare associationalism', such reluctance is no longer permissible.

Essentially, welfare associationalists insist that the dominance of the state and market sectors in social policy making is now detrimental to personal, social and ecological well-being. The state is still required as a guarantor of universal citizenship, and the market may still assist us in resisting the centralizing tendencies of the state, but welfare association-alists wish to move beyond the discourse of 'welfare collectivism versus welfare pluralism' in order to foster a civil society of equal autonomy (Lipietz, 1992; Hirst, 1994; Cohen and Rogers, 1995; Held, 1995). This means that the welfare state can no longer be a force separate from every-day lives and practices, nor something to be 'dissolved' into a series of impersonal, commercialized contracts. According to welfare association-alism, such (dis)integrative formalism must be supplanted by a 're-integrative informalism' of non-market decentralization and social parti-cipation, where individuals and groups either produce the welfare services which they consume or, where this is unrealistic, have the greatest practic-able control over their design and delivery.[6]

[...]

If this is to occur then a number of things must happen, one of which is that the employment ethic must itself give way to the second element of the ecological model: a work ethic. The work ethic implies a revaluation of the non-wage-earning, informal activity which is currently margin-alized by the wage contract. It may seem counter-productive to contrast an employment with a work ethic, when I have pointed out how easily people mean the former when they refer to the latter. Even so, it is important to understand that ecologists, like feminists, do not complain about work *per se*, nor about the centrality of work to human well-being, but about the reduction of work to employment or waged labour in the job market.

[...]

Against those who would reassert the centrality of the employment ethic as a necessary condition of social and family obligations, most ecologists regard non-employment work as the cornerstone of a sustainable society which is at ease with itself. Employment assessed in terms of non-employment criteria would reward individuals far more than the over-worked/underemployed economy in which we currently live. [...]

A work ethic which values informal, unremunerated activity also ques-tions the assumption that jobs should be the principal means through which income and status are distributed. As an alternative to the assump-tion that most people, most of the time, should depend upon either earn-ings or transfers, ecologists have promoted the idea of multiple sources of income. Earnings and transfers may then be received in addition to other forms of income: Social Dividend, Basic Income, Citizen's Wage, Green currency. The intended effect of this is not so much to devalue the formal economy as to revalue the informal one.

For instance, ecologists have been long-standing advocates of a Basic Income paid unconditionally to all.[7] [...]

Local Employment and Trading Systems (LETS) are often advocated as initiatives with a lot of ecological potential (Dauncey, 1988; Dobson, 1993; Lang, 1994). [...]

The final element of the ecological model, self-actualization, refers to what is a constant emphasis in the ecological literature: the necessity of changes in lifestyle expectations, values and, for some, consciousness itself. Such an emphasis deserves criticism if it is contained within an idealistic and non-materialistic frame of reference. It may be, for instance, that taxation should fall more heavily upon consumption than at present, as most Greens advocate, but unless such a shift in the tax burden is set within the overall context of a progressive tax and transfer system, then ecologists risk aligning themselves with the regressive policies of modern Conservatism.

Yet, without a post-materialist insistence upon divorcing our sense of personal worth from our standard of living, a progressive politics is unlikely to make much of a comeback in the future. A materialist society is always more likely to reward those who advocate self-interest and selfishness than those for whom altruism should be the social priority. Post-materialism, by contrast, offers a new basis for both self-interest and altruism.

[...]

Conclusion

[...]

Social welfare, as it has developed over the twentieth century, is very much a child of industrial capitalism and has internalized most, if not all, of the aims and assumptions of its socio-economic surroundings. The task for a Green social policy is not only to consider how social welfare may be made compatible with a sustainable society, but to speculate as to how social policies can themselves effect sustainability. But this is no longer a task for the future. The future is already here.

Notes

From *Critical Social Policy*, 18, 1, 1998, pp. 5–26. I would like to thank Hartley Dean and Michael Cahill for their encouragement and advice.

1 Though Michael Cahill reminds me that this is because of a desire to counter the Green fundamentalism of people such as Bahro (1986). Even so, few within the academy have dared follow in the footsteps of the visionary economist James Robertson (1983, 1985, 1989, 1994; cf. Cahill, 1995).

2 The [...] work of Claus Offe (1993, 1996) and James O'Connor (1988) falls largely into both ecological and neo-Marxist camps.

3 As has been long argued by one of the main influences on Green thought, Ivan Illich (1975).

4 We might think of William Morris (1970) as perhaps the earliest theorist of post-industrialism.

5 I leave aside the obvious point that the introduction of such indicators is unlikely to occur until popular awareness has already been raised to a certain level.

6 The terms integrative/disintegrative formalism and reintegrative informalism are all inspired by the political sociology of Habermas. Broadly speaking, the former corresponds to the productivist model of welfare, whereas the latter, as a strategy of welfare associationalism, corresponds to the ecological model. However, an exploration of these ideas and concepts will have to wait for another time.

7 See Johnson (1973) and Ekins (1986) as well as the debate conducted in *Critical Social Policy* [...] (Keane and Owens, 1986–7; Rustin, 1986–7).

References

Anderson, V., *Alternative Economic Indicators*, London, Routledge, 1991.

Bahro, R., *Building the Green Movement*, London, Heretic Books, 1986.

Beck, U., *Risk Society*, London, Sage, 1992.

Beenstock, M., *The World Economy in Transition*, London, George Allen and Unwin, 1983.

Brandt, W. (chairman), *North-South: A Programme for Survival*, London, Pan Books, 1980.

Cahill, M., 'The Greening of Social Policy?', in *Social Policy Review 1990–91*, ed. N. Manning Harlow, Essex, Longman, 1991.

Cahill, M., *The New Social Policy*, Oxford, Blackwell, 1994.

Cahill, M., 'Robertson', in *Modern Thinkers on Welfare*, ed. V. George and R. Page, Hemel Hempstead, Prentice Hall/Harvester Wheatsheaf, 1995.

Cohen, J. and Rogers, J., *Associations and Democracy*, London, Verso, 1995.

Daly, H. and Cobb, J., *For the Common Good*, London, Green Print, 1990.

Dauncey, G., *After the Crash*, London, Green Print, 1988.

Deleuze, G. and Guattari, F., *Anti-Oedipus: Capitalism and Schizophrenia*, New York, Viking Press, 1977.

Dobson, A., *Green Political Thought: An Introduction*, London, Routledge, 2nd edition, 1995.

Dobson, R., *Bringing the Economy Home from the Market*, Oxford, Jon Carpenter, 1993.

Ekins, P., ed., *The Living Economy*, London, Routledge, 1986.

Ferris, J., 'Green Politics and the Future of Welfare', in *Social Policy Review 1990–91*, ed. N. Manning, Harlow, Essex, Longman, 1991.

Ferris, J., 'Ecological versus Social Rationality: Can there be Green Social Policies?', in *The Politics of Nature: Explorations in Green Political Theory*, ed. A. Dobson and P. Lucardie, London, Routledge, 1993.

Fitzpatrick, T., 'Postmodernism, Welfare and Radical Politics', *Journal of Social Policy*, 25(3), 1996, pp. 303–20.

Fitzpatrick, T., 'Democratic Socialism and Social Democracy', in *New Political Thought: An Introduction*, ed. A. Lent, London, Lawrence and Wishart, 1998a.

Fitzpatrick, T., 'New Welfare Associations: An Alternative Model of Well-being', in *Storming the Millennium: A New Politics of Change*, ed. T. Jordan and A. Lent, London, Lawrence and Wishart, 1998b.

George, V. and Wilding, P., *Welfare and Ideology*, Hemel Hempstead, Harvester Wheatsheaf, 1994.

Gorz, A., *Critique of Economic Reason*, London, Verso, 1989.

Gorz, A., *Capitalism, Socialism, Ecology*, London, Verso, 1994.

Gould, A., *Capitalist Welfare Systems: A Comparison of Japan, Britain and Sweden*, London and New York, Longman, 1993.

Gray, J., *Beyond the New Right: Markets, Government and the Common Environment*, London, Routledge, 1993.

Held, D., *Democracy and the Global Order*, Cambridge, Polity Press, 1995.

Hirst, P., *Associative Democracy*, Cambridge, Polity Press, 1994.

Illich, I., *Tools for Conviviality*, London, Fontana, 1975.

Irvine, S. and Ponton, A., *A Green Manifesto*, London, Macdonald Optima, 1988.

Jackson, T. and Marks, N., *Index of Sustainable Economic Welfare*, Stockholm, Stockholm Environment Institute in co-operation with the New Economics Foundation, 1994.

Johnson, W., 'The Guaranteed Income as an Environmental Measure', in *Toward a Steady-State Economy*, ed. H. Daly, San Francisco, W. H. Freeman & Co., 1973.

Keane, J. and Owens, J., 'The Full Employment Illusion', *Critical Social Policy*, 6(3), 1986–7, pp. 4–8.

Kemp, P. and Wall, D., *A Green Manifesto for the 1990s*, Harmondsworth, Penguin, 1990.

Lang, P., *LETS Work: Rebuilding the Local Economy*, Bristol, Grover Books, 1994.

Lipietz, A., *Towards a New Economic Order: Postfordism, Ecology and Democracy*, Cambridge, Polity Press, 1992.

Meadows, D. H., Meadows, D. L. and Randers, J., *Beyond the Limits: Global Collapse or a Sustainable Future*, London, Earthscan, 1992.

Merchant, C., *Radical Ecology*, London, Routledge, 1992.

Morris, W., *News from Nowhere*, London, Routledge, 1970.

Naess, A., *Ecology, Community and Lifestyle*, Cambridge, Cambridge University Press, 1989.

O'Connor, J., 'Capitalism, Nature, Socialism: A Theoretical Introduction', *Capitalism, Nature, Socialism*, 1(1), 1988, pp. 11–38.

O'Neill, J., *Ecology, Policy and Politics: Human Well-Being and the Natural World*, London, Routledge, 1993.

Offe, C., 'A Non-productivist Design for Social Policies', in *Work and Citizenship in the New Europe*, ed. H. Coenan and P. Leisink, Aldershot, Edward Elgar, 1993.

Offe, C., *Modernity and the State: East, West*, Cambridge, Polity Press, 1996.

Pearce, D., *Blueprint 3: Measuring Sustainable Development*, London, Earthscan, 1993.

Pepper, D., *Eco-Socialism: From Deep Ecology to Social Justice*, London, Routledge, 1993.

Pepper, D., *Modern Environmentalism: An Introduction*, London, Routledge, 1996.

Pierson, C., *Beyond the Welfare State*, Cambridge, Polity Press, 1991.

Report of the Commission on Social Justice, *Social Justice: Strategies for National Renewal*, London, Vintage, 1994.

Robertson, J., *The Sane Alternative: A Choice of Futures*, Shropshire, James Robertson, 2nd edition, 1983.

Robertson, J., *Future Work*, London, Gower/Maurice Temple Smith, 1985.

Robertson, J., *Future Wealth: A New Economics for the Twenty-first Century*, London, Cassell, 1989.

Robertson, J., *Benefits and Taxes: A Radical Strategy*, London, New Economics Foundation, 1994.

Rustin, M., 'The Non-Obsolescence of the Right to Work', *Critical Social Policy*, 6(3), 1986–7, pp. 8–13.

Ryle, M., *Ecology and Socialism*, London, Radius, 1988.

Sherman, B. and Judkins, P., *Licensed to Work*, London, Cassell, 1995.

Solow, R., 'Intergenerational Equity, Yes – But What about Inequity Today?', in United Nations Development Programme, *Human Development Report 1996*, New York and Oxford, Oxford University Press, 1996.

Van Parijs, P., ed., *Arguing for Basic Income*, London, Verso, 1992.

Van Parijs, P., Closing address to the Sixth International Congress of the Basic Income European Network, Vienna International Centre, Vienna, 12–14 September 1996.

WCED (World Commission on Environment and Development), *Our Common Future*, Oxford, Oxford University Press, 1987.

Weisenthal, H., *Realism in Green Politics: Social Movements and Ecological Reform in Germany*, Manchester, Manchester University Press, 1993.

Weston, J., ed., *Red and Green: The New Politics of the Environment*, London, Pluto Press, 1986.

Basic Income and the Two Dilemmas of the Welfare State

Philippe van Parijs

Can we avoid a social tragedy? Can we help entering the next century with our welfare states in disarray, with labour's hard-won conquests under deadly threat, and with a growing minority of citizens losing all hope of ever getting a decent job and securing a decent standard of living throughout their existence? I believe we can, but also that it won't be easy. We shall badly need intelligence and will, to come to terms with two central dilemmas.

First Dilemma: Fighting Exploitation versus Fighting Exclusion

Improving the incomes and working conditions of the poorest workers – whether directly through a statutory minimum wage and other aspects of labour law or indirectly through improving the levels of the replacement incomes granted to those out of work – has long been a central objective of our welfare states. But because exclusion from paid work is also a major form of deprivation, another central objective must be to fight against unemployment. The tension between these two objectives generates our first dilemma. Under a number of (un-Keynesian) assumptions that have become realistic enough, the more you do to improve the material situation of the poorest among the workers, the scarcer the jobs become, and the more people there are who are deprived of the privilege of having one. Thus the two objectives potentially pull in opposite directions; and as soon as unemployment ceases to be a marginal phenomenon, this leads to an acute dilemma.

This dilemma can be highlighted by starting from the dramatic explosion of inequalities in gross earnings that has been observed in much of the Western world [since the early 1980s]. The exact pattern of causation is disputed. But it is bound to include such factors as worldwide outlet expansion, increased competition on both labour and goods markets and the nature and distribution of the skills made more crucial by the computer revolution. In both the US and Western Europe, the higher gross earnings have risen considerably; but at the bottom end, there is a striking difference. Owing precisely to the better social protection of both the employed and the unemployed, what has led in the US to a sizeable fall in the lower categories of earnings has led in Europe to a considerable permanent increase – across cycles – in the proportion of people excluded from gainful employment. The very success (however partial) of Europe's fight against exploitation is making exclusion the dominant form of social injustice. Is there a way out of this painful dilemma between the fight against exploitation and the fight against exclusion, between our concern with poverty and our concern with unemployment? Yes, there is.

Along with a growing number of people across Western Europe,[1] I have been arguing that any realistic and desirable solution to this dilemma must involve the introduction of a comprehensive minimum income guarantee that takes the form, *not* of a means-tested safety net in which people get stuck – as illustrated by the UK's basic social security, Germany's *Sozialhilfe*, France's *revenu minimum d'insertion*, etc. – but of a genuine unconditional floor. Under various names – basic income, social dividend, *Grundeinkommen*, *reddito di cittadinanza*, *allocation universelle*, etc., this idea is being proposed as a key component of the backbone of a positive progressive project for a post-neo-liberal, post-communist Europe. Of course, because of the principled though partial disconnection between labour and income it implies, this proposal calls for some quite radical rethinking – not least in those parties whose very name makes it clear that they regard (paid) labour as central. But contrary to what is sometimes said, it does not rely on some absurdly optimistic assumption of abundance. Nor does it give up the aim of full employment, at any rate in the important sense of trying to give everyone the possibility of doing meaningful paid work. Indeed, something like a basic income is part of any realistic strategy for achieving it.

Ever wider circles of people are beginning to see some sense in this bold claim, as they start realizing the narrow limits of what can be expected from such alternative policies as general working time reduction or active labour market policies, and as they start sharing the following crucial insights. Coupled with a corresponding reduction in all other benefits and in the net minimum wage, basic income can be viewed as an employment subsidy given to the potential worker rather than to the employer, with crucially distinctive implications as to the type of low-productivity job that is thereby made viable. Secondly, because it is given irrespective of employment status, the introduction of a basic income abolishes or reduces the unemployment trap, not only by making more room for a positive income differential between total idleness and some work, but even more by providing the administrative security which will enable many people to take the risk of accepting a job or creating their own. Thirdly, basic income can be viewed as a soft strategy for job-sharing, by providing all with a small unconditional sabbatical pay, and thereby making it more affordable for many either to relinquish their job temporarily in order to get a break, go self-employed or retrain, or to work durably on a more part-time basis.

The combined effect of these three processes should lead to a far more flexible working of the labour market, with significantly more stepping-stone, training-intensive, often part-time jobs. Such jobs must be paid little because they represent a risky investment on the part of the employer in a free human being who could leave at any time; and they could acceptably be paid little because the pay would supplement an income to which the workers are unconditionally entitled and which therefore enables them to filter out the jobs that are not sufficiently attractive in themselves or in terms of the prospects they offer.

Of course, the size of this effect will be very sensitive to the level of the basic income and to the package of labour-market and tax-and-benefit institutional adjustments that will need to accompany its introduction. But if embedded in an appropriate package, even a modest basic income could put a halt to the growing dualization and demoralization of our socio-economic system. Under present conditions, the indignation of the jobless who are morally and legally expected to keep looking for what many know they will never find is matched by the outrage of those who subsidize with their social security contributions the idleness of people who are overtly transgressing the rules of the game. Once it stops being utopian to believe that all those who wish to work can find a job which earns them (when added to the unconditional part of their income) enough to live on, the conditions attached to supplementary entitlements – typically, unemployment benefits restricted to active job-seekers – can more realistically and more legitimately be expected to be enforced. The introduction of an unconditional basic income would thereby also make it possible to rehabilitate the social insurance aspect of our welfare systems. Consequently, whereas a well-intentioned gradual increase in the real level of the safety net could rightly be feared further to disturb the working of the labour market, a well-embedded gradual lifting of the floor can be expected to address both the poverty and the unemployment problem.

Second Dilemma: Economic Capacity versus Political Capacity

Whether or not one is willing to introduce a basic income and make it a central component of our welfare states, one seems faced with a second dilemma which was neatly, though shockingly, illustrated by a full-page advert published some time ago in Belgian newspapers on behalf of the (socialist) president of the Walloon government. The advert starts with a copy of a number of large cheques made out by various companies which had decided to settle or expand in Wallonia. The headline, and the punch-line of the message, reads: 'What unites us today is no longer charity but business.'

Here is, then, our second dilemma. *Either* you try to formulate and implement your ideal of social justice in one region or in one nation, but then you soon find out that, for a number of mutually reinforcing reasons, the potential mobility of savings, investment, skilled labour and consumer demand is now such in Europe that the only aim you can afford in all areas of policy – social, educational, environmental and so on – is none other than 'business', as the advert put it. The economic constraints are so powerful that you are compelled to run the state as if it were a firm and to make competitiveness your paramount concern. *Or* you try to give yourself some leeway by attempting to formulate and implement your ideal of social justice on a large scale – typically, [. . .] the European Union – but then you are soon faced with the powerful obstacles that stem from a widespread distrust of highly centralized institutions, from a lack of identification and hence of spontaneous solidarity between residents of the various areas, and from the difficulty of generating a common public debate across national and linguistic boundaries about the extent and shape of the solidarity you advocate.

Is there a way out of this second dilemma? Once again, I think there is, and one in which basic income has some role to play. I shall here make no attempt even to sketch the broad outlines of what I believe [would be] an adequate solution. Let me just state two firm convictions to which I have been led by a close observation of the debate around the regional aspect of redistribution in Europe and in my own country [Belgium], whose very existence is contingent upon the preservation of a nationwide social security system. One is that a high level of structural redistribution across the borders of broadly autonomous political entities can be sustained only if it takes the form of an interpersonal transfer system, rather than of grants to the governments of the beneficiary entities. The other conviction is that, especially if the political entities involved are culturally and linguistically very different, such a system can be sustained only if on both the contribution and the benefit sides it can operate using extremely simple and uncontroversial information. Fatal resentment is far less likely to arise, for example, if all that needs checking on the benefit side is whether [particular individuals exist] and how old they are, rather than whether they really need psychiatric treatment or truly are involuntarily unemployed.

Because of the conjunction of these two convictions, I strongly believe not only that basic income does have a central role to play in solving the first dilemma of our European welfare states, but also that it has a significant role to play in tackling the second one, between the economic unsustainability of a generous national welfare state and the political unsustainability of a generous transnational welfare state. The argument sketched here would need to be elaborated and qualified along many dimensions. But I predict that as more and more people start realizing the full extent and exact nature of the two big dilemmas we face, basic income will be transformed from the pet idea of a handful of cranks who believe abundance has been reached at long last to a key weapon in the struggle for the preservation of social solidarity and the promotion of social justice.[2]

Notes

From *Political Quarterly*, 67, 1, 1996, pp. 63–6.
1 The Basic Income European Network, founded in 1988, gathers together individuals and organizations from fourteen countries. [...]
2 Several aspects of the argument sketched here are developed in Philippe van Parijs, *Real Freedom for All: What (if Anything) Can Justify Capitalism?*, Oxford, Oxford University Press, 1995.

The Welfare State and Postmodernity

Kirk Mann

It would be difficult to overstate the importance of the welfare state for the critics of modernity. It might be thought that social policy in the twentieth century embodies the modernist exercise and would therefore be condemned out of hand. As Williams (1996) points out, there are grounds for seeing welfare states and social policy as essentially modern and diametrically opposed to all things postmodern. Instead, criticism of public welfare tends to take two forms: first, the social engineers of 'the' welfare state got it wrong; and second the current defenders of the welfare state continue to get it wrong. As Taylor-Gooby (1993) demonstrates, the first claim is made by various critics of modernity but the second is most forcibly asserted by Giddens (1994) in his ambitious attempt to redefine radical politics.

First, the principal architects and so called 'founders' of the welfare state are portrayed as naive and short-sighted, which led them to promote well meaning but mistaken policies.

Thus, interviewed for *Intimations of Postmodernity* (1992) Bauman asserted that:

> The idea of welfare state provision really was to engage the state in order to create for the ordinary people, who didn't have freedom, the conditions for it. It was very much like Aneurin Bevan's view of the National Health service, that it was a 'one off' expenditure. You introduce it, then everybody would become healthy; and then there would be no expenditure on national health any more – at least, it would be going down and down, year by year. That was the idea. And it was the same with the welfare state. The welfare state was thought of as an enabling institution, as a temporary measure to provide a sort of safety cushion for people, so that they know they can dare, they can take risks, they can exert themselves, because there is always this safety provision if they fail. (Bauman, 1992: 219–20)

Bauman does in other respects provide a sensitive and erudite perspective on modernity that offers a number of insights (Bauman, 1993, 1995). However, and even allowing for the fact that interviews tend to generate rather shallow and narrow responses, this respondent has a remarkably benign view of both the architects and the intentions of 'the' welfare state. This view is reiterated when he discusses the dismantling of the Welfare State:

> The welfare state, wisely, institutionalized *commonality* of fate: its provisions were meant for every participant (every citizen) in equal measure, thus balancing everybody's privations with everybody's gains. The slow retreat from that principle into the means-tested 'focused' assistance for 'those who need it' has institutionalized the *diversity* of fate, and thus made the unthinkable thinkable. It is now the taxpayer's privations that are to be balanced against someone else's, the benefit recipient's, gains. (Bauman, 1993: 243; emphasis in original)

Bauman seems to applaud the initial good intentions but implies these were misplaced and have been overwhelmed by the concerns of the anxious taxpayer. An attractive feature of Bauman's account, highlighted by Rattansi (1994), is the idea of the architects of welfare as gardeners, weeding out the defectives. Despite this, however, there are difficulties to do with the picture of 'the' welfare state that is painted. 'The welfare state' is portrayed in an unambiguous and simple manner, but more of this later. Similarly, the clichéd dichotomy of benefit recipients versus taxpayers is reproduced uncritically. It may be that public welfare is more visible and makes the recipients of it more prone to disciplinary measures but that is largely a consequence of discourses that neglect other forms of welfare (Sinfield, 1978). Only if the observers gaze is fixed upon the poorest, and if the discourse is conducted in terms that problematize the least powerful, can such a view be sustained.

Smart (1990: 412) claims, 'It is through the work of Bauman (1988a, b) that the question of postmodernity has been placed firmly on the sociology agenda', while Giddens is cited on the cover of both *Postmodern Ethics* (Bauman, 1993) and *Life in Fragments* (Bauman, 1995) as saying, 'Bauman, for me has become the theorist of postmodernity. With exceptional brilliance and originality, he has developed a position with which everyone now has to reckon'. If so, then the possibility of finding common ground with a critical social policy looks rather difficult. Students of social policy might well be advised to simply 'Forget Foucault', 'Forget Baudrillard' and 'Forget postmodernism' (Rojek and Turner, 1993 in Rattansi, 1995: 339). To be fair 'the' welfare state does not occupy as central a position for Bauman as it does for Giddens (1994) or Harvey (1994).

It might also be claimed in Bauman's defence that he is discussing the ideas behind the welfare state, not the policies that were introduced. This is a rather lame response since it suggests a disjuncture between the good intentions of the architects and the actual construction of the welfare state. Nor is Bauman's suggestion that 'the' welfare state was 'meant' to cater for a commonality of fate or to enable risk-taking to pass without comment. When was this 'meant' to have happened? When was 'the' welfare state intending to cater 'in equal measure' for citizens? Perhaps I am too firmly grounded in the empiricism of social policy but some evidence in support of these remarkable claims is surely called for. In fact there is ample evidence that the founders of 'the' welfare state – whichever period and founders we care to choose – held ideas that were not, even in the eyes of their contemporaries, benign (Orwell, 1970; Shaw, 1987; Williams, 1989). What is more, such an account completely neglects one of the insights that postmodernists claim: that there is no unitary cause and no single 'idea' about the way society is, or should be. The patterns of consumption in the 1930s, the pressure from various groups representing women, the TUC, employers' organizations, the notion of a post-war settlement, intraclass divisions, racist and nationalistic ideas, employers' changes to the labour process, notions of the deserving/underserving, among other factors, all had an influence, and this suggests we might be a little more sensitive in the way we account for the establishment of 'the welfare state' (Mann, 1986, 1992, 1994).

The second major criticism of 'the' welfare state, that defenders of it continue to get wrong, is more closely associated with Giddens (1994). Indeed, Giddens places 'the' welfare state at the centre of his account of how we might go 'Beyond Left and Right'. His undoubted influence on sociology [since the late 1970s] combined with his ambitious project – establishing a future for radical politics as he sees it – and his [...] appointment as Director of the London School of Economics, means it is not unreasonable to single Giddens's work out for scrutiny. This is particularly important when it is asserted that, 'We should be prepared to *rethink* the welfare state in a fundamental way' (Giddens, 1994: 17; emphasis in original). He portrays 'the' welfare state as developing in response to 'misfortunes that "happen" to people' (1994: 18). Thus he sees welfare policy responding *post-hoc* to mishaps and instead proposes a pro-active role for welfare that: 'mobilizes life-political measures, aimed at once more connecting autonomy with personal and collective responsibilities' (1994: 18). Social policies are generally acknowledged to have served to maintain traditional gender roles with the myth of the male breadwinner and the female carer at their core. Although some (e.g. Dennis and Erdos, 1992; Green, 1993) might take issue with the claim that social policies have gone too far in promoting the traditional heterosexual family, and others might point to features that have been used to promote a measure of independence (Mann and Roseneil, 1994), Giddens takes a distinctly critical perspective on the role of the welfare state, mentioning the close link between social policies and economic policies in the post-war period and the accumulation and legitimation functions attributed to social policy.

Thus far, many who identify with a critical social policy may nod enthusiastically, although some may want to quibble with the peculiar reductionism employed – peculiar because it rests uneasily with a theoretical model that seeks to escape any hint of reductionism; reductionism because the idea of certain key functions is difficult to sustain in the light of various critiques, some of which Giddens goes on to cite. But leaving these quibbles to one side there are more profound and disturbing flaws in Giddens's account of social policy.

If, as Giddens (1994: 17) claims, 'the welfare state was formed as a "class compromise" or "settlement" in social conditions that have now altered very markedly', it might be worth considering who was party to that settlement and who was excluded. I have argued at length elsewhere that the foundations for contemporary social divisions were laid by a sectional, economistic labour movement pursuing a pragmatic strategy of social closure and exclusion (Mann, 1992). Although he acknowledges the way 'the' welfare state developed as an exclusive range of publicly funded insurance-based schemes that were never designed for those who most needed assistance, Giddens proceeds as if this were the case. That is, he acknowledges the sectional interests that promoted insurance but then turns to discuss why it is that 'the' welfare state failed to meet the needs of those who were excluded. In running through a series of failures that 'the' welfare state is held to be responsible for, Giddens highlights the failures of post-war social democracy and the Fabian strategy. The Left, he accepts, were consistently critical of both the strategy and the normative philosophy that informed the orthodox approach to social policy. However, it is Marshall and Crosland who Giddens takes as his representatives of the socialist tradition on welfare and how 'the' welfare state confronts a formidable list of problems (Giddens, 1994: 73–7). It is doubtful if these would be the representatives most readers of *Critical Social Policy* would nominate and Giddens has an equally cavalier approach to certain substantive areas of social policy.

Risky Welfare

It is important to note that risk and risk assessment are central features of the contemporary welfare state, according to Giddens. He undertakes a discussion of risk that potentially raises a number of themes that could engage with both critical and more 'orthodox' approaches to social policy.

In pointing to pensions he takes a good example, one that illustrates both the exclusionary features of insurance-based notions of risk and the inherent limitations for many of such schemes. Insurance-based schemes like those in Britain certainly did rely heavily on actuarial calculations, although it is doubtful if these actuarial considerations are still based on any meaningful sense of 'insurance funds' as was the case before the Second World War. There is not, for example, a pot of money held by anyone marked 'pension contributions'. The old Friendly Society principles of collective risk assessment are more likely to be carried on by occupational and insurance company pension fund managers. Giddens is surely correct, though, to point to the actuarial assumptions that underpin welfare regimes. However, he fails to appreciate, or if he appreciates it to address, the part occupational and fiscal welfare play (Titmuss, 1958; Sinfield, 1978; Rose, 1981; Mann, 1992; Ginn and Arber, 1993). This myopic view of the provisions available, and by implication of risk assessment, leads to some very serious misrepresentations of what welfare is and how it developed.

A misunderstanding of why and how social policy developed is not just a matter of fine detail: the traditional concern of the lamppost counting social policy person with 'facts' versus the sociologists' interest in the broad sweep of events or theory. That is not to say that an unblemished truth exists that all can agree upon, the history of social policy is as contested as any other. But if the claim is that the development of welfare illustrates the limitations of the modernist exercise, it might be more helpful to acknowledge the diverse and different forms that welfare has taken. Indeed, the history and development of social policy actually illuminates modernity and reveals it to be more complex and ambiguous than is often thought. It is the bizarre manner in which everything can be presented as complex, diverse and ambiguous, except the welfare services associated with the state, that is so frustrating. This is most obvious when Giddens discusses the role of the welfare state in addressing risk and need.

Giddens has a fixation with the costs and risks that public welfare recipients incur that obscures other forms of welfare. In contrast to the way he observes the role of risk assessment, actuarial principles and calculations about the behaviour of potential claimants are certainly not confined to public welfare recipients. Indeed, when it comes to pensions, an example Giddens cites, it is remarkable that he can discuss the demographic and funding 'crisis' and consider (confusingly) the potential for intergenerational conflict but make no mention of some of the most significant players in the pensions arena. With all pension funds in January 1992 holding assets in the region of £500 billion according to Goode (1993: 157) and with actuarial calculations so important to their future ability to fulfil the 'pensions promise', we have to ask why the focus is only on public welfare. Giddens also neglects, to paraphrase Sennett and Cobb

(1973), the hidden benefits of class. Thus the focus on risk and responsibility in respect of public-welfare, often associated with benefit fraud, can neglect other insurance, collectively calculated risk provisions, such as home contents, vehicle and holiday insurance. As Cook (1989) has emphasized, the benefits systems favour those that already access the more privileged services. The actuarial calculations used to assess risk often have regressive clauses. For example, for the poor and anyone living in an area where poverty is prevalent, the risk of burglary is greater but so is the possibility of being refused insurance cover or being charged additional premiums. If our notion of welfare includes the idea that it provides some form of protection against accidents, unforeseen circumstances and unwarranted hurt – a fairly narrow and conservative definition it might be thought – then some form of insurance or protection is vital. Denying or penalizing those most at risk could be seen as public dis-welfare. Unfortunately, Giddens sets an agenda that does not allow for a discussion of 'risk' in this context because he is fixated with existing public welfare policies.

Only if someone was unaware of the array of occupational and fiscal welfare measures that exist could they write:

> As a result of the way in which the welfare state developed, from a concern to assist (as well as to regulate) the poor, 'welfare' has generally come to be equated with improving the lot of the underprivileged. But why not suppose that welfare programmes should be directed at the affluent as well as those in more deprived circumstances? (Giddens, 1994: 193)

Concern that he is unaware of the welfare policies that the state already provides for the affluent is reinforced by his discussion of welfare dependency. Again the focus is, like so many of the tiresome discussions of the 'underclass', simply on public welfare recipients (Giddens, 1994: 144–50). There is also a tendency to invert the problems of the poor and claim that these are in some way shared across the social spectrum. Thus he emphasizes how the affluent also have welfare needs: 'Security, self-respect, self-actualization – these are scarce goods for the affluent as well as the poor, and they are compromised by the ethos of productivism, not just distributive inequalities' (Giddens, 1994: 193). Indeed, 'The relief of dependency becomes a *generalized* aim in a post-scarcity society. Overcoming welfare dependency means overcoming the dependencies of productivism, and both can be combated in the same way' (1994: 193–4).

Benefits provided by state agencies that reinforce traditional labour market and gender roles are blamed for promoting public welfare dependency. Nor does 'the' welfare state cater for the individual needs of either the poor or the affluent. Everyone, it would seem, is discontented and there is little that can be defended, despite the desperate attempt by 'the

Left' to do so. The answer lies, he claims, in the affluent accepting that paid work does not have to be at the centre of life, a situation the poor have learnt to accept and from which the affluent can learn (Giddens, 1994: 194–5). Thus Giddens makes a virtue out of something that the over-whelming majority of those who are poor regard as an unwarranted necessity. Instead of promoting universal welfare measures that can in turn promote welfare dependency (1994: 75) there is a need for:

> Schemes of positive welfare, oriented to manufactured rather than external risk, would be directed to fostering the *autotelic self*. The autotelic self is one with an inner confidence which comes from self respect, and one where a sense of ontological security, originating in basic trust, allows for the posit-ive appreciation of difference. It refers to a person able to translate potential threats into rewarding challenges, someone who is able to turn entropy into a consistent flow of experience. The autotelic self does not seek to neutralize risk or to suppose that 'someone else will take care of the problem'; risk is confronted as the active challenge which generates self-actualization. (Giddens, 1994: 192; emphasis in original)

Perhaps my sociological imagination needs to be stimulated in some way but it is very difficult to see the people of Basildon, Billericay and Harlow engaging in a discovery of the autotelic self. Of course 'well-being' con-sists of more than consumption and perhaps the people of Essex (for example) need to be a little more reflexive and a little less materialistic if they are to 'feel good'. Giddens is surely right to stress the more vulner-able, more dependent and more fragmented nature of contemporary social life. He may also be correct in highlighting the risks of everyday social and personal life that currently lie beyond the scope of public welfare regimes. The suspicion remains, though, that the discovery of the autotelic self is lower down the agenda of the people of Essex than the restoration of fiscal welfare measures. [...]

Lamppost Counters and a Critical Social Policy?

If commentators on postmodernity and post-traditional society have viewed social policy rather narrowly and inadequately, this should not detract from the implications of their critique for a critical social policy. There is a peculiarly postmodern irony in the fact that Taylor-Gooby (1993) has prompted JSP into publishing two articles in the same issue (Fitzpatrick, 1996; Hillyard and Watson, 1996) that address, if not pro-mote, postmodernism. For in 1981 Taylor-Gooby was lambasting 'the empiricist tradition in social administration' for its persistent 'repression of theory' (1981: 8). Taylor-Gooby in his critique of postmodernism was clearly not calling for a return to 'lamppost counting' and could be seen in other texts (e.g. Dean and Taylor-Gooby, 1992) to have used, albeit in a fairly restrained fashion, Foucault's work to account for the discourse directed at public welfare recipients. The irony seems even greater when we look at the number of former members of the *Critical Social Policy* editorial collective who contribute to JSP. In some respects this blurring of boundaries and positions epitomizes the uncertainties associated with the postmodernist critique. As the troops of various ideological armies clamber out of the trenches, they wander aimlessly in a no man's land of corpses and mines, but where does that leave a 'critical social policy'?

Note

From *Critical Social Policy*, 18, 1, 1998, pp. 85–93.

References

Bauman, Z., 'Is There a Postmodern Sociology?', *Theory, Culture and Society*, 5(2/3), 1988a, pp. 217–37.

Bauman, Z., 'Sociology and Postmodernity', *The Sociological Review*, 36(4), 1988b, pp. 790–813.

Bauman, Z., *Intimations of Postmodernity*, London, Routledge, 1992.

Bauman, Z., *Postmodern Ethics*, Oxford, Blackwell, 1993.

Bauman, Z., *Life in Fragments: Essays in Postmodern Morality*, Oxford, Blackwell, 1995.

Cook, D., *Rich Law, Poor Law*, Milton Keynes, Open University Press, 1989.

Dean, H. and Taylor-Gooby, P., *Dependency Culture*, Hemel Hempstead, Harvester Wheatsheaf, 1992.

Dennis, N. and Erdos, G., *Families without Fatherhood*, Choice in Welfare no. 12, London, IEA Health and Welfare Unit, 1992.

Fitzpatrick, T., 'Postmodernism, Welfare and Radical Politics', *Journal of Social Policy*, 25(3), 1996, pp. 303–20.

Giddens, A., *Beyond Left and Right*, Cambridge, Polity Press, 1994.

Ginn, J. and Arber, S., 'Pension Penalties: The Gendered Division of Occupational Welfare', *Work Employment and Society*, 7(1), 1993, pp. 47–70.

Goode, R., *Pension Law Reform: The Report of the Pension Law Review Committee*, vol. 1, CM2342–1, London, HMSO, 1993.

Green, D. G., 'Foreword', in *The Family: Is it Just Another Lifestyle Choice?* ed. J. Davies, Choice in Welfare no. 15, London, IEA Health and Welfare Unit, 1993.

Harvey, D., 'Flexible Accumulation through Urbanization: Reflections on "Post-Modernism" in the American City', in *Post Fordism: A Reader*, ed. A. Amin, Oxford, Blackwell, 1994.

Hillyard, P. and Watson, S., 'Postmodern Social Policy. A Contradiction in Terms?', *Journal of Social Policy*, 25(3), 1996, pp. 321–46.

Mann, K., 'The Making of a Claiming Class – The Neglect of Agency in Analyses of the Welfare State', *Critical Social Policy*, 15, 1986, pp. 62–74.

Mann, K., *The Making of an English 'Underclass'? The Social Divisions of Welfare and Labour*, Milton Keynes, Open University Press, 1992.

Mann, K., 'Watching the Defectives: Observers of the Underclass in Britain, Australia and the USA', *Critical Social Policy*, 14(3), 1994, pp. 79–98.

Mann, K. and Roseneil, S., 'Some Mothers Do 'Ave Em: The Gender Politics of the Underclass Debate', *Journal of Gender Studies*, 3(3), 1994, pp. 317–31.

Orwell, G., *Collected Essays, Journalism and Letters*, Harmondsworth, Penguin, 1970.

Rattansi A., '"Western" Racisms, Ethnicities and Identities', in *Racism, Modernity and Identity*, ed. A. Rattansi and S. Westwood, Cambridge, Polity Press, 1994.

Rattansi, A., 'Review Essay: Forget Postmodernism? Notes From De Bunker', *Sociology*, 29(2), 1995, pp. 339–49.

Rattansi, A. and Westwood, S., eds, *Racism, Modernity and Identity*, Cambridge, Polity Press, 1994.

Rojek, C. and Turner, B., eds, *Forget Baudrillard?*, London, Routledge, 1993.

Rose, H., 'Rereading Titmuss: The Sexual Division of Welfare', *Journal of Social Policy*, 10(4), 1981, pp. 477–502.

Sennett, R. and Cobb, J., *The Hidden Injuries of Class*, New York, Vintage Books, 1973.

Shaw, C., 'Eliminating the Yahoo, Eugenics, Social Darwinism, and Five Fabians', *History of Political Thought*, viii(3), 1987, pp. 521–44.

Sinfield, A., 'Analyses in the Social Division of Welfare', *Journal of Social Policy*, 7(2), 1978, pp. 129–56.

Smart, B., 'On the Disorder of Things: Sociology, Postmodernity and the "End of the Social"', *Sociology*, 24(3), 1990, pp. 397–416.

Taylor-Gooby, P., 'The Empiricist Tradition in Social Administration', *Critical Social Policy*, 1(2), 1981, pp. 6–21.

Taylor-Gooby, P., *Postmodernism and Social Policy: A Great Leap Backwards*, University of New South Wales Discussion Article, no. 45, September 1993; reproduced in *Journal of Social Policy*, 23(3), 1994, pp. 385–404.

Titmuss, R., 'The Social Division of Welfare', in *Essays on the Welfare State*, London, Allen and Unwin, 1958.

Williams, F., *Social Policy: A Critical Introduction*, Cambridge: Polity Press, 1989.

Williams, F., 'Somewhere over the Rainbow: Universality and Diversity in Social Policy', *Social Policy Review*, 4, 1992, pp. 200–19.

Williams, F., 'Postmodernism, Feminism and the Question of Difference', in *Social Work, Social Theory and Social Change*, ed. N. Parton, London, Routledge, 1996.

Positive Welfare

Anthony Giddens

[...]

Positive Welfare

No issue has polarized left and right more profoundly in recent years than the welfare state, extolled on the one side and excoriated on the other. What became 'the welfare state' (a term not in widespread use until the 1960s and one William Beveridge, the architect of the British welfare state, thoroughly disliked) has in fact a chequered history. Its origins were far removed from the ideals of the left – indeed it was created partly to dispel the socialist menace. The ruling groups who set up the social insurance system in imperial Germany in the late nineteenth century despised *laissez-faire* economics as much as they did socialism. Yet Bismarck's model was copied by many countries. Beveridge visited Germany in 1907 in order to study the model.[1] The welfare state as it exists today in Europe was produced in and by war, as were so many aspects of national citizenship.

The system Bismarck created in Germany is usually taken as the classic form of the welfare state. Yet the welfare state in Germany has always had a complex network of third sector groups and associations that the authorities have depended on for putting welfare policies into practice. The aim is to help these to attain their social objectives. In areas such as child care, third sector groups have almost a monopoly on provision. The non-profit sector in Germany expanded rather than shrank as the welfare state grew. Welfare states vary in the degree to which they incorporate or rely upon the third sector. In Holland, for instance, non-profit organizations are the main delivery system for social services, while in Sweden hardly any are used. In Belgium and Austria, as in Germany, about half the social services are provided by non-profit groups.

The Dutch political scientist Kees van Kersbergen argues that 'one of the major insights of the contemporary debate [about the welfare state] is that to equate social democracy and the welfare state may have been a mistake'.[2] He examines in detail the influence of Christian democracy upon the development of continental welfare systems and the social market. The Christian democratic parties descend from the Catholic parties that were important between the wars in Germany, Holland, Austria and to a lesser degree France and Italy. The Catholic unionists saw socialism as the enemy and sought to outflank it on its own ground by stressing co-determination and class reconciliation. Ronald Reagan's view, expressed in 1981, that 'we have let government take away those things that were once ours to do voluntarily' finds a much earlier echo in Europe in the Catholic tradition. Church, family and friends are the main sources of social solidarity. The state should step in only when those institutions don't fully live up to their obligations.

Recognizing the problematic history of the welfare state, third way politics should accept some of the criticisms the right makes of that state. It is essentially undemocratic, depending as it does upon a top-down distribution of benefits. Its motive force is protection and care, but it does not give enough space to personal liberty. Some forms of welfare institution are bureaucratic, alienating and inefficient, and welfare benefits can create perverse consequences that undermine what they were designed to achieve. However, third way politics sees these problems not as a signal to dismantle the welfare state, but as part of the reason to reconstruct it.

The difficulties of the welfare state are only partly financial. In most Western societies, proportional expenditure on welfare systems has remained quite stable [since the late 1980s]. In the UK, the share of GDP spent on the welfare state increased steadily for most of the century up to the late 1970s. Since then it has stabilized,[3] although the gross figures conceal changes in the distribution of spending and the sources of revenue. The resilience of welfare budgets in the UK is all the more remarkable given the determination of Margaret Thatcher's governments to cut them.

Expenditure on education as a percentage of GDP fell between 1975 and 1995 from 6.7 per cent to 5.2 per cent. Spending on the health service, however, rose over this period. In 1975 it was equivalent to 3.8 per cent of GDP. By 1995 it had risen to 5.7 per cent (a lower percentage than in most other industrial countries). Public housing experienced the greatest cut, declining from 4.2 per cent of GDP in 1975 to 2.1 per cent twenty years later. As happened elsewhere, spending on social security increased most. In 1973–4 it made up 8.2 per cent of GDP. This reached 11.4 per cent by

1995–6. Expenditure on social security went up by more than 100 per cent in real terms over the period. The main factors underlying the increase were high unemployment, a growth in the numbers of in-work poor, and changes in demographic patterns, especially a growth in numbers of single parents and older people.

Much the same developments have affected all welfare systems, since they are bound up with structural changes of a profound kind. They are causing basic problems for the more comprehensive welfare states, such as those in Scandinavia. Nordic egalitarianism has historical and cultural roots rather than being only the product of the universalist welfare state. There is a wider public acceptance of high levels of taxation than in most Western countries. But the benefits system comes under strain whenever unemployment rises, as happened in Finland – this in spite of the fact that the Nordic countries pioneered active labour market policies. Given its relative size, the Scandinavian welfare state is a major employer, particularly of women. Yet as a result the degree of sexual segregation in employment is higher than in most other industrial countries.

The large increase in social security spending is one of the main sources of attack on welfare systems by neo-liberals, who see in it the widespread development of welfare dependency. They are surely correct to worry about the number of people who live off state benefits, but there is a more sophisticated way of looking at what is going on. Welfare prescriptions quite often become sub-optimal, or set up situations of moral hazard. The idea of moral hazard is widely used in discussions of risk in private insurance. Moral hazard exists when people use insurance protection to alter their behaviour, thereby redefining the risk for which they are insured. It isn't so much that some forms of welfare provision create dependency cultures as that people take rational advantage of opportunities offered. Benefits meant to counter unemployment, for instance, can actually produce unemployment if they are actively used as a shelter from the labour market.

Writing against the backdrop of the Swedish welfare system, the economist Assar Lindbeck notes that a strong humanitarian case can be made for generous support for people affected by unemployment, illness, disability or the other standard risks covered by the welfare state. The dilemma is that the higher the benefits the greater will be the chance of moral hazard, as well as fraud. He suggests that moral hazard tends to be greater in the long run than in shorter time periods. This is because in the longer term social habits are built up which come to define what is 'normal'. Serious benefit dependency is then no longer even seen as such but simply becomes 'expected' behaviour. An increased tendency to apply for social assistance, more absence from work for alleged health reasons, and a lower level of job search may be among the results.[4]

Once established, benefits have their own autonomy, regardless of whether or not they meet the purposes for which they were originally designed. As this happens, expectations become 'locked in' and interest groups entrenched. Countries that have tried to reform their pensions systems, for example, have met with concerted resistance. We should have our pensions because we are 'old' (at age sixty or sixty-five), we have paid our dues (even if they don't cover the costs), other people before have had them, everyone looks forward to retirement and so forth. Yet such institutional stasis is in and of itself a reflection of the need for reform, for the welfare state needs to be as dynamic and responsive to wider social trends as any other sector of government.

Welfare reform isn't easy to achieve, precisely because of the entrenched interests that welfare systems create. Yet the outline of a radical project for the welfare state can be sketched out quite readily.

The welfare state, as indicated earlier, is a pooling of risk rather than resources. What has shaped the solidarity of social policy is that 'otherwise privileged groups discovered that they shared a common interest in reallocating risk with the disadvantaged'.[5] However, the welfare state isn't geared up to cover new-style risks such as those concerning technological change, social exclusion or the accelerating proportion of one-parent households. These mismatches are of two kinds: where risks covered don't fit with needs, and where the wrong groups are protected.

Welfare reform should recognize the points about risk made earlier in the discussion: effective risk management (individual or collective) doesn't just mean minimizing or protecting against risks; it also means harnessing the positive or energetic side of risk and providing resources for risk taking. Active risk taking is recognized as inherent in entrepreneurial activity, but the same applies to the labour force. Deciding to go to work and give up benefits, or taking a job in a particular industry, are risk-infused activities – but such risk taking is often beneficial both to the individual and to the wider society.

When Beveridge wrote his *Report on Social Insurance and Allied Services*, in 1942, he famously declared war on Want, Disease, Ignorance, Squalor and Idleness. In other words, his focus was almost entirely negative. We should speak today of *positive welfare*, to which individuals themselves and other agencies besides government contribute – and which is functional for wealth creation. Welfare is not in essence an economic concept, but a psychic one, concerning as it does well-being. Economic benefits or advantages are therefore virtually never enough on their own to create it. Not only is welfare generated by many contexts and influences other than the welfare state, but welfare institutions must be concerned with fostering psychological as well as economic benefits. Quite mundane examples can be given: counselling, for example, might sometimes be more helpful than direct economic support.

Although these propositions may sound remote from the down-to-earth concerns of welfare systems, there isn't a single area of welfare reform to which they aren't relevant or which they don't help illuminate. The guideline is investment in *human capital* wherever possible, rather than the direct provision of economic maintenance. In place of the welfare state we should put the *social investment state*, operating in the context of a positive welfare society.

The theme that the 'welfare state' should be replaced by the 'welfare society' has become a conventional one in the recent literature on welfare issues. Where third sector agencies are not already well represented, they should play a greater part in providing welfare services. The top-down dispensation of benefits should cede place to more localized distribution systems. More generally, we should recognize that the reconstruction of welfare provision has to be integrated with programmes for the active development of civil society.

Social Investment Strategies

Since the institutions and services ordinarily grouped together under the rubric of the welfare state are so many, I shall limit myself here to comments on social security. What would the social investment state aim for in terms of its social security systems? Let us take two basic areas: provision for old age and unemployment.

As regards old age, a radical perspective would suggest breaking out of the confines within which debate about pension payments is ordinarily carried on. Most industrial societies have ageing populations, and this is a big problem, it is said, because of the pensions time bomb. The pension commitments of some countries, such as Italy, Germany or Japan, are way beyond what can be afforded, even allowing for reasonable economic growth. If other societies, such as Britain, have to some extent avoided this difficulty, it is because they have actively reduced their state pension commitments – in Britain, for example, by indexing pensions to average prices rather than average earnings.

An adequate level of state-provided pension is a necessity. There is good reason also to support schemes of compulsory saving. In the UK the effect of relating pension increases to prices rather than earnings, without other statutory provisions, is likely to leave many retirees impoverished. A man who is fifty in 1998 and leaves the labour market aged sixty-five will receive a government pension amounting to only 10 per cent of average male earnings. Many people don't have either occupational or private pensions.[6] Other countries have come up with more effective strategies. A number of examples of combined public/private sector funding of pensions exist, some of which are capable of generalization. The Finnish system, for example, combines a state-guaranteed basic minimum income and earnings-related pension with regulated private sector provision.

The interest of the pensions issue, however, stretches more broadly than the questions of who should pay, at what level and by what means. It should go along with rethinking what old age is and how changes in the wider society affect the position of older people. Positive welfare applies as much in this context as in any other: it isn't enough to think only in terms of economic benefits. Old age is a new-style risk masquerading as an old-style one. Ageing used to be more passive than it is now: the ageing body was simply something that had to be accepted. In the more active, reflexive society, ageing has become much more of an open process, on a physical as well as a psychic level. Becoming older presents at least as many opportunities as problems, both for individuals and for the wider social community.

The concept of a pension that begins at retirement age, and the label 'pensioner', were inventions of the welfare state. But not only do these not conform to the new realities of ageing, they are as clear a case of welfare dependency as one can find. They suggest incapacity, and it is not surprising that for many people retirement leads to a loss of self-esteem. When retirement first fixed 'old age' at sixty or sixty-five, the situation of older people was very different from what it is now. In 1900, average life expectancy for a male aged twenty in England was only sixty-two.

We should move towards abolishing the fixed age of retirement, and we should regard older people as a resource rather than a problem. The category of pensioner will then cease to exist, because it is detachable from pensions as such: it makes no sense to lock up pension funds against reaching 'pensionable age'. People should be able to use such funds as they wish – not only to leave the labour force at any age, but to finance education, or reduced working hours, when bringing up young children.[7] Abolishing statutory retirement would probably be neutral in respect of labour market implications, given that individuals could give up work earlier as well as stay in work longer. These provisions won't as such help pay for pensions where a country has overstretched its future commitments, and this perspective is agnostic about what balance should be aimed for between public and private funding. Yet it does suggest there is scope for innovative thinking around the pensions issue.

A society that separates older people from the majority in a retirement ghetto cannot be called inclusive. The precept of philosophic conservatism applies here as elsewhere: old age shouldn't be seen as a time of rights without responsibilities. Burke famously observed that 'society is a partnership not only between those who are living, but between those who are living, those who are dead and those who are to be born'.[8] Such a partnership is presumed, in a relatively mundane context, by the very idea of collective pensions, which act as a conduit between generations. But an intergenerational contract plainly needs to be deeper than this. The young should be willing to look to the old for models, and older people should see themselves as in the service of future generations.[9] Are such goals realistic in a society that has retreated from deference, and where age no longer appears to bring wisdom? Several factors suggest they may be. Being 'old' lasts longer than it used to do. There are far more old people in the population and hence the old are more socially visible. Finally, their growing involvement in work and the community should act to link them directly to younger generations.

The position of the frail elderly, people who need continuous care, raises more difficult questions. There are twenty times more people over eighty-five in the UK today than there were in 1900. Many of the 'young old' may be in quite a different situation from that of those in the same age group a couple of generations ago. It is a different matter for the 'old old', some of whom fare badly.[10] The question of what collective resources should be made available to the frail elderly is not just one of rationing. There are issues to be confronted here, including ethical questions of a quite fundamental sort, that go well beyond the scope of this discussion.

What of unemployment? Does the goal of full employment mean anything any more? Is there a straight trade-off, as the neo-liberals say, between employment and deregulated labour markets – contrasting the US 'jobs miracle' with Eurosclerosis? We should note first of all that no simple comparison between the 'US' and the 'European model' is possible. As economist Stephen Nickell has shown, labour markets in Europe show great diversity. Over the period from 1983 to 1996, there were large variations in unemployment rates in OECD Europe, ranging from 1.8 per cent in Switzerland to over 20 per cent in Spain. Of OECD countries, 30 per cent over these years had average unemployment rates lower than the US. Those with the lowest rates are not noted for having the most deregulated labour markets (Austria, Portugal, Norway). Labour market rigidities like strict employment legislation don't strongly influence unemployment. High unemployment is linked to generous benefits that run on indefinitely and to poor educational standards at the lower end of the labour market – the phenomenon of exclusion.[11]

The position of the third way should be that sweeping deregulation is not the answer. Welfare expenditure should remain at European rather than US levels, but be switched as far as possible towards human capital investment. Benefit systems should be reformed where they induce moral hazard, and a more active risk-taking attitude encouraged, wherever possible through incentives, but where necessary by legal obligations.

It is worth perhaps at this stage commenting briefly on the 'Dutch model', sometimes pointed to as a successful adaptation of social democracy to new social and economic conditions. In an agreement concluded at Wassenaar some sixteen years ago, the country's unions agreed to wage moderation in exchange for a gradual reduction in working hours. As a result, labour costs have fallen by over 30 per cent [since 1988], while the economy has thrived. This has been achieved with an unemployment rate below 6 per cent in 1997.

Looked at more closely, however, the Dutch model is less impressive, at least in terms of job creation and welfare reform. Substantial numbers who would in other countries count as unemployed are living on disability benefit – the country in fact has more people registered as unfit for work than it has officially unemployed. At 51 per cent, the proportion of the population aged between fifteen and sixty-four in full-time work is below what it was in 1970, when it was nearly 60 per cent and well short of the European average of 67 per cent. Of jobs created [since 1988], 90 per cent are part-time. Holland spends the highest proportion of its income on social security of any European country, and its welfare system is under considerable strain.[12]

Strategies for job creation and the future of work need to be based upon an orientation to the new economic exigencies. Companies and consumers are increasingly operating on a world scale in terms of the standards demanded for goods and services. Consumers shop on a world level, in the sense that distribution is global and therefore 'the best' no longer has any generic connection with where goods and services are produced. Pressures to meet these standards will also apply more and more to labour forces. In some contexts such pressures are likely to deepen processes of social exclusion. The differentiation will be not only between manual and knowledge workers, or between high skills and low skills, but between those who are local in outlook and those who are more cosmopolitan.

Investment in human resources is proving to be the main source of leverage which firms have in key economic sectors. One study in the US compared 700 large companies across different industries. The results showed that even a marginal difference in an index of investment in people increased shareholder returns by $41,000.[13] The business analyst Rosabeth Moss Kanter identifies five main areas where government policy can assist job creation. There should be support for *entrepreneurial initiatives* concerned with small business startups and technological innovation. Many countries, particularly in Europe, still place too much reliance upon established economic institutions, including the public sector, to produce employment. In a world 'where customers can literally shop for workers', without the new ideas guaranteed by entrepreneurship there is an absence of competition. Entrepreneurship is a direct source of jobs. It also drives technological development, and gives people opportunities for self-employment in times of transition. Government policy can provide direct support for entrepreneurship, through helping create venture capital, but also through restructuring welfare systems to give security when entrepreneurial ventures go wrong – for example, by giving people the option to be taxed on a two- or three-year cycle rather than only annually.

Governments need to emphasize *life-long education*, developing education programmes that start from an individual's early years and continue on even late in life. Although training in specific skills may be necessary for many job transitions, more important is the development of cognitive and emotional competence. Instead of relying on unconditional benefits, policies should be oriented to encourage saving, the use of educational resources and other personal investment opportunities.

Public project partnerships can give private enterprise a larger role in activities which governments once provided for, while ensuring that the public interest remains paramount. The public sector can in turn provide resources that can help enterprise to flourish and without which joint projects may fail. Moss Kanter points out that welfare to work programmes in the US have sometimes foundered on the problem of transport. Companies offer jobs in areas which those available for them can't easily reach because of lack of adequate transport facilities.

Government policies can enhance *portability*, whether through common standards of education or through portable pension rights. Greater harmonization of educational practices and standards, for instance, is desirable for a cosmopolitan labour force. Some global corporations have already set up standardized entrance requirements, but governments need to take the lead. As in other areas, harmonization is not necessarily the enemy of educational diversity and may even be the condition of sustaining it.

Finally, governments should encourage *family-friendly workplace policies*, something that can also be achieved through public-private collaborations. Countries vary widely in the level of child care they offer, for instance, as do companies. Not only child care, but other work opportunities, such as telecommuting or work sabbaticals, can help reconcile employment and domestic life. The more companies emphasize human resources, the more competition there will be to have the best family-friendly work environments. Governments which help them will also tend to attract inward investment.[14]

Can these strategies produce a return to full employment in the usual sense – enough good jobs to go around for everyone who wants one? No one knows, but it seems unlikely. The proportion of jobs that are full-time and long-term is declining in Western economies. Comparisons between the 'full employment economies', such as the US or the UK, and 'high unemployment' societies, like Germany or France, are less clear cut when we compare not the number of jobs but the hours of work created. Net job creation for skilled work that is secure and well paid over the ten years 1986–96 was the same in Germany as in the US, at 2.6 per cent. Labour productivity doubled in Germany over that period, whereas in the US it rose by only 25 per cent.[15]

Since no one can say whether or not global capitalism will in future generate sufficient work, it would be foolish to proceed as though it will. Is the 'active redistribution' of work possible without counterproductive consequences? Probably not in the form of limits to the working week fixed by government – the difficulties with such schemes are well known. But if we see it in a wider context, we have no need to ask whether redistribution of work is possible. It is already happening on a widespread basis, and the point is to foster its positive aspects. One much-quoted experiment is that at Hewlett Packard's plant in Grenoble. The plant is kept open on a 24-hour cycle seven days a week. The employees have a working week averaging just over 30 hours, but receive the same wages as when they were working a 37.5-hour week. Labour productivity has increased substantially.[16]

Since the revival of civic culture is a basic ambition of third way politics, the active involvement of government in the social economy makes sense. Indeed some have presented the choice before us in stark terms, given the problematic status of full employment: either greater participation in the social economy or facing the growth of 'outlaw cultures'. The possibilities are many, including time dollar schemes [...] and shadow wages – tax breaks for hours worked in the social economy. As diverse studies across Europe show, 'more and more people are looking both for meaningful work and opportunities for commitment outside of work. If society can upgrade and reward such commitment and put it on a level with gainful employment, it can create both individual identity and social cohesion.'[17]

In sum, what would a radically reformed welfare state – the social investment state in the positive welfare society – look like? Expenditure on welfare, understood as positive welfare, will be generated and distributed not wholly through the state, but by the state working in combination with other agencies, including business. The welfare society here is not just the nation, but stretches above and below it. Control of environmental pollution, for example, can never be a matter for national government alone, but it is certainly directly relevant to welfare. In the positive welfare society, the contract between individual and government shifts, since autonomy and the development of self – the medium of expanding individual responsibility – become the prime focus. Welfare in this basic sense concerns the rich as well as the poor.

Positive welfare would replace each of Beveridge's negatives with a positive: in place of Want, autonomy; not Disease but active health; instead of Ignorance, education, as a continuing part of life; rather than Squalor, well-being; and in place of Idleness, initiative.

Notes

From *The Third Way*, Cambridge, Polity Press, 1998, pp. 111–28.

1 Nicholas Timmins, *The Five Giants*, London, Fontana, 1996, p. 12.
2 Kees van Kersbergen, *Social Capitalism*, London, Routledge, 1995, p. 7.
3 Howard Glennerster and John Hills, *The State of Welfare*, Oxford, Oxford University Press, 2nd edition, 1998.
4 Assar Lindbeck, 'The End of the Middle Way?', *American Economic Review*, vol. 85, 1995.
5 Peter Baldwin, *The Politics of Social Solidarity*, Cambridge, Cambridge University Press, 1990, p. 292.
6 Stuart Fleming, 'What we'll earn when we're 64', *New Statesman*, 5 June 1998.
7 Will Hutton, *The State We're In*, London, Cape, 1995.
8 Edmund Burke, *Reflections on the Revolution in France* [1790], London, Dent, 1910, pp. 93–4.
9 Daniel Callahan, *Setting Limits*, New York, Simon and Schuster, 1987, p. 46.
10 Ibid., p. 20.
11 Stephen Nickell, 'Unemployment and Labour Market Rigidities', *Journal of Economic Perspectives*, vol. 11, 1997.
12 Dominic Vidal, 'Miracle or Mirage in the Netherlands?', *Le Monde Diplomatique*, July 1997.
13 Rosabeth Moss Kanter, 'Keynote Address', Centre for Economic Performance: Employability and Exclusion, London, CEP, May 1998.
14 Ibid., pp. 65–8.
15 Ulrich Beck, 'Capitalism without Work', *Dissent*, winter 1997, p. 102.
16 Jeremy Rifkin, *The End of Work*, New York, Putnam's, 1995, p. 225.
17 Beck, op. cit., p. 106.

Subject Index

Page references in *italic* indicate tables.

accident insurance 21, 23
action, collective 79–80, 90, 145, 310
  and social class 86–7
Adjusted National Product 349
administration *see* bureaucracy
affirmative action 114
age
  and intergenerational conflict
    293–304, 364, 374–5
  and mandatory savings 274, 275–9,
    281–5, 288–9, 373
  and poverty 11, 12–13, 15, 279, 300
  and social insurance 21, 23, 185
  and voting behaviour 299–300
  and welfare provision 155, 271–80
  World Bank study 6, 271, 276, 279,
    281–92
  see also pensions
agriculture
  and coalition-formation 165–6,
    167, 194
  Common Agricultural Policy 260
Aid to Families with Dependent
    Children (AFDC, USA) 136,
    139, 201
American Association of Retired
    People (AARP) 297, 311
assistance, social 159, 161, 247, 286–7

and de-commodification 158
and means testing 155, 162, 325,
    329
and retrenchment 328–31
associationalism, welfare 349–50
Australia
  and armed forces 134
  and family allowances 142–3
  and female dependency 135, 136,
    138
  and feminism 146
  feminist health and welfare services
    122, 144–5
  as liberal welfare state 162, 192
  and pensions 274, 279
  and taxation 139
Austria
  and social service delivery 370
  and state corporatism 159, 162, 186
    n.8, 191–2
  and welfare expenditure 155
autonomy
  government 6, 258, 263–4, 266
  individual 56–7, 62, 115, 148–9,
    228, 378

bargaining
  and citizenship 38

and European model   209, 212, 218, 223–4, 225
and social change   82–3, 85
societal   83–4, 87–8, 222
and union power   29, 67, 69, 80, 216
Belgium
and income inequality   323
and pensions   21
and social service delivery   370
benefits
in cash   21, 39–40, 67, 96–100, 162
citizens'   158–9
and cohabitation rule   119–20, 138–9
contributory   135–6, 158, 161, 288–9
earnings-related   161, 163, 173, 187 n.20, 373–4
fringe   29, 162, 166
functions   44–5, 47
and gender   136, 137
in kind   21, 55, 67, 98–100, 203 n.4
and labour force participation   241
sickness   21, 140, 158–9, 240, 242, 339
supplementary   128
for women   119, 143–4
Beveridge, William
and feminist critique   120, 139, 141
Full Employment in a Free Society 28
and minimum standards   21, 47
Social Insurance and Allied Services 139, 372
Unemployment   28, 139
and welfare state   269, 378
Beveridgism   28, 158, 160–1
birth and state allowances   14, 15
Bismarck, Otto von, and social security legislation   21–4, 68, 159–60, 191–2, 200, 244, 369
Brandt Report (1980)   349
Britain
and armed forces   134
compared with USA   20
and dependency politics   114
and economic policy   263, 268
and education and training   243
and employment insecurity   337–41

and European social model   210, 220–1, 224–5, 228
and expenditure   155, 315, 316, 322, 327, 341, 370
and family allowances   142–3
and female dependency   135, 138
and feminism   146
feminist health and welfare services 122
and income distribution   60, 247, 274, 323, 325, 337
and industrial relations   29, 217, 220
and intergenerational conflict 293–4, 297, 299–302
and labour market flexibility 220–1, 247, 337–40
as liberal welfare state   168, 192, 248–9
and pensions   284–5, 290, 373
and political coalition-building 165–6
and public employment   328
and retrenchment   329–32
and social conflict   67, 68
and taxation   139, 301
and underclass   111, 114, 249
and unemployment   240, 249, 337–9, *338*, 341
and universalism   160–1
welfare bureaucracy   94
Brundtland Commission (1987)   349
bureaucracy, welfare   74, 93–4, 344, 370

Canada
as liberal welfare state   162, 167–8, 247
and pensions   290
and unemployment relief   27
and universalism   160
capital
accumulation   63–6, 69–70, 72, 74, 75
human   79–80, 235, 242–3, 249, 373, 375–6
and labour   67, 70–1, 73, 80, 81–3, 123–4, 129, 217

capital (*cont'd*)
  markets 211, 236, 240, 254–6, 258, 277–9, 283, 289–90
  monopoly 65
  as power resource 79–80, 226
  social 63–6
  supply 235–6, 240, 242, 246, 249
capitalism
  and citizenship 36–8, 40
  and critique of welfare state 69–72, 76, 321
  and the family 127
  feminist critique 123–4
  liberal 67
  and power resources 78–80
  stakeholder 223
  and the state 63–4, 67, 77, 234–50
  welfare *see* welfare capitalism
Central Europe and European social model 215–16
change, social
  and demography 6, 250, 271–307, 331
  and power resources 81–3, 85
  role of welfare state 135
charity
  limitations 26
  v. rights 57
Child Benefit 126, 191
child care
  as female responsibility 126–7, 135, 139
  and labour force participation 110, 121, 139, 377
  and social democracy 163
children
  and dependency politics 112–13
  and state allowance 14, 15, 163
  in work 23, 24, 35, 255
Chile and pensions 285, 286–8, 289
choice and individual liberty 93
Christian democracy 228, 247, 370
Christian socialism 68
Christianity
  and corporatism 162
  and welfare provision 22, 24–5, 370
citizenship
  and civil rights 32, 33–4, 35, 37–8, 54, 135, 156, 160
  and defence of the state 133–4
  economic 202
  and employment 134, 191, 198–9, 202
  and equal worth 37, 54–5, 56, 62, 137, 141, 147
  European 198–203, 228, 261
  and independence 99, 113, 133–5
  industrial 38
  and patriarchy 142
  and political rights 32, 34, 35, 37–8, 54, 83, 202
  and self-government 134
  and social class 32–41, 114, 157, 159
  and social rights 32, 34–6, 38–40, 42, 157, 191–2, 200–2, 261
  and welfare rights 29, 114, 157
  of women 35, 133–4, 137–44, 146–9
civic culture 378
civil service
  and state corporatism 159–60
  and state welfare 155, 166
Claimants' Union 124
class, social
  and citizenship 32–41, 114, 157, 159
  and coalition-building 83, 165–6, 167–8, 266, 332–3
  and conflict *see* conflict, social
  in Marx 85–6
  and patriarchy 135
  and political rights 34, 85–8
  and politics 85–8, 107, 115
  'post-industrial' 162
  and power resources 77–88
  and right to work 33
  and social rights 38–9, 162
  in Weber 85–6
  and welfare regimes 5, 18, 22–4, 29, 121, 159–61, 162, 164
  see also middle classes; underclass; working class
coercion by the state 63, 90–3, 115, 370
cohabitation rights 119, 129, 138–9
Commission on Social Justice 2, 51–62, 243

compensation, welfare benefits as 44, 46–8, 73, 192, 212
competitiveness
labour market 220–1, 228, 248–9, 259–60
regulatory/locational 255–6, 257, 259
and social welfare 5–6, 7, 93, 222, 223, 234–53, 332, 358; compatibility/incompatibility theories 235–46, *237*, 248, 249; contingency theories 246–50; and equality 243–5; regime differences 239–43, 247–50, 268
compromise and power resources 82–3, 88
conduct, politics of 107–8, 111–14
conflict
and democracy 85–8
institutionalized 87
intergenerational 6–7, 277, 293–307, 364, 374–5
social 67, 68, 71–3, 75, 77, 81–8, 108, 115
consciousness, social 81
consensus
as role of state 266–7
and welfare provision 2, 75, 99, 161, 220, 228, 244, 249, 291, 331
conservatism
and critique of welfare state 69–73, 75–6, 107–8, 110, 309–19
and ecologism 345
and economic growth 65, 69–70, 114
and social reform 22, 24, 68, 111, 113, 116
and women in labour market 163
see also state corporatism
consumption
private 65
social 64–6, 68, 123–4
contingencies, social 18–20, 25–7, 73
see also age; unemployment
control, social 27, 74–5, 111–12, 115, 121, 124, 344
corporatism *see* bargaining, societal; state corporatism

crime
and economy 244–5
and poverty 1, 3, 11, 15, 108–9, 114, 245

death grant 52–3
decentralization and European social model 221–4, 225, 228
democracy
and class conflict 85–8, 115
industrial 146, 147, 225
and power resources 83
and welfare bureaucracy 94
and welfare demands 29, 67
see also social democracy
demography and social change 6, 250, 271–307, 331, 373
Denmark
and decentralization 222
and pensions 21, 280
and social democracy 249
and unemployment 241, 249
union membership 217
dependence, mutual 29, 122, 148
dependency 234, 365–6, 371
female 119–21, 125–6, 128–9, 133–6, 138–45, 148–9
and politics 107–17
and poverty 3, 100, 101–2, 107–11, 162
wage dependency 125, 129–30
desert
and eligibility 74, 109, 135–6, 156, 201
and social justice 52, 58–60, 300
differentiation in welfare state provision 8
disability benefit 23, 125
disaggregation and feminism 127, 128–9
discrimination
and fair reward 60–1
positive 48–9
diswelfare allocation 44–7, 365
divorce and poverty 129, 136
dualism, social, welfare-state 159–61, 162–3, 166, 247, 357

Dutch Socio-Economic Panel Survey 185–6 n.6

ecology
  and social conflict 87
  and social welfare 7, 260, 343–51
economics
  classical 65, 90
  demand-side 238
  historical 22
  Keynesian 68, 84, 238, 254, 263, 267
  monetarist 68–9, 234, 263
  and monetary union 224, 226–7, 259
  neo-classical 235, 240
  positive policies 27–8
  supply-side 234, 263–4, 267
economy
  and boundary control 254–5, 258, 259–61
  as challenge to welfare 5–6
  and competitiveness 234–53
  efficiency and social policies 5, 6, 18–19, 43, 70, 235, 238, 241–3, 271, 340–2
  and European social model 5, 207–8, 210–21, 226–9
  and globalization 6, 244, 246, 254–6, 257–9, 263–9, 376
  hidden 249
  interdependence of 210
  liberalization 214, 215
  and national economic governance 254–6, 263–9
  political 22, 28, 155, 159, 275, 303
  and recession 68, 74, 109, 210, 226, 338
  social 378
  and war on poverty 101–2, 105, 109, 111
  and welfare regime 173, 182–3
  see also fiscal policies; justice, social; market economy; monetary policy
education
  and citizenship 32, 35–6, 38
  and dependency politics 112–13, 115

and economic growth 242–3
  educational leave 158
  and equality 56, 248
  and European social model 211–12
  and expenditure 64, 249, 370
  as investment 45, 46, 377
  and poverty 12, 13–14, 15, 108–10, 115
  and social justice 55, 56, 58
  and social mobility 159
  state provision 68, 72, 90–1
  and universal services 42
effort
  and fair reward 6
  and social justice 59–60
eligibility 47, 156
  and gender 135–6, 137–8
  nature 44
  and need 46, 74, 158
  and retrenchment 312, 315, 321–2, 331, 341
  rules 44, 46, 162
  and social justice 52, 57, 58–60, 62
emancipation and social democracy 163
employment
  casualized 337–8
  and citizenship 134, 191, 198–9, 202
  European policies 198–9, 209, 226
  full 147, 149, 241, 356, 377–8; and welfare regime 155, 163, 165–6, 173, 192, 194, 214
  insecurity 337–41
  and job creation 376
  part-time 323–4, 338–9, 341, 357
  policies 247
  protection 112, 241, 339–40, 356
  public 4–5, 14–15, 57, 115, 124; female 121, 191, 371; and retrenchment 312, *313*, 322, 326, 328, *329*
  restrictions on 33
  self-employment 199, 339–40
  and social justice 58
  see also industrial relations; labour market; work

employment ethic 347–8, 350
entitlement *see* eligibility
entrepreneurialism 376–7
Equal Opportunities Commission 127
Equal Pay Act (1970) 61
equality
  and citizenship 36–41, 114
  and competitiveness 243–5, 248–9
  and efficiency 235, 241–2, 243
  and feminism 125–9
  of income 166, 173–4, 178–80, 184
  of opportunity 56, 62, 80, 110, 260
  and social democracy 5, 163
  and social justice 52, 54, 56–7, 58–61, 92, 107, 180
  and welfare provision 18, 21, 23, 29, 160, 173
European Community
  and basic income 191–4, 201–2
  Common Agricultural Policy 260
  and competitiveness 249, 358
  and European social model 224–7
  harmonization measures 5, 190, 194, 195–7, 201, 377
  and immigration 111
  internal market 256, 259
  and labour market 210–11, 213–14, 247, 260
  and Maastricht treaty 190, 199, 202, 225–6, 260, 264
  and monetary union 202, 224, 226–7, 259, 264
  regional funds 260
  and social charges 236
  and social policy integration 5, 190–203, *198*, 207, 227, 244, 331
  welfare regimes 5, 190–203, 208–10, 212–13, 247–8
European Community Household Panel 185 n.5
European Management Forum 239
European social model 5, 207–32, 260–1
  and common crisis 209–11, 216
  and convergence 207, 209–10, 216

and co-ordinated decentralization 221–4
and divergence and decentralization 208, 213–16, 225
and the European Union 224–7
identification 208–9
lean production and social adaptation 218–20
and limits to flexibility 220–1
and loss of functionality 211–13
and trade unions 209, 216–18
European Union *see* European Community
Europeanization
  as challenge to welfare 257, 259–61
  and poverty policy 195–203
exchange relations and power resources 81–2
exclusion, social 221, 227, 228, 337–8, 355–7, 364
  and the third way 372, 375, 376
expenditure
  acceptance 28
  changing composition 329–3, 370
  and competitiveness 249
  crisis 138, 167, 296
  and debt interest payments 211, 236, 249, 288
  and employer contributions 28
  and European model 209, 211
  impact on poverty 97–8, 100, 101–2
  as measure of welfare effort 4, 154–6, 236–9, 245–6, 249, 321–2, 325–31, 341, 370–1
  and monopoly industries 64–6
  reduction 7, 70, 74, 111, 114–15, 116, 138, 213, 226, 249, 288, 312–15
  and social capital 63–5
  and spending service cliché 74
  on state pensions 6
expenses, social 63, 64–6
exploitation and exclusion 71, 355–7

factory legislation 21, 23–5, 26, 28, 35
fairness
  and free market 51

fairness (*cont'd*)
  and social justice   53, 54, 55, 56, 58,
    60–1
family
  in corporatist state   162, 249
  and employment ethic   347
  and employment insecurity   339–41
  and female dependency   119–20
  and feminism   127–8
  and male breadwinner   134–7,
    141–3, 172, 247, 249, 362
  poverty and family breakup   103–5,
    110, 111, 113
  and provision of welfare   138, 157
  in social democratic state   163
family allowances   26, 142–4
  and universal provision   42
  and women   119–20
feminism
  and coalition-building   145–6
  and disaggregation   127, 128–9
  and domestic labour   347
  and family allowance   143–4
  and feminist agencies   122, 144–5
  and labour movement   123, 128,
    130, 146–8
  liberal   141, 142, 146–7
  libertarian   119–20, 123
  and men   130–1
  'new'   125–7
  and organization   130
  and politics   122–4
  and social policy   3, 119–31, 136, 345
  socialist   127–30
  and women's liberation   120,
    126–31
Finland
  and pensions   373–4
  and unemployment   371
fiscal policies   226, 264–6, 285
food stamps   99
France
  and debt interest payments   211
  economic policies   210, 227, 263
  and industrial relations   217
  as 'Latin rim' regime   194, 203 n.6
  régulation school   218

social policies   24, 377
  and state corporatism   159, 162,
    247
  welfare expenditure   28
friendly societies   160, 364
funerals and state allowance   14, 15

GDP
  and pensions provision   274, *275*
  and welfare state effort   182–3,
    238–9, 312, *313*, *314*, 321, 326–7,
    326, 370
gender   *see* feminism
generations, economic/sociological
    297–301
German Socio-Economic Panel   185
    n.6
Germany
  and decentralization   222–3
  and economic growth   182–3, 223,
    253 n.57, 268–9
  and European social model   222–4
  and expenditure   312–15, 327
  and income inequality   60, 178–80,
    323, 325
  and income instability   181–2
  and industrial relations   217, 222–3
  panel studies   170–1
  and pensions   373
  and political coalitions   165
  and poverty   174–8, *196*
  and regional government   267
  social policies   21–4, 68, 158, 161,
    197–9, 202, 204 n.7, 214, 222–3,
    369–70
  and societal bargaining   83–4
  and state corporatism   159, 162, 172,
    174–83, 191–2, 194, 223, 247
  and taxation   238
  and unemployment   211, 212, 223,
    240, 377–8
  unification   214, 223
globalization
  as challenge to welfare   6, 244, 246,
    257–9, 376, 378
  and national economic governance
    254–6, 263–9

GNP and social policy expenditure 74, 101–2, 274–5
goal displacement 87–8
government *see* state
Great Society and reduction of poverty 97, 99, 101–3, 106, 108, 111, 116
Greece and resource distribution 224
growth, economic 114
  and equality 243–5
  and European social model 208, 210–11
  and expansion of welfare state 68–70, 75
  Green critique 345–6, 348–9
  and old-age provision 271, 276–7
  and social capital 63–6
  sustainable 343, 348–9
  and war on poverty 101–2
  and welfare expenditure 239, 240
  and welfare regime 5, 173, 182–3, 192

hazard, moral 371, 375
health, personal
  and national insurance 25, 47, 55
  and privatization 300
  and social justice 55–6, 58
  and the state 20–1, 55, 68, 72, 99, 244, 370
  and universal provision 42, 43, 209
health, public, and the state 20
housework
  as female responsibility 126
  wages for 122, 124–5
housing
  benefit 341
  deregulation of provision 242
  and negative equity 242, 340, 341
  public provision 26, 68, 72, 98, 99, 315, 370
human nature and poverty 116–17
human relations movement and welfare capitalism 28

ideologies as power resources 78
ignorance and poverty 12

incapacity benefit 338
income
  basic/minimum 8, 92, 124–5, 147, 191–4, 201–2, 350–1, 355–9, 374
  distribution 39–40, 48, 59, 73, 159, 173, 235, 247
  and economic growth 182–3, *183*
  and family breakup 104–5
  household 136
  inequalities 323–4, *324*, 356; and competitiveness 248–50; and external constraints 258; and gender 128, 323–4; and market economy 60; and old age 300; and welfare regime 110, 166, 173–4, 178–80, *179*
  and labour force participation 103, 112
  protection 163, 356
  volatility 171, 173–4, 175, 179, 180–2, *181*, 184–5, 337, 340–1
income support 339, 340, 341
income transfer 7, 8, 18, 64, 139
  and income inequalities 179–80
  and income instability 181–2
  intra-European 197–8, 201, 224, 260
  and liberal regimes 162, 174, 175–6, 192
  and poverty levels 96–101, 106 n.5, 174–6
  and Scandinavian regimes 191
  and social-democratic regimes 163
independence
  and citizenship 99, 113, 133–5
  and defence of the state 133–4
  and self-government 134
  and self-protection 133
  and social democracy 163
  of women 119–20, 133–5
Index of Sustainable Economic Welfare 349
individual
  de-commodification 157–9, 162–3, 247
  and economic freedom 33–4, 35, 38, 90–1, 93–4

industrial relations   29, 69
  and competitiveness   241
  and European social model
    209–10, 212–16, 218–23, 224–6,
    228, 261
  and trade unions   209, 216–17
  see also bargaining
industrialism
  Green critique   345–6, 349
  and welfare   19, 154–5
industrialization and class formation
  165, 208
industry
  and industrial injury   44
  and industrial policy   263–4
  and labour market   211
  monopoly   64–6
  and welfare conditions   26, 28
inequality
  and capitalism   36–7, 107
  increasing   108, 321, 322–5
  in pay   61, 143
  and power resources   81
  reduction   39–41
  and social justice   54, 58–61, 62,
    107
  see also income
insurance, private   155, 160, 162, 166,
  340, 365
insurance, social   27–8, 64, 68, 357
  in Britain   25, 27, 139–40, 364
  and corporatism   159–61, 162, 163,
    167, 172–3
  and European model   209
  in Germany   21–4, 158, 166, 172–3,
    198–9, 369
  and labour market performance
    157
  reduction   249
  and retrenchment   329–32
  and role of the state   90–3, 158
  and social stratification   159–61,
    162, 167
  and universal provision   42, 162–3
  in USA   136
  and women   139–40, 162
integration, European

and loss of boundary control   6,
  254–6, 259–61, 268
negative/positive   190, 254–61
and social policy   5, 190–203, *198*,
  207, 227, 244, 331
integration, social   39, 45, 48, 203, 221,
  228
interest rates and global markets
  254–5, 263
International Labor Office   27
Invalid Care Allowance (Britain)   138
invalidity insurance in Germany   21,
  23
investment
  and global finance   254–5
  of power resources   78
  private   65, 69–70, 236, 240, 245,
    250, 282–3, 289
  social   45, 46, 64–6, 274, 373–8
Ireland
  and industrial relations   222
  and resource distribution   224
Italy
  and debt interest payments   211
  and income inequality   323
  and industrial districts   222
  as 'Latin rim' regime   194
  and pensions   273, 274, 373
  and political coalition-building
    165
  and regional government   267
  and state corporatism   84, 159, 162,
    222, 249
  welfare expenditure   28

Japan
  and employment policies   247,
    250
  and income distribution   60, 248,
    250
  industrial systems   219
  and pensions   290, 373
  and social expenditure   236, 239,
    249–50
  and social integration   203, 268–9
justice, distributive   *see* justice, social
justice, right to   32

justice, social   19, 22, 37, 40–1, 51–62,
    81, 164, 173
    and conflict   54, 57–8
    and desert   52, 58–60
    and ecology   343–51
    and equal worth of citizens   54–5,
        56, 62
    and equality   52, 54, 56–7, 92, 107
    and free market   51, 60–1, 107, 258
    and merit   52, 53, 58
    and need   52, 53, 55–6, 62
    and opportunities and life-chances
        56–8, 62
    theories   53–4

Keynes/Keynesianism   28, 68, 84, 238,
    254, 263, 267

labour
    and capital   67, 70–1, 73, 80, 81–3,
        123–4, 129, 217
    costs   236–8
    protective legislation   23, 25, 68, 70,
        73, 126–7, 130
    reproduction   64, 123–4, 137
    reserve army   71
    sexual division   347
    supply   235, 236–8, *237*, 240–2, 246
Labour Code (Germany, 1891)   24
labour market   102–3, 105, 109–10,
    112, 249
    decentralization   228
    and de-commodification   157–9
    deregulation   220–1, 225, 248, 249,
        256, 337, 375
    effects of welfare state   237–8, 240,
        323
    and European social model   210–11,
        213–14, 247, 260
    flexibility   220–1, 244, 247, 248–9,
        357
    and human capital as power
        resource   79–80
    and poverty   174
    regulation   5, 7, 191–2, 194
    and unemployment benefit   71,
        240–1

    women in   260, 345; and casualized
        work   338–9; and
        competitiveness   241–2, 249–50;
        and dependency   128, 137–42,
        147; and social democracy   163,
        191, 238; and state
        corporatism   162, 163, 194;
        working hours   23, 35, 126–7
    see also employment; industrial
        relations; retirement
labour movement
    and civil rights   38
    and collective power   69, 70, 73
    and feminism   123, 128, 130, 146–8
    and public policy   67
    and social consumption   66, 68,
        123–4
    and socialism   29, 88, 164
    and state corporatism   159–60, 191–2
    and welfare state regimes   164
    see also trade unions
language and social conflict   86–7
law and order
    as central concern   109
    as role of state   90–1, 245
liberalism
    alternatives to   24
    and Christianity   24–5
    and coalition-building   249, 250
    and de-commodification   247
    and economic growth   184
    'embedded'   258
    and employment   247
    feminist   141, 142, 146–7
    and income inequality   178–80, 248
    and income instability   181–2
    and the market   162, 163, 167
    and monopoly capital   65
    and old-age provision   295–6
    opposition to   24
    and poverty   26, 107, 110–11, 112,
        115–16, 174–7
    and residual welfare state   47, 156,
        166, 167–8, 172–3, 191–4, 201,
        247–9, 329–31
    and welfare state regime   4, 5,
        162–8, 172–83, 247

liberalism (*cont'd*)
  see also Beveridgism
libertarianism
  feminist 119–20, 123
  and social justice 51
liberty
  and aims of welfare state 90–4
  as civil right 33–4, 35
  and coercion by state 63, 90–2, 115, 370
  and equality 23
  individual 3, 33–4, 35
  and social justice 54–5, 56–7
Local Employment and Trading Systems (LETS) 351
London and state provision of employment 14–15
Luxembourg Income Study (LIS) 170, 325

management and power resources 80
market economy
  and boundary control 255, 258
  and inefficiency 242, 340–2
  and market society 67, 69
  and Poor Laws 34–5
  and poverty 25–6, 36–7
  and power resources 84
  and social capital 66
  and social justice 51, 60–1, 107
  and social rights 37–8, 40, 42, 157, 162, 202–3
  and social security 18, 72, 124, 162
  and social-assistance welfare state 158
  and social-democratic welfare state 163
  and state corporatism 162, 192
  and Weberian theory of class 85–6
  and welfare state 18–19, 21, 25, 28, 72, 73, 112, 161, 167, 235
marriage
  and female poverty 136–7
  and private provision of welfare 138
  and rape 134
  and social security 14, 15, 128–9, 139–40

Marxism
  and class 85–6
  and feminism 121, 123
  see also structure, social
maternity leave in de-commodifying states 158
means testing 39, 45, 124
  and disaggregation 128
  and European policy 201
  and liberal regimes 27, 162, 171, 172
  and need 158, 192
  and pensions 289
  and retrenchment 312, 321, 325
  and social assistance 155, 162, 325, 329
  and social stratification 159
  and stigmatization 47, 157, 159, 162
  and women 136
Medicaid 99
Medicare 99
men
  as citizens 133–5, 148
  and feminism 130–1
  and welfare benefits 136
  as workers 134–7, 139, 142–3, 146, 148
merit and social justice 52, 53, 58
Michigan Panel Study of Income Dynamics 171, 185 n.6
middle classes
  and occupational fringe benefits 166
  and old age 295
  and opt-outs 6, 155, 331
  and political coalitions 83, 166, 167, 247, 332–3
  and universalism 160–1, 162–3, 166, 316
monetarism 68–9, 234, 263
monetary policy 214, 226, 236, 258–9, 263, 264–6, 285
Moneylenders Act (Britain) 24
monopoly sector and social capital 64–6

National Health Insurance 25, 47

National Health Service and
  universalism 48
National Insurance Act (Britain, 1946)
  139–40
National Providence League 24
nationalism and welfare provision 43
need
  and causality 73
  and eligibility 46, 74, 158
  and market society 67, 192
  and social justice 52, 53, 55–6, 62
  and social policy 197
neo-corporatism
  and distribution of power 77, 85,
    155
  and European social model 213, 222
  and societal bargaining 83–4, 87
neo-liberalism 220, 256, 371, 375
Netherlands
  and economic growth 182–3
  and income inequality 178–80, 274
  and income instability 181–2
  and labour costs 375–6
  panel studies 170–1, 184
  and poverty levels 174–8
  and social service delivery 369–70
  and unemployment 376
New Deal 164, 165
New Zealand
  and income inequality 323
  and labour market flexibility 247
  as liberal/residual welfare state 192,
    248
  social security legislation 27
Newsom Report 47, 48
NICs (newly industrialized countries)
  and competitiveness 257–8, 268
Norway
  and political coalitions 165
  and social insurance 161

obligations, social, and rights 3
OECD
  and competitiveness survey 238,
    240–1
  and economic growth 182
  and pensions provision 274, 331

and unemployment 375
and welfare retrenchment 312, *313,
  314,* 320, 323–8, *324, 326, 328, 329,*
  340
opportunity
  equality of 56, 62, 80, 110, 260
  and underclass 107, 110

Panel Comparability (PACO) Project
  185 nn.2,5, 186 n.10
parental leave 158, 225
participation
  in labour force 102–3, 109, 110,
    112, 121, 138–42, 148–9
  social 147–8
parties, political
  and class 86, 87–8
  and power resources 80, 83, 311
  and welfare state regimes 164–6
partnerships, public-private 21
paternalism and welfare 29, 93–4, 111,
  115–17, 222
patriarchy
  challenges to 140–9
  and citizenship 142
  and class 135
  and welfare state 133–50
pensions 271–80, 281–92, 372
  and annuities 279, 282
  and citizenship 40
  in de-commodifying states 158
  and demographic change 271–80,
    300, 373
  and European social model 212
  and inflation 275, 284
  and intra-European transfer 197–8
  invalidity 140, 194
  pay-as-you-go 240, 271–4, 276–7,
    279, 282–3, 288–9, 317
  and postmodernity 364–5
  private 6, 240, 276–9, 282–6, 289,
    290, 317, 340
  and social investment strategies
    373–5
  state provision 6, 13, 21, 23, 24, 26,
    166, 249, 259, 317
  and universal provision 43, 209

pensions (*cont'd*)
  war 44
  for women 140
Plowden Report 47, 48
politics
  and coalition-building 68, 83,
    145–6, 165–6, 167–8, 249–50, 266,
    332–3
  of conduct 107–8, 111–14
  and democratic class struggle 85–8,
    115
  of dependency 108–17
  and feminism 122–4
  generational 303–4
  interest-group 311, 316, 320–1,
    331–2
  and participation 32
  and political change 75–6
  of poverty 3, 7, 107–17
  and the private sphere 141–2, 147
  and social justice 53–4
  and state expenditure 66, 331
  third way 8, 369–78
  and the underclass 107–17, 171, 249
  and welfare state regimes 164
  and welfare state retrenchment
    309–17, 320–33
  see also rights, political
pollution, environmental 44, 265–6,
  378
Poor Law
  and citizenship 34–5, 40
  and eligibility 186 n.15, 197
  opposition to 12, 15, 24–5, 26–7
  and social stratification 159
postmodernity and the welfare state
  8, 304, 360–7
poverty
  and civil rights 35
  and competence and motivation
    107, 111–12, 115–16
  and crime 1, 3, 11, 15, 108–9, 114,
    245
  'culture' 110–11
  definition 174
  and desert 74, 109, 116, 135–6, 156,
    201, 300

duration 170, 177–8
  and education 12, 13–14, 115
  European policy 195–203
  and family breakup 103–5, 110, 113
  female 128–9
  feminization 141
  and labour force participation
    102–3, 109, 112
  latent 99–100, 102–5
  and market system 25–6, 36–7
  measurement 96–8, 174–8, *175*,
    176, 234–5, 327
  net 98–9, 100, 102, 105, 174–7
  new politics of 3, 7, 107–17
  official 96–8, 100, 102, 105, 176
  panel studies 171–4
  passive 110–11, 113, 115–17
  and political rights 35
  'poverty line' 96, 110, 112, 170, 174,
    177, 287
  and prevention 43
  primary/secondary 21, 26
  recurrence 170–1, 177–8, *177*
  and social control 74
  and social rights 34–5
  state relief of 12, 14–15, 25, 97–8,
    174–8, *176*
  and stigmatization 28, 35, 40, 157
  'trickle down' effect 97, 101
  and unemployment 355–7
  wars against 96–106, 171
  welfare regimes compared 174–8,
    249
  see also exclusion; means testing;
    Poor Law; underclass
power
  collective 69, 80
  inequalities 58, 61, 67, 84
  private appropriation 66
power resources model 77–88, 320,
  332
  basic/derived 78
  and control of capital 79–80
  distribution 77, 80–2, 84, 85, 87–8
  and human capital 79–80
  and means of violence 78–9
  and social change 81–3, 85

prevention and social service
    provision 43, 73
privatization
    and pension provision 6, 240,
    276–9, 282–6, 289, 290, 317
    and welfare state retrenchment 312
production and Marxian class theory
    85–6, 87
productivism
    and Giddens 365
    Green critique 346–8
    and social policy 249–50
productivity
    and competitiveness 216, 235, *237*,
    239, 241–4, 248, 249–50, 259
    and disincentives to work 69, 70–1,
    242, 248
    and expansion of welfare state 6,
    43, 69–70
    and social capital 63–6, 378
professions and state control 25
profitability and welfare costs 69–70
property
    and class 86
    and inheritance 58
    and self-respect 56
    and state intervention 73
    and women 134

race
    and class and social conflict 86–7
    and dependency politics 114
    and family breakup 103–5
    and labour force participation
    102–3, 110
rape in marriage 134
rationing of services 47–8
recession and welfare reduction 68,
    74, 109, 226
redistribution *see* justice, social
religion and social conflict 86–7
repression
    by state 83
    by welfare state 74
Rerum Novarum (encyclical of Leo
    XIII) 24
resource distribution

coalitions 266
    and efficiency 235, 238
    and European Union 224, 228, 260
    and health care 55–6
    and intergenerational conflict
    293–4, 297, 301–2, 364
    and pension provision 277–8, 294
    and power 77, 80–2, 191
    and taxation 310
    and unemployment 57
    see also justice, social
respect, mutual, and citizenship 147
retirement, early 212, 273, 295, 299,
    338
reward, fair 60–1
rights
    civil 32–4, 35, 37–8, 54, 125, 135, 156
    de-commodified 4, 158, 162
    legal 125
    political 32, 34, 35, 37–8, 54, 83,
    85–8, 125
    property 157
    social 19, 32, 34–6, 38–40, 42–3,
    137, 157–8, 162, 200
    and social obligations 3
    v. charity 57
    to welfare *196*, 199, 201
risk 67, 363–7, 372, 375
    and pensions 281–2
    and welfare retrenchment 310
Royal Commission on the Aged Poor
    (Britain) 38
Royal Commission on the Poor Laws
    (Britain, 1905–9) 27
Royal Commission on Population
    (1949) 293–4

savings
    and competitiveness 240
    and old-age welfare 274, 275–9,
    281–5, 288–9, 373
Scandinavia
    and industrial relations 217
    and social democracy 163–4, 167,
    173, 214–15
    welfare regimes 191, *193*, 194,
    247–8, 250, 258, 321, 322, 371

school meals provision 43
security, social *see* welfare
Seebohm Committee 48
selection
  and positive discrimination 48–9
  and quality of services 47–8
selectivity and universalism 42, 46–9,
  156, 192
self help and welfare 20, 28
self-protection and citizenship 133
self-respect and social justice 56, 57,
  62
Sex Discrimination Act (Britain, 1975)
  138
sickness insurance 21, 140, 158–9,
  240, 242
social democracy
  and coalition-building 165, 166, 250
  and competitiveness 247, 249
  and economic growth 5, 182–3
  and European social model 214–15,
    228
  and income inequality 5, 178–80,
    184, 247, 249
  and income instability 181–2, 184
  and monetary policy 214, 258–9
  and poverty levels 5, 174–8, 184,
    249
  and power resources 87
  welfare regimes 2, 4, 23–4, 68,
    162–6, 167, 172, 173–7, 370
social policy
  and ageing population 295, 296
  and competitiveness 234–53
  critical 362–3, 366–7
  and dependency 112–13, 116–17,
    162, 365–6
  European 190–203, 207–32, 244
  and feminism 3, 119–31, 136, 345
  Green 343–51
  and integration 45
  and modernity 8, 360–6
  post-industrial 113
  reform 224
social services, universalism v.
    selectivity 42–9, 156, 160–1,
    162–3, 173

Social Work and the Community 48
socialism
  alternatives to 24
  Christian 68
  and critique of welfare state 73–5,
    76, 124
  and feminism 127–9
  and labour movement 29, 88, 164–5
  and liberty 91–2
  opposition to 24
  reformist 88, 124–5
  and rural economy 165
  and social policy 124–32, 160
  state 7, 22
  and universalism 160
society
  30/30/40 337–42
  and allocation of diswelfare 44–7
  market 67, 69
  Marxist-Leninist model 77, 78–80,
    82, 85–6
  and poverty 26
  protection 44, 46
  and social change 81–3, 85
  and social conflict 67–9, 71–3, 75,
    81–8
  'work-centred' 191, 192, 321
  see also structure
solidarity
  class 160, 166, 247
  intergenerational 301–3
  national 160, 163, 266, 268–9, 344
  social 155, 228–9, 244, 370, 372
Spain
  and labour market reforms 221
  and societal bargaining 83–4
  and unemployment 211, 214, 221
standards, minimum 21, 39, 57–8
state
  and borrowing 236
  and capital accumulation 63–6,
    69–70, 72, 74, 75, 77
  and class conflict 67, 71, 75, 82–4,
    87
  and coercion 63, 90–3, 115, 370
  defence 133–4
  and female dependency 120, 125

fiscal crisis   63–6, 73–4, 207–8, 296
and fiscal policies   264–6, 285
legitimacy   63, 64–5
minimal role   90
and national economic governance
  254–6, 263–9, 285–6
and the professions   25
and provision of employment
  14–15
and provision of welfare   12–15,
  19–20, 21–9, 55, 68, 72, 90–4, 107,
  295
and regional government   267
and repression   83
'social service' state   18
structure   155–6
territorial boundaries   6, 254–6, 258,
  259–61
and use of violence   79
see also expenditure; welfare state
state corporatism   4, 5, 63–4, 83–4, 87
and competitiveness   244, 247, 249,
  268–9
and decentralization.   223
and de-commodification   247
and economic growth   182–3, 244
and European Union   225
and income inequalities   178–80,
  192, 247
and income volatility   180–2, 184
and monetary policy   258
and poverty levels   174–8
and social insurance   159–61, 162,
  163–4, 167, 172–3
state socialism   7, 22
stigmatization
and means testing   47, 157, 159, 162
and poor-law provision   28, 35, 40
and universalism   43, 48
stratification in welfare state   88, 157,
  159–61, 162, 167, 247
structure, social
Marxist-Leninist model   77, 78–80,
  82, 85–6
neo-corporatist model   77, 80
pluralist-industrial model   77, 79,
  80, 85–6

power resources model   77–88
subservience and welfare   23
subsidiarity and state corporatism
  162–3, 225, 261
Supplementary Benefits Commission
  48
sustainability   343, 348–9, 351
Sweden
and de-commodification   344
and dependency politics   114
economic policy   210, 214
and European social model   214–15
and income distribution   60, 191,
  214, 274, 325
and labour mobilization   164
and panel studies   186 n.10
and political coalitions   165
and Poor Law   26–7
and public employment   328
and retrenchment   312, 316, 321–2,
  329–31
and social conflict   67
and social democracy   172, 191, 203
  n.3, 244, 247, 249
and social insurance   27, 161
and social service delivery   370
and unemployment   210, 241, 249,
  323
and welfare expenditure   327
Switzerland
and national insurance   21
and pensions   279–80

talent
and desert   59–60
and fair reward   61
taxation
and capital accumulation   63, 69
child allowance   120
and disaggregation   128
and education   12, 15
effects on income   39
and energy consumption   265–6
evasion   273
and fiscal welfare   155
income tax   120, 128, 237–8, 265,
  341

taxation (*cont'd*)
and labour supply 237–8
and married man's allowance 139
of mobile factors 226, 265
and pensions 13, 271–4, 279, 288–9, 301
of the poor 11–12
and private welfare 161, 249
reduction 228
tax credit proposals 119–20
and tax-transfer system 139, 172, 186 n.9
and unemployment 15
and welfare expenditure 28, 112, 116, 249–50, 310, 371
Thatcher, Margaret; Thatcherism
and disincentives to work 70
and intergenerational conflict 303
and welfare state 7, 72, 138, 146, 155, 315, 332, 370
tourism, social 204 n.11
trade unions
and civil rights 38
and collective power 69, 70, 73, 80, 83, 87, 340
decline in membership 217–18
and European social model 209, 216–18, 223
and fraternal welfare 160
and globalization 255–6
and goal displacement 87–8
and labour party formation 164–5
and protective legislation 127, 130
and public policy 67, 68
reform 220
and welfare benefits to women 120, 143
and welfare regimes 164
and welfare state retrenchment 316–17
see also labour movement
training, vocational
and economic growth 243, 249, 377
and European social model 211–12, 223
transfer *see* benefits; income transfer

underclass
and European policy 201
female 141
and new politics 107–17, 171
and opportunity 107, 110
and welfare state 3, 108–11, 114, 170–1, 249
unemployment
chronic 19, 97
and economy 102, 103, 238, 249, 337–9
and European social model 210–11, 212, 214, 221, 223, 227
and expansion of welfare state 6, 25, 27–8, 312
and exploitation 71, 355–7
and income inequality 324, 337–8, *338*
increase 114, 338, 341, 371
and industrialism 19
involuntary 27
as social disservice 44
and social investment strategies 375–6
and social justice 57
and state responsibilities 84
youth 212
unemployment insurance
in de-commodifying states 158
as disincentive to work 71, 240–2
and eligibility 74, 316
and welfare regimes 24, 27, 43, 323
United States
and armed forces 134
compared with Britain 20
and crime 245
economic policy 28, 182–3, 268
Equal Rights Amendment 133–4
and expenditure 28–9, 312, 327
and female dependency 136
feminist health and welfare services 122
health care 99, 241
and income inequality 178–80, 247, 248, 274, 324–5
and income instability 181–2
industrial systems 218–19

and intergenerational conflict 295,
296–7, 299, 302
and investment in human resources
376
labour market flexibility 220, 247,
248–9
labour movement 29
and labour supply 240
and liberal feminism 141, 146
as liberal welfare state 162, 163–4,
167–8, 172, 174–83, 194–5, 247,
248–9
and male violence 133, 149 n.2
panel studies 171–2
and pensions 284, 288, 290
and personal health 20, 55
and political coalitions 165
and poverty; levels 174–8; new
politics 107–17, 135;
persistence 170–1; policies
96–106, 195–6, 197, 199–200, 201,
203
and regulation 255–6
and social charges 236
and social conflict 67
and unemployment 27, 356, 375,
377–8
and welfare bureaucracy 94
universalism 42–9
and European welfare state 191–2,
201, 203, 209
and retrenchment 329–31
and social insurance 42, 162–3
and welfare regimes 156, 160–1,
165–6, 173, 247, 321
urbanization and European social
model 208, 217

victimhood and dependency politics
114
violence
male 133
as power resource 78–9

wages
and differentials 61, 110, 143, 223,
323–4, *324*

efficiency 221
family wage 137, 143
for housework 124–5
minimum wage 68, 112, 124, 198,
241, 355
and poverty line 112, 228
and productivity 70
and reproduction of labour
power 123–4, 137
reservation 240
stabilization 215
wage dependency 125, 129–30
wealth and welfare provision 90, 92
welfare
and allocation of diswelfare 44–7,
365
and citizenship 32
and competitiveness 5–6, 7, 93,
234–53
and decentralization 222
definition 43–4
and disaggregation 127, 128–9
as disincentive to work 70–1, 117,
162, 184, 212, 240–2, 248
and ecology 7, 260, 343–51
and economic policies 27–8
eligibility rules 44, 47
and family breakup 103–5, 110,
111, 113
as female contribution 137–40, 142,
147–8
fiscal 155, 364, 365, 366
international comparisons 21–3,
27, 207, 271–80
as investment 45, 46, 64–6
and latent poverty 106 n.5
and market forces 18, 72, 124
non-state provision 19
positive 8, 366, 369–79
private 137–8, 158, 162, 166, 167,
249–50, 300–1
state provision 92
terminology 20
universalism v. selectivity 42–9,
156, 160–1, 162–3, 173
as waste 46, 47
see also desert

welfare capitalism
  contradictions   2, 67–76
  and industrial betterment   25, 28
  and investment control   254–5
  regimes   *see* welfare regimes
'welfare mothers'   144
welfare regimes   4, 154–69, 255
  Anglo-Saxon   158, 192–4, *193*, 194,
    197, 201
  'Bismarck' countries   *see* Austria;
    Germany
  and cause of differences   164–6, 167
  comparative studies   170–85, 247
  conservative   *see* state corporatism
  and economic growth   5, 173, 182–3
  and economic impact   246–50
  European   5, 190–4, 260
  and income inequalities   5, 178–80,
    184, 247–50
  'Latin rim' type   5, *193*, 194, 197
  liberal   4, 5, 162, 163, 166, 167–8,
    172–83
  and poverty   174–8
  and 'regime shopping'   259
  social-democratic   *see* social
    democracy
welfare society   373, 378
welfare state
  aims   91–3
  comparative approach to   4, 20,
    155–6, 170–85, 207, 217
  components   *see* assistance;
    insurance, social; universalism
  constraints   4, 5–6, 7, 257–61
  contradictions   2, 67–76
  crisis   138, 167, 207–8, 209–11,
    215–16, 296, 315
  critique   *see* conservatism; feminism
  de-commodifying   4, 157–9, 162–3,
    247, 344
  definitions   18–20, 154–6
  European   5, 190–203
  expansion   6, 25, 27–8, 68–70, 73,
    75, 309, 312, 317, 320, 332
  and feminist agencies   122, 144–5
  gender division in   3, 135
  historical perspective   18–31

  impact   170–85
  as inefficient   3, 73–4, 241–2, 271
  institutional   156, 192
  Keynesian approach   68
  meaning   90–5
  means of provision   20–1
  methods   92–4
  patriarchal structure   133–50
  and political change   75–6
  power resources model   77–88
  regimes   *see* welfare regimes
  as repressive   74
  residual   *see* liberalism
  re-specification   157–9
  retrenchment   7, 111, 114–15, 167,
    259, 309–17, 320–33
  and social administration   2
  and social harmony   63–4, 67–9,
    71–2, 75, 291
  social-assistance   158, 159, 161, 247
  socialist critique   73–5, 76
  as system of stratification   88, 157,
    159–61, 162, 167, 247
  typology   *see* welfare regimes
  see also bureaucracy; expenditure
welfare to work programmes   377
women
  in armed forces   133–4
  as citizens   35, 133–4, 137–44,
    146–9
  and civil rights   33, 125
  and dependency   119–21, 125–6,
    128–9, 133–6, 138–45, 148–9
  health   140
  in labour force   *see* labour market
  and minimum income   124–5
  as mothers   144
  and pay inequalities   61, 143
  and political rights   34, 125
  and private provision of welfare
    137–40
  as property holders   134
  and social rights   35, 137
  and underclass   141
  and welfare provision   30, 119–20
  as workers   137–40, 148, 194
  working hours   23, 35, 126–7

Women's Aid refuges   122
work
  right to   24, 33, 56–7, 135, 156, 163,
    191, 192
  and social democracy   163
  working hours   341, 348, 356, 376,
    378; female   23, 35, 126–7
work disincentives   69, 172, 212, 248
  and conservative critique   70–1
  and economic growth   184
  and unemployment benefit   71,
    240–2
  and welfare dependency   101–2,
    109–10, 117, 162
work ethic   71, 162
  and employment ethic   350
workfare programmes   113, 115, 116
working class
  and citizenship   37–8
  control of   124
  and false ideology   73, 75
  and feminism   146, 147
  in Germany   22–4
  and liberalism   162

mobilization   154–5, 157–8, 160,
    164–5, 167, 173
  and political coalition   83, 165–6,
    167–8, 332–3
  and poverty   112
  and power resources   81–3, 85, 87–8
  and social democracy   163
  and state corporatism   84, 87,
    159–61
  and underclass   108–11
  in United States   29
  and wage dependency   125, 129–30
  and welfare legislation   22–4, 25, 29,
    121
  and 'welfare mothers'   144
  see also labour movement; trade
    unions
World Bank
  Averting the Old Age Crisis   6, 271,
    276, 279, 281–92
  and education   243

youth, and dependency politics
    112–13

Name Index

Abrams, P. 298–9
Achenbaum, W. A. 295, 298
Adenauer, Konrad 161, 166
Ash, T. G. (quoted) 203
Atkinson, A. B. 239, 240, 241
  & Mogensen, G. V. 240–1

Bacon, R. & Eltis, W. 236
Bahro, R. 352 n.1
Baldwin, Peter (quoted) 372
Bane, Mary Jo & Ellwood, David
  T. 171, 185 n.4
Barr, N. 235, 243–4
Bauman, Z. 360–2
Beattie, R. 6, 281–92
Bentham, Jeremy 20
Blackley, W. L. 24
Booth, Charles 25–6, 30 n.15, 38
Boulding, K. E. 45
Bowles, S. & Gintis, H. 245
Boyer, Robert 218
Briggs, Asa 18–31
Brittain, Vera 141
Burke, Edmund 374
Burns, E. M. (quoted) 29
Burtless, Gary 323
Bush, George 108, 112

Cahill, Michael 352 n.1
Callahan, D. 296–7

Calmfors, L. & Drifill, J. 248
Cameron, D. R. 155
Campbell, B. (quoted) 138–9
Carter, Jimmy 112
Chadwick, E. 22
Charlton, Val 121
Cheal, D. 302
Clapham, J. H. 24
Clayton, Richard 7, 320–34
Coase, Ronald H. 221
Cole, T. R. 295–6
Colquhoun, Patrick 36
Cook, D. 365
Cutright, P. 155

Daly, H. & Cobb, J. 349
Daniels, N. 301–2
Dawson, W. H. (quoted) 21–2, 24
Dicey 20
Dirven, Henk-Jan 5, 170–88
Disraeli, Benjamin 24
Dukakis, Michael 108
Duncan, Greg 171

Eisenhower, Dwight D. 97
Ekins, P. 349
Engels, Friedrich 147
Esping-Andersen, Gøsta 203 n.2, 253
  n.57, 331
  and competitiveness 239, 246–7, 248

and definition of welfare state 154–6
and regime types 4–5, 161–9, 172, 246–7, 322–3, 329
and re-specification of welfare state 157–61
and welfare expenditure 312

Fanon, Franz 121
Featherstone, M. & Hepworth, M. 295, 304
Finch, J. & Mason, J. 302
Finegold, D. & Soskice, D. 243
Fitzpatrick, Tony 7, 343–52
Flora, Peter 310–11
Foucault, Michel 367
France, Anatole 54

Giddens, Anthony 8, 360–6, 369–79
Gieve, Katherine et al. (quoted) 120
Gilbert, B. B. 43
Goode, R. 364
Goodin, Robert E. 5, 170–88
Gough, Ian 6, 74, 234–53
Grahl, John 5, 207–32
Gramsci, A. 219
Gregg, P. et al. 241
Gregg, Paul 339

Habermas, Jürgen 352 n.6
Hagestad, G. 302
Harvey, D. 361
Hayek, Friedrich von 3, 51, 90–5
Headey, Bruce 5, 170–88
Heberle, 298
Heclo, H. 303–4
Hegel, G. W. F. 141, 148
Hewitt, C. 155
Hirst, Paul 6, 263–9
Hobbes, Thomas 133
Hutton, Will 7, 337–42

James, Estelle 6, 271–80
Jessop, Bob 87
Johnson, L. B. 97, 99, 101–2, 106, 171
Johnson, P. & Falkingham, J. 294

Katzenstein, P. 244
Kennedy, J. F. 97
Kenworthy, L. 245
Kersbergen, Kees van 370
Ketteler, von 24
Kolberg, J. & Uusitalo, H. 247
Korpi, Walter 2, 77–88, 155, 320, 332

Land, Hilary 126, 149 n.9
Lassalle, Ferdinand 23–4
Leibfried, Stephan 5, 190–204
  & Rieger, E. 244
Lijphart, A. 86
Lindbeck, Assar 371
Lloyd George, David 25
Lohmann, Theodor 23, 24

McGillivray, W. 6, 281–92
McIntosh, Mary 3, 119–32
McLaughlin, E. 241
Mann, Kirk 8, 360–7
Mannheim, K. 298
Marmor, T. R. et al. 297
Marshall, T. H. 2, 95 n.4, 363
  citizenship and social class 32–41, 135, 137, 139, 157, 159
Marx, Karl 85–6
Mead, Lawrence M. 3, 107–17
Meade, James 60
Miles, David 341
Mill, J. S.
  and female dependency 145
  and male violence 133, 149 n.2
  and welfare bureaucracy 95 n.3
Mitchell, Juliet 121
Morris, William 352 n.4
Moss Kanter, Rosabeth 376–7
Moynihan, Daniel Patrick 113
Muellbauer, J. 242
Muffels, Ruud 5, 170–88
Mun, de 24
Murray, Charles 3, 96–106, 116–17
Myles, J. 155
Myrdal, G. 235

Napoleon III of France 24
Nelson, B. (quoted) 136, 139

Neugarten, B. & Neugarten, D. 301
Nickell, Stephen 375
Nixon, Richard M. 63, 112
Nozick, Robert 59

Oastler, R. 22, 24
O'Connor, James 2, 63–6, 352 n.2
Offe, Claus 2, 67–76, 352 n.2
Okun, Arthur 184, 235
Owen, M. (quoted) 136

Paine, Thomas 1–2, 11–16
Panitch, L. 87
Parijs, Philippe van 7–8, 355–9
Parkin, Frank 86–7
Pateman, Carole 3, 133–50
Pesch, Heinrich 24
Phillips, Kevin 108
Phillipson, Chris 7, 293–307
Pierson, Paul 7, 309–19, 320–2, 325–6,
    331–2
Piven, F. Fox (quoted) 144
Polanyi, K. 235
Pontusson, Jonas 7, 320–34
Pound, Roscoe (quoted) 94
Prais, S. 243
Preston, Samuel 294

Rathbone, Eleanor 125–6, 143–4
Rattansi, A. 361
Rawls, John 53, 58–9, 116
Reagan, Ronald
    and poverty 116
    and welfare state 7, 72, 108, 111,
        112, 138, 146, 370
Reddin, M. J. 45
Regini, Marino 222
Rhodes, Martin 6, 257–62
Ricardo, David 22
Riley, M. et al. 298
Ringen, S. 241
Rodbertus, J. K. 22
Roosevelt, Franklin D. 28
Rowntree, Seebohm 24, 25–6
Rowthorn, R. 248

Saunders, P. & Klau, F. 236

Sawer, M. (quoted) 144–5
Scharpf, Fritz 6, 254–6
Schmidt, M. G. 155
Schmitter 77, 87
Schmoller, G. von 22–3
Schumpeter, J. A. 24
Schwartz, Herman 332
Sen, Amartya 54
Sennett, R. & Cobb, J. 364–5
Singh, Ajit 289–90
Sismondi, 30 n.5
Skocpol, T. (quoted) 135
Smart, B. 361
Smeeding, Timothy M. 106 n.2
Smith, Adam 56
Spencer, Bruce 284–5
Steele, Shelby 114
Stephens, J. 155
Stiglitz, Joseph E. 289
Swenson, Peter 332
Szyszczak, Erica 231 n.43

Taffe, von 159
Tawney, R. H. 33–4
Taylor-Gooby, P. 360, 366–7
Teague, Paul 5, 207–32
Therborn, G. 155–6
Thompson, Grahame 6, 263–9
Thompson, William 136
Thomson, D. 297–8, 301
Titmuss, Richard 2, 25, 55, 186 n.14
    quoted 29
    and residual and institutional
        regimes 156
    and universalism v. selection 42–9
Tocqueville, A. de 29
Townsend, P. 47
Traxler, Franz 210
Trevelyan, G. M. (quoted) 32

Vogelsang, von 24

Wagner, Adolf 22
Wallace, S. et al. 299
Webb, Beatrice 21, 26, 27, 33, 43
Webb, Sydney 21, 33, 43
Weber, Max 85–6

Weisskopf, T. 248
Wilensky, H. 155
Wiles, P. (quoted) 94
Wilkes, John 33
Wilkinson, R. 244
William I of Germany 30 n.9

William II of Germany 24
Williams, F. 360
Wilson, Elizabeth 3, 120
Wilson, William Julius 116–17
Wollstonecraft, Mary 142, 144, 148